THOMAS J. WISE IN THE ORIGINAL CLOTH

THOMAS JAMES WISE: 1859–1937
Hon. M.A. (Oxon), and Honorary Fellow of Worcester College

THOMAS J. WISE IN THE ORIGINAL CLOTH

THE LIFE AND RECORD OF THE FORGER
OF THE NINETEENTH-CENTURY PAMPHLETS

By
WILFRED PARTINGTON

WITH AN APPENDIX BY
GEORGE BERNARD SHAW

De mortuis nil nisi verum

1974
Reprinted
DAWSONS OF PALL MALL
Folkestone & London

First published 1947
Reprinted 1974
DAWSONS OF PALL MALL
Cannon House,
Folkestone, Kent, England.

ISBN 0 7129 0617 7

Printed by Unwin Brothers Limited
The Gresham Press, Old Woking, Surrey

To
ELISABETH O'NEILL

ERRATA

P. 13, line 8, should read: "John Ruskin, Dante Gabriel Rossetti, and William Bell Scott."

P. 24, line 1 of verse should read: "Full many a time and oft my soul"

P. 211, line 30: "persons" for "person."

P. 257: the date of the third letter—Feb. 29, 1813—follows the book quoted. It is an error of the original writer of the letter, whether Byron, de Gibler, or whoever he was.

P. 306, line 35: "aplomb" for "apomb."

ACKNOWLEDGMENTS

¶The considerable contribution of Thomas James Wise himself to this biographical and critical study appears from the text.

¶I was greatly obliged to Dr Philip Gosse for the unrestricted use of his father's letters and for much other help; and also to the Brotherton Collection Committee of Leeds University for putting the originals of the Gosse-Wise Correspondence at my disposal—an arrangement in which Dr R. O. Offor, the University Librarian, was very considerate.

¶As ever in our long acquaintanceship, George Bernard Shaw was kind and also responsive with his reminiscences, even if we duelled about the 'fun'. And Dr F. E. Loewenstein, who is his bibliographer and promises to be his Boswell, made an impartial second as the pens blazed at Welwyn and Wimbledon. 'Blazed' is not entirely figurative. G.B.S. occasionally fired with bloody-coloured ink—in the same manner as Wise (see page 235).

¶To the officials of the British Museum Library generally—and in particular to the ex-Keeper of Printed Books, Wilfred A. Marsden, and to A. I. Ellis, A. F. Johnson, and H. Sellars—for courteous assistance over a long period, my indebtedness cannot be too warmly expressed.

¶The ladies played their part characteristically. It is pleasant to acknowledge the letters and interest of Miss Olivia R. Garnett, Miss Sylvia Gosse, the late Mrs Florence Hardy, Mrs Flora V. Livingston, Miss Audrey Lucas, Mrs Clara Watts-Dunton, and Miss Irene Cooper Willis.

¶To Sir John Murray, Cecil Clay, C. S. Evans, F. S. Ferguson, S. F. Sabin, Sir Stanley Unwin, *The Times*, and William H. McCarthy, formerly of Texas University Library, my inquiries involved considerable trouble which was readily and generously undertaken.

¶For letters of information, for facilities, etc., I was obliged to

9

the Viscount Esher and Sir Sydney Cockerell; to Roland
Baughman, H. F. B. Brett-Smith, A. E. Calkin, John Carter (the
industrious *Enquirer*), H. M. Cashmore, Dr R. W. Chapman,
Richard Curle, Henry Danielson, Alban Dobson, E. Eisler, F. H.
Evans, Maurice Buxton Forman, Herbert Garland, John A.
Gedge, C. G. Des Graz, John Kelly, P. R. Kimber, John Kirkby,
Dr R. B. McKerrow, Benjamin Maggs, W. Marchbank, J. G.
Millward, Dr Alexander Mitchell, de V. Payen-Payne, Professor
A. W. Pollard, Graham Pollard (the twin *Enquirer*), H. C. Rham,
Seymour de Ricci, William Roberts, Percy Simpson, M. H.
Spielmann, Gleb Struve, George Sutcliffe, Charles Vivian, and
C. H. Wilkinson; to the Ruskin Literary Trustees, and the exe-
cutors of the estates of Thomas J. Wise, Joseph Conrad, and
Mrs Florence Hardy; and to the Council of the Bibliographical
Society, J. M. Dent & Sons, the Oxford University Press, Wm.
Blackwood & Sons, Methuen & Co., and the proprietors of
Punch.

WIMBLEDON, 1945   WILFRED PARTINGTON

CONTENTS

ILLUSTRATIONS

*Photographs by the National Portrait and the Tate Galleries, Downey,
Elliott and Fry, Hay Wrightson, H. W. Barnett, etc.*

13

CHAPTER I

INTRODUCING THE SECRET EMPEROR OF BOOK FORGERS AND SOME OF HIS FORERUNNERS

If a man is to write A Panegyrick, *he may keep vices out of sight; but if he professes to write* A Life, *he must represent it really as it was.*
Dr Johnson to Boswell

I sincerely hope that now that both Wise and Mrs Wise are dead there will be no need for further concealment as to the motives and inception of the frauds, and that the facts may be stated in plain language so that in future we may know who was guilty and who was not.
Dr R. B. McKerrow (in a letter to the author)

I

I WAS VERY CURIOUS to see him—this successful business man looming into such prominence in the world of books; already something of a dictator, referred to with the familiarity of fame as 'Tommy' Wise. And he, as was later revealed, was anxious to meet me. But our reasons were different.

There is nothing unusual in a man of commerce taking up book-collecting as a hobby. For the weary and disillusioned fugitive from the daily round and the damned office, it is of all relaxations the happiest, most enthralling, most honoured. But here, one reputed to have spent a strenuous if obscure career in the City amassing his wealth, was such an expert in rare books as only a lifetime of study could make him, and was the author of a most imposing array of instructive works. No bookman had ever before produced such a mass of valuable and fascinating information. How was it done? Where lay the secret? What manner of man was he?

It was on a late and darkening autumn afternoon in 1919 that I was shown into the already widely-known Ashley Library. My first impression was of a pink bald head bent over a large handsome desk against a background of books shining in the gay

15

parade of new gilt and many-coloured moroccos. Then a short, chubby figure, bespectacled and smiling, approached briskly and greeted me also briskly. My second impression was of the keenness of the eyes twinkling behind their large lenses, and how ferret-like they became searching mine—as if trying to read their imprint. My third impression was that this plump, alert, confident man of sixty years looked remarkably shrewd and determined.

I was also curious as to what of his famous treasures he would select to show me. First was a case preserving Mary Shelley's long account of the shipwreck and cremation of the poet, locks of hair of Shelley and Mary, and some of 'his' ashes 'snatched ... from the funeral pyre', and said to have been given to Byron's former mistress, Jane Clairmont, by Trelawny when that old adventurer and satyr was pressing his affections on her. The few dead cinders seemed unimpressive compared with the moving pathos of Mary Shelley's living epistle. And I did not care to comment on the surprising absence of reference to them (which might have supplied the needed authentication) in the accompanying detailed Deed of Sale of Jane Clairmont's effects. Already I divined that under his joviality Wise was a testy man, brooking no argument.

The owner next showed me, with pride and obvious anticipation of my astonishment, some of Swinburne's manuscript aberrations in verse and prose on the subject of flagellation.

'Amusing, are they not?' he asked.

'No! They strike me as being puerile and pitiable.'

'Eh?'

Was he going to print this stuff? He dismissed the question vaguely as he reached to his shelves for some specimens of his private-printings. Such indiscretions were safe with him, he assured me. When he added, with many laughing asides, that he had spent some three thousand pounds to save the poet's unpublished manuscripts getting into wrong hands and to preserve them for posterity, I was deeply impressed. That favourable impression remained for many years until my researches brought out the truth to be told here.

During the years I was editing the *Bookman's Journal* (1919–31) and later writing the book-collecting section of the American *Bookman* (1931–3), almost to the time of his death in 1937, I was in the habit of meeting Wise frequently and also of being in correspondence with him for rare-book and kindred discussions.[1] In the collecting boom that made those years memorable, the increasing prevalence of fabricated first editions and manuscripts became a subject of anxiety to those concerned for a hobby so delightful and valuable to literature. Wise, when he became aware of my views, enthusiastically pressed me to 'block the forger's path'—to use his own words. 'Carry on the good work', and 'You ought to expose this', he urged. The support of his great authority and world-wide reputation at the time it was offered would naturally be regarded as worth having. And so I innocently regarded it. Little did I suspect that the man who sometimes provided me with powder and shot for the campaign against fakers, whose clarion cry against fraud was heard afar, was himself the secret Emperor and Grand Lama of Forgers: that he would go down to history in the line of succession to William Henry Ireland, John Payne Collier, and De Gibler.

For after the boom came the bomb. In 1934 it was revealed[2] that over fifty purported first-edition pamphlets of writings by Victorian authors, copies of which were in the Ashley Library of Thomas James Wise, were forgeries or of very doubtful authenticity. The authors included the Brownings, George Eliot, Kipling, Ruskin, Swinburne, Tennyson, and Thackeray. The classification of these highly-esteemed pamphlets as first editions, their reputed literary and bibliographical importance, and their commercial value as rarities, had depended almost solely upon the authority of Wise. He was not then accused of

[1] The association was hardly of the character implied by the endearing style of address affected in his correspondence with the author. The visits were not those for hospitality, but arranged by one or the other to discuss pre-specified bibliographical matters. Nor was the author the recipient of any one of his pamphlets—spurious or legitimate. Some half-dozen of the Ashley Library catalogues and bibliographies were sent to him for professional purposes; but two of these were returned unopened in consequence of a reference that represented them as gifts—a circumstance which led to a temporary intermission in the relationship. The association was so circumscribed, in fact, that Wise would protest at the other's independence, for example, in pre-paying the postages when their biblio-graphical collaboration involved correspondence.

[2] In *An Enquiry into the Nature of Certain Nineteenth Century Pamphlets* by John Carter and Graham Pollard. Some additions have since been made to their list of condemned or suspect printings. See pages 343–5.

being the fabricator of these forgeries, though the circumstances of his connexion with them were suspicious. The bomb bursting in the charming stillness of the libraries of the collecting and literary worlds was the sensation of the time. Then followed a strange silence.

It will be illustrative to say something of the genesis of this study and its development. In 1932 I had designed to devote a considerable article in the American *Bookman* to Wise's career as a collector and bibliographer; and for that purpose he at some of our meetings told me certain things incorporated in this book. But in 1933 the article (which was being built up at leisure) was still uncompleted when the *Bookman* ended its long career. In the following year came the sensation concerning those spurious first editions in the Ashley Library.

In 1936 I informed Wise of my plan to extend the article into a larger study, expressing my wish to quote from our correspondence. He was then preserving an obstinate silence in the face of the exposure of his rare pamphlets. His reaction to my request was both surprising and revealing. He promptly placed an embargo upon the use of any of his letters to me. The copies I had sent to him were returned with passages viciously and heavily scored out in blue pencil in an effort at censorship which was abandoned for a total ban. That ban, however, has been without the intended effect, and has not prevented me from setting forth what I have considered it a duty to write of a man who so amazingly won for himself a threefold claim to fame.

The object of this biographical and critical study of Wise is to present fresh information and give hitherto unpublished evidence of Wise's responsibility for the forgeries, to trace the curious and little-known ramifications of his career, to show the inner character of the man in relation to his friends and ambitions, and generally to indicate the extent and value of his achievements. In these respective aims I hope to do him impartial justice. For my purpose is to preserve Thomas James Wise as he was—in the original cloth: not to present him changed and furbished up after his own habit of rebinding things all decked up in scarlet, apple-green, and royal-blue moroccos—like his lamented

25, Heath Drive
N. W. 3.
2 3. 4. 3 1.

My dear Partington,

Here's another chance for you to carry on good work, & block the path of the Forger. You will doubtless have seen in the Catalogue of [   ]

And why did his son, Lord [   ] know nothing whatever about it? And where has it lain hidden all these years? And who has produced it now?

Very truly yrs

T. J. Wise

Reduced reproductions of the first and last pages of a letter in which Wise urges the author to block the Forger's path

Byrons and desecrated Wordsworths, that ought to have been left in their primary condition.

II

It is almost certain that the earliest literary forgeries were of religious writings, a fact which induces some amusing reflections. After the religious fraud came the political forger, who, even if he made statecraft the excuse for his methods, was more usually concerned to secure for himself or his associates some valuable consideration. But neither religion nor politics has had much to do with the activities of later practitioners, in their making of forged manuscripts, spurious printings, piracies, faked first editions, and the like. These mainly developed in the latter part of the eighteenth century (though there were earlier ones); for it was by then that collecting had ceased to be confined to learned institutions and wealthy noblemen, and was becoming more and more developed through the spread of education and wealth.

As the numbers of book-collectors have increased, so have these 'wrong' books and manuscripts been multiplied to cater for them. Almost every country has produced literary fabricators. Their annals are adventurous, gay, sad, and generally incredible. Of all the bold and clever gallery, taking ability with offence, and the two often coincide, the English breed must surely be awarded first place—notwithstanding that France can claim Lucas Vrain, who confessed to manufacturing for a wealthy dupe 25,000 spurious autographs, including letters by Cleopatra, the resurrected Lazarus, and Mary Magdalene: all in modern French!

The Irelands, father and son, were a curious pair. Sam, the father, had a passion for collecting; and William Henry (1777–1835), the boy, likewise picking up many rare books, studied mediæval literature, and amused himself writing verse in imitation of early authors. How this led to his producing, in his 'teens, the 'newly discovered' Elizabethan manuscripts that he rained upon a delighted father, is too well-known to need re-telling. In 1795 proud Samuel held at his house in Norfolk Street,

London, an exhibition of his clever son's 'finds'. The pundits, sublimely hoaxed, lifted up their voices in wonder and gratification; and Boswell kneeled down in his best breeches to kiss the relics! Eventually the Irelands were exposed; and Samuel died broken-hearted, still protesting the innocence of his son, who had already confessed the forgeries and disappeared.

It is never too late to repent; though later book-world forgers, perhaps not relishing the fate of the Irelands, have tended either to brazen out their deeds or to lie low, hoping doubtless to go down to posterity as beautiful mysteries.

Contrary to the case of William Henry Ireland, life did not become exciting for John Payne Collier (1789–1883) until he was sixty-three years old, at which time he was enjoying a Civil List Pension of one hundred pounds in recognition of his bibliographical work and scholarly services to learned societies. Then he surprised the world by producing a copy of the Second Folio Shakespeare (1632) bearing annotations which, if genuine, provided a corrected text earlier than any other known. Shakespearean students of repute declined to accept these; and, while the ink was flying in another battle of books, he added sensation to sensation by bringing forward documents concerning Shakespeare and his contemporaries. All were proved to be spurious; and it was also found that he had planted forgeries in the Dulwich College Library and even in the British State Paper Office. Collier fought back and managed to find a few optimistic champions, such as are usually at hand in a case of the kind.

The examples of Ireland and Collier are only mentioned by way of brief introduction to our subject and as prominent figures in the gallery of delinquents. It is usually extended to include poor Thomas Chatterton (1752–70), the one genius of them all, who committed suicide at the age of eighteen after producing immortal verse attributed to a fifteenth-century 'Thomas Rowley'. Pity for the tragedy of Chatterton, however, prompts the plea that his case is arguable: he was no worse than Horace Walpole, who so badly treated him, and who put out a novel purported to have been done by someone else. Yet Walpole is never included in the infamous gallery.

But there is another figure of whom it is necessary to say something. In the middle of the nineteenth century there was operating in London, and for a time also in America, a clever scoundrel named De Gibler, who was to sow a great deal of trouble. His speciality in crime was the forging of what probably totals hundreds of letters purporting to be by Byron and Shelley (but chiefly the former) and making faked association books. This De Gibler called himself George Gordon Byron, claiming to be the illegitimate son of Lord Byron by a Spanish lady, the 'Countess de Luna'—as amusingly named as the 'Dr Underwood' who will be met later. The rogue is said to have been remarkably like the poet; and that fact, the 'peculiar circumstances' he had to relate, and his pretty little wife's[3] ability to embroider the tale must have made his career a lively one, and provided a never-ending source of amusement to the De Giblers in their connubial chamber. The alleged Don Juan Junior remains a mysterious person. But he will reappear later in these pages, for his misdeeds were constantly coming under the rake of Thomas James Wise, whose own life and character afford a study even more remarkable than those of the delinquents mentioned, and whose achievements included a new departure in literary frauds.

[3] Wife or mistress? Mary Russell Mitford, writing to Mrs Ouvray (7 April 1852), gives an account of the De Giblers that she had received from Dr W. C. Bennett, who figures here. De Gibler's partner is described as a most elegant young woman, who was educated at a finishing school at Blackheath: and 'Mrs Byron, it is now said, was not his wife'.

CHAPTER 2

EARLY AND EVENTFUL YEARS

Full many a time and oft my souι
Has nursed upon its faltering breast,
The light of some long cherished goal,
Yet vainly clutched the wished-for rest!
Oft bursting on the heart's cold strand,
Hope's wave has borne a gladder ray;
But full as oft my eager hand,
Missing the wave, clasped but the spray!
Thomas J. Wise: *Verses*

I

WHEN IN 1937 I began my researches for this biography I found that practically nothing had been recorded, and little seemed to be known among many who might be expected to know, about the family, unbringing, and early career, of Thomas James Wise. Modern fashion favours the supply of biographical information, even by the subject of the biography. The dearth in this case was largely due to Wise's own determined reticence. In the few statements he made about himself and his career, biographical details were always lightly skirted. He was once offered handsome terms—'a thousand pounds down on account before putting pen to paper', as he told me—to write a book about himself and his experiences. Asked why he had not done so when assured of commanding wide attention, his reply was: 'All that's of 'interest about me is in my books. My life is in the bibliographies 'I've compiled and the books I've collected. The rest doesn't 'matter to anyone.'

This modesty, or contempt for biographical fashion, is hardly in keeping with the character. Nevertheless, it is true enough that there is much that is revealing of their author to be gained from his specialized works—so much indeed that he was speak-

24

ing either with cynicism, or with that surprising naïveté that makes his strange psychology stranger. Most biographers, however, are able to begin with at least a nucleus of information about their subjects that offers opportunities for filling the gaps. But until 1937 the personal history of Wise was largely a mystery. The few biographical facts about him which had been stated (and some of those were wrong) could have been contained on the first page of a book, leaving the rest a succession of teasing and inviting blanks. Owing to a combination of incredible luck and his own astuteness, some of the blank pages in the record will never be filled.

They are significant circumstances that nearly all with whom he was associated in his early and middle life—among them eminent men of letters—predeceased him, and that the accounts he subsequently gave involved some of them in the shady phases of his career.[1] It is equally remarkable that the few early associates who survived him mostly professed inability or great reluctance to contribute to the blank pages—even if all 'controversial matters' (which was the usual euphemism for the forgeries) were ruled out of discussion.

The few details Wise gave out about himself were not always accurate. In a letter to John Henry Wrenn he was 'once betrayed'[2] into a piece of family history—namely, that he was related to the well-known Irish family of Wyse whose tree is set forth in Burke's *Landed Gentry of Ireland*. He claimed—with affected modesty, and linking up his own interest in Shelley— that Sir Thomas Wyse, K.C.B., a supporter of the poet in 1812, was his paternal grandfather's first cousin; explaining that the spelling of the name was changed by his grandfather, and that the 'simpler form' was continued by his father, and also by himself 'of course'. The claim is very unlikely to be establishable.[3] For reasons which will hereinafter be apparent, it was made to impress the wealthy American. If there was any substance in it the

[1] See Appendix III.

[2] As Miss Fannie Ratchford, editress of *Letters of Thomas J. Wise to John Henry Wrenn* (1944), quaintly put it, apparently accepting the morsel of 'history' with relish. The taradiddle is quoted in full twice, in addition to a briefer reference.

[3] Some genealogical inquiries have been made under the names of Wise, Wyse, Wyes, and Weiss. But owing to the non-return—due to the war—of the official Records to their normal depository, it has not been possible to go as far as desired in the research. This is a case which future investigators will find presents problems outside the normal routine.

fact would not have been reserved exclusively for consumption across the Atlantic—where it would be safely remote from the difficult sources in which such a pretence could be decided. Wise's brother and confidant, in 1945, knew nothing of the relationship; and, answering a specific genealogical inquiry, he said that according to all the records of their family, which dated 'back for four hundred years', its name was never spelt with a 'y'.

II

Thomas James Wise was born on 7 October 1859, at 52 Wrotham Road, Gravesend, the first-born of Julia Victoria Wise, formerly Dauncey. His father, Thomas Wise, was a 'manufacturing traveller'—his own peculiar description—and subsequently he became a tobacconist. He has been otherwise described as a builder; and also as a general merchant in Fenchurch street, E.C. The son invariably stated his father's rank or profession to be that of 'Gentleman'. Three other children were born to Julia Victoria and Thomas Wise—two sons and a daughter. The daughter Julia died in infancy. One son, Henry Dauncey, died in 1915; the other, Herbert Athol Wise, enlisted in the army in 1891 and served most of his time abroad, retiring in 1908 with the rank of acting sergeant-major. He was twelve and a half years junior to Thomas James, the eldest of the family, and survived him. The mother died of consumption in 1881. The widower was afterwards twice married: first to Hannah Waldock (who pre-deceased him); and then, at the age of seventy, to his nurse, Jeannie Donald Carden (or Garden). He died in 1902, leaving his estate of £2,362 entirely to his relict, who was remarried to one Avenell. These facts correct the misstatements made in usually accurate quarters as to Thomas James Wise's parents. It is not true that he inherited any family business; or that he derived wealth from his parents. He was a 'self-made' man, who gained fortune and fame in divers extraordinary ways.

Wise senior was a Baptist; and young Thomas James's upbringing, if not very strongly influenced, was at least under the auspices of that denomination. Among the two or three recollections of boyhood he permitted himself to give, one was of his devotion to his invalid mother, whose interest in literature led to his reading poetry to her—especially that of Shelley, for which he developed a partiality. Shelley readings in a Baptist home sounds rather incongruous, but the readings may have been selected and such as would have appeared innocuous to the Brethren, who believe in the confession of sins.

Maternal leanings to literature guiding a child's taste and career is a circumstance fairly common in biography; but it cannot be recorded in this instance that mutual affection and kindred tastes between mother and son were ever commemorated by the latter in outward sign such as a book dedication or written tribute. The 'family grave of Julia and Thomas Wise' in Highgate cemetery was found in a neglected state in 1938, appearing to have been left uncared for after the burial of Julia, the mother of Thomas James Wise. The lower inscriptions on the headstone were partially illegible. It also records that buried in this family grave is one 'Amelia Groseman, died July 13th, 1874, aged [10 or 19 years]'. The Registry of Deaths at Somerset House contains no entry for 1874 respecting this mysterious Amelia Groseman. Thomas James Wise was not buried here.

The Wise family early left Gravesend for North London where its first abode (there were two other Thomas Wises who were residents in the locality) was apparently at 127 Devonshire Road, Holloway, from 1866 to 1878. In 1880 the local records show it as occupying 3 Thornhill Grove, Barnsbury; which address was given in 1882 by the eldest son, Thomas James, in a letter to the Press. The family remained there until 1883, and the following year was back at 127 Devonshire Road; where it settled, and where we shall find our subject making an independent home under the paternal roof.

Thomas James Wise, in his later years, was wont to describe himself as having been educated privately.[4] His schooling was, according to another statement of his, received at the City of London School, in Milk Street off Cheapside, where he stayed until the age of sixteen; but according to the present headmaster, Francis Richard Dale, there is no record of his being there. His

[4] For example, the *Who's Who* for 1925 (the issue to which Wise first contributed his biographical entry) and for the years following. It was in that same work that for fourteen years the information supplied by him gave a wrong year—1901—for his second marriage (see Chapter 11).

brother says that Thomas was educated at home owing to his
delicate health. He was early placed in a junior capacity with the
firm of H. Rubeck, of 14 Mincing Lane, E.C., and afterwards of
59 Mark Lane, E.C.3, an essential-oil merchant.

The beginning of the lad's career was not auspicious. At the
end of six months he was sacked by Hermann Rubeck, the proprietor—who, however, on the representations of the father
agreed to give Tommy another chance. Little could Hermann
have guessed the surprising sequel to his clemency. With the
Rubecks, Wise was to be associated for the whole of his city
career. There was little, if anything, he did not come to
know about essential-oils; but the products Hermann Rubeck
specialized in possess (according to the encyclopedias) an
aromatic smell, and as a rule leave no permanent grease
spots.

Most boys at some time collect something or other—birds'
eggs, black eyes, stamps, vermin, etc. Tommy, who had soon
shown inclination for literary pursuits, at seventeen began book-
collecting. The stories which have been printed about the lad's
starving in order that he might buy books are inventions;
although it is true that on occasions he walked to and from his
work to put the fares thus saved towards the cost of some par-
ticularly-desired volume—a little economy not unfamiliar among
keen youngsters. Arundell Esdaile, in a notice in *The Library
Association Record* for November 1937 to be referred to later,
stated that Wise used to say his father 'gave him a little money
'to play with, observing that poets were safer than racehorses or
'actresses'. There are, of course, some quite unsafe poets for a
young man; and not all actresses are as dangerous as they are
painted. But granting the well-meaning implication of the dictum,
it rather airily suggests that father Wise was sufficiently well-off
and indulgent to give little Tommy the means to play with book-
makers and belles of the chorus had he been so disposed. It is
unlikely that the small and not very well-established tradesman
was at the time so affluent. Moreover, the dictum is not original.
The 'reminiscence' came from Wise in his late period when he
was famous; though this is the only instance I have heard of its
being told in connexion with him. Perhaps it owed more to his
lively imagination and desire to impress such a welcome guest

as the Secretary of the British Museum than to biographical accuracy.

The favourite hunting ground of Thomas was at first the Farringdon Road, where book-laden barrows and stalls still line the sidewalk. Afterwards he adventured into the picturesque old bookshops up Fleet Street and along the Strand and in its more dubious backwaters that have now fallen before palatial offices and gorgeous cinemas plastered with their grotesque 'lovelies'. If priceless treasures in Elizabethan manuscripts and old books were not to be found 'plenty as blackberries' as in the London of Halliwell-Phillipps, nevertheless the city's bookshops were still El Dorados for the wise. Thomas, of that ilk, was a shrewd lad. Not only did he browse and occasionally buy a volume, but he began paying visits—naturally shy at first—to the better-class antiquarian shops further West, noting their prices, and the finer condition of the books as compared with those of the dirty untidy piles on street stalls and barrows. He was learning: ideas were fertilizing—ideas that were to lead to the acquisition of wealth and fame.

His visits to the old bookshops became more frequent as he grew more familiar and confident with their proprietors. Sometimes he would make a much-debated purchase; at other times, to raise funds, he would sell to a bookseller a volume picked up cheaply from a rival shop close at hand. But at all times he asked questions. Young Wise in quest of wisdom was as quick as a ferret after a rabbit.

One never-to-be-forgotten day, when aged eighteen, he spent no less than twenty shillings on Thomas Moore's *Epicurean* and Shelley's *Cenci* (this was the order in which he mentioned them); and these he declared to be the foundation of the Ashley Library now honoured in the British Museum with its own special room. The price made him wince, but they were both first editions. The antiquarian booksellers on their part were only too ready to encourage the intelligent, pert young man, neatly dressed in his black cloth and bowler hat—a book-collector obviously determined to go far in a delightful pursuit. His inquisitiveness was already remarked. He would start as many queries as a good researcher with his nose in a bad catalogue. Among other things that impressed him in this early stage of his private education was that the more entertainingly a bookseller talked about a particular work he was showing, the more desirable the volume seemed to become, and the higher its price.

That observation was to have a result affecting the whole of book-collecting and book-selling; for he had now determined to form a fine library for himself, and also to supply others forming libraries.

III

In 1881 there settled in London a middle-aged merchant who for some years had been interesting himself in literary subjects and contributing to the transactions of learned societies: he was James Dykes Campbell. To him literature was more than Mammon; and at forty-three years of age he retired from business on a moderate competency to become a man of letters—devoting himself largely to the study of Coleridge, whose biography he wrote. Young Wise was an admirer of Campbell and was much impressed by his example. He was not to be such an idealist himself: for him Literature was too often spelt with a £ for the first letter—that plan of his to build a fine library required capital. Nor was he ever equal in scholarship to Campbell or those other contemporaries whose abilities he was to use, as we shall see, to such advantage and so unscrupulously.

But he had all the energy and determination necessary to achieve the ambitions now clearly before him; he had also plenty of patience when he chose to exercise it. If any man's life ever exemplified what triumphs can be effected, what revenges taken, by watchful, silent, biding-the-time, it is that of Thomas J. Wise.

For all his materialistic outlook, however, he had his romantic moments, the results of which were seen when in 1882 he printed his *Verses*. Of this, his first publication, thirty-five copies (including 'five upon vellum') were produced; and a further six copies, reimposed within red borders on larger and superior paper, bearing the date 1883. The twenty-three-year-old author took for his title-page quotation this from Martin Tupper:

> Thoughts that have tarried in my mind and peopled
> its inner chamber.

Wise's poetry was pretty much of the *Keepsake* variety, and contained the usual sprinkling of 'last Trumps', 'throbbing bosoms', and 'Fancy's ears'. He came to be very shy of his little book of *Verses*. It appeared for sale in his disguised bookseller's list of 1895, but he never admitted it to his *Ashley Library Catalogue*. Three examples of his poetizing are quoted here for their peculiar appropriateness—one at the head of this chapter, and two later.

The most interesting points about this booklet are the printer of it, and that limiting of the edition which was to become so famously associated with Wise's publications. The man chosen for the honour of printing Thomas James's muse was William Fullford, of 251 Pentonville Road, N.1,[5] which place was within easy reach of Wise's home in Holloway. Fullford was little more than a jobbing printer; but he hitched up his trousers and did his best with red and black inks and ruled borders to please his new customer—who hinted at lots of work to follow. For among other thoughts peopling Wise's 'inner chamber' were some exceedingly novel ones requiring the services of a printer who could do just what he was told, and would be too busy to ask a lot of questions.

Fullford's next job for his new customer, a few months later, was to make a reprint of Keats's *Ode to a Nightingale* in an edition of twenty-nine copies, including a few on vellum. Perhaps there wasn't much difference between the two poets for William Fullford, to whom the cash result was eminently satisfactory—for Wise was always prompt in paying his accounts, and settled without a quibble those for printing and binding. But the result was not so satisfactory for the customer; who soon realized that Fullford was not the man for his purpose.

Wise needed a printer with a large range of types—one with skilled compositors, one who could print anything, match anything. For what reasons will transpire in the next three chapters.

---

[5] Subsequently the firm moved a few doors away. In 1945 the premises of 'Fullford & Son Ltd.' were vacant and dilapidated. Although not numbered, they appeared to be then No. 263, and still bore the sign 'Cheapest High-Class Printers & Stationers'. The P.O. Directory for 1886 described Fullford as a printer and stationer, but did not include him among the bookbinders. See footnote page 239.

IV

Wise's commercial instincts were in keeping with his shrewd character. He was always on the lookout for profit, however small. Any mission in the city was keenly explored for its commission. Even visits to restaurants had to yield their return, according to the recollection of a later colleague. On returning from a meal in a nearby café, Wise was noticed invariably to go to a shelf in the sample room, take down a large tin used as a container for saffron, and drop into it a few lumps of sugar. When filled, the tin disappeared, and an empty one took its place. There is nothing very original, it is true, in this practical application of the old saw that many a pickle makes a mickle: the mickle fortunes of some of our most prominent snobs have been thus begun.

The keen short-statured clerk was something of a hustler. But he was also a thoughtful young man—even a man of vision. At this period he had a number of inspirations which, opportunist as he was, were to be exploited to the full. One of these was the realization of the collecting possibilities in the galaxy of early nineteenth-century authors that included Scott, Wordsworth, Byron, Shelley, Keats, and Leigh Hunt. After all, he was not so far removed from their time. When he was twenty-one, that hardy adventurer Trelawny was walking the earth 'without greatcoat, stockings or underclothing this Christmas',[6] telling tales of his friend Lord Byron, discussing the affair of Jane Clairmont[7] whom he had liked (she had been kind to him), lauding his 'ever glorious Shelley', and abusing that poet's widow (she had refused to marry him after all).

When Wise in his early hunts saw the first edition of *Endymion* and also the Pisa *Adonais* procurable for ten guineas or less, he pondered deeply. There could not be so many of these treasures about—especially in fine condition and in the original boards. The time would come, and that soon, when the world would be seeking them and willing to pay high prices for them (he was actually to see some of them realize as many hundreds as

---

[6] At eighty-seven years of age, as D. G. Rossetti recorded in 1879.
[7] Mother of Byron's Allegra.

they had once been priced in pounds). Here was his immediate field, then, with Shelley in the centre. It says much for his imagination and courage that at twenty-five, earning a salary well under four pounds a week, he gave what was then the record sum of forty-five pounds for a superb copy of the Pisa *Adonais*; and a little while afterwards forty pounds for a set of two Shelley items (from the Glasgow booksellers, Kerr and Richardson)—all original issues. Such instances of his commercial foresight and youthful confidence he was wont to recall with pride in later years: as when he told an acquaintance: 'Some forty 'years ago I was laughed at by Forman, Furnivall, W. M. Rossetti, 'and others, for giving as much as fifty pounds apiece for what 'they called Shelley "impossibles". But I backed my own 'judgment, and was satisfied to wait. For these I could get 'five hundred pounds and more each to-day.' Those high prices, as they were considered in the early 'eighties, caused a stir in the antiquarian book-trade and gave Wise a reputation. Such buying required pluck; it also required resources.

Although at first only earning a young clerk's salary, he had the advantage of living at home—127 Devonshire Road, Holloway, N.,[8] one of a long row of three-storied, single-fronted houses in a dull, somewhat dingy thoroughfare. Living thus with his parents there (as he continued to do until he was thirty years of age) meant a substantial economy: Thomas James Wise was a careful sort. Assisted by occasional book deals and other side-line earnings, he was able both to pursue his collecting and to save money for that great chance which comes sooner or later for the commercially ambitious—and which, seized with the cash in hand, leads on to fortune. Sometimes when he had his small but slowly-growing capital tied up, he was hard-pressed to meet the demands of his book-buying. But he never faltered. He could afford to tease the booksellers about his impending insolvency. 'I'm stony broke,' he would chaff them. 'It looks like 4/9 in 'the pound for you.' They, who believed him to be a wealthy young City merchant, joined in the joke.

[8] Renamed Axminster Road since the above was written.

V

All this time he had been making rapid progress in the essential-oil business. By the most diligent attention to his and everyone else's duties, as well as by extraordinary perception and opportunism, he soon made himself not only indispensable to but the confidant of his employer. Before he was thirty, he was Rubeck's chief clerk and cashier. He has been described by an intimate friend as one of the shrewdest buyers on the Produce Market. But in office life he has also been compared unflatteringly to a Dickensian character in somewhat similar circumstances, although Hermann Rubeck was hardly Mr Dombey.

This was his daily or city life; and although his rare-book activities were allowed to obtrude into his office routine, it was all part of the young man's scheme—a scheme to be pursued with relentless and indefatigable vigour, and to succeed even beyond his wildest dreams. Once the City was left behind him for his home in that dingy Holloway thoroughfare, his evenings and nights were almost entirely given up to his books, to the research involved by them, to occasional literary meetings (all part of the great scheme), and to private and far-reaching projects as to which his friends were told no more than it was strictly useful that they should know.

But however unattractive the neighbourhood, Thomas set himself up in some state under the domestic roof. Two rooms on the ground floor were given up solely to his use. He had the larger one in front of the house furnished by Messrs Jones Bros. of Holloway as a library and sitting-room where he could occasionally entertain his friends, and the one behind as his bedroom. This making of a home within the home shows something of the independence and ambition of the industrious young bachelor, and was encouraged by his father, whose favourite he is said to have been. The privacy of this front room was jealously guarded. It was his habit to shut himself up there, and work far into the nights except when meetings of the Browning and Shelley Societies, or occasional evenings in town or boating on the Thames, brought necessary relaxation. It has been related by a member of his family that he was visited in this sitting-room by George Bernard Shaw, T. P. O'Connor, Stopford Brooke, Dr Furnivall, and Harry Buxton Forman. In this reminiscence, however, there seems to be some confusion with his literary society contacts; of which, in his later years of celebrity, Wise was never tired of speaking.

Bernard Shaw's recollection, as written for me, is: 'I made his 'acquaintance when we both belonged to Furnivall's Shelley 'Society. We were both playboys then. . . . I never visited him 'privately; and when the Society perished I lost touch with him 'for many years. Later, when we both became famous, we corre-'sponded, as he was keen on collecting rehearsal copies of my 'plays (I print little private editions for use in the theatre) and 'I was the only person he could get them from.' Of this sidelight it only remains to be said that, however Shaw's description may have applied to himself, Thomas James Wise was not then, or at any time, a playboy. His life and habits were much too otherwise fixed.

Of natural qualifications other than those already mentioned, one was his extraordinary memory. Another was his gift of observation, as an illustration of which this story of his later years may be told here. In a discussion with Sir John Murray, a question arose over a disputed document attached to a manu-script. 'You have seen the manuscript; I have not,' he told Sir John. 'You can judge from the appearance of the pin whether 'it was placed where it is subsequently to 1900, or whether it is 'a pin of a century or more ago.' It is a clue worthy of Sherlock Holmes. How many people to-day would know that the head of the old-fashioned pin was merely stuck on, and was liable to slip down the stem?[9] It was by such pinpoint observation that Wise developed his faculty for examining books and making his bibliographical descriptions.

This period between the ages of twenty and thirty was most fertile for him in ideas. Not only did he realize the great scope in collecting the famous early nineteenth-century authors, but it occurred to him that there must be living some descendants of those romantic figures. What an inspiration! They would be sure to possess interesting relics, perhaps unpublished pieces, certainly

[9] Of the kind that the proverb spoke: 'It takes ten men to make a pin.'

letters. Letters from and to those passionate lovers and erratic geniuses would be revealing. There is often dramatic history in private communications. For all the parade of critical commentary in Wise's books, the truth is that he was generally more captivated by the story behind the story than by the work itself.

So he set to business, putting out cautious inquiries here, burrowing like some human mole there, in order to reach the quarries. Bold as he was, not even Wise could have foreseen the harvest he reaped from time to time. Those descendants were doubtless amazed to find themselves traced by the prim, efficient little man who knew so much about their family heroes, of whom he could usually tell some new and amusing stories. What an enthusiastic collector to go to so much trouble! How nice to be so wealthy and want to buy old papers and books, of which (one suspects in some cases) the possessors were rather tired! And the dear man was so generous; at least, that is what some of the descendants thought, knowing nothing about the rare-book market.

In 1886, when he was twenty-six, he found out Mrs Cheltnam, and bought from her Shelley's *Epipsychidion*, which the poet had given to her father, Leigh Hunt. Next, he traced the son of Sir John Bowring, to whom Mary Shelley gave the MS. of her husband's *Hellas*; and this changed hands in the following year. Also he acquired through Harry Buxton Forman (who had bought them from Jane Clairmont's heiress and executrix) Shelley letters and relics of the first importance, and Jane's own series of diaries—so enthralling, and mostly unpublished.

A few years later he secured one of the seven copies saved from destruction of the suppressed *Œdipus Tyrannus* as the result of finding Lieutenant-Colonel Call, husband of the daughter of the ubiquitous Trelawny to whom the author had presented the copy. This happens to be one of the comparatively few instances in which Wise recorded the price he paid—thirty-six pounds; and he adds that in 1920 a copy (apparently with far less interesting association) was sold for six thousand one hundred dollars (say one thousand two hundred and twenty pounds). This last example evidences the shrewdness of his buying. But his reward in hunting down these single items was nothing compared with his amazing coup when Swinburne's library came to be cleared at The Pines, and with his deals with Charlotte Brontë's husband and George Borrow's daughter—the stories of which will be told in their order.

VI

It was not only as a book-hunter and book-buyer that he was keen and far-sighted. I remember, at the time he had retired from business and was immersed in the compilation of his great catalogue, telling him of a reader who had written to me asking where or how a copy of one of Wise's privately-printed bibliographies could be obtained. I inquired what he did with his spare copies, whether he sold them, and could the reader be advised to write to him? I shall not forget the momentary scene that followed. We were in the room that housed his famous library. Wise leapt off his seat as if he had been severely bitten there, exclaiming: 'Sell my books? Never! I am NOT a bookseller.' From his extraordinary indignation, and in that sumptuous room surrounded as we were by bookcases crammed with gold-tooled, morocco-garbed treasures, I supposed that I had uttered an incongruity. I murmured an apology: Wise calmed down. The next instant he was telling me the firm to which he sold all copies beyond those he required himself.

The fact is—although it was not known to me then, nor to ninety-five per cent of the book world—that for the most of his career Wise was a bookseller himself. He was the equivalent of what are called in some of the commercialized sports the 'professional amateur'—the person who makes money out of his playing engagements and connexions while posing as unpaid. In other words, he was a private dealer in rare books and manuscripts. The business was done by negotiation—often as 'friendly offices' for acquaintances, especially Americans—mainly from his home addresses. Apart from one deceptive instance, he issued no catalogues: there was no need to do so, for he dealt not so much in quantity as in quality. This phase of his activities was kept *sub rosa* with the same skill that he showed in other enterprises.

There is nothing derogatory in dealing in books and manuscripts: on the contrary, it is one of the most respected trades, of whose fortunate members many an author has declared his envy. But some explanation (for his clients immediately, and the world ultimately) was necessary to account for a reputedly wealthy collector of his vaunted independence and character engaging in book-selling. So there was propagated the plausible fiction that he sold duplicate copies acquired in the process of collecting and improving his collections. If this was the case, then Wise had an abnormal number of duplicates, and did amazingly well out of their re-sale. No doubt he had a few which he disposed of as such: most collectors have. But the explanation in general was as fictitious as are the imprints of some of his pamphlets. Light will be thrown in later chapters on his dealings, the full scope of which will probably not be revealed for many years. The subject is introduced here because, although it was during the 'nineties and onwards that the business flourished, it began in the period under consideration.

VII

A haunt of Wise's in his twenties was the shop of Bertram Dobell, who is now fittingly canonized as one of the illustrious of antiquarian booksellers for his literary discoveries, and for being a good Samaritan to poor poets. This worthy had his shop (started as a stationer's and newsagent's on a capital of ten pounds) in Queen's Crescent, Kentish Town—which was convenient for Wise. It was also convenient for Harry Buxton Forman, Wise's very friendly rival in collecting. So handy for both that it was 'damned awkward', as Thomas James exclaimed one early morning when both men, laughing to hide their chagrin and confusion, met outside the shop waiting for Bertram to open. They had received one of his catalogues by that morning's post, and were there after the same bargain!

On another occasion Wise called at the bibliopole's shop just before closing. The Dobells were giving a Christmas party for their children. Bertram used to recall the scene: the shrewd hustling young 'merchant', attracted by the gay lights and glad tumult from the interior, going to the glass doorway separating shop from domesticity, opening the curtains a few inches, and peeping into the cheery room where the infant Dobells and their school friends were playing. After a long silent contemplation, he turned hurriedly, and with a subdued 'Good night' plunged into the darkness of the snow-carpeted street—to make his way to the grim house in Holloway.

The picture supplies another Dickensian hint. Perhaps for a while the busy ambitious young bachelor felt that there was something else in life besides the scramble to find and sell rare books and manuscripts, his daily strivings for mastery with old Hermann Rubeck, and those secret projects now filling his thoughts every spare minute. But the reflection would soon pass. No! He was not ready to settle down in a home of his own. There was so much to do. He had so many irons in the fire.

And there were those literary circles he was getting into. What scope they offered him!

CHAPTER 3

ROBERT BROWNING, HIS *PAULINE*, AND OTHER AFFAIRS

Sweet innocent, the mother cried,
And started from her nook,
That horrid fly is put to hide
The sharpness of the hook.

Ann and Jane Taylor: *The Little Fish*

I

IN THE 'SEVENTIES and 'eighties poetry was still widely read. If the Victorians of those times did not devour it with the same whole enthusiasm and feeling that their parents and grandparents did, nevertheless cultured taste included not only appreciation of the classic Muse, but an admirable desire to do justice to contemporary poets. Among these was Robert Browning, whose works, with their strange mixture of religious expression and of daring originality of thought, attracted two opposite camps of admirers and fascinated both by some obscurities of meaning. He himself, when asked to explain a passage in one of his early poems, said, so the anecdote goes: 'When that poem 'was written, two people knew what it meant—God and Robert 'Browning. And now God only knows what it means.' Well! if the poet was uncertain, his admirers could excuse themselves for their doubts. But those doubts made them more curious. Why should not they get together and debate them? There were literary societies for the study of dead master poets like Chaucer and Shakespeare. Why not one for a living poet? And so it came about that in 1881 was founded the Browning Society—the forerunner of a series of societies associated with later living writers. It was an immediate success, drawing to it those who wrestled with Robert and also those who loved Elizabeth Barrett Browning and her *Sonnets* with their revelation that never varies—whether in an age of stuffy bonnets and crinolines or in one of shorn hair and short skirts.

The official founder of the society was Frederick James Furnivall. Any such institution simply had to owe its birth to him; for had he not the prestige of having formed the Early English Text, the Chaucer, the Wiclif, and the New Shakspere Societies? Dr Furnivall's record as the fecund father of literary societies is unique. But he was much more than that: a fruitful scholar and philologist to whom the *Oxford English Dictionary* owes so much, a practical idealist, a hard-working pioneer, and a magnificent oarsman who took a lively interest in the adoring young ladies he taught to row. Something more than a passing introduction of him is necessary here because he figures considerably in the story of Thomas James Wise.

The big cheerful bearded scholar was as fearless as he was industrious. He had a revealing flair for inconvenient truths, and an inconvenient flair for revealing them. For example, he was one of the most ardent admirers of the verse of Browning, and an esteemed friend of the man himself, for whom he did much. When the poet died, his biographers were concerned to make the most impressive show of his pedigree, giving credence to Browning's fond and often vaunted belief that he was descended from a noble Anglo-Saxon family that bore in Norman times the name of De Bruni. This snobbery was intolerable to Furnivall, whose regard for truth caused him to make researches which traced the poet's family back to a great-great-grandfather who was a footman-butler. He published a long and interesting protest against the biographical suppression of the worthy footman 'for the sake of the contemptible vanity of successors', adding that readers could not help asking themselves in how many other cases this kind of thing had been connived at.

II

Wise was soon influenced by the vogue for the Brownings and began collecting their writings in 1880. When the Society was founded, he early became a member, taking—young as he was—as active a part in its affairs as the older and more influen-

tial members allowed. In 1883 (when he was twenty-three) the
committee recorded their regret that the calls on their funds
precluded them from publishing the Browning concordance he
had undertaken, so they 'released him from his promise'. In the
following year he was elected to the committee, much to his
satisfaction. He would henceforth have a voice in its activities.
Subsequently he became the Society's secretary for a short
time.

The references he was wont to make in later life to his friendship with Robert Browning rather tended to give the impression
that it was a long and intimate one. Dr Thurman L. Hood says
it began through membership of the Society, the collector 'often
'calling on Sunday afternoons with questions from his colleagues
'for the poet to answer (that, at least, was the excuse)'.[1]

The introduction was apparently made in 1886 through the
kindness of Dr Furnivall. The first of the poet's few brief letters
to Wise concerns the visit at which it was made. Wise's own
account of the meeting is instructive.[2] One spring morning
Furnivall took his young protégé to call on Browning at his
home, 19 Warwick Crescent. The aged poet—he was then
seventy-six—was found burning letters and documents from an
old trunk dragged from the top of the house. How this destruction lacerated the collector's feeling is conveyed. Then Browning
fished out two copies of the extremely rare first edition of his
Pauline (1833), his original essay into print. The keen eyes of the
visitor widened. 'Had I upon the instant asked Browning for
'one of them, I am convinced he would have given it to me. But
'delicacy forced me to hesitate, and I allowed the opportunity
'to pass,' he says. After he had left the house, however, he began
thinking how he could make good the regretted lack of enterprise. Furnivall, he declares, suggested that he should write
asking for one of the copies, and offering to pay to charity such
subscription as might be named. But before the suggestion was
acted on, Wise was again in the company of Browning—this
time with Dykes Campbell as host—when the poet, walking
round the room looking at the books, observed: 'I see you have

---

[1] *Letters of Robert Browning Collected by Thomas J. Wise.* Edited by Thurman L. Hood
(1933).
[2] See his *Browning Library* (1929).

'A fruitful scholar and philologist to whom the *Oxford English Dictionary* owes so much, a practical idealist, a hard-working pioneer, and a magnificent oarsman who took a lively interest in the adoring young ladies he taught to row'—Dr FREDERICK JAMES FURNIVALL (Chapters 3, 8, 14 etc)

everything of mine, Campbell.' 'No,' was the reply, 'I still lack *Pauline*,' upon hearing which, Browning promised to send him one of the two copies he had just found. 'Here', continues Wise, 'was an opportunity for me to ask for the other copy. But once more modesty restrained me.' Next day modesty was overcome. He wrote to Browning, who replied that, having given one to Campbell, he was keeping the other for his son.

Wise, whenever he talked about the authors he had met, used to lay stress on his friendship with Browning, and to describe him as 'a charming man, without any "side". You would 'have taken him for a well-to-do stockbroker.' The indications, however, are that the 'friendship' was somewhat one-sided. The poet was affectionately demonstrative to friends like 'my dear Gosse', and Furnivall, and Dykes Campbell. He kept a strictly 'neutral' attitude towards the Society of his admirers (who were 'fair game for criticism', as he told Edmund Yates), although he appreciated its usefulness when a little book of his verse had 'got itself sold . . . at the rate of 2,000 copies very early, and is 'now reprinting. It all comes of the Browning Societies.'[3] Likewise, supposedly wealthy enthusiasts such as our book-collector were not to be discouraged. But the poet's dozen communications to 'Dear Mr Wise' are either short notes of thanks for the never-failing presentation copies, or slightly longer ones that are mostly courteous, but formal and confined to answering questions. The snappiest is a postcard acknowledgment of a letter telling him the price Wise had paid for a first edition of the much-desired *Pauline*:

'Thanks, unwise Wise'

was all Browning's comment. It is true that subsequently, when Wise got him to inscribe this copy, the poet wrote: 'I see with 'much interest this little book, the original publication of which 'can hardly have cost more than has been expended on a single 'copy by its munificent proprietor and my friend—Mr Wise.' Perhaps Browning considered the occasion called for a little flattery: he was as susceptible to munificence as the many others who were later to be blinded by the radiance of the Ashley

---

[3] Furnivall's Browning Society had a family of no less than twenty little (or branch) societies!

Collection. But the proprietor was not so 'unwise', as we shall see on reaching the time when he comes to pay off old scores—one in regard to this very book.

III

When Robert Browning was a youth, playing 'at verses and 'letters, instead of cricket and trapball', he had a passion for Eliza Flower, elder sister of Sarah Flower Adams who won celebrity as the authoress of the hymn 'Nearer, my God, to Thee'. Eliza—who remained single, and died aged forty-three in the year of Robert's marriage—was the inspiration of some poems which he wrote, showed to her, and then destroyed. One of them began:

> *Pauline, mine own, bend o'er me—thy soft breast*
> *Shall pant to mine—bend o'er me—thy sweet eyes*
> *And loosened hair, and breathing lips, and arms*
> *Drawing me to thee. . . . .*

A few years later, at the age of twenty-one, he printed this poem under the title of *Pauline; A Fragment of a Confession* (1833)—the very book that Wise's modesty failed to get for him from the author. 'Robert Browning told me,' he was never tired of recalling, 'that not a single copy of *Pauline*, his first book, was ever 'sold. A relative gave him thirty pounds to pay for the produc-'tion and advertising of the little work in a small edition. But 'not a single copy was sold.' There is some evidence to corroborate that Wise was told by the poet of this experience of his first appearance in print. But not content with the telling, Wise—now so keen a collector of autograph material—must needs have it in writing! So we find Browning replying testily to the request: 'If it really does interest you to have my statement '"in black and white", I willingly repeat that to the best of my 'belief no single copy of the original edition of *Pauline* found a 'buyer.'

In 1886 the Browning Society—apparently at the instigation of their energetic young member, Thomas J. Wise—produced, in an edition of four hundred copies, a 'type-facsimile' reprint of this same *Pauline*. It was prepared under the superintendence and editorship of Wise, who asked the author to write an introduction. Browning jibbed, replying dryly: 'I really have said 'my little say about the little book elsewhere, and should only 'increase words without knowledge'; and he also declined to see the proofs. It is clear that he disliked the idea of the reprint, but consented to it as (in his own words) 'a concession to the 'whim of the more than friendly members of the society'.

Was such a distinction for this piece of juvenilia distasteful to him (it was in his *Collected Works*)? Or did he suspect that trouble might result from facsimile reprinting? Previously, according to the Society's report for 1884, he had 'withdrawn his leave' for the reproduction of *The Ring and the Book*. He was a careful man; he knew more about the ways of forgers, pirates, and fabricators than most people. For example, he knew all about Thomas Powell, who made a timely flight from England's shores to the United States. There the immigrant won success and a warm notice in the Dictionary of American Biography which is silent about his former forging activities exposed by both Dickens and Browning.[4] The latter also had been taken in by the forged Shelley letters of De Gibler. Wise himself provided examples of Browning's readiness to suspect: as in the case of the purported 1849 printing of *The Runaway Slave*. Incidentally, of the *Pauline* edition done by his special permission for members only, Wise was selling a bundle of copies to his agent, Herbert Gorfin, for two pounds as late as 1910. But the Society was dead by then.

It was the page-for-page type imitating of the 1833 *Pauline* and of Shelley first editions that most probably started Wise on his series of typographical forgeries. We have seen Fullford in 1884 reprinting for him Keats's *Ode to a Nightingale*, but not attempting typographical imitation—probably owing to his lack of material. But the idea was in Wise's mind. Now he had taken his work to Richard Clay and Sons—a well-known firm of printers, then in Bread Street Hill, London, E.C., with almost unlimited type equipment and with men skilled in using it. What ardour he applied to this task of imitating *Pauline* may be gathered from

---

[4] See the monographs "Should a Biographer Tell?" (in *The Atlantic Monthly*, 1947) and "Thomas Powell's Forgeries" (in *The Dickensian*, 1947) by the author.

his triumphant comment in his preface: 'In all respects save 'the paper, which it has been found absolutely impossible to 'match exactly, the present reprint may be considered a very good 'and precise representation of it.' Evidently feeling that there was some call for defence of such efforts at close imitating, he says:

There is a sentiment attaching to the very form in which a book of this description first appeared which is entirely wanting if the same work is perused in another dress; and therefore, failing the original, we are only too glad of the opportunity of providing ourselves with a good likeness of it. It is in this sentiment that the true book lover finds his pleasure, and not in the mere massing together of many volumes, simply because they are 'curious' or 'scarce', as persons who are not collectors frequently suppose.

The pleading here is specious. But with Wise it is nearly always a case of sufficient for the day is the argument thereof. Keats, sitting in the garden of the Grove at Hampstead, weak in body but with soul inflamed with poetic fire, did not listen less enraptured to the nightingale because it sometimes sang from a neighbour's tree. And his ode to the 'Light wingéd Dryad' is not less appealing to us when read in an edition having a stanza to a page instead of a stanza-and-a-half, as in the first edition. The absurd craze for imitative reprints, that Wise encouraged, will be referred to again. Strangely enough it was himself who, thirty-eight years later, revealed the fraudulent uses to which his own facsimiles were put. In the March 1924 number of the magazine I was editing he made public a long statement, of which the chief part is as follows:

Sir,—May I be permitted, through the columns of *The Bookman's Journal*, to enter a warning against two impudent forgeries of rare books, of which a number of copies appear to have been planted upon the unwary, and which are certainly enjoying an unfortunate success? The two books in question are the first editions of Shelley's *Adonais*, printed in Pisa in 1821, and *Hellas*, printed in London in 1822. The forgeries now circulating have been prepared by taking copies of the very close reprints issued by the Shelley Society to its members in 1886, removing my own introductions, and then rubbing them in dust to impart an appearance of age. That the result is sufficiently misleading is testified by the fact that among the persons who have fallen victims to

the fraud are two of the foremost and most widely experienced antiquarian booksellers in London, each of whom was misled by the
apparently genuine appearance of the books. How many of the smaller
dealers and private collectors have been likewise defrauded, and how
many copies of the books have crossed the Atlantic, it is impossible to
say. Both books are valuable (the *Adonais* in mint condition is now
worth about three hundred and fifty pounds), so the temptation to
the fabricator to do his best—or worst—is a strong one.

In the spring of 1886 I produced for the Browning Society a facsimile reprint of Browning's first book, *Pauline*. Almost immediately
copies of this reprint, 'faked up', were offered as originals. . . .

Actually, apart from the papers used, a comparison of Wise's
reprint with the original *Pauline* reveals easily distinguishable
differences between the types employed. But the fabricator of
copies of the reprint to pass for the valuable original would trust
that the fake would be bought without expert, or even close,
comparison. Long before Wise's warning, both J. H. Slater and
H. B. Wheatley exposed the faking of the *Pauline* reprint, the
latter commenting: 'The forger is abroad whenever prices rule
high.' Coincident with the experimental work on close imitating
of *Pauline*, Wise had still more opportunity in 1886 for typographical experience and for getting acquainted with the range of types
of Clay and Sons when he produced the Shelley reprints, which
will be dealt with in Chapter 5.

IV

While never encouraged by any warmth in Browning's letters,
Wise was extraordinarily thrustful in his to the poet. One contained three queries regarding Robert's poem, *The Statue and the
Bust* (1855), that Wise said had been raised by a member of the
Society who signed himself—it was averred—'Ball-goer'. To
this Browning replied: 'Dear Mr Wise, I have seldom met with
'such a strange inability to understand what seems the plainest
'matter possible: "ball-goers" are probably not history readers,
'but any guide-book would confirm what is sufficiently stated in
'the poem." He then appends some notes to show what a stupid
fellow (whoever he might be) the inquirer was, the last of which

concludes: 'My vagueness leaves *what* to be "gathered" when all 'these things are put down in black and white? Oh "ball-goers"!' Browning would have been still more sarcastic and pointed had he known that young Mr Wise, the sender of the queries, made a spurious edition of *The Statue and the Bust*.

Then there was the still more surprising correspondence in August 1888, when the determined young collector-dealer wrote to the poet about a twenty-eight-page printing dated 1849 of Elizabeth's poem, *The Runaway Slave*—to receive the disappointing reply: 'I never heard of a separate publication, and am pretty 'certain such a circumstance never happened. I fear this must be 'a fabricated affair.' Wise, desperately anxious to get the aged[5] poet's authoritative acceptance of the printing as genuine, came back with a clincher—sending a copy of the pamphlet for inspection. Browning's suspicions were lulled by the appearance of the print; for he returned the pamphlet with this comment: 'I dare-'say the fact has been that, on the publication of the Poem in 'America, the American friends (in London) who had been 'instrumental in obtaining it, wrote to the Authoress (in Flor-'ence) for leave to reprint it in England, and that she of course 'gave her consent—probably wrote the little advertisement. The 'respectability of the Publisher and Printer is a guarantee that 'nothing surreptitious had been done.' But the fact that it gave the name of Edward Moxon as publisher and Bradbury and Evans as printers did not prove they had produced it. Browning's first opinion that it must be a fabrication was correct. The imprints were both fictitious. The thing was one of Wise's forgeries.

As a relief to these unpleasanter aspects of Wise's activities, two stories of his collecting of Browning first editions and manuscripts may fittingly come here, although out of their chronology. In 1914, Mrs Fanny Browning, the widowed daughter-in-law of the poet, sent a tiny lock of Browning's hair to the collector. He had it enclosed under a glass panel let into a superb binding to adorn his copy of the most notable of his forgeries—Elizabeth's *Sonnets* (Reading: 1847)—thus adding association interest and value to a pamphlet whose Judgment Day had yet to come. Fanny Browning accompanied the lock of hair with a letter in

[5] Browning was seventy-six. He died the following year.

which she wrote: 'You remember I said I had sent it to be 'cleaned, as I fancied it had got moths in it.'

Some time after the death of Sir Edmund Gosse in 1928, his son, Dr Philip Gosse, was having lunch with Wise in the hotel of a southern seaside resort. A discussion on books led to talk about the Brownings—a natural turn of the conversation because the party included Fanny Browning. Dr Gosse recalled that when a small boy he, together with his sisters Teresa and Sylvia, always visited 19 Warwick Crescent (which was close to their own home) on Robert Browning's birthdays, taking bouquets. The young visitors were received with delight by the poet, who promptly found chocolates for them. After tea together, Browning, to amuse his little guests, drew pigs for them on scraps of paper. 'Those sketches would be even more interesting now,' added Dr Gosse reflectively. 'I often wonder where they have got to.'—'Oh,' replied Wise promptly, and with a laugh, 'I can 'tell you that. They are in the Ashley Library. Your father showed 'them to me, and I persuaded him to let me have them.' Dr Gosse tells the little story as an example of the collector's omnivorousness.

V

When Robert Browning had passed from the scene of his triumphs and Wise was at the height of his, the book-collector and dealer was fond of saying, both in conversation and in print: 'I am one of the few persons still living, and I believe the sole 'remaining man, who broke bread at Browning's table.' Again, in the introduction to his *Browning Library*, he speaks of his love of the poet's books, and concludes: 'Robert Browning was a 'great poet and a great gentleman, and one of the kindest and 'most noble-hearted of men.'

How strange the psychology of the man who, while writing thus of his affection for the poet and living in the daily presence of a bust of him, yet knew that he had produced spurious editions of the Brownings![6]

[6] They were Robert's *Cleon* (1855), *The Statue and the Bust* (1855), and *Gold Hair* (1864), the last-named being only suspect of forgery; and Elizabeth's *Sonnets* (Reading: 1847) and *The Runaway Slave* (1849). See pages 273 and 340 for details.

CHAPTER 4

THE LAKE POETS: *LYRICAL BALLADS* FAKED

The occasion is the first upon which a really full and faultless set of the original editions of the writings of either master has been drawn together. I very much doubt whether the achievement will ever be repeated.
Wise's Introduction to his
Two Lake Poets

I

IT WAS IN 1884 that Wise turned his attention to Wordsworth. In that year, he has recorded in his somewhat affected account,[1] he began the 'frequent' habit of paying after-dinner visits to the home in Manchester Square of the Reverend Stopford Brooke, whom he had got to know through the Shelley Society. That ardent bookman's study, on the top floor of his tall Victorian house, had volumes lining every wall, heaped on the tables, and piled up on the floor. The friendly atmosphere and charming disorder probably both attracted and irritated the young business man. Anyhow, there in his host's delightful room 'we smoked our honest pipes'—a pretty touch.

One evening Stopford Brooke handed to Wise a description he had received from John Pearson, the bookseller, of a clean, uncut first edition in the original boards of Wordsworth's *Poems* (1807), saying: 'This is a book you ought to take.' Wise continues: 'I replied that I never bought a book I could not read 'with satisfaction, and that, with few exceptions, I derived but 'little pleasure from the shorter poems of Wordsworth, whilst the 'longer ones attracted me not at all.'

In reply to this sweeping pooh! pooh!, so typical of Wise, came the kindly host's over-optimistic prophecy: 'One day 'you'll read nothing else.' But that day had not dawned when Wise, over seventy years of age, added: 'The time when I shall

---

[1] In *Two Lake Poets* (1927).

'feel driven to revel in the poetry of Wordsworth to the exclu-
'sion, even the comparative exclusion, of the works of other
'great poets, is never likely to arise.' Incidentally, this is not one
of the best illustrations of the theory advanced by Richard Curle
(in one of his introductions to Wise's catalogues) that 'Mr Wise
'collects an author primarily because his literary sense is appealed
'to and his literary instinct aroused'. Could the poet have known
of his bibliographer's intolerance, he would probably have said
that lack of enthusiasm from one who required to be 'driven to
revel' in his poetry was no great loss. To turn one of the *Peter
Bell* satires:

> *This Wordsworth verse that did from Nature rise*
> *Mere books of numbered pages were to Wise,*
> *And they were nothing more.*

Notwithstanding the plain hint that his literary taste forbade
his buying the rare first edition of Wordsworth's *Poems*, he was
round at Pearson's the next morning, and bought the strongly-
recommended item for three guineas—a price which was low
enough then, and makes the mouth water now. The commercial
instinct working after the smoking of 'honest pipes' would tell
him that he certainly ought to overcome his exquisite prejudices
when such a bargain was to be had.

The incident is typical of Wise's opportunism. In a way, he
deceived Stopford Brooke, who, hearing the almost indignant
protest of his guest against buying anything other than what it
pleased him to read, might well have presumed the rarity would
still be available for himself or another of his friends. As for the
treasure itself, the old drab boards covering what Wise himself
describes as 'this very satisfactory example of the 1807 *Poems*'
were broken. So instead of preserving the book in its original
state he had it bound in apple-green levant morocco.

At that time he could no more resist apple-green morocco
than Adam could refuse Eve's green apple. He later acquired
another copy of Wordsworth's *Poems, in Two Volumes.* This had
been in Robert Southey's library, and was still in what is now
punningly known as the original 'Cottonian' binding with which
Edith Southey was wont to clothe her husband's books out of
her cast-off petticoats and dresses. Was this jolly binding pre-

served? No! Away it had to go, for the binders to replace it by
morocco and gold. So-ho! for the apple-green levant. Much
smarter than Edith's old petticoats.

But much less interesting.

II

Poets are reputed to be, and indeed often are, the most careless
and happy-go-lucky of men—except where their own work is
concerned. Then they can be as exacting and meticulous as anyone—plagues to their printers, terrors to their publishers. Of
such was William Wordsworth. He must very nearly hold the
record for having leaves reprinted (now known as *cancellans*) to
alter or correct his work.

For example, there was his pamphlet the *Convention of Cintra*
(1809), the production of which had its amusing aspect—although
Wordsworth was probably far from seeing it at the time. The
pamphlet, one of the poet's prose writings inspired by his love
of justice, was in the printer's hands. De Quincey had been
deputed to be its censor, and told that if any dangerous passage
should be found the leaf bearing it was to be cancelled regardless of expense. One day, in an idle moment, Wordsworth picked
up an old magazine and read a paragraph which made him start.
It told of a pamphleteer having been fined one hundred pounds
and imprisoned in Newgate for a libel 'as it was termed' upon
a bishop.

The poet was a good deal shaken by the fear that something
he had written might be 'made a handle for exercising upon my
person a like act of injustice'. Such a passage in the *Cintra*
pamphlet came under the voluntary censorship, and publication
was subsequently delayed while the necessary two leaves were
reprinted and substituted.

Similar delay occurred in connexion with the first publication
of Wordsworth's *Lyrical Ballads*, in which Coleridge's *Ancient
Mariner* originally appeared. This is one of the outstanding books
in English poetry. The few existing copies of the unamended first
edition are naturally classed among the high prizes of book-
collecting—'the black tulip of that sort of literature', as Swin-

burne described the rarity that made him 'break the tenth com-
mandment into shivers' when he thought of it. Wise, of course,
possessed one of the black tulips.

He also possessed a second copy of the rare *Lyrical Ballads*. It
was another tulip, whose blackness hid a fake.

III

Wise was very proud of the section of his library devoted to
the Lake Poets: on the whole he was right to be proud. Of the
five variant issues of the first edition of *Lyrical Ballads* (1798),
he possessed three, two of which he claimed to be unique copies.
The adventures of the printing and publishing of the ballads
make an involved study. He, with his fondness and ability for
pursuing tortuous paths, revelled in it; and his triumphant satisfaction at owning two varieties of the first edition that no one
else possessed is not disguised. Some forty pages in his *Bibliography of Wordsworth* (1916) and thirty in his catalogues of 1926
and 1927 are devoted to the 'points' constituting the rarity of
his specimens. Between 1916 and 1927 he seems to have had his
own personal adventure with *Lyrical Ballads*; for only in 1926
and 1927 did he describe the peculiarity of one of his two unique
copies—a copy which has since been the object of much inquiry
and had the distinction of examination under ultra-violet rays at
the British Museum.

This copy, which is of the issue bearing the 'J. & A. Arch'
imprint, contains a *cancellans*—in this case, a leaf reprinted in
place of pages ninety-seven and ninety-eight. The chief textual
difference between the original issue and the one corrected by the
cancellans is that on page ninety-seven the second line is altered
from 'Than fifty years of reason', to 'Than years of toiling reason.'
and on page ninety-eight a poem's title is abbreviated. Wise
suggests that this reprinting of the leaf was one of the changes
undergone by the book immediately after printing in 1798. To
explain why the textual changes made on the reprinted leaf were
not followed in subsequent editions, he suggests that the second
edition was set up from a copy of the first which had not been
corrected by the insertion of the *cancellans*. The alterations thus

went unmade, according to Wise, through successive editions until 1836, or thirty-eight years later, when Wordsworth altered the line to read: 'Than years of toiling reason.'

Wise was the first bibliographer to call attention to the issue containing this *cancellans* that is apparently peculiar to his collection. If genuine, it constituted one of the most important and valuable of his Wordsworth rarities. But it is a fake—and a bad one at that.

The *cancellans* is printed from a type larger than, and of a face different from, that used for the book—a type known as Old Style which was first cut by Miller and Richard of Edinburgh about 1860. As it had not been designed when *Lyrical Ballads* was printed in 1798 the substituted leaf, which could only have been run off at a very much later date, is a fraud. With exception of the paper (which is 'all-rag' like that used for the book), all the other evidence—the appearance of the ink, the size, etc., goes to corroborate that this purported *cancellans* is a fake.

It happens that the first issue of *Lyrical Ballads* has an admittedly genuine *cancellans* (pages sixty-three to seventy),which the printer had to produce to substitute for Coleridge's *Lewti; or the Circassian's Love Chant*; and this is in the same type as the remainder of the book. Why should the printer have departed from his practice and general custom if he really had been called upon to reprint pages ninety-seven and ninety-eight in 1798?

Again it was important that Robert Southey, high priest among literary critics and future Laureate, should have an early and a correct copy of *Lyrical Ballads*. In fact, he received an advance copy containing the genuine *cancellans*; and, true to his book-collecting instinct, he recorded in his copy now in the British Museum: 'The Advertisement[2] and the Circassian Love 'Chant in the volume were cancelled. R. S.' If what may be called the Wise *cancellans* was really produced by Wordsworth's printer, why was it also not sent to Southey?

The second edition of *Lyrical Ballads* was carefully prepared, the two poets making a number of alterations. There is even documentary evidence of Coleridge warning the printer not to print from an early copy containing the cancelled *Lewti*. But he said nothing about any other *cancellans*.

[2] i.e., the list of contents, which shows the title substituted for the withdrawn *Lewti*.

One moment now may give us more
Than fifty years of reason ;
Our minds shall drink at every pore
The spirit of the season.

Some silent laws our hearts may make,
Which they shall long obey ;
We for the year to come may take
Our temper from to-day.

97

One moment now may give us more,
Than years of toiling reason :
Our minds shall drink at every pore
The spirit of the season.

Some silent laws our hearts will make,
Which they shall long obey :
We for the year to come may take
Our temper from to-day.

Wise's faked Lyrical Ballads. [*A*] *is a reproduction of the upper portion of page 97 of the genuine and very rare first issue of the first edition of the book. Below* [*B*] *is the upper portion of the fake* cancellans, *i.e. substitute leaf, purportedly printed in 1798 with the textual changes which Wordsworth did not effect until 1836. The attempt at type imitation is a poor failure, as will be seen by comparison.* (*Chapter 4, section III*)

The change of the line to 'Than years of toiling reason' appeared in the 1836–7 collected edition of Wordsworth's work. Yet Wise's story is that the poet altered the line in 1798 and then for thirty-eight years allowed edition after edition to come out without the correction—attributing this action to a man so meticulous about his work, which he was constantly revising and reissuing, as Wordsworth was.

Lastly, no other copy of the first edition of *Lyrical Ballads* with this *cancellans* of pages ninety-seven and ninety-eight is known; and Wise has not a word to say of the provenance of what, were it genuine, would be a copy of the very highest importance.

All these considerations are merely supplementary to the main fact that the *cancellans* is condemned on its type. It is possible to theorize that Wise acquired the volume with this faked *cancellans* in the ordinary way of book-collecting and was deceived. But it is hardly possible to believe that, when he observed the biblio-graphical differences and came to consider all the circumstances, he could feel other than suspicious. Why should he lend his authority to establish as genuine this fake *cancellans*, and that by the ridiculous proposition that Wordsworth, of all men, let his corrections remain unmade for so many years? The weakness of any theorizing exculpatory of Wise, however, is that the type of the false *cancellans* is the same as that used for some of his spurious pamphlets.

Apart from the attempt to fabricate a rarity of great value, the result was that the bibliographical history of such an important book was falsified in the Ashley Library catalogues. Further, that copies of the 'J. & A. Arch' issue with pages ninety-seven and ninety-eight uncorrected were forced up to fictitious values —the presumption in the rare-book trade being that naturally, of the copies extant, the majority would bear the *cancellans* or corrected leaf. Whereas, in fact, not one is known to exist except Wise's very black tulip.[3]

---

[3] Professor John Edwin Wells was apparently the first to express doubt of this issue of the first *Lyrical Ballads* (see *The Times* Lit. Supp., 23 June 1932); and Professor G. F. Whicher in *The Colophon* (1937) subsequently added to the doubt, but left the verdict open pending 'expert examination of paper and type'.

IV

The discovery in regard to this 'unique' issue of the first
edition of *Lyrical Ballads* means that other hitherto unsuspected
rarities in the Ashley Library will be the subject of investigation
in the future. To what extent there has been fabrication of others
of the library's rarities may not be known for many years.[4]
Nevertheless, Wise's collecting of the two Lake Poets was successful in gathering printings and manuscripts of undoubted
genuineness and of the highest interest to students of the two
authors.

One of his manuscripts is of Wordsworth's nine-line poem on
childhood, beginning:

> *My heart leaps up when I behold*
> *A rainbow in the sky:*

and is famous for containing the line which has now passed into
everyday language as a saying: 'The child is father of the man.'
But Wise's note on this MS. reveals the critical limitations of the
bibliographer—and something more.

The manuscript was written by the seventy-two-year-old poet
and sent to his publisher, Moxon, in 1842, with the instruction
added in faltering script: 'The above sonnet I wish inserted first
'of my Poems refering [*sic*] to the period of Childhood.' Comparison of this late script with the definitive printed version
shows important differences in four lines. This caused Wise to
add the characteristic note to his catalogue description of the
MS.:

> For some unknown reason Moxon failed to obey the poet's instruc-
> tions. Not one of Wordsworth's editors has been aware of the revisions,
> and consequently the text of 1807 has always been reproduced in
> subsequent editions of the poet's work.

For some equally unknown reason Wise failed to observe—
or rather to record—that across the manuscript, in a more faltering script even than the poet's, Moxon (presumably) has writ-

[4] Other examples I have discovered during my researches are described in Chapters 13
and 16.

ten, 'Corrected from Mr Wordsworth's last copy'—indication that the version thus minuted had not been followed.

It is fairly obvious that Wordsworth wrote the 1842 version from failing memory, and only to indicate clearly to Moxon that this was the particular 'Childhood' poem to have first place in the series. The hurriedly-written script sent with the instruction to his publisher was never intended as a textual revision—as Moxon rightly understood. The four lines as they appear in Wordsworth's imperfectly remembered version are inferior to those in the poem as printed and approved by the poet from time to time.

Which is precisely why, if they knew of what Wise mistakenly calls the 'revision', the various editors of the poet have not altered the poem. It was foolish of Wise to boost the importance of this scrap of Wordsworth's writing, with the evidence of what it really was so clearly before him. He had enough manuscripts of indisputable value in his collection.

V

A privately-printed four-page brochure of Wordsworth's poem, *Grace Darling*, was produced for his own use in 1843. The poem, wrote the poet to Henry Read (27 March 1843), 'I threw 'off two or three weeks ago . . . to do justice to the memory of a 'heroine whose conduct presented a striking contrast to the in-'humanity with which our countrymen shipwrecked lately upon 'the French coast have been treated'. This printing is now a rarity. Because every surviving copy of it that Wise had inspected was inscribed by the author, he states: 'There can be 'no doubt that each example of *Grace Darling* distributed by 'Wordsworth was given by him personally as a friendly gift.'

This is a perfectly reasonable conclusion and in accordance with custom. Authors who go to the trouble of privately printing a piece of their work usually inscribe the few copies and distribute them among their friends. Yet, with the knowledge of what he had written, Wise is silent about the curious feature of that other example of a private Wordsworth pamphlet, the dedicatory verses *To The Queen*.[5] Printed for the author (Kendal, 1846)—'one of the most uncommon of the First Editions of Wordsworth,' says the collector. Neither his own nor any other is recorded as being a presentation copy, although the production is of the same class as the *Grace Darling*. That fact is remarkable, though not remarked on. Wise seems to have always a blissful confidence that his readers will accept his conclusions without question or comparison. But there was good reason why a copy of this edition of the verses *To The Queen* had *not* been inscribed by Wordsworth.

It was one of Wise's forgeries, produced long after the poet's death.

5 See also Chapter 7, Section III.

CHAPTER 5

SHELLEY STORIES: THE PIRATE IN FULL SAIL

'By Jove, I will; he was my father's friend!'
Thus Dr Furnivall, in choice blank verse,
Replied when he was asked by Mr Sweet
(Sweet of the pointed and envenomed pen,
Wherewith he pricks the men who won't elect
Him a Professor, as he ought to be),
'Twas thus, we say, that Furnivall replied
To the bold question asked by bitter Sweet.
And what that question? Briefly, it was this—
'Why do not you, who start so many things,
'Societies for poets live and dead,
'Why do not you a new communion found—
'"Shelley Society" might be the name—
'Where men might worry over Shelley's bones?'
'By Jove, I will; he was my father's friend,'
Said Furnivall: and lo! the thing was done . . .
Andrew Lang: *The Shelley Society*

I

IN THE AUTUMN OF 1885 the idea of a Shelley Society occurred to Professor Henry Sweet, whose grievance it was that his services as a philologist were not readily acknowledged. Of course the fiat of Dr Furnivall had to be obtained for the plan. The father of literary societies must not only be persuaded to accept the role of paternity, but the literary doctor must also be the man-midwife.

He was willing as usual—indeed more so in this interesting case. He remembered that his own father, a surgeon, had attended Mary Shelley at her confinement. The poet, when he lived at Marlow, had often rowed up the Thames to Windsor, left his man and boat there, and sat on the surgery counter chatting with Furnivall senior. Shelley would refuse all refreshments except a dish of milk and a piece of bread. Although the surgeon did not believe in the poet's theories, he had been delighted with the young man's society.

All this Dr Furnivall told at the inaugural meeting of the Society at University College on the 10th of March 1886. He explained that when Mr Sweet had asked, 'Why not found a 'Shelley Society,' he had replied: 'By Jove, I will; he was my 'father's friend.' And proceeded to remark that had the proposal been made with respect to a Tupper or a Gosse [this was a side dig at young Edmund, whose poetical aspirations were once acute] people might naturally have wondered. But as Shelley was one of England's greatest poets, etc., etc., etc.

When Andrew Lang read Furnivall's speech in the newspapers, there followed an incident that led to the production by Wise of one of his most attractive privately-printed pamphlets. Like many more of his printings, this was produced *sub rosa*. It was not until seven years had passed that he revealed his hand by sending Gosse a copy of the pamphlet—drawing from Sir Edmund this reminiscence:

> . . . I well recollect that Thursday in March 1886. I was busy in the garret I used to occupy in the Board of Trade when Lang came in like a whirlwind, and waved a newspaper. He read the report of the Shelley Society's meeting with shouts of laughter, and said 'I must do this 'for the Saturday Review—for Shelley was my father's friend—give 'me some paper!' 'Won't you do it in verse?' I suggested. And right away, seated on the edge of the table and sprawling across it, he scribbled the blank verse, murmuring it out aloud as he wrote. I contributed two or three lines to it as it proceeded. The whole thing was done in fifteen minutes, folded up, addressed, stamped, and sent off with splutters of laughter. You cannot think how delighted I am to possess this charming memorial of a delightful episode. . . .

The opening lines of Lang's amusing poem, with its effective reiteration of Furnivall's 'By Jove, I will; he was my father's friend!' preface this chapter, which tells of some strange sequels when 'Lo! the thing was done'. The poem was promptly put out by Wise in one of his limited editions as *Lines on the Inaugural Meeting of the Shelley Society*. Reprinted for Private Distribution from *The Saturday Review* of 13 March 1886. The pamphlet is advertised in his 1895 bookseller's list, which presumably would only be circulated to his clients. He did not include it in his 1905–8 catalogue of the Ashley Library. He had written to Lang (whose name is not mentioned) about permission to print the *Lines*, but only received a cold, curt, reply referring him to the publishers.

II

Wise, the twenty-six-year-old bookman, member of the Browning Society, and known to be collecting Shelley, was among the first to be enlisted in the new project. From the beginning, he was one of those who ran the Shelley Society. It was just the field for enterprise that he needed: the activities of the Browningites were rather too circumspectly controlled by men like Furnivall and Dykes Campbell, and overwatched by the cautious poet himself.

This is a very notable period in the development of the Shelley Cult. The poet's sisters were still alive. His son and daughter-in-law, Sir Percy and Lady Shelley, were intensely active—especially the latter—in clearing the poet's name and doing justice to his work. Professor Dowden was nearing the end of long labours on his *Life* of Shelley. Within the Society were two groups: one of scholars like Dr Richard Garnett, and Dowden, and Furnivall, concerned only with the genius and interpretation of the poet; the other, of collectors like Wise, whose interests were rather more materialistic.

Something of the division that separated these inner and outer circles was indicated by Miss Olivia R. Garnett, daughter of the British Museum's great Keeper of Printed Books. 'My father', Miss Garnett wrote to me, 'was reticent in this sort of Shelleyan 'controversial matters, and generally turned off inquiries by non- 'experts with a humorous expression or a quotation from the 'Classics. In such a manner he would refer to Mr Wise, whose 'cognomen struck him in such connexions as singularly and 'amusingly inappropriate. Far otherwise was it with reference to 'Mr Buxton Forman. . . . If my father met Mr Wise in person it 'must have been in the Reading Room.' In short, there emerges the conclusion that young Wise's interest in Shelley and Browning was far less that of the student than that of publisher, collec-

tor, and dealer. One of the Societies even makes the nice distinction. In a report some of the members of the Committee, including Wise, are grouped as 'Shelley Workers'; while others are
described as 'Students of Shelley'. The reading of papers—and
admirable many of them were—was a natural feature of both
societies. There is no record of a single paper ever having been
contributed by Wise to either of the institutions.

But he was at least as active as anyone. The obsession for
facsimile reprinting was now upon him, and also the urge to
be among the types of Richard Clay and Sons. From the beginning, it was the Society's policy to publish facsimiles of Shelley's
printings, and distribute them to members for the purpose of
attracting subscriptions. The printing arrangements were put
entirely under the control of Wise. The Reverend Stopford A.
Brooke, in an inaugural address, outlined the programme, with
some misgivings: 'It pleases us to have facsimiles of the first
'editions of Shelley, and other bibliographical curiosities. I do not
'say that this is a very high ambition, nor that it has anything to
'do with the love of poetry.' Here possibly young Wise or somebody tugged at the clerical coat-tails, for the worthy Brooke
side-stepped with ecclesiastical agility, continuing: 'Yet it is a
'harmless and innocent fancy. . . . A lover likes everything that
'puts him in mind of his mistress, even a picture of the room she
'dwells in.' True! so true!—always providing that the mementoes
are not faked, or the picture not made by another lover.

Wise lost no time. The Society was launched on 10 March
1886; and a month later his type-facsimile of the first edition of
Adonais (begun while his Browning Society's *Pauline* reprint was
still in preparation) was ready for delivery to members. There
followed in the same year type-facsimiles of Shelley's original
Hellas and *Alastor*, in addition to other publications—all from
Clay and Sons; and the programme was continued in 1887. The
prefatory note to *Hellas* gives an indication of Wise's triumphant
feelings about his typographical success: 'Of this 1822 edition,
'the present is as exact a representation as it has been found
'possible—with types—to obtain . . . each "printer's error,"
'"dropped letter," or other peculiarity of the original being care-
'fully retained.'

The young bachelor spent laborious nights in his Holloway

home straining over the proofs. He found it fascinating, certainly useful, to make these imitative reprints of rare first editions. What an experience it was for him! Watching for wrong founts, a comma missing here, a slug (i.e. a space) there; learning the dodges—legitimate dodges—of the printing trade, the publishing trick of working off old-edition sheets with new title-pages, the cancelling of leaves, etc., etc. Eagerly he drank of the cup of bibliographical knowledge which was later to bring him fame. The cup was filled at the pumps of the Shelley and Browning Societies from the common well of Richard Clay and Sons.

It is only fair to say that there were other type-facsimiles being produced at this time. That there was money in them, he himself shows in citing the case of Harry Buxton Forman, who, having bought a copy of the elusive first edition of Byron's earliest work, *Fugitive Pieces*, for seventy pounds, made a facsimile reprint of it in the same year, 1886. 'The profit derived from the 'sale of the reprint,' says Wise, 'exactly equalled the sum For-'man had paid for the original copy.'[1] It was a cheap way of acquiring rarities.

The Victorian bookmen and collectors were sincere, enthusiastic, and not a little impressionable. The arguments advanced to them were that the rare first editions of collected poets and prose writers were becoming harder to get as competition grew, especially from America; and that it was the 'right thing' to have these facsimile reprints, which were the best of alternatives and worthwhile substitutes for the unattainable. In consequence, collectors and librarians paid their guineas. The reprints multiplied until now they can be bought in bundles at a shilling a time. The British Museum and offices of rare-book sellers must echo with the curses of experts wearied by optimists bringing these type-facsimiles in the hope that they are rare originals and worth small fortunes. The same places must also be filled by the ghostly sighs of the disappointed inquirers.

The production of imitative reprints without proper safe-guards—i.e., without the use of dated watermarked paper, and also the facsimile itself bearing a printed statement that it is a facsimile—is playing into the hands of the unscrupulous. Both the law and printing practice ought to have made it impossible

[1] *Byron Bibliography* (1932), Vol. i, page 4.

for such reprints to be made. Whether those who produced them in 1886 and 1887 appreciated the objections that could be made to their work, it is useless to argue. What is certain is that the typographical experience Thomas James Wise gained in his considerable share of facsimile reprinting was utilized in producing the spurious nineteenth-century pamphlets.

I have met with no evidence of Wise faking his own facsimile reprints. The 'doctoring' of individual copies of a seventy-two-page book, 1or example, the discoloration of paper to give the appearance of age so that they would pass for genuine first editions, would be a long and troublesome business, with uncertain results and the risk of immediate discovery. On the other hand, the production of small pamphlets of from eight to about twenty-four pages of matter already published, putting on them false imprints, and also dates earlier than those on any printings of the same matter—thus making them appear as rare first editions hitherto unknown—would involve much less labour for much greater return. In the latter case the printers did the work as directed by the clever customer in the background. And that was the highly ingenious idea conceived in the mind of Thomas James Wise about this time. His manufacturing of facsimiles for the Shelley and Browning Societies had accustomed the printers to accept from him predated title-pages.

III

While the young man was now advancing in his business career with Hermann Rubeck and busying himself with the Shelley and Browning Societies, his rare-book collecting and dealing went on apace. He surprised me in later years by saying that he had picked up few bargains, explaining that this was due partly to the fact that he insisted on having only the finest specimens, and partly to the fact that he had bought mostly as the result of booksellers reporting rarities to him. He was, however, silent about some of his big coups which, as will be shown, brought him thousands of pounds profit. Perhaps he did not call them bargains.

It was an opportune time for a shrewd, well-informed man like

Wise, who realized that books in their original boards and in fine condition, especially books with 'points' or association interest, would soon be in greater demand. There were plenty of good things about for those with courage and determination—even bargains. For instance, he called at a bookshop to learn of a man who had just found a first edition of Shelley's *St Irvyne* in the original state, for which he had paid only a shilling. 'Cuss him!' was Wise's comment.

But he had his finds also. An exciting one was in a book auction lot of three volumes containing about forty tracts on Catholic emancipation. Someone had begun to catalogue the volumes, but had given up the task. Had that cataloguer turned over one more tract he would have come across a rarity— Shelley's *Address to the Irish People* (Dublin: 1812. Price 5d.). Wise's keen eyes spotted it, however; later they stared anxiously at a London bookseller when he in turn examined the volume. Nevertheless, no one else detected the lurking treasure; and presently Wise secured the lot for two pounds ten shillings. He resold the tracts, with the exception of Shelley's *Address*, to the British Museum for the same sum; so that the Shelley rarity cost him nothing. Subsequently he sold it for two hundred pounds, when he replaced it by a finer copy having the association interest that it had been given by the poet to Byron's Jane Clairmont.

Another story about Wise, which can be supplemented here, illustrates not only his determination to have the rarest of the rare, but the very romance of collecting. That excessively scarce first edition *Original Poetry* by 'Victor and Cazire', Shelley's 1810 work, was suppressed because a poem by 'Monk' Lewis was accidentally included in it—and possibly also because the poet's sister ('Cazire') was offended by its publication. *Original Poetry* was so rigidly suppressed, indeed, that for fifty years it was an unknown book. In 1859 a reference to it was found, but thirty-eight more years passed before the first copy came to light at Dorchester in 1898. The find caused a sensation, and Wise captured the unique item—paying one hundred and fifty-five pounds for it, according to a letter from him to me. In 1903 a second copy was found at Barnsbury, London; being a slightly taller copy containing words erased in the other. It had been bought for sixpence by an old gentleman who died in ignorance both of its authorship and of its great value, bequeathing it among other effects to his housekeeper. Wise bought this one at auction for six hundred pounds; and it eventually went via F. R. Halsey to the library of that great American collector Henry E. Huntington.[2] Then a third copy came to light. It was notable for containing the autograph inscription: 'Given to me at Eton by the Author Percy Bysshe Shelley, my friend and schoolfellow. 1810. W. W.'—i.e., William Wellesley, fourth Earl of Mornington. Wise was fortunate enough to pay no more than six hundred pounds for it, selling his original copy (i.e., No. 1) to John H. Wrenn. Thus, the only three copies of this Shelley rarity with such a romantic history all came into Wise's hands.[3]

'During the first twenty years of my search for Shelleyana,' Wise recalled, 'I met with no opposition I was unable to defeat, 'and Mr [F. R.] Halsey of New York became my first serious 'and successful competitor.'[4] There in his own words is the determination of the man.

It was with Halsey that Wise had an auction-room duel in 1903 for the Shelley political pamphlet, *Proposals for an Association of those Philanthropists who convinced of the inadequacy of the Moral and Political state of Ireland . . . are willing to unite to accomplish its regeneration.* Only one other copy of this rarity was known at the time; and it was anticipated that there would be a keen fight for this second copy, which, when Wise was a boy of ten, had been catalogued for sale at ten pounds. The protagonists did not appear, being represented by agents. Wise left with the auctioneer, Tom Hodge of Sotheby's, an instruction to 'bid for it to an amount limited only by his judgment'. Not for a moment did he anticipate defeat, he says, although why not it is difficult to see. Anyhow, the fight came on. At five hundred and thirty pounds the auctioneer exercised his discretion, and Wise lost the rarity to his New York rival. His disappointment was acute

[2] Wise told Wrenn (*Letters to Wrenn, op. cit.*, page 333) that he bought this copy No. 2 on behalf of a London agent acting for an American client. But for a more remarkable aspect of his dealing in these three famous copies, see page 127 here.
[3] To a specific inquiry Wise replied for publication (25 October 1924): 'Yes, I have owned each of the three "Victors". Each as it turned up was a better. . . . Alas, neither was a "find"' [he meant, of his].
[4] *A Shelley Library* (1924).

—although the auctioneer assured him he was well out of the business, that the price would have gone soaring up, and that Wise was certain to get another copy at a smaller price. But he had to wait twenty-eight years, and then pay nine hundred pounds for the uncut copy which had belonged to Denis MacCarthy, the author of *Shelley's Early Life* (1872). It was the 'other copy' whose existence was on record, but which had been long lost. After it was found by MacCarthy's son among his father's papers, the rarity was eventually sold to Wise privately through Sotheby's in 1931.

IV

The foregoing stories have been selected as illustrative of the adventure of Wise's collecting. Two others, of the more involved course his career was now taking, should be told here.

In 1887 Thomas James Wise became Charles Alfred Seymour. The object of this disguise was to mislead any unsympathetic person who might chance upon a copy of *Poems and Sonnets. By Percy Bysshe Shelley. Edited by Charles Alfred Seymour, Member of the Philadelphia Historical Society* (Philadelphia: 1887). Of course it was printed for 'Private Circulation Only', and as usual 'Limited to thirty copies'; and of course the Philadelphia imprint was false. Wise's long preface is a mixture of cynicism, humbug, and wholesale quotation from Dowden.

These *Poems and Sonnets*, which were originally contained in a manuscript volume, express Shelley's feelings for the comely and seductive Harriet, his first wife, at a time when they were happy in the full ardour of fresh and mutual love. 'Thou wert the in-'spiration of my song,' he dedicated the volume to her:

> *Then press into thy breast this pledge of love,*
> *And know, though time may change and years may roll,*
> *Each floweret gathered in my heart*
> *It consecrates to thine.*

The poems remained in manuscript until they came into the possession of Professor Dowden, to be included in his *Life* of Shelley. Now we come to Wise's justification for the imposture.

He asserts that 'Dowden, Rossetti, Forman, and *other friends*
'were with me in my desire to have these poems in a convenient
'form' [the phraseology should be particularly noticed]. 'But
'Lady Shelley expressed dissent (as she did with most projects
'connected with Shelley not originating directly with herself)
'although she held no interest whatever in the copyright of the
'verses.' [Then why was Lady Shelley's permission sought—
if it was sought?] 'To avoid discussion with her Ladyship the
'name of Charles Alfred Seymour was invented, and Philadelphia
'was selected as the nominal place of printing.'

Wise described the book fully in his *Ashley Library Catalogue*
of 1922–36 and in his *Shelley Library* (1924). His chuckling justi-
fication says that the book was printed in London by Clay and
Sons, and prepared and edited by him in collaboration with
Professor Dowden—who, it is alleged, 'elected the mythical
Charles Alfred Seymour to the equally mythical Philadelphia
Historical Society'. But Dowden's *Life* of Shelley, in which these
Poems and Sonnets were first printed, was issued in November
1886. For Wise, alias Seymour, to reprint the poems in a separate
edition in 1887 and call it a first edition looks like an attempt to
manufacture a rarity. Moreover, Dowden's letter to Wise which
was inserted in the Ashley Library copy hardly confirms his
collaboration in the affair. He writes to his 'friend':

My dear Sir,   Dublin, Aug., '88.
    You are very good to give me (on behalf of 'Mr Charles Alfred
'Seymour') the beautiful quarto. When a gentleman of the road makes
you stand and deliver, and then courteously hands you back your purse,
you can do no less than make a bow and say that he has the manners
of a Prince. . . .

No gentleman of the road could have mistaken the sarcasm
here. But, having, in the pleasantest way possible, called Wise a
highwayman, Professor Dowden evidently thought that there
was a more fitting description to be applied. His letter continues:

And so I feel to that amiable member of the Phila. Hist. Soc. He
has done his work with the greatest care and correctness as far as I
can see, and I hope you will greet him from me in the words of Shelley
in his Homeric hymn which tells of the light-fingered doings of the
first of pirates . . . I will keep the veil of darkness over his misdeeds,
but I fear I cannot help him to the 'other songs'.

What had happened needs no explanation. Dowden's letter does not even require to be read between the lines. The fact is that by 1887, the pirate was in full sail. It is significant that the account of this Shelley piracy was not given by Wise in his original *Ashley Library Catalogue* of 1905–8 when Professor Dowden was alive. The story implicating him in the imposture was only printed after his death, which occurred in 1913—a circumstance we shall see paralleled in regard to other men who were useful to Thomas James Wise. But one lamentable result of the *post-mortem* libel on the worthy professor was that in the British Museum's Catalogue of its printed books the pseudonym Charles Alfred Seymour was for years recorded as that of both Wise and Dowden, the latter thus being made a co-pirate on the statement of the sole perpetrator. The attribution was, of course, made innocently and naturally enough at a time when Wise's authority was unquestioned and his true character unrevealed. The British Museum's Catalogue entries were amended and the piracy removed as a Dowden title when attention was called to the matter after the original publication of this work.

V

There is in the Ashley Library a series of six important little volumes of Shelley letters. Their abbreviated titles with the alleged dates of printing are as follows:

[1] *Harriet Shelley's Letters to Catherine Nugent* (1889);
[2] *Letters from Percy Bysshe Shelley to Jane Clairmont* (1889);
[3] *Letters . . . to Elizabeth Hitchener*, 2 vols. (1890);
[4] *Letters . . . to William Godwin*, 2 vols. (1891);
[5] *Letters . . . to J. H. Leigh Hunt*, 2 vols. (1894) and
[6] *Letters . . . to Thomas Jefferson Hogg*, vol. 1 [only] (1894).

Although Wise admits in the *Ashley Library Catalogue* (Vol. V) that all these were his publications, an examination of them shows mysterious characteristics. They are all 'Privately Printed', but bear neither publisher's nor printer's imprint. The first four contain no identification with Wise; but the fifth (which came out after a lapse of three years from the date of the fourth) and finally the interrupted sixth work, are identified, and bear the Ashley Library book device at the end.

It is obvious from the volumes themselves that the first four were issued surreptitiously. Why the suppression of the imprints? Why, with the exception of Harriet's letters, the absence of any reference to the source of the material? Why the cataloguing of them in such an inadequate and uncandid way? I was for a long time mystified. Then, in the same week that brought a timely communication from America, I was shown a letter written by Wise, dated 13 January 1893. Both communications refer to Shelley's *Letters . . . to Elizabeth Hitchener*—that sex-repressed schoolmistress who, for a short time, was the 'soul-sister' of the poet; but who was soon to be seen by him as that 'ugly hermaphroditical beast of a woman', that 'brown Demon' whose avaricious jaws snapped at a pension of £100 from the poet as the price of her riddance.[5]

The letter from America was written to me by William H. McCarthy, of the University of Texas Library, and contained the following:

You select for inquiry one of the Shelleys we very much would like to own! Since the Carter and Pollard book, that Shelley item has struck me as having marks of being an overture to the forgeries themselves. We have proof sheets of the first edition of Shelley's *Letters to Elizabeth Hitchener*, heavily corrected throughout. These proofs are stamped with Clay's regular proof-sheet stamps of various dates in 1887 and 1888, but the title page has a New York imprint dated 1886. There was an ambiguity about the ownership of these letters, Elizabeth Hitchener having disappeared through a Continental marriage, leaving the MS. in the possession of an attorney. He lost track of her and her heirs, and the trial New York imprint with the faked date were apparently planned to obviate trouble. The small edition was not run off, however, until 1890, and the imprint was given then as London. Trouble must have blown over by . . . 1908. . . . The entry for these proof sheets in

---

[5] Her story is summarized in one of the admirable letters of Harriet, Shelley's unfortunate first wife, to whom biography now does justice. Harriet writes to Catherine Nugent, 14 November 1812: 'The lady I have often mentioned to you, of the name of Hitchener, 'has to our very great happiness left us. We were entirely deceived in her character as to 'her republicanism, and in short everything else which she pretended to be. . . . She built 'all her hopes on being able to separate me from my dearly loved Percy, and had the artful-'ness to say that Percy was really in love with her, and [that it] was only his being married 'that could keep her within bounds. . . .'

the Wrenn Catalogue uses the title page of the 1890 edition, and says nothing about a projected New York imprint. These proofs were *a gift* from Mr. Wise to Mr Wrenn.

The other communication is from Wise to a London bookseller and helps to complete the explanation of the *Hitchener Letters* mystery. Wise is writing, three years after his publication of the *Letters*, because the bookseller had copies for sale, guessed or knew that there was some difficulty about the publishing, and naturally asked questions. Wise explains that the possessor of the original letters was a Mr Slack, who had allowed him to take copies of them upon his giving the undertaking that they would not be circulated among outsiders. Wise says he does not desire to incur the owner's displeasure, chiefly because he anticipates buying the originals at some time. He adds that he does not wish to seem to be going back on his undertaking of honour, and indicates that he does not wish publicity to be given to the publication—presumably by having it advertised for sale in a catalogue.

This letter exemplifies the liberties which Wise took with the truth in his dealings and correspondence. Actually what happened was that Henry J. Slack, of Forest Row, Sussex, a barrister, had allowed William Michael Rossetti to copy these letters solely for future use in a Shelley compilation by Rossetti that was never published. Wise borrowed the transcripts, and made his privately-printed edition without the knowledge of Rossetti or Slack. Subsequently he seems to have feared trouble; and in the autumn of 1888 he attempted to buy the originals. Rossetti, becoming cognizant of the printing, suggested to him to offer Slack an indemnity against all possible claimants for the use which had been made of the letters; for 'I am quite persuaded there will be none such, and you will get off scathless'. How the business ended is not clear from Rossetti's correspondence with Wise (Ashley Coll.). What is clear is that Wise printed Shelley's letters to Miss Hitchener secretly and without authority.

These facts about the origin of his volumes of the *Hitchener Letters* illustrate the surreptitiousness of his publishing methods. The Clay proof sheets in the Wrenn Library are important as showing his use of a false title-page date and faked imprint in 1887. Further, the *Hitchener Letters* were not the only ones in the Shelley Series to be so printed. Apparently he was going to issue a similar volume of Shelley's *Letters to Robert Southey and Other Correspondents*. 1888. London: Privately Printed—described in the Wrenn Catalogue as 'The Revised Proof of the 'First Edition, with corrections in the "handwriting of the '"Editor, Mr T. J. Wise...." The volume was never completed'— a description passed by Wise, who edited the catalogue. When the Ashley Collection came to be removed to the British Museum, a set of page-proofs on vellum of this item was found. Contrary to Wise's practice, even in the case of his suppressed publications, he made no mention of this projected 'First Edition' in his own catalogues; probably because its false imprint would require explanation. For the title-page imprint on the vellum proofs reads: '1886. New York: Privately Printed. (Not for Sale).' To complete the exposure of this project it has to be added (1) that the printing of this 'New York' publication was done for him by Clays; and (2) that the Shelley Letters to Southey had already been published in 1881 by Dowden in *The Correspondence of Robert Southey with Caroline Bowles*.

Wise's explanation in the *Ashley Catalogue* for the abrupt stoppage of the series of Shelley correspondence volumes (of the sixth and last selection in 1894, Vol. II never came out) is that 'I had proposed to print the whole of the letters of Shelley 'arranged in volumes each of which was to contain the letters 'addressed to one particular correspondent. But the preparation 'by Mr Roger Ingpen of Shelley's correspondence complete in 'one series rendered it unnecessary to continue my own work, 'and the project was relinquished accordingly.' Unfortunately for that explanation, which leaves so much to be accounted for, the fact is that Ingpen's edition of the complete correspondence did not appear until 1909—twelve years later. If everything was straightforward, if there was no objection to his procedure, why so abruptly stop (even half-way through the last work) this production of correspondence of the highest importance in volumes that he could claim to be genuine first editions—unauthorized though they were?

These six Shelley publications had all to be bought by the British Museum Library. Not one was sent in accordance with the requirements of the Copyright Act or as a gift from a

Shelley student, worker, highwayman, pirate, or whatever the publisher may be called.

VI

To conclude the account of Wise's activities with the Shelley Society, that institution, which was popular enough in its early days to secure four hundred members, got badly into debt. For this, the Society's recital of *Hellas* with music, involving a loss of ninety pounds, was largely blamed. But it is now apparent, from private correspondence put into my hands, that the expenditure on those facsimile reprints and also the offprints done for himself was the greater cause. In the Society's first year, Wise's printing (over which he had entire control) at the works of Clay and Sons came to one hundred and ninety pounds. In the next year, from 10 January 1887 to 17 January 1888, Clay's printing bill had gone up to three hundred and eleven pounds out of the Society's total expenditure of four hundred and twelve pounds. Eventually, in the 'nineties, the Shelleyites found themselves in debt, mostly to their printers, to the extent of eight hundred pounds—and subscriptions falling off! There ensued a most unphilosophical row. Clays were patient: they looked to Wise, by whom they were much impressed. But there is a limit of credit to be given, even to literary societies backed by eminent and respectable gentlemen. An arrangement was made for the debt to be paid off at the rate of one hundred pounds per annum by private levies on a few of the leading members. Here, for example, are the chief contributors for two years to pay the piper for the facsimile-reprinting tune called by Wise:

1893	£	1894	£
W. M. Rossetti	13	W. M. Rossetti	14
Dr Furnivall	10	H. Buxton Forman	18
H. Buxton Forman	13	R. A. Potts	18
R. A. Potts	13	T. J. Wise	18
T. J. Wise	13	[John] Todhunter	5
[Another]	3	Dr Furnivall	10

Wise, in conversation, used to be fond of recalling that he put his hand in his pocket to pay for the Society's losses on the

Hellas venture. But that he got some cash return (apart from the invaluable typographical experience at Clays) for his own levied contribution he himself partly discloses. In his catalogue there are certain Shelley publications whose presence called for some explanation. So he has this note: 'When the Shelley Society 'issued under my superintendence its series of type-facsimile 'reprints of a number of the original editions of Shelley's works, 'I took advantage of the opportunity of having the type set for 'some of them[6] specially reimposed to suit a crown quarto page, 'and printed three copies of each upon fine vellum. Each was 'printed with a certificate signed by the printers Messrs Richard 'Clay and Sons, Ltd.' Further, his private bookseller's list of 1895 contained under the heading 'Shelleyana' no less than nineteen pamphlets of papers read to the Society. These pamphlets, with two or three exceptions, were all run off for Wise from the type set for the Society's *Records*, after reimposition and provision of new preliminaries. Not all the authors desired, or were even given, the option of refusing to have their papers produced in this way by Wise,[7] but these small editions were a publishing side-line of Wise—and not an unprofitable one either. And, as in the case of the *Pauline* facsimile reprint, 'done for 'members of the Browning Society only', he was in 1910— eighteen years after the end of the Shelley Society—selling to his agent, Herbert Gorfin, a bundle of these publications for six pounds.

It may be reasonably conjectured that Messrs Rossetti, Furnivall, Potts, Todhunter, Buxton Forman, and others, who joined him in paying off the debt which his printing adventures had piled up, did not recoup themselves by the methods of the smart and reputedly affluent young merchant.

---

[6] In all, nine books.   [7] See page 326.

CHAPTER 6

REVELATIONS OF THE CONTEMPORARY
DIARY OF MR Y. Z.

I du believe in bein' this
Or thet, ez it may happen
One way or t'other hendiest is
To ketch the people nappin';

It ain't by princerples nor men
My preudunt course is steadied,—
I scent wich pays the best, an' then
Go into it baldheaded.

J. R. Lowell: *The Biglow Papers*[1]

I

ONE OF THE most debated questions—hitherto unanswered—
in connexion with Thomas James Wise and his spurious pamphlets is: When did the manufacture of the forgeries begin? The
authors of *An Enquiry into the Nature of Certain Nineteenth-
Century Pamphlets* observe: 'The actual dates between which the
'forger was engaged in production cannot, of course, be pre-
'cisely determined. Kipling's *The White Man's Burden* shows that
'he was at work as late as 1899.' For the earliest indicated date,
they mention 1886, the year Wise 'discovered' Dr W. C. Bennett's copies of Elizabeth Barrett Browning's *Sonnets* with the
Reading: 1847 imprint. But when the *Enquiry* was written, its
authors did not know that subsequently Wise was to retract his
highly romantic story of how these forgeries came from Bennett
—hence the date 1886 means nothing as a guide here. They are
on certain ground, however, in mentioning 1888, for we have
seen the collector in August of that year bringing forward his
spurious 'first' edition of *The Runaway Slave* in order to entrap

---

[1] The American poet, when Minister in London for the United States, was a member of
the Browning Society.

Browning into a declaration of its genuineness. This year 1888 is also the earliest assigned (at the time this chapter is being written) by the British Museum Library's Catalogue as the date of production of any of the forgeries.

There is one source from which light might have been thrown on the question of dates—indeed, on the whole story of this unparalleled manufacture of forgeries, the record of which is in the Appendix. That source, naturally, would be the printing-house that did the forger's work. Unfortunately, the records of Richard Clay and Sons are no longer available. Cecil Clay, the present managing-director of the firm, told me that in 1911— consequent upon a decision by the Board of Directors—all the firm's old correspondence was destroyed. It is useless to lament the destruction of what might have been so valuable. But there is other evidence—circumstantial though it may be. It is an axiom in our Courts of Law that circumstantial evidence is often the most convincing. Many criminals are convicted on it.

In the case of some of these nineteenth-century literary forgeries there is contemporary evidence not only about the date of their manufacture, but about the forger.

II

In the course of gathering material for this study, I made the acquaintance of one whose father became a well-known and highly-esteemed member of the literary circles of the 'eighties and 'nineties. There followed a delightful and memorable visit to the home of the son. Our initial talk naturally concerned Wise. Unexpectedly came the question to me: 'Would you be surprised 'to learn that at the time the pamphlets were being fabricated his 'connexion with them was known?'

Myself: 'Hellup! That it was known Wise was actually pro-'ducing the forgeries?'

My host: 'Yes! There were evidently a few people who knew 'the source they came from.'

Myself: 'That news is indeed important. Is it hearsay, or is 'there evidence for it?'

My host did not reply for a few seconds. Then he rose—went to a bookcase—selected a small volume—returned to his chair facing me—opened the book at what seemed to be an already-marked place. These things were done with a silent deliberation that was impressive. At last: 'This is my father's 'diary for the year 1888. See what he says there,' said my host, handing me the open manuscript volume and indicating an entry. There I read under the date 11 January 1888:

... Went to Shelley Society meeting. At this gathering Wise, Forman, Tegetmeier, Furnivall, Rossetti, &c were there, but not Mr Salt, whom I had expected to see. Wise is still proceeding on his wild career of reprinting or pirating Browning, Shelley, Swinburne, &c. . . .[2]

It is unfortunate that for the time being the writer of this diary must remain under the anonymity of Mr Y. Z. His identity would reveal with what authority it speaks. But after it had been shown to me without the least reservation or condition, and also after its owner had produced other data which have assisted me in reaching my conclusions in regard to Wise, he provided a second surprise by stipulating that 'in anything you say I do not wish my father's or my name mentioned at all'. Notwithstanding the absence on my part of any promise as to the use of the material shown—material that was bound to influence me—I have come reluctantly to the conclusion that in the circumstances the request not to divulge names is one that in fairness ought to be complied with. But I hope that in due course the amiable and proud possessor of the diary will agree to this veil being lifted from a figure to shroud which there has been so remarkable a combination of design and accident.

This diary entry says more than is perhaps at first evident. Taking the date 11 January 1888, in relation to the statement about 'still proceeding on his wild career', the reference connotes that Wise's particularized activities covered an appreciable part, if not all, of the immediately preceding year, 1887—it may even have referred back to 1886. Next, the description 'wild career' conveys not only the diarist's very proper condemnation of Wise's pursuits, but that they were already considerable in extent.

[2] In the preliminary edition of this book the Diary entry had (line 2 here) 'Dr Salt'. For the correction to 'Mr Salt', and also a minor one concerning the diarist later in the narrative, I am obliged to the diarist's son.

He would not have used such a sweeping term as 'wild career' in relation to two or three reprints or unauthorized printings. This reasoning is confirmed by the use of the word *etcetera*, indicating that there were *other* authors besides Browning, Shelley, and Swinburne, who were the objects of the wild careering. Next, we come to the objective words 'reprinting or pirating'. It is clear beyond a doubt—not only on the knowledge that the diarist proceeds to reveal, but on the fuller information we now possess—that he did not intend the expression 'reprinting' to be interchangeable with 'pirating'. Diary entries such as this are often written hurriedly; the conjunction 'or' in such a case is commonly used where 'and' is really intended. What the diarist meant here—and shows indisputably that he meant—was 'reprinting *and* pirating'.

The proof is thus: The diarist, as a member of the Shelley Society, would know that Wise had done type-facsimile reprinting of both Shelley and Browning. These were activities open and aboveboard. But, as he never did any mere facsimile printing of Swinburne, the term 'pirating' must refer at least to that author. The preceding chapter has shown that it did, in fact, also apply to Wise's publications of Shelley's *Poems and Sonnets*, and to some, if not all, of the volumes of his *Letters*. Lastly, the term 'pirating' is ambiguous. Leaving aside the question of any unauthorized printings of Shelley, the diarist, at that early date, was perhaps at a loss how to describe the printings of Swinburne and others that he speaks of as emanating from Wise—as the following pages show they did. So in his hurriedly written diary entry he grouped the Swinburne things as 'piratings'. But they were worse than that.

III

Thanks to Mr Y. Z. and his diary, the beginning of Wise's 'wild career' can be fixed certainly as not later than 1887: it was more probably 1886 when he (at the age of twenty-six or twenty-seven) had the false New York imprint set by Clays for the proposed Shelley *Letters to Southey*,[3] if not earlier. There is other illuminating evidence as to this dating. In 1888, some months

[3] See page 74.

after the entry was written, there were advertised for sale in the secondhand-book catalogue of Messrs Matthew and Brooks, of Bradford, Yorks, certain privately-printed items to which the diarist, evidently in wonderment, drew Wise's attention by letter. That collector-dealer-publisher was so moved to wrath that he swore. He damned as only an Englishman damns. And the reason? That Matthew and Brooks were asking prices too low for these books!

It seems incredible that a book-collector would make such a complaint. But in this case Wise did not want to buy: he wanted to sell. The explanation is that two of the three books in the Matthew and Brooks catalogue were his own productions— namely Swinburne's *Cleopatra* (1866) and his *Siena* (1868). Wise replied in writing to the diarist that Brooks had these pamphlets at the cost price of about half-a-crown apiece, which was why he could catalogue them as cheaply as three shillings and sixpence —damn him! He could have asked half-a-guinea easily. And side by side with these he was asking six guineas for D. G. Rossetti's pamphlet *Hand and Soul* (1869). What a damn shame! To complete the explanation of Wise's bitter anger, it has to be added that his *Siena* is now condemned as a forgery, and the *Cleopatra* classified as a suspected forgery. And as the diarist could refer to such things as 'piratings' in January 1888, it follows (Wise having produced no other Swinburne printings at that date) that both were fabricated in 1887—if not in 1886.

IV

Something needs to be said here about Wise's initial marketing of the forgeries.[4] The manufacture of them was only the first part of the business. There remained the more difficult part—the establishing of them and their sale; then the reaping of the harvest. It has been mentioned in the opening chapter that he was almost solely responsible for establishing these spurious 'first' editions, and making them the desiderata of the collecting world. Examples of the clever ways in which this was effected will be given later. The reason for releasing a few copies of the pamph-

4 See also Chapter 9, Sections IV and VI.

lets at cost price to provincial booksellers like Matthew and
Brooks is that he realized the need for getting some copies into
circulation as far removed from him as possible. It was not
desirable that they should all emanate directly from him: a
circuitous distribution would make them look more genuine.
He himself would see to it that their values were boosted. If he
let a few copies go cheap, he could make his profit on the rest
of the supply in his hands. By the autumn of 1888, the forgery
ramp was at high pressure, and he was beginning to get his
profits—mainly through his private book-dealing and through
indirect channels.

Instances of sales by indirect methods are provided by the
British Museum Library's list of acquisitions of the now condemned pamphlets.[5] On 16 August and 23 October 1888, the
authorities bought Mrs Browning's *The Runaway Slave* and George
Eliot's *Brother and Sister* for five and three guineas respectively
from one E. Schlengemann, a fellow employee of Wise's in
Hermann Rubeck's firm. In 1890 the Museum bought copies of
the Swinburne *Cleopatra* (catalogued by Brooks at three shillings
and sixpence—damn him!) for five guineas, two Ruskin pamphlets *The National Gallery* and *The Nature and Authority of
Miracle* for two guineas each; and the Matthew Arnold *St
Brandon*, also for two guineas. The vendor in these latter cases
was Hermann's son, Otto P. Rubeck, with whom we shall find
Wise entering into an important partnership in the city.

Between 16 August 1888 and January 1926 the British
Museum received twenty-nine pamphlets, now condemned or
suspect as Wise's book-forgeries or piracies, of which twelve
were bought by that institution and seventeen presented to it
by Wise;[6] who also made gifts to the Cambridge University
Library and the Bodleian Library of his spurious printings.
These were not thrown as sops to Cerberus, or as crumbs from
the pitying rich man's table to fill the lacunae of hungry
libraries. The gratuitous planting of the pamphlets, coincident
with indirect sales of others similar, was all part of the essential

---

[5] The *Enquiry, op. cit.*

[6] It is probable that the total of Wise's 'generosity' in planting wrong things on the
Museum was greater. The two Kipling piracies in the Condemned List were presented
anonymously, as were other items. The above figure of twenty-nine is one more than
given by Carter and Pollard (see also footnote page 188 and Appendix II).

scheme of getting the things established. That they were entered and unquestioned in the British Museum's great Catalogue immediately gave them an appearance of genuineness. But what a nuisance that there should be such a punctilious registering of how, whence, and when, things pass into the State's keeping!

It may be reasonably assumed that the worthy officials of our Record Office of Literature never dreamed in their worst attacks of private indigestion that the generous donor was the fabricator of both his gifts and those other pamphlets on which they had been innocently spending the nation's money. It is equally feasible that this consideration was not absent from the mind of the astute young builder of the Ashley Library. But it is an ironical thought, in view of the nation's ultimate purchase of that library, that it was built partly out of the profits of these forgeries. If he got nothing on the swings when he released a few of the pamphlets at the cost price of half-a-crown each, he made up on the round-abouts when the same worthless frauds immediately brought him from two to five guineas each. He was to make even better prices than these—that is, when his gigantic bibliographical and cataloguing publicity schemes got working. Some of the pamphlets were to acquire temporary values—fictitious as themselves—of nearly one hundred pounds each, the highest recorded auction-room price for one being one thousand two hundred and fifty dollars.

Thus did the young man 'scent wich pays the best, an' go 'into it baldheaded'. A posthumous acknowledgment is due to our Mr Y. Z., who would surely not regret that his Diary had been the means of throwing light on the mystery of Thomas James Wise and his nineteenth-century forgeries.

CHAPTER 7

THE ROLES OF HARRY BUXTON FORMAN AND SIR EDMUND GOSSE

How doth the little busy bee
Improve each shining hour,
And gather honey all the day
From every opening flower!

I. Watts: *Against Idleness*

THEY WERE HECTIC days for Wise in the 'eighties when he was forging ahead, mastering trade and trader of essential-oils, making his type-facsimiles, printing those mysterious little pamphlets, attending meetings of the literary societies. It was a life of driving work, ceaseless scheming, severe concentration. His script in those days had just the same characteristics as in his late years—scrawling, sprawling script, showing hand and pen hopelessly unable to keep pace with his ideas and the urge to get things done.

But he liked going to the theatre, especially to music-halls of the type whose passing is now lamented: those with the open bars running alongside the stalls, where the whiskered Victorian beaux could sip champagne or sherry and keep an eye on the billowing petticoats of the dancers at the same time. On such occasions young Wise left his Baptist home at Holloway, and went up West. One night, in '88, he joined a party of officers from the P. and O. *Verona*. The programme began at the Alhambra; where it ended is not recorded. But he did tell his friend ******* ****** that he had his gold tiepin—very handsome pin, heart-shaped, and set with a diamond—collared by some something girl. And he added that he 'got into no mischief whatever'. He was not always so fortunate, however, in his escapes from the verse and letters of immortal poets and the inks and types of mortal printers.

Thomas James Wise was never a bibliophilic recluse. No Dryasdust was he.

84

II

We have seen how his membership of the Browning and Shelley Societies introduced him into literary circles of his day. This led to a few lifelong associations with men of letters, who put their knowledge at the disposal of the reputedly rich collector always so generous with his little privately-printed first editions. For the most part, his relations with men like Furnivall, Stopford Brooke, Dykes Campbell, and Edmund Gosse, depended on the communion of book-collecting interests rather than on friendship. Such visits as he paid at this time were usually made in the evenings when the recipients had dined.

It was in May 1882 that there began the long and fruitful association with Henry Buxton Forman, C.B. (1842–1917), a Controller in the General Post Office, where he was sometime Second Secretary. The acquaintance was sought by Wise, but did not reach visiting terms until 1886. It was a valuable contact to establish, because he was becoming acutely aware of his lack of educational and literary qualifications for the part he was envisaging for himself. The early correspondence between the two men shows Forman correcting the other's transcriptions, attempts at critical commentary, etc.

Moreover, the G.P.O. official (how seminal the siestas of Civil Service employment—shade of Trollope!) was also a most successful book-collector; and as a student and editor of Keats and Shelley he did useful work. Wise, in conversation, used to give the impression that it was himself who was the pioneer in Shelley collecting and bibliography. The truth is that Harry (as he preferred to be called) Buxton Forman was the Shelley expert when the younger man was a groping novice in the same field. But Wise saw to it that his friend was denied the honours.

In 1886 there was published *The Shelley Library An Essay in Bibliography* by Forman, a book of one hundred and twenty-eight pages crammed with the most valuable and surprising information. Nothing like it had been done: it is the fountainhead of Shelley bibliography. Thereafter the collecting and bibliographizing of that poet was comparatively easy. Nevertheless, the reader will look in vain throughout Wise's books for one solitary tribute to this work of his friend to which he was so greatly indebted. Instead, there is an endeavour to divert attention from it. Wise had to catalogue his copy, of course; but he adds: 'No 'further portion of this projected work was produced'—a note well calculated to put off anyone interested. But that it is deliberately misleading by the use of the word 'projected' is obvious from the work itself; for Forman made it clear that this Part 1 dealt with Shelley's first editions and their reproductions; whereas the second part, which for some reason he never completed, was to be devoted to minor and miscellaneous matters. Even if it was an 'essay' and had the faults of most pioneer efforts, it was a source book; it had considerable merits; and it was extremely useful to Wise. His treatment of it was shabby in a bibliographer, and mean in a friend.

Much the same thing happened regarding the bibliography of Mrs Browning. Here again, Forman was the pioneer and allowed his material—*Elizabeth Barrett Browning and her Scarcer Books* (1896)—to be printed in the *Literary Anecdotes* (1895–6), produced by Wise and Sir W. Robertson Nicoll, editor of the *British Weekly*—surely one of the most curious combinations ever seen in literary harness; though Nicoll was very much the sleeping partner in the affair, which was used by the other for sponsoring some of the forgeries. Wise made his usual off-print edition of the bibliography; but he did not send a copy to the British Museum—the very first place to which such a book ought to have gone.

Apart from these two considerable obligations as to a pioneer, Wise was under a private indebtedness. Harry Buxton Forman was used in the furtherance of Wise's schemes to boost his spurious first editions. There were, indeed, other contemporary bookmen similarly used by Wise—men like J. H. Slater and Colonel W. F. Prideaux, whose reputations were, as they are now, above suspicion. Buxton Forman, however, was the most useful. He it was who first began the business of establishing the forgery *The Runaway Slave*. It seems to have escaped notice that as early as 1891, in the introduction Forman contributed to Wise's type-facsimile of Mrs Browning's *Battle of Marathon*, he went out of his way to incorporate material purporting to authenticate the fraud, material that could only have been supplied by Thomas James Wise.[1]

III

Immediately after the exposure in 1934 of the nineteenth-century pamphlets the view that someone else 'must have been' involved with Wise in the production of the forgeries was persistently put forward in private discussion. The man whose name was most frequently joined with Wise's in this aspect of the affair was Harry Buxton Forman. Whatever suggestion was implied by the conjunction of the two names probably derived its force, if not its origin, from the remarkable correspondence in *The Times* Literary Supplement to be dealt with in its chronological place.

In 1939 I gave[2] the gist of a letter written 7 December 1916 by Wise to Forman, when the latter was aged seventy-three, concerning the former's fraudulent edition of Wordsworth's verses *To the Queen* (1846). The letter accompanied a signed presentation copy of Wise's *Bibliography of Wordsworth*, then just published, which in describing the edition has the statement: '. . . it was 'at one time believed that only two examples had survived. But 'a few years ago a tiny "remainder", consisting of some half- 'dozen copies, was unearthed. . . .' The material passage in the letter assures Forman that what is said in the *Bibliography* about the examples of the pamphlet in existence is right, and tells him (with seeming casualness) that most of the copies that were in the 'remainder' they had shared were destroyed. This ambiguous passage only says that the two men shared the spurious edition which was made artificially rare, and not that Forman had any thing to do with its production. But why the need for such assurances about what he would hardly forget—unless, perhaps, Wise wanted to make the letter (which the recipient would

---

[1] Says Forman: 'It [the first edition of *The Battle of Marathon*] is probably even rarer 'than the separate issue of *The Runaway Slave* . . . which was also unknown to Mr Browning 'until a year or two before he died—a circumstance, however, which he readily explained.' But Browning did not explain: what he did was to theorize about the pamphlet's origin, which he was misled into pronouncing as genuine. Forman proceeds to quote the letter from Browning to Wise—which has been given here (see page 48).

[2] In *Forging Ahead* (Putnam's Sons, New York, 1939), the preliminary edition of this biography. See pages 59 and 60 here.

be likely to preserve: as he did) an instrument of secret purpose.[3]

In the matter prefatory to the *Letters to Wrenn*[4] published in 1944, which was peculiar for reasons apart from its sensationalism, there was an effort to 'raise the swindle from an individual crime to a national scandal', which—it was suggested—had gravely affected world confidence in British honesty. But the editress did not proceed with the wholesale charge implicating the nation in Wise's forgeries. In the first place she was concerned to convict Harry Buxton Forman and Sir Edmund Gosse as fellow-criminals in what she described as the 'Wise-Forman-Gosse 'factory'. ✶✶ ✶✶✶✶✶✶✶✶✶✶✶✶✶✶✶✶✶✶✶✶✶✶. There is instanced an alleged forged receipt sent to Wrenn which 'seems to be in Gorfin's hand', disguised by the use of a fine nib, and which is twice thereafter declared to be in his handwriting. Whatever the 'tool' (as we shall find Gorfin confessing himself to have been) was induced to do by his masterful and all-powerful employer, this method of argument was not convincing.

Another example related to the private issue of William Morris's *The Pilgrims of Hope* (1886)[5] which Forman produced (he states in his preface) after unsuccessfully trying to persuade the author to publish it immediately in volume form. This private-printing the editress first described as a 'near piracy', and afterwards as an 'unauthorized publication'—that is, an unqualified piracy. She explained, professing to quote Forman's preface: 'Failing to carry his point [i.e., with Morris], he deter-'mined "to have the poem in book form somehow." "Being 'forbidden", he proceeded to print a "dozen or two copies".' But what Forman actually says is the very reverse: his words are: '. . . Being unforbidden, I have proceeded to carry out my pro-'ject; and indeed it has not been difficult to persuade the poet

---

[3] For the letter would read innocently enough to anyone without knowledge of the fact—which was not to be proved and made public until many years later—that the pamphlet was a fraud. The term 'remainders' is significant: it is to figure largely in Chapter 21 where is described how Wise tried to shift his responsibility on to Forman. The latter's library was sold at the Anderson Galleries, New York, for £44,622 (approx.), the forgery realizing thirty-three pounds (approx.).

[4] *op. cit.* (pages 58 and 109-110).

[5] It was produced while Morris was alive. But it bears no printer's imprint or certificate of the limited issue—as it ought to have done.

'that a dozen or two copies cherished in libraries where the rest 'of his poems are lovingly guarded do not add one whit to the 'publicity of the book pending . . . general circulation.'

This, again, was not a convincing way for the editress to present her case. Also, she overstretched her conclusions drawn from debatable matters such as Forman's possession of a large number of the forgeries (of which other people innocently held large groups) and his sponsoring of some of them (as others were induced to do). In short, on the evidence, inferences, and surmisings, that she put forward, her main charge against Harry Buxton Forman of co-partnership in the production of Wise's spurious pamphlets was—to choose the Scottish verdict—not proven.

As for her allegations against Sir Edmund Gosse, they were astonishing for their weakness and perversity, and had been better left unmade. Further, the intimate correspondence between him and Wise brought out in this work provides the strongest circumstantial evidence against the existence of any conspiracy. This evidence was very well known in 1944:[6] it is increased later in these pages.

The rest of the British nation, included in the *Further*—and hopeful—*Inquiry* conducted 'way down in Texas, were Wm. M. Rossetti, George A. Aitken, Clement K. Shorter, W. B. Slater, R. A. Potts, H. T. Butler, and 'other English collectors', who were all more or less exonerated by the kindness of the American editress.

But she left out Uncle Tom Cobleigh.

There is extant, however, another Wise-to-Forman document (secured by Carl Pforzheimer at the sale of the latter's library)[7] which could not be produced by the editress of Wrenn's correspondence, though her cognizance of it was thrown into the scales to weigh them heavily against Forman. The document is a paper found in a packet consisting of Forman's manuscript, proof, and revise, of his article 'The Building of the Idylls' (contributed to Wise's *Literary Anecdotes*, 1896) together

---

[6] See footnote page 126.

[7] Printed in *Between the Lines Letters and Memoranda Interchanged by H. Buxton Forman and Thomas J. Wise* (Austin, Texas, 1945). This handsome but poorly-edited little volume has a Foreword by Carl H. Pforzheimer.

with letters and messages from the writer to Wise which the latter had returned with his customary interlineations in script to answer points made by the other. Apparently Forman had been writing 'testy letters' which made Wise 'quite miserable'. On the crucial piece of paper the former criticized the inadequacy of Wise's certificate as to the number of copies produced of one of his privately-printed Ruskin pamphlets (a subject dealt with in the following chapter). Forman was a severer critic than perhaps would be expected of one who has now been accused of co-partnership in forgery. 'There is more than an appearance of dishonesty' [dishonesty underlined by Wise], he wrote of the certificate in question; and he proceeded:

The appearance is this—that you are reluctant to say how many are printed; & say "a few" because some will understand that to mean 3 or 4 [the figures 3 or 4 have been struck out by Wise], some 10 or 12, some 20 or 30, & so on. There cannot on the face of it be an honest reason for wanting the number printed to be differently conjectured by different people; and it turns out that the appearance is borne out by the fact that printing 30 (more or less) you want someone to think you only print 10 or 12. However, that is all your affair. . . .

In reply to this forthright criticism, Wise wrote between the lines of Forman's note:

Quite so. And we print "Last Tournament" in 1896, & want "someone to think" it was printed in 1871! The moral position is exactly the same! But there is no "dishonesty". Mrs Severn does not buy her copy under the impression that only 10 or 12 are printed: I give it to her gratis!

That is all. But in regard to Thomas J. Wise it is more than enough: for it is an admission in his own script of his responsibility for the forgery of Tennyson's *Last Tournament*[8] and consequently for the whole series of pamphlet frauds.

As regards Forman, the document implicates him—but to what extent? Wise's comment is tantalizing and capable of raising a host of questions and theories. For example, Wise may have printed the pamphlet without the other's co-operation or approval, though Forman had got to know when (and probably where) it was printed: just as our diarist Mr Y. Z. had

[8] See Appendix II.

earlier got to know of Wise's 'wild career'. And angered into making the revealing retort, Wise may have purposely used the pronoun 'we' to involve his critic. He was sufficiently unscrupulous for that trickery, as these pages demonstrate. If in his morality there was 'no dishonesty' in antedating the pamphlet in order to pass it off as something other than it was, then there was none in incriminating Forman merely because of his knowledge of the spurious dating. Alternatively, 'we' could be said to mean himself (i.e., Wise) and Clays; which was literally true so far as the actual printing was concerned. But such conjectures could be piled up without reaching any satisfactory result.

What is certain about the document as affecting Forman is that

(a) it is only an *ex-parte* statement, and that of a man who is to be shown as so anxious to find a scapegoat.

(b) Forman's reaction to it is not known. He may have strongly denied the implication, which could be corrected as adroitly as the alternative meanings allowed.

(c) in a court of law such an *ex-parte* statement by a man self-convicted of forgery and systematic untruthfulness in connexion with his printings would not be accepted *per se* as proving Forman's joint responsibility for *The Last Tournament*, even if his knowledge of the thing being spurious was thus established. Still less could such an *ex-parte* statement be accepted as proof of Forman being Wise's co-partner in the whole series of frauds.

It is pertinent, however, to recall that when in January 1888 Mr Y. Z. wrote that significant entry in his diary,[9] he named Wise—and Wise only—as the person engaged in the 'wild career' at the printing-press. The diarist was a very well-informed man who certainly knew as much about Forman and his activities as he did about Wise and his. Had he known of anyone else being concerned in the illegal printing he would not have withheld the knowledge from the secrecy of his journal. Again, when Wise in the hour of his exposure was 'giving himself away' as his printer said, there was no hint or mention of Forman in what passed at the desperate interview.[10]

[9] See pages 77–83.

[10] See page 268. Further to this, Cecil Clay wrote to me (13 March 1946): '. . . To my knowledge no one other than Wise was concerned with getting the illicit pamphlets printed.'

It is Wise all the way. All the known and reliable evidence is against him. He was the cute conceptor, the arch-schemer, who carried through the most original and extensive frauds in literary annals. Harry Buxton Forman's association with him, whether it was one of foolish connivance or of the limited complicity of a tool, is—until evidence to the contrary is forthcoming—a comparatively minor phase of an historic affair.

IV

'Three hundred and sixty-five days were included in the year '1886. One of these days was a red-letter day for me . . . it was 'with a thrill of delight that I was one day informed by Miss 'Mathilde Blind that she had asked and obtained permission to 'bring me to The Pines'—says Wise,[11] telling of his meeting with Algernon Charles Swinburne. Judging from the poet's brief correspondence with Wise, 1888 would appear to have been the year of the red-letter day, and not 1886. With the exception of two notes of thanks for gifts in 1886,[12] the correspondence was confined to the period 1888 to 1896, during which, Wise relates, he received from Swinburne 'some twelve or fourteen letters of interest and importance'; but of these only seven letters and notes were found 'after diligent and protracted search'. Wise was a careful man: it is incredible that he could not put his hand on all he received. The significance of the alleged missing letters will be seen in Chapter 13, where it is shown that Watts-Dunton was threatened with the production of one of them.

Whenever it was, the meeting with the poet was a curious affair, from what may be read between the lines of the visitor's account. To see Swinburne's original editions of Shelley 'was the 'professed object of my visit to Putney. In about half an hour 'from the moment I had been ushered into Swinburne's study 'the door slowly opened; Watts-Dunton stole silently into the 'room and gently shepherded me away.'

The gently-shepherded visitor considered that he must have found favour in the poet's sight, because an appointment was

---

[11] In *A Swinburne Library* (1925).
[12] One printed by Wise; and the other left unprinted.

made for the following Sunday for him to see some first editions of Elizabethan plays. But Wise, for once, was late. 'Watts-'Dunton himself admitted me. He was obviously nervous, and 'quietly reproved me for my lack of punctuality,' saying that Swinburne had been expecting his visitor for the last half-hour, and was 'quite excited by your non-arrival'. Very excited he was, according to the account. But Wise has nothing to say about such treasures as an English black-letter book (not in the British Museum or Bodleian!) that Swinburne proudly displayed, and that most bookmen would have expected to be a subject of reminiscence.

The first two printed letters of 1888 from the poet were concerned with the '1866' pamphlet of *Cleopatra*. Working precisely the same trick as that on Browning, Wise had written telling Swinburne about his 'discovery' of a copy of this rare edition of *Cleopatra*. The poet cried to Heaven in wonderment at Wise 'wasting good money' on a 'trumpery ephemeral', of the printing of which in that form the author knew nothing. 'Seven guineas!' exclaimed the poet. It would have been 'dear at as many shillings'. He thought it a shame to deprive Wise of his copy. But that it could easily be spared (though that fact the innocent author never guessed) may be fairly argued, since it is now known that Wise had a stock of copies which he sold in subsequent years. This pamphlet is the suspected forgery mentioned in the previous chapter.

It was after the subject of book-collecting had been introduced in the two above-mentioned letters that Swinburne wrote in May 1888, about his Shelleys and Elizabethans; which fact suggests the origin of Wise's 'intercourse with the circle at The 'Pines'. The association, however, was obviously never a close one in the time of Swinburne, notwithstanding his polite interest as a 'bit of a bibliomaniac' himself.

But we shall not tarry longer in this remarkable year of three hundred and sixty-five days, because the amazing sequel to Miss Blind's introduction of Wise to The Pines belongs to the year 1909—which also had three hundred and sixty-five days, including some scarlet-lettered ones for the collector-dealer. But these require chapters themselves.

V

To Sir Edmund Gosse is attributed the *bon mot* 'I am sure that 'on the Day of Judgment Wise will tell the good Lord that 'Genesis is not the true first edition'. Gosse, the happy essayist and richly-informed literary critic, sometime Librarian of the House of Lords, was—like so many of his kind—an ardent book-collector. He came to have what now seems a pathetic confidence in and esteem for Thomas James Wise as a bibliographer and collector. But he died before the exposure of rare Ashley Library printings—some of which he received as gifts (to be greatly prized), and others he bought. Those of us who knew the proud and sensitive critic can well imagine his horror and dismay if he has heard a confession to the good Lord that certain nineteenth-century pamphlets also are not true first editions.

Wise got to know Gosse in the late 'eighties. Miss Sylvia Gosse, Sir Edmund's artist daughter, sent me the following dry-point reminiscence: 'He used to come and see father at 29 Dela-'mere Terrace—our home then—*after* dinner. As a small child, 'in my bedroom, I heard them through the ceiling. They would 'mumble, mumble, mumble into the night. Mr Wise was in the 'wholesale and importing chemist world, and therefore only free 'in the evenings and week-ends to chase the Arts.' Gosse's friendship was one of the luckiest of the many boons that befell Wise. There were times when he was positively humble to the 'literary gent' as he described the critic. An instance is contained in a very illustrative letter from Wise (18 October 1912) that gives this faithful self-portrait:

No: I am by no means "gracious". On the contrary, I fear that I am frequently pugnacious to a militant degree! But my mind is not altogether in a state of atrophy,—and I am sufficiently acute to be able to perceive when, and to what degree, I fall short of par. When any matter of mere business regulation is before me, I cannot help but lean upon my own opinion; &, when opposed, I quickly develop into a pig-headed and obstinate beast. But, on the other hand, I do not fail to appreciate how terribly short I fall of the standard necessary to the holding of any opinion on matters or questions of literary expediency, or of critical judgment. Thus, when you (who are overlord in all that pertains to literature or criticism) are generous enough to express an opinion, I appreciate that the opinion you express is a correct one, even though it does not coincide with any determination at which I may previously have arrived. Hence I naturally follow without question whatever path your finger points to!

Nothing could be truer. Unfortunately, he did not always follow the path. Here, for once, Wise draws aside the veil and reveals himself. After examination of many of his own papers, the foregoing is the fullest of the few examples of introspection and humble confession I have found.

The Gosse-Wise collaboration was of incalculable value to the Ashley Library publications. More of the critic's prefaces to the privately-printed pamphlets were unsigned than signed; and he was also one of the most generous of unnamed contributors of notes for the bibliographies and catalogues that displayed intimate knowledge of the Elizabethan dramatists, poetical insight, and critical acumen. In one of the *Letters to Wrenn* (page five hundred and forty-seven), where Wise is returning thanks for appreciation of the Preface to Swinburne's *Queen Fredegond*, he says it could not be signed either with his name or Gosse's because it was so much the work of both. This was not the truth, as well he knew—although apparently the editress did not know or she would surely have enlightened her readers. Gosse's hand in the production of the Swinburniana was kept secret because of the animosity between Watts-Dunton and him. The *Fredegond* preface, for example, was wholly his. In fact Wise gave himself away in the next sentence with the admission that all the really important information in it derived from Gosse. There is no doubt that Wise's reputation was greatly enhanced by the belief of those who early handled these private-printings that the anonymous prefaces to them were all his work although years afterwards much fuller acknowledgments to his mentor were made in his bibliographies.

Wise was constantly indebted, besides, to persons better informed than himself, for notes, hints, sources, etc. But although in certain of his own introductions he paid tribute to some— notably Sir Edmund Gosse and Sir John Murray—there were others, among them Furnivall, Forman, Aitken, and Herne Shepherd, to whom he owed much, yet who were passed over. Only those who have had the opportunity of learning the sources of information, and seeing the original documents, can fully appreciate how much of the best in the Ashley books originated with Wise, and how much otherwise. More frankness regarding these sources would have added interest to his commentaries, and not left him open to the criticism of allowing the scholarship of others so often to appear as his own. He could do enough himself for merit.

Gosse was forever pricking bubbles in Wise's editing, and sending corrections. For example, the critic warned him (6 July 1909): 'But I hope you will forgive me if I urge you to collate 'the text with the greatest care. At present it is full of what can 'hardly but be errors of transcription. I send you my sugges-'tions. . . .' Three typical protests made during one of the spates of private-printing—of the George Borrow pamphlets—were (4 February 1913) '. . . I do very strongly hold that if these 'pamphlets are to be of value they must be *exquisitely* edited. . . .' (30 November 1913) '. . . You have got this thing into a great 'muddle. It will be best to print the thing again. . . .' (17 July 1914) '. . . I protest, as so often before, against these pamphlets 'going out without any statement of what they are or whence 'they came. . . .'

As an instance of how Gosse, from his booklore, directed the bibliographer: 'Who wrote *The Meretriciad*? I should think that 'he was, very likely, also the author of *Cooper's Well*. . . . I think 'you will probably find, if you look closely into the memoirs of 'the time, that Miss Cooper was a fashionable prostitute in 1767, 'and this would give point to the title, which is otherwise mean-'ingless . . .' [Discussing the possibility of John Hall Stevenson's authorship] 'but I think not, for he had enjoyed a college educa-'tion, and would hardly have been guilty of several false quan-'tities—*Priapus* and *Illium*, etc.'

And here is part of a letter (22 June 1924) which could hardly have pleased the man who had edited the *Faerie Queene*:

My dear Wise Let me at once express my horror at finding the author of the *Faerie Queen* called
                                        Spencer
in your proofs, as if he were a cunning bookseller or an effete philo-

sopher. My first idea was that the c was a printer's error, but no! it is repeated. What possible authority can you have for spelling Edmund Spenser with a c? It looks horrible. I entreat you to correct it in every case. . . .

Now do, I entreat, restore Spenser to his proper spelling. You might as well write

Biron
Coalridge
Driden
Po
Chawcer

as (oh ye Gods)

SpenCer.

An amusing example of Wise's false readings caused Gosse to write on another occasion (15 April 1907): 'The Coleridge letter 'wants careful collation. Some of it is quite unintelligible.

"He never saw a *Byron* in his life but has heard of *thine* they are quite *backwards*."

'I guess this should read:

"He never saw a *Bear* in his life, but has heard of *them*; they are quite *backwoods*."

'Try if this isn't right?'

VI

There was a grave occasion, however, when Gosse—fearfully perturbed—tried to restrain Wise. Among his manuscripts was one entitled 'Algernon's Flogging' that he chose to assert was 'autobiographical'. This MS., which certainly appears to be in Swinburne's script, is inserted in a Holywell Street type of publication entitled *The Whippingham Papers. A Collection of Contributions in Prose and Verse, chiefly by the Author of the 'Romance of Chastisement'* (London: 1888). 'Although Swinburne's name 'does not occur anywhere in the volume, a large portion of the 'contents, both prose and verse, was written by him,' says Wise. On receiving a proof containing the entry of this sorry trash, Gosse at once wrote to Wise (4 July 1920):

Now comes the question of N. 226. You must take the responsibility

of it. But I should not be honest if I did not tell you that I am greatly
distressed. What does it matter whether any dirty fellow should
"pounce upon" the W. Papers and hold them up as "a rarity
unknown to Wise and Gosse"? Any little vanity which we might
possibly feel seems to me nothing beside the dishonour done to a
great name.

However, you have printed this, and I know you too well to expect
you to cancel the entry altogether. But I do entreat you to modify it.
It is absolutely needless to dwell on the details, and gloat over the
thing. It must be sufficient to quote the nasty title, without exciting
prurient interest by quoting the sub-titles and first lines of the four
sections. I *entreat* you not to do this. I think it will be a cruel offence
against Swinburne's memory to do it. And to what purpose? Merely
to gratify the last pedantry of bibliography. It is surely enough, since
you were so anxious to be "complete", to mention the publication.
That will preserve you from the charge of not knowing its existence,
an ignorance which might (however) be well considered honourable.
But to print these titles and first lines is to give away the whole secret,
which I have done my very best to hide. You might just as well publish
the whole hideous rubbish in full as print these titles and lines. They
expose the whole disgrace.

I entreat you not to be so cruel to Swinburne's memory.

Wise could hardly ignore this forceful and moving appeal. He
suppressed the sub-titles and quotations in his 1920 *Bibliography
of Swinburne*, tucking away the entry in the appendix of 'Contribu-
'tions to Periodical Literature, etc.' But in his later and bigger
catalogues it was promoted to a place among the *Editiones
Principes* of Algernon Charles Swinburne.

It was in a philosophical mood that Gosse wrote to Wise in
February 1901: 'As life goes on, it seems more and more to run
'in a rut, and the adventurous grows more difficult to grasp.
'Friendship and letter-writing are really adventures. . . .' How
adventurous will be revealed in Chapters 12 and 13.

Edmund Gosse   Sylvia Gosse

For Wilfred Partington
S.G.

SIR EDMUND GOSSE IN HIS STUDY
From the original Etching by his daughter, Sylvia Gosse, R.B.A., R.E.
(Chapters 7, 12, 13, etc)
Size of the plate 6⅞ × 5⅝

CHAPTER 8

MARRIAGE, SECRET PUBLISHING, AND RUSKIN RUSES

My dear Friend. . . . If, then, you must have Leoni *out of his inaccessible hiding-hole of an annual, christened under an evil star, be it even so. . . .*
From the Preface to Wise's forgery of John Ruskin's *Leoni*—a preface not now accepted as by Ruskin.

I

IN 1890 THE thirty-year-old cashier, bookseller, collector, and publisher, found time from his absorbing avocations to make two important moves: the first, into matrimony; the second, consequently, into a new house—52 Ashley Road, Crouch Hill, North London. The former was not to be so distinguished as the latter, which gave its name to his now fast-growing collection—the Ashley Library.

His first bride was Miss Selina Fanny Smith, aged twenty-two, daughter of Frederick Smith, a salesman. Thomas James Wise and Selina Fanny were married on 12 July 1890, in the Parish Church of Kentish Town, Wise describing himself as a commercial clerk and giving his age as thirty-one. He was actually thirty: it is an instance additional to those given of his inaccuracy in such details.

Shortly before the marriage, Wise had left the paternal home in Holloway, and made a temporary abode at 33 Leighton Grove, N., Miss Smith's home being 174 Leighton Road. After the marriage, however, they moved into 52 Ashley Road, which leads from Hornsey Rise to Crouch Hill. What with his improved position at Rubeck's, and the money he was making out of his book-deals and those rare little pamphlets, he was doing well. The chosen home for his library and his wife reflected his new status and confidence. No. 52, standing in a good-sized

99

pair of grass plots with privet hedging, and wearing a showy
gable—as respectable as a cashier in white spats and shining
topper—was a great improvement on the house in grim
Holloway.

No doubt Selina, who was little and lively, thought it was all
very imposing. There was plenty to occupy her time—at first.
As for her chosen life-partner, he became busier than ever. He
was no longer living cheaply at his parents' home. There was
this establishment to keep up. And there were all those private
enterprises of his.

II

The production of the spurious pamphlets that we have seen
initiated in 1886 or 1887 was certainly continuing at this time,
although there is a lack of evidence at present by which most of
their dates can be precisely assigned. Also the rare-book business
was developing as his private list of clients grew—a list aug-
mented by Browning Society and Shelley Society contacts. But
it is the third phase of his private activities with which this
chapter is concerned: his publishing business. For at all times
from the middle 'eighties Thomas James Wise was a publisher
—under the usual cloak of anonymity, of course; as he was a
bookseller.

It was publishing in a small way, maybe; but publishing of a
particularly ingenious and novel kind. The method generally was
this: he would get hold of a series of an author's letters or a
manuscript of verse or prose; print the material neatly but inex-
pensively; serve up as first editions purportedly limited to a small
number of copies; and sell hot. His editing, unless he derived
help from others, was often superficial. Where there was some
effort at proper presentation and annotation the work was poor
and inadequate. For example, Charles Augustus Howell was one
of the recipients of Rabelaisian letters from Swinburne's 'festive'
pen. When some of these got into the hands of a dealer, the poet
(through the offices of Richard Herne Shepherd) was glad to
buy back the indiscretions; and after his death Wise seized the
chance of printing such a festivity. Some of these, he says elsewhere in relating the episode, were included 'with necessary

omissions' in his privately-printed *Letters from . . . Swinburne to Richard Monckton Milnes and Other Correspondents* (1915). But there is a complete absence in the book of any indications that Swinburne's letters have been castrated.

At first, as in the case of the Shelley first editions issued by Wise, original manuscripts were borrowed, publication being sometimes made without authority. Later, however, when he had more capital, he mostly printed only such material as he bought. There is little doubt that the proceeds from the sale of these small books and pamphlets often covered the cost of acquiring the original manuscripts, plus the comparatively insignificant printing charges. If Buxton Forman could buy a Byron rarity for seventy pounds and pay for it out of the sale of a mere facsimile reprint, Wise went one better in being able to produce first editions of the manuscripts they were to pay for. It was buying your cake, eating it, selling it at a profit, and yet keeping it in the pantry all the time. Thus another way in which the Ashley Library grew is illustrated. Providing that no copyrights were being infringed, and providing also that the subscribers to these editions were always getting what these publications were represented to be, the enterprise was legitimate enough, notwithstanding the secrecy.

While Wise throughout his career always had something or other in course of production at his printers, there were—apart from the printing of the spurious nineteenth-century pamphlets and his own large compilations—five periods of publishing of certain authors. They were:

> Shelley, from 1886 to 1897;
> Ruskin, from 1890 to 1897;
> Swinburne, from 1909 to 1920;
> Borrow, 1913 and 1914;
> Conrad, 1919 and 1920.

Between the earliest of these dates and 1929 he also published privately-printed first editions of Matthew Arnold, J. M. Barrie, the Brontës, the Brownings, S. T. Coleridge, Charles Dickens, Edward FitzGerald, George Gissing, Thomas Hardy, Walter Savage Landor, D. G. Rossetti, E. J. Trelawny, William Wordsworth, and lesser authors. Although not all the publications are

important, the material on the whole includes much of literary
and biographical value. The list (it is given fully in Appendix II)
is one of which Wise was proud. On the face, it is a list on which
he could well pride himself. The pity is that a record of useful
publishing should have been besmirched by piracies and other
objectionable features.

In all, so far as I have been able to trace, Wise published
privately two hundred and fifty-one separate works, exclusive of his own bibliographies and catalogues, and exclusive
also of the nineteenth-century pamphlets condemned or suspected that are also detailed in Appendix II; but including piracies.
Approximately sixty-four per cent of the two hundred and fifty-
one items are from twenty to fifty pages; twenty per cent are
lesser in content; and sixteen per cent greater. The following is
an analysis:

Privately-printed publications by Wise 251
Examined 250
Bearing no printer's imprint 184
With Clay and Sons' imprint 58
With other printers' imprints 9
Bearing no identification with Wise as publisher .. 63[1]
Not delivered to the British Museum Library 47

III

Wise represented—both in talk and in his books—that these
private publications were done for the purpose of preserving
the manuscript material in print, and thereby making it available
to students. Very laudable and usual are such purposes. But in
some cases the material was already in print, and the greater part
of it was fairly certain to be printed sooner or later. However, let
us take the avowed purposes without these reservations.

The very first place in which a person printing such material
for preservation is anxious to see it deposited is the British

---

[1] This figure includes some half-dozen items which bear statements that they were
'edited' by Wise. Also the ten printed with Conrad's imprint, and the nine with Watts-
Dunton's imprint, because they were produced by Wise (by arrangement in these cases),
he retaining the bulk of the editions.

Museum Library. Nor is this a voluntary matter. The Copyright Act requires, under penalty for non-compliance, that a free copy of every work published[2] shall be delivered to the British Museum Library and also to each of five other libraries—of Oxford and Cambridge Universties, and the National Libraries of Scotland, Ireland, and Wales—if these five make written demand. Yet here we have a bibliographer with the knowledge and reputation of Thomas James Wise, whose privately-printed books were alleged to be done as records and for students, failing in forty-seven instances to send a copy to the British Museum—which at various dates, usually long after production, had to buy twenty-three of the books (several from Wise himself), and never possessed the remainder until 1937, when the Ashley Library was bought for the nation. Even of those of his publications that reached the British Museum, at least four (three certain piracies and one suspect of piracy) were sent anonymously; and eight—mostly unauthorized printings of Shelley and Ruskin letters—were bought by that institution, at prices ranging from sixteen shillings and sixpence to three pounds, from the Shelley Society whose printing and publishing were controlled by Wise.

The absence of any identification with him as publisher in sixty-three of the works, regarded in conjunction with his pirating, suggests an obvious reason—at least in some cases—for his not using either his imprint or the more usual Ashley Library book sign, which is a feature of his publications after 1894—in nearly every instance. The absence of a printer's imprint in such a large proportion of the works is an equally serious matter. Here was a long-sustained course of illegality, for the law is that with a few exceptions such as Parliamentary Papers, Bank of England Notes, certain legal and financial documents, and sale catalogues:

Every printed paper or book which at the time it is printed is meant to be published or dispersed must have upon the front of such paper, if it be printed upon one side only, or upon the first or last

2 There is an uncertainty which ought to be removed about the applicability of this statutory requirement to private printings. Wise, by himself and through agents, both distributed and sold copies of publications so designated. Irrespective of sales or restriction of circulation, such distribution surely comes within the Copyright Act's definition of publication as 'the issue of copies of the work to the public'. But apart from the legal aspect, there was a moral obligation on Wise to deposit copies with the B.M. Library.

leaf if it consists of more than one leaf, the name and address of the printer.

See 32 and 33 Vict. c 24. Schedule II.

The one hundred and eighty-four publications issued by Wise without a printer's imprint are most of them identifiable typographically as Clays'; and there is no reason for doubting that the omission was procured by him. Clays had innocently printed for him the spurious nineteenth-century pamphlets, and certain of them were also identifiable with some of these two hundred and fifty-one privately-printed first editions, the majority of which bore the Ashley Library book device. He may have deemed it undesirable, as he had been in charge of the Browning and Shelley Societies' printing done at Clays, to have such a series of uniform volumes as his Shelley and Ruskin letters labelled by the same printers. As for his piracies, the less said about their printing origin the less risk of detection.

Discussing with me Wise's practice, Cecil Clay said that his firm would always include its imprint on a work unless it was a printing where omission was permissible. They did not know how the imprints came to be left off Wise's publications. That customer's instructions were always taken by the firm's London manager, J. R. Maylett; and presumably the omissions were due to a request by Wise that 'unfortunately went unnoticed and unquestioned'. It is pertinent to this statement to add that Maylett died in 1929 before the investigations into the pamphlet forgeries. His part-responsibility in the affair, so far as regards the printing aspect of it, is obvious.

The fact is that, however much Wise claimed to be doing disinterested service to literature, the publishing of these things was first and always a commercial proposition. If the profits were small, the returns were quick, the labour light, and the risk of loss almost negligible. For him it was good business although not always legitimate business. When he declared—as he so often did after the 1914–18 World War—'this boom in modern first editions is preposterous,' he was silent about the extent to which he had so ingeniously played a hand in it.

Apart from the sale of these private-printings to his clients, he reserved a few as 'gifts' to authors, to obtain in return interesting autograph letters and services. Browning, Swinburne, and

Sir Edmund Gosse, have been mentioned as illustrative cases. The last-named was a particularly favoured recipient of the first editions from Wise: what abundant value he received for them is only now demonstrable. The profits these privately-printed editions brought their publisher will almost certainly never be known. Probably they varied considerably. But that they must have been appreciable is indicated by the reminiscence of Herbert Gorfin. He related that in 1913, on the publication of the long series of George Borrow first edition pamphlets, he sold to an Oxford Street bookseller ten of them for eighty pounds on behalf of Wise, who accompanied him, and who waited in a neighbouring café for the proceeds of the transaction.

I have also been shown a list in the handwriting of Wise giving the prices at which he suggested five of his privately-printed Swinburne pamphlets should be catalogued for sale. They were: *Queen Fredegond*, thirty pounds; *The Worm of Spindlestonheugh*, twenty-five pounds; *Letters on the Elizabethan Dramatists*, eighteen guineas; *Border Ballads*, twenty-five pounds; *Liberty and Loyalty*, twenty-one pounds. This was perhaps a case of forcing his market. But these figures—for pamphlets that at the rates then prevailing (as supplied by Messrs Clay) did not cost, on the average, more than twenty shillings per copy to print—show what prices he was aiming at, and probably asked from his private customers, who were invariably men of wealth.

IV

When Wise in his bibliographies and catalogues described books that did not meet with his approval, he was severe in his criticisms. 'This pamphlet is one of the most impudent examples 'of exploitation I have yet encountered,' is an example. 'Extortionate', 'not a legitimate first edition', 'this unsightly scrap' are other instances of his outspoken disapprobation. Yet irrespective of his nineteenth-century forgeries, his privately-printed publications include some that come within the same terms of censure. As late as 1930 he produced a little volume, *Autobiographical Notes with Comments upon Tennyson and Huxley*, by George Gissing, consisting of three long letters to Edward Clodd. But these three letters had already been included by Wise among the thirteen which he had privately printed in 1914 under the title *Letters to Edward Clodd*. The three letters of the 1930 reprint are the longest in the 1914 edition, and the versions are practically identical except for a few corrections of faulty transcription, the omission of a four-line paragraph, and a postscript: nor can the duplication be justified by the autobiographical grouping. Yet Wise catalogued both as first editions, and presumably sold them as such.

Another example of his loose publishing methods is the private-printing of George Borrow's *Letters to his Mother Ann Borrow & Other Correspondents* (1913). The reader will be surprised to find that the little book consists of one letter of twelve lines to Borrow's mother, and the remainder (fourteen) to his wife Mary, with the exception of two to other correspondents. But Wise had already produced a selection of Borrow's *Letters to his Wife*—hence the other misleading title.

This manufacturing of first editions was not without alarms and excursions. On one occasion, when older and wiser, he came into possession of copies of letters from Swinburne to Pauline, Lady Trevelyan—an accomplished lady whom for her sagacious encouragement and corrective advice Swinburne had cause to revere. Here was something for Wise's market . . . away went the transcripts to the printers . . . and back came the proofs. But he was afraid to take this trip under the pirate's flag. He therefore asked Gosse to forward the proofs to Sir George Trevelyan for his permission. Sir George came down on the project in no uncertain manner, and without bouquets too. He insisted that the letters must first appear in public form 'in some work of authority'. Gosse told Wise that the inevitable must be bowed to, and the pamphlet suppressed—which was done, save for the usual few copies of the proofs. There was apparently much concern about a long paragraph in one of the letters. It referred to some 'venomous backbiter' to whom was attributed the story of a mutual acquaintance having boasted of murdering his own illegitimate children. Wise, in his *Ashley Library Catalogue* (Vol. VII, page forty-four), points out that the long paragraph of scandal was omitted when the correspondence was officially published. But the result was that he had made another rarity for the Ashley Library, and an unexpurgated version also available for the general public to read in the proof copy he sent to the British Museum—if there is any satisfaction to be gained from the absurd scandalous talk. This was not the only Wise pamphlet to be suppressed.

Sir George Trevelyan had not only banned the printing of these Swinburne letters in Wise's private pamphlet, but he insisted that his long letter portraying Lady Trevelyan, which accompanied them, must be given in its entirety or not at all, and in Gosse's *Life* of the poet. The thwarted publisher was much chagrined, his expressed annoyance drawing upon him one of Sir Edmund's occasional reproofs (5 July 1916):

> My dear Wise I quite understand—and share—your vexation. But we must not think of Sir George Trevelyan as a "dull and dense old sinner". He is neither "dense" nor "dull". We must remember that he is one of the most distinguished of living Englishmen, the nephew and biographer of Macaulay, a very eminent historian, and a Cabinet Minister of long and honourable experience. . . . Such a man is justified to himself in saying how a communication—a studied piece of his celebrated prose—shall be given to the public. . . .

V

A surprising feature of Wise's first-edition publications is their certificates as to copies printed. In the case of limited editions the object of such certificates is to record in the work itself the actual number of copies produced, and—when published for sale, as were those by Wise—to provide a guarantee for the subscriber, who is usually charged a higher price by reason of the restriction on copies. Wise's publications generally bear statements that the 'edition of this book is limited to a few copies', or (more usually) variations of 'Of this book Thirty copies only have been 'printed'. The numbers vary up to about fifty copies. Wise's catalogue descriptions of his own publications frequently give figures different from those in his certificates. For instance, the number of copies of Shelley's *Letters to Elizabeth Hitchener* is certified to be twenty-nine (twenty-five on handmade paper, and four on vellum) while in the *Ashley Library Catalogue* the number is given as thirty-four (thirty and four respectively).

But apart from such discrepancies, which ought not to have been made by a bibliographer in regard to his own books, what number, in the case of a certificate of 'a few copies', constitutes 'a few'; and who is the arbiter? And where a number only is specified, what guarantee is there that it was not exceeded, bearing in mind the unfortunate fact that other circumstances in Wise's publishing preclude trust in his honesty? A rare-book expert, through whose hands many of these limited first editions have passed, surprised me during my researches with the question:

'How many copies do you think Wise printed and sold of his 'private editions certified to be limited to thirty copies?'

Myself: 'Do you suggest that he overprinted the numbers 'stated in the certificates?'

Expert: 'All I know is that some of these books have been 'appearing with enough regularity to suggest that there were 'nearer one hundred and thirty copies.'

What that expert says is surmise, and not evidence, and should be so regarded. A copy may circulate and appear in the market more than once. It would take many years and a careful census to get at the truth of this matter. Some independent corroboration of the expert's experience is, however, supplied by Herbert Gorfin, who sold many of the publications. He gave me his view that in the case of the earlier publications Wise printed more copies than he certified; but he thought that the stated numbers of the later first editions, like those of Swinburne, Borrow, and Conrad, were pretty closely adhered to. It is possible that the pamphlet Charlotte Brontë's *Adventures of Ernest Alembert* (1896) would be illustrative. The printing is stated by Wise to have been limited to thirty copies. There must surely have been plenty of subscribers for such a small number of a purported Charlotte Brontë first edition.[3] Yet Wise was still selling the edition in 1910—disposing of a bundle of fifteen copies for six pounds nineteen shillings, fourteen years after the production of 'thirty copies only'!

---

[3] It was actually an off-print from *Literary Anecdotes of the Nineteenth Century* (1895-6), edited by Wise and Robertson Nicoll, in which it first appeared.

There is one form of certificate of limitation—and one only
—that fulfils its object: it is the one that not only specifies the
total of copies printed, but enumerates each copy, and is signed
by the publisher or printer. Wise, with his bibliographical experience, ought never to have permitted himself such looseness in
regard to his certificates. That he did so is in keeping with his
publishing principles. Strangely enough, it was Harry Buxton
Forman's criticisms of Wise's certificates specifying a 'few
copies' that drew the dramatic admission in Wise's script (given
in the preceding chapter) of his responsibility for one of the
pamphlet forgeries.

VI

In spite of his success in making acquaintance with authors,
and of producing their letters and fragments with or without
permission, Thomas James Wise had one great disappointment
in his active and varied career. He never could get in with John
Ruskin. Try as he might, write letters, seek introductions, that
proud, sad, disillusioned idealist would have nothing of him, and
never wrote a single letter so far as I can ascertain; on the few
occasions that it was necessary to reply to the collector-dealer-
publisher, he did so through a third person. This was all the
more grievous to Thomas because for a long time Ruskin was a
great shining orb in the book-collecting constellation. Wise paid
him homage (in collaboration with James P. Smart) with a
monumental *Ruskin Bibliography* (1893). All to no purpose: it
did not bring him grace. But he was wholly undaunted. There was
a rhinocerotic quality in his psychological skin. Sesame and
Lilies open or closed, he would find something for Clays to
print—something of which to make Ruskin rarities. Result: six
pamphlet forgeries, two suspected forgeries,[4] and eleven privately-printed first editions—of the last some, if not all, under
very doubtful authority.

The first five of the privately-printed editions were issued by
Wise under his cloak of anonymity, although in the fifth he gave
his name as editor. After that one—in 1893—there seems to have

---

[4] For details, see Chapter 11, 'The Writing on the Wall', in which the story of the first
exposure of some of them is told; and also Section IV of Appendix II.

arisen a cloud of suspicion: apparently lenders of original material required assurances as to Wise's rights, and there was some objection to the paucity of acknowledgment. For example, the Reverend J. P. Faunthorpe was really obstinate, insisting upon having a declaration from Wise that no copyright was being infringed, and that he was printing Ruskin's letters to him with the author's knowledge and approval. Another lender was Charles Fairfax Murray, who supplied his own annotations, but who insisted on a proper printed acknowledgment, and on having his footnotes initialled. In the case of ten of the Ruskin private-printings the subscribers had to be content with the assurance of the editions being limited to 'a few copies only'. It was only with the eleventh—the *Letters to Frederick J. Furnivall*—that the certificates specified thirty copies as the limitation. Furnivall was just the man to insist on a little detail like that.

Now that people were worrying themselves and him about copyrights, it meant submission of material to authors. The character of Ruskin's acquiescence will emerge. But coincident with the stricter attitude of lenders, we find Ruskin in the intervals of his mental afflictions giving closer attention to those proofs that were submitted to him. In one set he made two suppressions: the first of a passage which referred to his forbidding study of 'the act of Copulation, and the process of Generation in the Womb'; the other, of a saying of his that when there was the least chance of getting a kiss he felt 'all scrubbing brush' about his lips owing to cutting his moustache. When such suppressions were made, the lenders of the original letters doubtless congratulated themselves on their caution, even if it was not so agreeable to the publisher. He, however, usually had his way in the end. Years later, when he came to compile his catalogues, the censorship imposed as an understood condition of publication was evaded by his custom of quoting the suppressed passages in annotations.

VII

A most pertinent example of Wise's methods is supplied by Dr Furnivall in regard to one of these Ruskin editions entitled *Two Letters concerning "Notes on the Construction of Sheepfolds"*

(1890)—a pamphlet, by-the-bye, which has nothing to do with agricultural architecture. However anonymously it might be published, Furnivall was having no hanky-panky about the facts, which he boldly gave away in his 'Forewords' as follows:

Of late years Mr Wise has most kindly given me, who could not afford to buy them, many of his privately-printed rarities. Thinking what I could do in return for these benefits, I askt Mr Wise if he'd like to print privately my copies of the *Sheepfold* correspondence between Maurice and Ruskin in 1851. He said Yes, but ultimately determined to print only Ruskin's two letters, as Maurice's theology had no interest for him. He has also just shown me Ruskin's letter from Brantwood, '29th May 1889', to some correspondent, part of which has already appeared in print:—'. . . You may print this . . . where and 'whenever you like; *as anybody else may, whatever I write, at any time, or say* '—if only they don't *leave out* the bits they don't like!' Under this authority the present print appears.

Six years after the candid and cautious Furnivall made the above explanations, which have several points of interest in this study, Wise in the second volume of *Literary Anecdotes* (1896) gave pride of place to a contribution by himself on this *Sheepfolds* correspondence. It begins:[5]

In October 1890, Dr F. J. Furnivall caused to be issued for private circulation a tiny volume which contained within its thirty pages matter of greater interest and higher importance than is to be found in any of the many pretentious volumes of *Ruskiniana* which have made their appearance during the last decade.

The tiny volume referred to is the very *Sheepfolds* pamphlet described above that was printed by Clay, and published and sold by Wise, and for which Ruskin's original letters had been made available to him by Furnivall as carefully recorded in the latter's 'Forewords'. The distortion of facts about the responsibility for publishing is repeated by Wise a few pages later:[6] 'It is to be regretted that, for quite sufficient reasons, Dr Furni- 'vall printed Mr Ruskin's letters only, contenting himself with

---

[5] This scissors and paste affair was not signed. But it was off-printed—'Edited by Thomas J. Wise'—as usual (see page 334).

[6] Wise was probably nervous about taking responsibility. Five years before, Ruskin had brought a successful action-at-law against a London firm of auctioneers to restrain them from dealing in piratical copies of his works printed in New York (see *The Times* of 31 October 1885).

'quoting three short passages from those of Maurice.' For 'Dr Furnivall' the reader needs to substitute 'Thomas James 'Wise' in these last two quotations—as I found, during my researches, an unknown person had actually done in the British Museum's copy of *Literary Anecdotes*.[7]

But consider the impudence of it all. First Wise obtained his materials from Furnivall (who obviously would have preferred to have Maurice's letters included in the private printing). Then, on the loose and doubtful authority of the seventy-year-old and mentally unbalanced Ruskin's remark that anybody could print whatever he wrote, Wise printed that material in one of his first editions, suppressing his connexion with it. Finally he put the responsibility for the publishing on to Furnivall. But why all this Machiavellian manœuvre? Why the deception? The short answer is FOR PROFIT. That answer is unintentionally supplied by Wise himself in the first page of *Literary Anecdotes*. After saying that Furnivall had caused the 'tiny volume' to be printed, Wise sets out its title-page—*Two letters concerning . . . Sheepfolds*—appending the footnote:

Naturally this little volume has become of considerable scarcity, and upon more than one occasion a copy has realized some five or six guineas.

So here we have Wise boosting the price of the tiny pamphlet he had surreptitiously published and then foisted on Furnivall. How it came about that Dr Furnivall, a man of fearless and independent character, allowed to pass Wise's wilful distortion of the facts in a work of importance like the *Literary Anecdotes* is difficult to understand. The distortion, however, may not have been seen. Furnivall was seventy-one years old when Wise wrote that paper in the *Anecdotes*, forgetting what the doctor had written in his 'Forewords' to the tiny volume, or else trusting that it would be overlooked.

One result of this piece of deception is that the *Dictionary of National Biography* in its article on Furnivall was led into error by accepting Wise's account of the origin of the pamphlet, quoting his *Literary Anecdotes* as its authority.

[7] The unknown reader, in defiance of one of the B.M. Library's sternest rules, had written in ink, in a minute script, above the two citations of Furnivall's name—'t.i. T. J. Wise'. The t.i. was presumably his contractions for 'that is'.

CHAPTER 9

THREE MEN AND A BOY

Thy bounteous hand with worldly bliss
Has made my cup run o'er,
And in a kind and faithful friend
Has doubled all my store.

Joseph Addison: *Spectator*, 453

I

EVERYTHING WENT well for Wise from the time he settled in his new home. The enterprising bookseller and private publisher was soon making partnerships of another kind—two of them being furthered by, if not due to, his choice of Ashley Road for residence. After his move to No. 52, 1891 and 1892 proved to be the wonder years for him. In these two years he begun four friendships of outstanding importance. Three of them were with men all his seniors, who predeceased him—as did most of his other friends whose connexion was turned to great advantage. In the order of acquaintance the three men were: first, Clement King Shorter, aged thirty-five, editor of the *Illustrated London News*—who was a neighbour, and who is credited with having suggested to Wise the naming of his library after Ashley Road. The second was William Robertson Nicoll, aged forty-one, editor of the *Bookman*, and also a neighbour—he was not yet knighted. The third was John Henry Wrenn, the fifty-year-old principal of an esteemed banking and brokerage house in Chicago, who was then about to extend his book-collecting in the grand manner of American millionaires.

The fourth friendship was with a bright happy lad of fourteen, just beginning as office-boy at Rubeck's—Herbert Gorfin. As in the three other cases, the friendship that was fostered with this smiling, perky youngster was turned by the firm's rising employee Thomas James Wise to benefit for himself. But it had a remarkable sequel forty-two years later.

II

Clement King Shorter for a time managed, with that by no means uncommon facility of Civil Servants, to combine a job at Somerset House with journalism, for which he had a flair. Obtaining an editorship, he became something of a figure through a weekly literary causerie which was sometimes refreshingly individual, but which was not conspicuous for the soundness of either its judgment or its style. *Punch* satirized him as the 'Wee Cham of Literature'. He was philosophical about his literary limitations, however: it was as well, for not even his friends spared him their wit or their criticism. Like Wise, he was not a man to be easily abashed; he was of the determined, thrustful sort, although along more conventional lines. Also, he was a successful collector of books and manuscripts. His collection— which after his death realized twelve thousand one hundred and twenty-four pounds at auction in 1928—practically cost him nothing, he once told Herbert Garland. It was built up by means of what he termed 'judicious exchanges', and was constantly 'vetted' by Wise.

Dr J. M. Bulloch, who knew Shorter intimately for many years and who edited his autobiographical fragment, described him to me as 'a man who was always making other men do what they did not want to do', and 'a pusher'. It was Mrs Florence Hardy who gave me an enlargement of Bulloch's miniature. Shorter once visited Thomas Hardy, and begged to see the manuscripts of any of his works. Obligingly, the author produced some bundles out of a drawer. Shorter seized them, urged that they ought to be bound to preserve them safely, and finally insisted upon taking them away with him for that purpose, to save the owner trouble. Hardy appreciated that the MSS. would be better in bindings; but, somehow, the way the service was proffered irritated him. However, his reluctance to be under an obligation to Shorter was weakened by a courteous desire not to hurt his guest's feelings—whose toughness he little knew. But Shorter was overwhelming; and in the end he departed from Max Gate hugging the precious manuscripts. In due course he had them bound, and they were returned to Hardy—except one

HENRY BUXTON FORMAN, C.B.   CLEMENT KING SHORTER

'Wise was the master; I was the servant. Before long I realized that I was merely regarded as a tool.'—HERBERT E. GORFIN, from a self-taken photographic study (Chapters 9, 15, 20, etc). On the left is the Ashley Library sign printed at the end of many of Wise's publications

that Shorter asked to be allowed to keep, suggesting that it might set off the binder's bill, which he had already settled. When Shorter's library was sold it included two Hardy manuscripts— *An Ancient Earthwork* (fifteen leaves) and *The Lost Pyx* (five leaves) which brought six hundred pounds and three hundred and ten pounds respectively; also three single leaves which yielded one hundred and ten, one hundred and five, and one hundred and eighty-five pounds.

These reminiscences are illustrations of the character of Clement Shorter, but they have a reflective interest.[1] He was Wise's boon companion. In each other's merry company they would relieve themselves from the tiresome poses that other contacts required: they could hail each other beneath their veneers. If few men are heroes to their valets, not many more are gods to their bosom friends.

Another flair of Shorter's was for hunting down autograph material, as Wise did. Many a mutually advantageous deal there was between the two men. Shorter once made a fateful haul of Brontë manuscripts on behalf of Wise, who was not only the wealthier of the two but the bolder and more confident speculator. In 1895 Shorter 'became possessed', to use his own words, of a packet of letters written by Charlotte Brontë. Of course he wanted to publish them; for to a small extent he copied Wise in private-printing, but was more scrupulous in the matter of certificates. To secure the copyright, and also to buy any other relics of the Brontës, he determined to seek the Reverend Arthur Bell Nicholls, one time curate of Haworth, whom Charlotte married in 1854 for a happy union of a few months. Nicholls was traced to Banagher, King's County, Ireland, where he was farming, having left the Church. He had married a woman who remembered Charlotte on her honeymoon, and who spoke kindly of her illustrious predecessor in the affections of Nicholls.

---

[1] The import of them was confirmed in a recollection to me by Dr Bulloch of a dramatic incident at a London première when he accompanied Thomas Hardy, and Shorter was observed to be present. It is possible that the correspondence of the master, and also of Mrs Florence Hardy, gives no hint of the personal antipathy indicated. Probably it was a case where absence made the heart more tolerant. Most authors have a sentimental regard for the periodicals that help to make known their early work; and perhaps Hardy could not forget that some of his had appeared in the *Illustrated London News*. Anyhow, here—as elsewhere in these pages—I have faithfully recorded what was told me with an authority and a sincerity that I had neither right nor reason to doubt.

Shorter, accompanied by Robertson Nicoll, crossed the sea, found the 'genial little' Nicholls at the 'precise psychological moment' when he was ready to talk, not only about Charlotte but about business. Apparently the ex-curate was not doing better than most farmers at the time, and was glad to see the cash that Clement held out for a brown-paper parcel full of manuscripts and letters by the Brontë children, including those tiny MS. books of tales that were the first amazing efforts in authorship of Charlotte & Branwell. These relics had lain by for forty years. According to Shorter, Charlotte's husband intended to burn them all; but perhaps this was embroidery to lend romance to the tale of the 'find'.

They changed hands for about four hundred pounds, Shorter has related. Wise used to boast that the Brontë manuscripts cost him 'in all' a sum variously stated as one thousand one hundred or one thousand five hundred pounds. The final figure, whatever it was, would include a similar transaction with Nicholls, through the agency of Harry Buxton Forman in 1892. Shorter 'retained' what copyright there was in the material he himself acquired; and the two cronies proceeded to issue the inevitable first editions. It must be noted, however, that Clement's contribution to Brontë literature in consequence of these dealings was by far the more considerable and appreciated, even although he passed over the Angrian cycle of MSS. as worthless.

But consider Wise's way with the unique scripts that thus came into his charge. From them some fifty or sixty thin little volumes in expensive bindings were made. After he had selected what he wished to keep, the others were disposed of to clients and friends in England and America: of the unbound MSS. some were kept for exchanges with or gifts to acquaintances, the remainder being sold to a London bookseller. The result was that the editors of *The Miscellaneous and Unpublished Writings of Charlotte and Patrick Branwell Brontë*[2] had to admit that, owing to large sections of the manuscripts thus being missing and untraceable, they had not had access to the whole of the young

---

[2] Vol. 2 (Oxford. The Shakespeare Head Press, 1938). This work is described on its general half-title as 'edited by Thomas James Wise and John Alexander Symington'. But the first volume, dated 1936, states that the transcripts and notes in it are by Symington and C. W. Hatfield. The second volume (1938) says: 'The long illness and death of Mr 'Wise robbed us of his assistance.'

Brontës' fantastic story, the 'History of Angria'. Although the editors do not say so, Wise's procedure was vandalism for the sake of profit. His few printings are set out in the Appendix, and need not detain us here. A sequel to his haul of the Haworth relics—the story of his printing of Charlotte's love letters to Professor Heger, and of *The Times*'s heavy hand on Shorter—will be related in its chronological place.

III

While the two men worked in the very closest harmony and co-operation, Wise was much given to chaffing his friend, and even to scoring off him. When he made his astonishing coup at The Pines in 1909, Shorter was allowed to have a little finger in the pie. Among other things, he was lent the MSS. of some unpublished fragments, including poems rejected by Swinburne when sending his *Songs before Sunrise* to press; and these fragments were produced by C. K. S. in two crude pamphlets of twenty-five copies each. But he was more Grundyish than Wise, and considered that some bowdlerizing was necessary. For instance, when transcribing 'Moonrise by the Sea' says Wise, teasing his friend, 'Mr Shorter unfortunately overlooked a 'line included in the manuscript. . . . In place of the second line 'we should therefore read:

> '*The small dark body's Lesbian loveliness*
> '*That held the fire eternal.*'

The development of the friendship between Wise and Edmund Gosse, with its promise of usefulness to the former, led to an awkward situation which was long handled with masterly skill by Thomas. Shorter disliked Gosse, an attitude even more thoroughly reciprocated. C. K. S. characteristically vented his prejudice through his weekly causerie, once observing: 'Personally I do not like either Mr Gosse or Sir Sidney Colvin'—an outburst which prompted some sarcastic lines in *Punch* from E. V. Lucas, of which these touch our subject:

> *Alas, alack, for Sidney C!*
> *Alack, alas, for Edmund G!*
> *On both must History's verdict be*
> *That Shorter did not like them.*

In vain poor Edmund's enterprise
In baring Putney to the skies,
And linking up with T. J. Wise,
For Shorter doesn't like him.

On the occasion of another of the weekly causerie attacks, Gosse wrote (4 April 1914) to Wise: 'Will you explain to me 'why I have suddenly received over my head and shoulders this 'bucketful of Mr Clement Shorter's bedroom slops?' The friend-of-the-enemy replied soothingly in terms that are implied in Gosse's acknowledgment of Wise's 'excellent advice' about the 'irresponsible little journalist'.

'Tommy' and 'Clem', as they called each other affectionately, were wont to spend a day together every week, visiting book-shops and hatching their schemes. Just after the first World War, I often met them slowly making their way up the Strand, and into West End booksellers'—laughing and confiding. Except that 'Clem' was hairy and 'Tommy' was pink and almost hairless, they were two for a pair in their chubbiness, joviality, and shrewdness. Seeing them thus together used to remind me of a poem entitled 'Twin Souls' from Wise's *Verses* previously quoted—his solitary effort in print as a poetaster. Here is the first verse:

Calm and bright
In the fading light
Two hearts together singing!
Sweet and fair,
In the summer's air,
Two forms together clinging.

How they did enjoy their days out, this clinging pair of book-men! And there was that weekly lunch, of which Wise told me the arrangement between them was that one week Shorter should settle the joint bill, and the next week Wise should pay —and so on, alternately. Now Clement Shorter was ingenious in drawing famous authors into correspondence with him. How this affected the feasts of the twins is best described in Wise's own words to me: 'On the days that it was Shorter's turn to pay, 'he would tell the waiter to make out the bill "all on one". 'Then, while this was being done, he would take out his wallet 'from an inside pocket, carefully select a letter he had received

'from Thomas Hardy, or George Meredith, or some other
'author, and—holding it high between finger and thumb—
'slowly advance it to me, saying: "Well, Tommy; if you settle
'"the bill and I give you this, we shall be quits—eh?" This,
added Wise, 'became a regular thing; and so I nearly always
'found the cash for our luncheons.'

IV

Leaving the bosom friends at their trading in friendships'
tokens, the cheaply-acquired letters of unsuspecting authors, we
come to the other neighbour, the editor of the *Bookman*. Robertson Nicoll in person does not figure much in this study of Wise's
career. But his *Bookman* does. For in 1892 Wise began a journalis-
tic association with that monthly that was not only witness to his
shrewdness, but calculated to be of great value to him—alike
in his legitimate publishing and in the other sort.

There was no use in producing spurious pamphlets by
nineteenth-century authors, and also piracies, if they were not
established as collectors' items, and their commercial values
correspondingly forced up. We have seen one way in which
Wise put them into circulation, by selling a few cheaply to provincial booksellers; the majority, of course, would be reserved
for his private clients at profitable prices moving upwards with
whatever 'market' quotations he could manipulate. But it was
publicity that was now wanted for the things. The *Bookman*
provided just such an opening as was needed. It is almost unnecessary to add that Robertson Nicoll, as also the proprietors Messrs
Hodder and Stoughton, were unaware that the *Bookman* was being
utilized to boost publications that were to be proved forgeries.
Good Heavens! No!

Wise began in 1892 with a few notes of general interest
on book-collecting. Then, in 1893, Robertson Nicoll proudly
announced that Mr Thomas J. Wise, the 'well-known collector
and bibliographer', had undertaken the 'editorship' of their
'Recent Book Prices' reports, and that he would add, 'out of
'the fullness of his knowledge and experience', comments
'particularly valuable to book-buyers and booksellers'. The

description, 'well-known bibliographer', was a little premature, however inspired. Wise had not then published a single bibliography; that of Ruskin (done in collaboration with Smart) appeared later in the year.[3] Nevertheless, it was intelligent antici= pation; and no one could quarrel with the compliment to the fullness of Wise's knowledge and experiences of rare-book prices. No one!

In this year the *Bookman* contained long puffs of one of Wise's Ruskin forgeries, and of three of his volumes of privately-printed Ruskin letters. In 1894, however, the publicizing had a twofold object. Earlier in that year there had been some lively controversy in various periodicals over the new craze for collecting the first editions of modern authors—even living ones. William Roberts, a specialist writer on the subject, was unpleasantly outspoken. Of the 'First Edition Mania' he wrote: 'Time was 'when the craze existed in a perfectly rational form, and when the 'first editions in demand were books of importance and books 'with both histories and reputations, whilst their collectors were 'scholars and men of judgment. Now, every little volume of 'drivelling verse becomes an object of more or less hazardous 'speculation, and the book market itself a stock exchange in 'miniature.' Roberts was still more pointed with references to 'rubbishy tracts by living authors', and 'operators working the market', and '*too-zealous persons who feed their own vanity by hanging 'on to the coat-tails of eminent men and claim the title of public benefactor 'by "resurrecting" from a well-merited obscurity some worthless tract or 'obsolete and ephemeral magazine article, and trumpeting it about as a 'masterpiece*'.[4]

All of which shows the suspicion that was abroad concerning the artificial manufacturing of first editions—although the time had not arrived for exposure of the full extent of the evil, the faking of rarities then being unloaded upon the public. Roberts's sweeping criticism laid him open to counter-attack.[5] And Wise, the very leader in the new fashion, joined issue in his April

[3] The *Bookman* for January had an effusive paragraph heralding the coming Ruskin bibliography by Mr Thomas J. Wise, whose co-author—Smart—was not even mentioned.

[4] The italicizing is mine. The article appeared in the *Fortnightly Review* for March 1894.

[5] Roberts was then representative of the traditional type of book-collecting, with its heavily-bound fat quartos and tall folios. The resentment against the new tendencies of the 'eighties and 'nineties went too far. The collecting of contemporary authors always offers its fair field. Nevertheless, in the immediate object of his attack Roberts was sound enough.

article. It is instructive that he is more concerned with prices than principles. Out of twelve selected cases discussed, ten are treated from the point of view of cash values. In refutation of the criticisms about worthless ephemera, he blandly instanced Browning's *Cleon, The Statue and the Bust,* and *Gold Hair,* as being worth ten or twelve guineas each—the first two his own forged productions; the third, one of his suspected pieces: the cost of printing which we can estimate from his own figure of half-a-crown for similar things. The remainder of his reply to Roberts was an effort to support what had been rightly conjectured was the falling market in Ruskin first editions.

Wise, who had previously been Roberts's host at Ashley Road, never forgave his criticisms, which were taken personally. The course of their 'friendship' is illuminating. As recalled by Roberts forty-seven years later: 'I first met him in 1891 or '92, 'and was on friendly terms for a year or two, when I sensed 'some sort of antipathy on Wise's part; and for years I neither 'wrote to him nor saw him at Sotheby's and such places.'— But the specialist writer advanced in his profession. Wise, wanting to keep up with the times, evidently trimmed his sails. For Roberts's reminiscence continued: 'Then suddenly, by whose 'means I don't remember, we became very friendly, and nothing 'was said about the interval. He from time to time sent me copies 'of the special volumes of his Library Catalogues—Browning, 'Byron, and others. . . . I have no doubt he did me many an ill 'turn.'—At least attempts seem to have been made. Throughout the revived and useful 'friendship' Wise continued his secret enmity, as may be judged by his correspondence with Gosse and others that contained derogatory references to the erstwhile critic of 'operators working the market' and of hangers-on 'to the coat-tails of eminent men'.

In his next *Bookman* article (May 1894) Wise gave publicity to some of the 'first-edition' productions of writings by Matthew Arnold, George Eliot, William Morris, Ruskin, Rossetti, Swinburne, and Tennyson, that he issued, and that are now condemned as forgeries or suspected forgeries. That he quoted a sale price in 1892 of forty-two pounds for his sixteen-page spurious Ruskin, *The Scythian Guest,* indicates both his pride in and the success of the dark enterprise.

There were other channels used for disseminating the news of these nineteenth-century 'rarities' and their rising prices—Harry Buxton Forman's introduction has been mentioned, for one example. Worthy of employment in a better cause was Wise's skill in priming various writers with exactly the information he wanted brought out, in order that he could quote them as independent expert opinion about these precious 'first editions' he was so zealous to champion. Equally diplomatic was the quieting, if not winning over, of some who were critical, and even suspicious.

V

Wise's acquaintance with John H. Wrenn began in the summer of 1892. It quickly ripened into friendship under the influence of the American's admiration for the other's book knowledge. Every year thereafter, Wrenn's annual visit to Europe included a Continental trip, and also other excursions on which he used to take Wise and his wife. There was at least one occasion when Wrenn paid all the expenses; but, objecting to the bother of the constant tipping, he stipulated that Wise should settle with the politely-insistent seekers for gratuities on leaving the various hotels visited. Back home, the gratified guest described enthusiastically the royal time he had enjoyed with the millionaire. 'But mind you,' he added, 'it wasn't cheap—having to pay all those tips!'[6]

Under Wise's encouragement and guidance the Chicago banker built up a library in the magnificent tradition of old American book-collectors like General Rush Hawkins, John Boyd Thacher, and Hoe, while he had such contemporary rivals as Henry E. Huntington, J. P. Morgan, and F. R. Halsey. It would be gilding the lily to praise these generous men now for what they have done for American culture by forming noble

---

[6] Since the above reminiscence appeared in the U.S. edition of this work, it has been asserted, though without corroboration, that the Wrenn papers show the expenses 'of travel and entertainment' on the joint trips to have been 'prorated' between the two men. The reminiscence was a recollection, signed by Gorfin, of Wise's words. In view of an uncertainty whether it referred to the annual trips or—more probably—to a single excursion, it has been amended as applying to one occasion. It should be added that in various cases I had independent confirmation of the truthfulness of Gorfin's information supplied to me.

collections from Britain's rare books representative of her literature, and leaving them for the people of the United States. They
form a unique and lasting bond between the two countries—
although this view was not shared by the B.B.C. censor who, in
the script of one of my broadcast Talks (vide *The Listener*,
14 August 1929) on America's rivalry in scholarship as a result
of acquiring our book and manuscript treasures, deleted the
comment: 'What a happy part for these old books to play in the
'relations of two great English-speaking nations!' The reason
given for this stupid suppression was that the sentence touched
on international politics.

There has a been a tendency among the less-informed public
opinion in Britain to deplore the passing of so many of our
literary relics across the Atlantic, the belief being that we were
denuding our libraries. Never was there a greater error or more
short-sighted view. For the most part we could amply spare the
rarities that America paid us the compliment of coveting. With
a few exceptions they are well represented in our national collections—not to speak of our private libraries, which, notwithstanding the dispersals of the last few decades, still make a handsome showing. For example, it is probable that there are now in
America few short of seven thousand fifteenth-century works—
about half the total in Britain's public libraries alone. And if
ardent American bookmen had a big and natural appetite for the
good things from the Old Country, they did not begrudge paying handsomely for the feast.

With growing competition, the grand hobby became more
exciting—sometimes unpleasantly exciting, alas! as rogues and
opportunists on both sides of the Atlantic saw their chance of
illicit gleanings from the harvest. American collectors, shrewd
and keen though they might be, were not always, and could
hardly be, adequately informed in the often tortuous mazes of
the original editions of old English writers. Naturally, they
placed much trust in British booksellers of repute, and in other
advisers presumed to be independent of commercial interests. Of
the latter class Wise came to be regarded as the chief figure. It
is doubtful whether any English bookman, supposedly unpro-
fessional, has ever attained quite the same eminence and wide
reputation, alike for his knowledge and for his boasted intoler-

ance of anything second-rate, shoddy, or spurious. For over twenty years he was helping Wrenn to build his library. During those years, the American, with his almost childlike affection for and curiosity about the books he was amassing, must have prided himself in having such a high and distinguished mentor. Wrenn died before the exposure of his friend's forgeries and disloyalty, and so was spared a terrible disillusionment.

Wise related his connexion with the Wrenn Library in his introduction to its five-volume catalogue (1920) which he edited. The material part reads:

... For two decades we worked together. To prevent needless competition and to avoid any possible cause of friction, we agreed that each should have the first claim to the books of certain authors as they came into the market. For example, whilst I had "first call" on Shelley, Dryden, Prior, and the early quarto plays, Wrenn had "first call" on Pope, Wither, and other authors. To carry out this arrangement, Wrenn looked after my interest in America, whilst I attended to his interest here. As a result, *a few by no means unimportant* items came back to me from the United States, whilst quite a substantial proportion of the books now safely and finally housed at Austin were purchased by me in this country.

This is a very carefully concocted statement. Wise could hardly help acknowledging his considerable part in the forming of the Library. It is intended to convey the picture of two wealthy book-collectors combining in a friendly alliance not to compete in their hobby, and to help each other in their respective countries. A very pleasant picture too! But it is misleading—as such of Wise's explanations often are misleading. The arrangement actually in effect was that Thomas James Wise, the private dealer, was selling rare books (including, of course, the forgeries) to Wrenn—undoubtedly the best of his several rich clients, among whom were Lord Brotherton, Sir Algernon Methuen, Walter B. Slater, Colonel W. F. Prideaux, John Morgan of Aberdeen, R. A. Potts, and William Law; and in the United States: William Harris Arnold, Judge Klein, A. E. Newton, E. K. Butler of Jamaica Plain, Bonnell of Philadelphia, and Harry Elkins Widener. In addition, Edwin N. Lapham, Henry W. Poor, and others, were probably supplied with the forgeries by someone else. The extent to which Wrenn the banker was the agent of

Wise in America may be dismissed as comparatively negligible. Moreover, the purported division of their interests, as recorded when Wrenn was no longer alive, does not read very convincingly. For example, it is certain that for Pope rarities he was not given much preference by Wise, who was specializing in that author.

However friendly was the relationship between the two men (collectors are usually on good terms with their trusted booksellers), and however zealously Wise played his part—subservient to his own interests as a collector in several of the American's special 'fields'—the fact is that from his transactions with Wrenn he profited greatly. It was related by his assistant, Herbert Gorfin, that on one occasion, when they were busy dispatching books to America, Wise, in a burst of confidence, said: 'Wrenn 'is worth a thousand pounds a year to me.'

This figure is not difficult to accept. The Wrenn Library comprises some six thousand items. It entailed an average yearly rate of acquisition of about three hundred books and manuscripts, the individual prices of which would vary between five and five hundred pounds. Of these, Wise says himself he bought a substantial proportion for the Library. The dealings would, of course, include the sales to Wrenn of Wise's privately-printed books, and also his nineteenth-century forgeries (about seventy, including duplicates). As to the latter, the Keeper of the Wrenn Collection, which is now housed in the Library of the University of Texas, estimated the approximate total cost to Wrenn of the forged and suspect pamphlets alone as between five thousand and six thousand dollars.

Apart from planting his spurious printings on the Chicago collector, Wise occasionally faked a 'rarity' to sell him. Large deals were concerned with lots of up to one hundred and fifty or more titles at a cost ranging between thirty and eight hundred pounds per lot, the books mostly coming from Wise's stock or bought by him through Gorfin and other alleged employees. Some of these lots were given appropriate 'literary' provenances which were as impressive as they were fictitious. By correspondence and cables they were dangled before the eager client, and the purported negotiations for them were reported, with elaborate cunning and infectious enthusiasm calculated to be highly agreeable and stimulating to the ambitious bookman across the Atlantic.

The selection from this correspondence with the American banker issued in 1944, although so largely concerned with the business aspect of a single association, illustrated in detail the technique of Wise and the extent of his book-dealing. It also corroborated completely the evidence both as to the real character of Wise and the true nature of his relations with Wrenn that had already been published in the United States.[7] But in the prefatory comment of the editress there is a strange attempt to represent Wise's financially considerable transactions over some seventeen years in the altruistic light claimed for them by the London dealer. Reference is made to the 'unpaid service' of Wise, who is described as 'not greedy by nature, always fair and just to others in trading'. It is triumphantly declared that he never received any commission from Wrenn. Elsewhere, it is 'categorically' denied that a statement (which nonplussed the editress) at the end of one of the letters (11 November 1906), about them seeing the year close with a six per cent rate, referred to commission paid to Wise.

Of course it didn't. It referred to the London bank-rate which on 19 October 1906 was raised from five to six per cent—the forecast being just such as the interested produce-merchant would make to the equally interested Chicago banker and broker. And of course Wise was not paid a commission by Wrenn. He work for six per cent! To have accepted a commission on the books he supplied to Wrenn would have been to expose the 'friendly offices' as humbug, to have detracted from his reputed and self-vaunted position as a collector and bibliographer free of commercial bias. In short, to have accepted payment by commission would have been to tell the world (for the news would have leaked out) that he was the rival of the Antiquarian Book Trade's members. Instead, he took secret profits. Here are two typical examples:

[7] The original publication in the U.S.A. only of *Thomas J. Wise in the Original Cloth* under the title of *Forging Ahead*, preceded the appearance of the *Wise Letters to Wrenn* by five years. There is some reason to believe that this fact was at first unwelcome to the editress of the *Letters*: however, a perusal of her work shows that the precedence was very useful to her, ** *************.

He offered a first edition of *Paradise Lost* at eighty pounds. Wrenn countered with an offer of seventy pounds, which Wise —protesting he could never bargain!—took, adding that he originally paid ninety pounds for the copy. But on page one hundred and eighteen of the *Letters* is included one from Wise to Harry Buxton Forman which came into Wrenn's possession (how, is not stated) in which the dealer says he bought the Milton for fifty-five pounds. Profit fifteen pounds. But this was merely bread-and-butter earning. Now for a different example. It concerns the rare suppressed *Victor and Cazire*, the story of which has been told earlier.[8] In 1899 he told Wrenn that he paid two hundred and fifty-five pounds for the first known copy, which had recently been discovered. The American wanted to secure the next copy that should chance to turn up; and when number two was found in 1903 his bid of three hundred pounds for it was not nearly enough, the rarity realizing six hundred pounds. The publicity that resulted immediately brought copy number three to light; and it being the most desirable of the three Wise determined to acquire it, making this extraordinary offer to his customer: he could have Thomas's original copy (i.e. number one) at three hundred pounds on condition that if Wise had to go to more than that sum for number three Wrenn should give him for the number one whatever price the third copy cost less fifty pounds. In the result Wise paid six hundred pounds according to his letter to me which has been quoted; and so Wrenn fell to pay five hundred and fifty pounds for the number one. But the dealer had deceived his client by saying that number one cost him two hundred and fifty-five pounds; for his letter to me states one hundred and fifty-five pounds as the sum paid for it. Therefore his profit on the re-sale, less probably the auctioneer's fee for arranging the matter, was three hundred and ninety-five pounds for one book. And yet, with this evidence before her, the editress talks about the dear friend's 'unpaid service' and the fairness of his trading. Wrenn was systematically lied to, diddled, and defrauded by Wise. To try to gloss over the facts is merely stupid.

Whether Wrenn knew or guessed the true nature of the 'arrangement' with Wise it is idle to speculate. The provenance

[8] See page 67 *ante*.

of the proof sheets of Mrs Browning's *The Runaway Slave*, now condemned as a forgery, is given in a note in Wrenn's hand as 'Underwood. 4/10/1908'. But the Wrenn Librarian has traced the sale of these proofs through Wise, who stated in editing the Wrenn Catalogue (1920) that the Swinburne *Cleopatra* pamphlet, now condemned as a suspected forgery, was bought by the American collector from 'the late Dr Underwood', who does not figure in *The Times* indices of obituaries between 1908 and 1920, and who has not otherwise been identified. It was, moreover, from him that Wise alleged he bought a lot of eighty-four books sold to Wrenn for six hundred and fifty pounds. If there was 'no such a person' as Dr Underwood—and it is almost certain that he was invented to provide one of Wise's fictitious provenances—the choice of pseudonym is an amusing cynicism.

If, again, Wise made one thousand pounds a year out of Wrenn alone, as seems likely enough, it is now evident that a substantial part of his fortune accrued from rare-book dealing—remembering that the 'arrangement' with his American friend lasted for nearly seventeen years. The remarkable thing is that throughout his life he so successfully veiled these activities from most of his acquaintances and from the general public. As I write these words, again that scene in the Ashley Library comes back, when he declared to me with such angry vehemence: 'I am NOT a bookseller.'

VI

Another of Wise's American collector-clients was William Harris Arnold. The contact was made in 1896. It was timely, for some of the spurious Tennyson pamphlets were probably printed in the five preceding years. The first editions of that poet were collected by Arnold, who bought the forged rarities avidly. As Appendix II shows, there were more of them than of any other author. What touching confidence Wise was able to establish through his reputation and tact is evidenced by the American, who has recorded in his *Ventures in Book Collecting*:

Through the kind offices of my new, but now dear old, friend, the distinguished collector and bibliographer, Thomas J. Wise, . . . I obtained one Tennyson rarity after another, most of which at the time were unknown to American collectors.

It is clear that Arnold was another bookman who did not recognize Wise as a bookseller. The dealings were all 'kind offices'. He prints an excitedly flattering letter of 1898 from Wise who had negotiated the sale to him of two Tennyson rarities (apparently genuine in this case), of one of which the dealer says: 'If you were disposed to part with it I could sell it 'for you half-a-dozen times over at a considerable advance upon 'the price you have paid for it.' He speaks of 'we collectors', whose ways and ends are looked after by the gods; and 'honestly confesses' that had he seen the book before cabling for Arnold's offer he would have bought it for himself. 'Ah, well! From all I 'hear you are a good fellow, and well deserve your luck.' Reading this letter, so calculated to appeal to the very retiring but enthusiastic collector, it is easy to understand Wise's success in his tradings with wealthy private clients. He applies to Arnold the proverb 'whom the gods love die young' because of his good fortune in making his new Tennyson 'finds', forecasting the early demise of his 'good' correspondent if the saying were true.

As a fact, Arnold died in January 1923, at the age of sixty-eight, a few months before his book was published. Once more there is the remarkable circumstance of a trustful, almost reverential, client who did not live to know the nature of some of the things he had so eagerly bought through the 'kind offices' of friendship, or the character of the man who was so quick to plant frauds on him. Wise contributed the preface to Arnold's posthumous book, from which this gem shall point the tale: 'For me it must suffice to tell in ever so small a whisper that, 'whilst living, his society encouraged me, and that I hold his 'memory dear.'

Here is a short list of some of Wise's nineteenth-century pamphlets that were sold at the dispersal of Arnold's library. The details are a revelation of what was paid by the American bookman for each of the pamphlets whose production cost (as we have seen Wise admitting) averaged about half-a-crown apiece; and also of what profit they realized before the exposure of them. 'C' within parenthesis after the title means that this pamphlet is now condemned as a forgery, 'S' that it is classified as a suspected forgery. The word 'Collector' or 'Bookseller' is Arnold's indication of the source from which he got the pamphlet: the collector is undoubtedly Thomas James Wise. In the case of the three items indicated as exchanges, the cost prices against them are presumably nominal:

				Cost	Sold for
E. B. Browning's	*Sonnets* (Reading)	(C)	Collector	$115	$440
„ „	*Runaway Slave*	(C)	Collector	30	25
R. Browning's	*Cleon*	(C)	Collector (exchange)	10	80
„ „	*The Statue and the Bust*	(C)	Collector („)	10	91
„ „	*Gold Hair*	(S)	Collector („)	13.60	68
A. Tennyson's	*Falcon*	(S)	Bookseller	350	410
„ „	*The Promise of May*	(S)	Collector	330	430
„ „	*Lucretius*	(C)	Bookseller	25	32.50
			Totals:	$883.60	$1,576.50

VII

Young Herbert Gorfin, the bright intelligent office-boy at Rubeck's—the essential-oil merchant—soon commended himself to Mr Thomas James Wise, who, the youth found, ruled the office outside the closed door of Hermann Rubeck's inner room; and who took an interest in him. Before long, Gorfin was permitted to help the cashier in the dispatching of books: some of those parcels were mailed to America. Thus, in due course, the keen youth got to know that his immediate Lord-and-Master-of-the-Outer-Office was a dealer in rare books. This greatly interested Gorfin, who was fond of books.

There was one occasion each summer which Gorfin came to anticipate with GREAT EXPECTATIONS. It was when Mr Wise brought with him, for a short call at the office, a small-built, kindly-looking American, who was told that this was the youth who packed his books. With a few words of praise for the care with which the parcelling was done, the gentleman from Chicago (John H. Wrenn, it was) would dip a finger and thumb into a capacious top pocket of his waistcoat, extract two sovereigns, and present them to the awed youngster as encouragement for his attention.

'That proud, sad, disillusioned idealist' JOHN RUSKIN, arm-linked
with his friend DANTE GABRIEL ROSSETTI, and with a truculent-
looking admirer on his right (Chapters 8, 10, 11, 15, etc)

But the joke of the pleasing little annual ceremony was that the master himself actually did more of the parcelling than did his assistant. For Wise would pack a parcel as deftly as he could collate a book. He never lost the tradesman's pride in delivering the goods. Even when he had retired on his comfortable fortune, and when he was producing the imposing catalogues and bibliographies of his fine Library, the recipients were able to observe that they had evidently been packed and addressed in his sprawling hurried script by the compiler himself.

Here, for the time being, we must leave Gorfin, the bright promising youth, who is next to prove so useful to Wise—and then so devastating.

As we are in the 'nineties, two of Thomas James Wise's essays in literary work should be recorded here. In 1894 he edited the edition of Spenser's *Faerie Queene*, concentrating chiefly on the bibliography of the work. The edition, which was lavishly illustrated by Walter Crane and produced by George Allen, was a failure, more than half the copies being sold as remainders. Wise's remuneration was one hundred guineas; while Crane received nearly one thousand five hundred pounds. In the following year Wise also edited a new edition of Ruskin's *Harbours of England* (George Allen) for a fee of fifteen guineas.

CHAPTER 10

ENDINGS SWEET & BITTER: FIRST DOUBTS
OF CERTAIN XIXth CENTURY PAMPHLETS

It is a strange story, and the world knows little about it, and some men have condemned him, as some women have censured her. But the two men and that one woman who know best have been happy and contented with the change that John Ruskin's pure unselfishness brought into their lives. And so the world should not complain.

[Anon.]: *Ruskin's Romance*: 1889

I

IN 1892 THE PARENT Browning and Shelley Societies were wound up. The Girton College branch of the former had been dissolved very sweetly a few years before. The girls not only voted that the balance of funds in hand should be spent on chocolates, but 'have actually bought and eaten them', as Furnivall reported in the *Academy*. The Scottish branch, however, was hardiest of the whole family; for it braved the giddy rush of Twentieth-Century life until 1935, leaving behind a mass of transactions.[1] Wise in the days of his celebrity, when few of the original English members remained, was wont to refer to the two institutions with something of the self-righteous air of Mr Lingley in *Outward Bound* who boasted that he owned six cinemas, four music-halls, two public-houses, and a Methodist chapel. But although Wise often spoke of the societies to me, propagating the myths exploded here, I never once heard him regret their passing. They were, perhaps, better dead. But—like the widow who continues wearing her weeds because they become her—for over ten years after the official demise of the Shelley Society he

---

[1] In cataloguing his set of the parent society's transactions, Wise says no Part 6 was issued, that number having been reserved for the list of Contents, Index, etc.; but 'though this work had been completed by me, the Browning Society was wound up before the 'printing had been commenced'. If the work was done the useful MS. was not preserved with his set; which when removed to the British Museum was not only uncut, but mostly unopened.

used its notepaper for writing to clients in the rare-book department of his business activities. This notepaper bracketed him as hon. secretary with William Michael Rossetti as chairman. Thus the defunct institutions still served his purposes.

He was now concerned in promoting a venture which has escaped notice in connexion with his career, and which promised to replace them more usefully in his present scheme of things. This was the inauguration in 1893 of The Society of Archivists and Autograph Collectors. The Society's design was stated to be the publication of a *Reference Catalogue of British and Foreign Manuscripts*. This catalogue was composed of separately-issued monographs on the scripts of various authors, each part being contributed by a specialist 'giving hints for guidance in the detection of forgeries'.

Between 1893 and 1898, seven parts of the catalogue were published, the authors and their autographs dealt with being (1) Charlotte Brontë, (2) Robert Burns, (3) Charles Dickens, (4) John Keats, (5) Alexander Pope, (6) Matthew Prior, and

OH, THOSE GIRTON GIRLS!

who—as Furnivall said—'proved faithless to Mr Browning', and who are seen here as caricatured in Funny Folks *(27 March 1886) with the poet lachrymose and handkerchief in hand, regarding them ruefully (see beginning of this chapter)*

(7) Lord Byron. Of these, Wise contributed those on Charlotte
Brontë and Charles Dickens, in addition to 'editing' the other
parts. In his prefatory note to the first monograph, he said: 'It
'must, I suppose, be considered matter for congratulation that
'no forged or spurious letters of Charlotte Brontë are known;
'none, at all events, have ever occurred for sale.' Against this he
subsequently wrote in the British Museum's copy (breaking the
Library's rule): 'This statement is now, unfortunately, incorrect!' No doubt it was.

These archivistic activities of Thomas James Wise are not
surprising when we consider his interest in autograph material,
and how largely manuscripts figured in his dealing and collecting. He once said that he had made some study of the chemical
constituents of ink. It will be seen that five of the seven authors
chosen as subjects for monographs were authors in whom he
specialized as a collector. But it is a strange circumstance that in
the various books he compiled he is silent about the Society,
and that he did not include its monographs—not even his own
—in his Ashley Library catalogues.

The Archivists whose aim was the detection of forgeries
seem to have taken a patriotic as well as a cosmopolitan turn.
They issued two more parts—Number Eight, dealing with the
autographs of Beethoven, in 1899; and Number Nine, with
those of Her Majesty the Queen, in 1900. The inclusion of
Queen Victoria in this gallery is curious. Even more curious are
the facts that Wise's name disappeared from these two parts;
and that, at the time of writing, neither part was in the British
Museum Library.

II

Every young husband and wife in the Victorian days had
experience of those embarrassingly solicitous friends who had
the curiosity to inquire of one or the other (but never of both
together): 'When may we expect . . . ?' Thomas Wise used to
turn off such inquiries with the remark: 'Children! I can't
'afford children. They cost a thousand pounds each; and what a
'lot of books I can buy for that!' Presumably this was his idea
of humour. All the same, Selina had her own ideas.

Their occasional visitors in the early 'nineties found the young wife rather attractive, with her unexpected turns of speech, her quaint ways, and her natural gifts. Once, when a guest was sharing the evening meal, Wise remarked with considerable brusqueness—as though Selina had omitted the pagination in a book collation—that there was no cheese upon the table. Where-upon she left the room, and was heard calling down into the kitchen: 'Mary! Bring up the cheese-pot.' Thomas's petulance having increased, the amused guest asked about the unfamiliar term; and it was explained that 'cheese-pot' was the name for that kind of receptacle in Selina's native county. 'But the 'hurried appearance of the pot in no way mollified my host,' added the narrator; whose impression it was that, however increasingly prosperous its master, the Ashley Road ménage was under a cloud.

III

Wise was even busier at the printing-press in the 'nineties than in the previous decade; and, except for some Ruskin and Swinburne items, there was a marked tendency to more-openly-acknowledged publishing, which included his first three biblio-graphies. Indeed, the year 1899 is the last date attributed by Carter and Pollard for any of his wrong things—Kipling's *The White Man's Burden*. But he will be shown producing a piracy as late as 1914.

One of his 'nineties productions was of Swinburne's *Grace Darling*, a poem which had appeared in friend Shorter's *Illustrated London News* of June 1893. Wise in his *Swinburne Bibliography*, issued long after the poet's death, proudly describes it as 'one 'of the most interesting volumes in the Ashley Library Series 'of Privately Printed Books'. If it is true, as he says, that he printed the poem at Swinburne's expressed wish, it is curious that the twenty-page pamphlet bears no mark of identification with Wise or his Library, that it was not described in his 1905-8 catalogue, that the British Museum had to buy its copy—in this case from the publisher himself at ten shillings and sixpence, and that the claim as to the thing having been produced for the poet was not repeated in the later *Ashley Library Catalogue* or in the *Swinburne Library*. Moreover, textual comparison with the poet's manuscript rather suggests that the pamphlet was printed from Shorter's periodical. The inferences from various circumstances are that *Grace Darling* and also Swinburne's *Ballad of Bulgarie* (privately printed in the same year by Wise, a copy being sent anonymously to the British Museum Library) are piracies. More is to be said about these when we come to a startling letter from Wise.[2]

Similarly, his production of J. M. Barrie's poem, *Scotland's Lament* (1895), is almost certainly a piracy, and one which had a surprising and amusing sequel. This ode on the death of Robert Louis Stevenson appeared in January 1895, in Robertson Nicoll's *Bookman* from whose office Wise derived the manuscript. From this he promptly printed, in a more correct text than the *Bookman*'s, his 'first edition' purporting to be limited to twelve copies. But he kept very quiet about it, sending no copy to the British Museum and omitting this desirable item from his 1895–8 catalogue.

Now comes the comedy. In 1918 his twin soul, Clement Shorter, made a great discovery. He found out about this ode to R.L.S. and where it had appeared serially, and then rushed out one of his editions for private distribution, limited to twenty copies. He was only twenty-three years too late! Nevertheless Shorter could at least say that he had obtained Barrie's authority for the printing.

When Herbert Garland was completing his Bibliography of Sir J. M. Barrie, and inquired about these two separate editions of the same poem printed by the well-known friends and collaborators, Wise evidently felt that some explanation was necessary. He told Barrie's bibliographer '. . . this pamphlet [i.e. his own] was originally printed with the intention merely of providing a text to accompany the MS. which is also in my possession'. The adroitness of the explanation and the way it is left in the air are characteristic. For the original purpose as alleged, it would be sufficient to print one copy of the poem, not necessarily in pamphlet form. But Wise's edition bears a certificate of the number of copies printed—for what it is worth. In the not very likely event of his being challenged about the authority for the print,

[2] See Chapter 13.

when it was revealed twenty-seven years later, he would probably have said that it was produced by arrangement with Robertson Nicoll. Had this equally adroit explanation been offered, it would have been accepted by Barrie for the sake of the seventy-one-year-old Robertson Nicoll, the author's friend and early patron.

IV

If Wise was unable to establish other than the most formal and infrequent relations with John Ruskin, far different was the association of that author and Dr Furnivall. After Ruskin's unfortunate marriage in 1848 with Euphemia Chalmers Gray (Effie) had been annulled on the wife's unresisted petition (on the grounds of alleged impotency), and she had married the artist John Everett Millais, the devoted Furnivall received the poignant confidences of the divorced husband. Ruskin was, and continued to be for many years, much maligned; but he kept a chivalrous silence, allowing the gossips to slander at will.[3] The marriage was arranged by the parents. The young couple were incompatible. There is much in the theory that Ruskin married on the rebound, as his hero Sir Walter Scott had done; and that his life story would have been a happy one had he not been disappointed in 1847 in failing to secure Miss Lockhart, Scott's granddaughter. 'As to the accusation of my having 'thrown my late wife in Mr Millais' way,' he wrote to friend Furnivall in a remarkable letter, 'I should as soon think of simply 'denying an accusation of murder. Let those who say I have com-'mitted murder, prove it.' He ended with the bitter but true philosophizing: '. . . for she hated me as only those hate who 'have injured'.

When Furnivall, after Ruskin's death, showed that letter to Wise, the collector coveted it almost more than anything else he had ever sought. There was in it a dialogue which had a particu-

[3] There is a rare and mysterious pamphlet, *Ruskin's Romance* (1889), that purports to be a reprint 'From a New England Newspaper', and contains at least two errors of fact that were for long in general currency. It has features characteristic of Wise's printings. He described it in his *Ruskin Bibliography*, and sold copies of it to his agent, Gorfin, one for one pound five shillings in 1910. Clay and Sons, however, say that it was not printed by them. It is not included in the record of Wise's privately-printed editions given in Appendix II.

lar fascination for him. Furnivall, who lost his considerable fortune in a bank failure and was afterwards a poor man, was persuaded to sell the original letter to Wise, who used to show it as one of the most revealing documents in his store of manuscripts. For a reason not difficult to guess, he never made a private-printing of this letter. But he allowed Shorter to do so, freely quoting his friend's pamphlet in the *Ashley Catalogue* (from both of which my illustrative quotations are made).[4] The passage that so irresistibly attracted Wise was written by Ruskin as an illustration of his wife's attitude and moods. It is:

> For instance, would the kind of temper indicated in the following dialogue—which I happened to put down one day as an example of our usual intercourse—be believed in a woman who to all strangers behaved with grace and pleasantness?
> Effie is looking abstractedly out of the window.
> John: 'What are you looking at, Effie?'
> Effie: 'Nothing.'
> John: 'What are you thinking of then?'
> Effie: 'A great many things.'
> John: 'Tell me some of them.'
> Effie: 'I was thinking of operas, and—excitement—and (angrily) a great many things.'
> John: 'And what conclusions did you come to?'
> Effie: 'None—because you interrupted me.'
>
> *Dialogue closed.*

Possibly the explanation of that letter's fascination for Wise was the recollection of his own experiences. It was in 1895 that the difference in temperament and outlook of Thomas James (aged thirty-five) and Selina Fanny (twenty-five) reached a crisis. The young wife had become increasingly restless of late; and, being spirited and energetic, and feeling neglected, she sought the distractions of a tennis club and other social amenities. One day she blithely stepped out of Ashley Road . . . out of Thomas's life . . . into the blue.

'Into the blue' is not an extravagance. There was a considerable

---

[4] It was apparently printed under the 'authority' described on pages 111, 112. Shorter's item is notable for his introduction, in which he makes a point that seems to have escaped biographers—namely, that the unresisted allegation of impotency was later disproved when Ruskin fell in love with young Rose La Touche and was prepared to furnish proof that he had been cruelly slandered by his wife.

and costly quest for the five years' wife before the sequel—which was, of course, in the Divorce Court. This occurred on 28 October 1897, when a *decree nisi* was made at the husband's petition for divorce on the ground of his wife's adultery. Selina's subsequent experience of life was far from being as happy as her prospects had appeared to promise. The fact is only mentioned to do justice to Thomas James Wise, whose compassion—and perhaps regret—were sufficiently touched, it is said, to make him responsive when the time came to be helpful to the first and disappointed sharer of his domesticity.

In the meantime, in 1896, Wise left forever the road whose name was given to his library of future fame. A bachelor again, he took up his abode at 15 St George's Road, Kilburn, N.W., (now called Priory Terrace); where he remained until he entered his second and more successful edition of matrimony.

V

Almost the last of his jobs before leaving Ashley Road was the printing of a twenty-page booklet which has an importance greatly out of proportion to its small size. It bears the title:

THE ASHLEY LIBRARY. A List of Books Printed for Private Circulation by THOMAS JAMES WISE 52, Ashley Road, Crouch Hill, London. N. 1895.

This title is ambiguous, whether intentional or not. The second title, 'A List of', etc., may be taken as meaning either that the list was compiled by Wise, or that he had printed the books listed. Either way, the booklet has the apparent design of recording books in the Library. It details the titles, authors, dates, sizes, and limits of edition, of forty-seven items composed of eight Ruskin titles, six Shelleys, nineteen Shelleyana,[5] eleven miscellaneous, and three 'in preparation'. Among these titles are several of his piracies.

The items were those Wise had for sale; the booklet is nothing

---

[5] These were off-prints of Shelley Society papers that he 'took advantage' to make when in charge of the Society's printing as described (see pages 75 and 76 and Appendix II), rigging them up with the usual preliminaries and labelling them 'First Editions'.

more or less than his bookseller's catalogue in a disguised form. As if the title were not sufficiently calculated to conceal the list's object, there is a statement on the reverse of the title-page which says:

The following list is printed as a Record, not by way of Advertisement. Books printed in short numbers for private circulation become so rapidly and entirely absorbed, that it is exceedingly difficult to obtain information regarding them when such is required for bibliographical or other purposes. Hence the necessity for the present Catalogue.

This is a statement in keeping with his angry protestation to me: 'I am NOT a bookseller.' But if it is only a bibliographical record, as suggested, and not an advertising medium, how strange that the bibliographer did not send a copy to the British Museum Library (which had later to buy the one described above), and did not mention it in his exhaustive catalogues. This was an expanded edition of the List issued two years earlier from the same address, and reissued again in 1897. It is the only printed bookseller's list issued by Wise that I know of, unless some of his larger publications—like the *Bibliography of Borrow*—were also intended to serve the same purpose. The necessity for such a list indicates that his private publishing business was now in a considerable way.

VI

In the following year, 1896, as the result of the initiation of a Burns Centenary Club, appeared the pamphlet *Robert Burns. A Poem*. By Algernon Charles Swinburne (1896), which contains such masterly stanzas as:

> The daisy by his ploughshare cleft,
> The lips of women loved and left,
> The griefs and joys that weave the weft
>   Of human time
> With craftsman's cunning, keen and deft,
>   He carved in rhyme.

Its title-page said it was printed for the Club. Wise, describing his copy, says that thirty copies only were printed, and the circulation limited to the sixteen members to which the Club was 'rigorously restricted'. But the ultimate distribution of the precious first edition could hardly have been so rigorous or so equal; for I find that Wise kept three copies for the Ashley Library, two other copies found their way to his client, John H. Wrenn, and the collector-dealer had at least one copy to sell Gorfin fourteen years later!

Apparently the pamphlet was produced by Wise, who says of the holograph MS. of the poem in his possession that it is of somewhat unusual importance, for it supplies a stanza which was perhaps wisely deleted although restored in subsequent editions. The stanza, which—it may have been feared—might have led to the drawing of claymores north of the Tweed, runs:

> *And Calvin, night's prophetic bird,*
> *Out of his home in hell was heard*
> *Shrieking! and all the fens were stirred*
> *Whence plague is bred:*
> *Can God endure the scoffer's word?*
> *But God was dead.*

The pamphlet, however, follows the text of the poem as it had been printed in the *Nineteenth Century* for February 1896. If, as Wise affirms, Swinburne gave his 'ready consent' to the private-printing, it is nevertheless exceedingly doubtful—all things considered—whether he agreed to the suppression of the stanza. Incidentally, the British Museum did receive a copy of this item, but it came from an unknown donor. Why should it not have come from Wise, why the anonymous sending to the Museum? These are characteristic mysteries where Wise was at the printing-press.

VII

In January and February 1898 there was a correspondence in the *Athenæum* about an eighteen-page pamphlet by Robert Louis Stevenson entitled *Some College Memories*, which purported to have been printed in Edinburgh for members of the University Union Committee, 1886. It bore neither printer's nor publisher's imprint. Messrs T. & A. Constable of Edinburgh wrote of this pamphlet, 'at present being offered at extraordinary

prices', that *Some College Memories* was first contributed by
Stevenson to a little volume called *The New Amphion*, which was
printed by them for the Edinburgh University Union in November 1886. They said that the pamphlet was unknown to them or
to Stevenson's friends, who would certainly be expected to know
of it. The thing was pronounced to be 'not a first edition—merely
a pirated reprint, of which the sale is illegal'.

To this emphatic declaration the *Athenæum* appended a note
saying that Messrs Constable were in error, that Stevenson had
some copies printed off in 1886 for his friends connected with
the University, and that they had been informed by 'a bibliographer of note' that he had seen a copy inscribed by R.L.S.
Such a note not unnaturally angered the Constables, who replied
with truncheon strokes giving detailed reasons for their damning description of the pamphlet.

Wise, almost certainly the 'bibliographer of note' who had
inspired the *Athenæum*'s editorial 'reply', then entered the lists
(31 January 1898) in defence of the pamphlet's genuineness. He
insisted, in a variety of vague and differing expressions, on
Stevenson's responsibility for the thing. It was a most unsatisfactory and side-tracking defence for any kind of bibliographer to
make. But there are two strange features about his letter, written
from 15 St George's Road, N.W. *First*, that nothing was said
about the copy alleged to have been inscribed by Stevenson, the
production or corroboration of which might have provided a
clinching argument. If it ever existed, it has never been heard
of since. *Second*, that Wise, declaring the pamphlet to be no
"piracy", added, 'neither is it in any way a "spurious print",
'as it was printed in 1886, as duly set forth upon its title-page'.
No one had used the expression 'spurious print': the comment
indicates the trend of the writer's thoughts.

Then Frank T. Sabin, the bookseller, wrote a satirical skit
which effectively showed up the hollowness of the defence and
the absurdity of linking the production with Stevenson. This
pamphlet is now condemned as in Messrs T. & A. Constable's
censure. Even Colonel Prideaux, the innocent tool of Wise,
could not swallow the 'justification' of the 'bibliographer of
note'; as he showed in his *Bibliography of Stevenson*, when he
referred any 'curious reader' to the pages of the *Athenæum*.

While this affair was being thrashed out, Robert Proctor, the typographical expert and friend of William Morris, wrote to the *Athenæum* (22 January 1898) giving convincing reasons for describing as 'an unauthorised and later reprint' a pamphlet entitled *Sir Galahad A Christmas Mystery*. 1858 (from Morris's *Defence of Guenevere*. 1858). This Christmas mystery is now completely cleared up by its inclusion among Wise's forgeries by Carter and Pollard, who condemn it on the evidence of its paper as well as on that provided by Proctor.

The 'bibliographer of note' did not draw sword or even pen in defence of *Sir Galahad*. He had the attack on *Some College Memories* to cope with—and that was more than enough. But these exposures in the *Athenæum*, while not connecting the denounced things with him, of course, seem to have determined Wise for the future to keep out of controversy when he was on such dangerous grounds.

The closing years of the 'nineties found him at his temporary home in St George's Road, producing bibliographies of Browning (1897) and Swinburne (1897) which were forerunners to the completer ones of the same subjects. He was also working on his Tennyson bibliography (1908). These advanced his reputation as a bibliographer and collector; they also publicized his forgeries and piracies, and assisted his bookselling to an extent that can be better guessed than definitely assessed. In the Swinburne work he announced as 'in preparation' uniform bibliographies also of Robert Louis Stevenson and Dante Gabriel Rossetti. But these never materialized, probably because Colonel W. F. Prideaux was specializing in the former, and Rossetti's brother William in the latter. So that it may justly be said that there really were cases where Thomas James Wise did not ride rough-shod over all pioneers—as he did over Harry Buxton Forman and Herne Shepherd.

CHAPTER 11

RE-MARRIAGE, AND THE WRITING
ON THE WALL

Belshazzar the King made a great feast. . . . In the same hour came forth fingers of a man's hand, and wrote over against the candlestick upon the plaster of the wall of the King's palace: and the King saw the part of the hand that wrote. . . .

Daniel v.

I

WITH THE NEW CENTURY came a new turn in the career of Thomas James Wise. By this time he had probably finished with the production of the forged pamphlets, although his pirating continued as late as 1914. As a result of what could only have been extraordinary labours and ingenuities in bookselling and publishing since 1880, not forgetting his City employment as cashier with Hermann Rubeck, he now had capital at command and a considerable and growing income. The time had arrived when he could build up the Ashley Library on foundations begun on small savings and large discrimination. He had a reputation— even then somewhat exaggerated—as a bibliographer; and as such his plans were ambitious. Last but not least, at the age of forty he was entering on a new matrimonial partnership, and of course in a new home.

His second marriage, on 27 June 1900, was to Miss Frances Louise Greenhalgh, of Southend, who was his junior by twelve years. Her father had been a bank-manager. The ceremony took place at the Registry Office, Rochford, Essex. The usual particulars, presumably supplied by the bridegroom, are interesting. He described himself as a merchant; his father's rank as that of 'Gentleman'; and the bride's deceased father as 'Banker'. For this marriage Wise had made a new home at 23 Downside Crescent, Hampstead, where he lived until removing finally to 25 Heath Drive, Hampstead, in 1910.

When in the course of time Wise's career blazed into high fame and his circle of friends and acquaintances extended, there were not more than half-a-dozen who were aware of his previous marriage. But those who met the second Mrs Wise could hardly doubt that he had been as happy in his domestic partner as he had been successful in his worldly dealings. Added to the shrewd and practical virtues of a North-Country woman, she brought a sympathetic interest in the higher and open activities of this, the second part of his career, and a particularly watchful loyalty in the final catastrophic years. Then, when he produced his last publication—the concluding volume of his formidable *Catalogue* —he paid a deserved tribute by gracing it with a pleasing portrait of her. She survived her husband by nearly two years; her death occurring on the 6th of May 1939, at the age of sixty-six.

II

It was during the first decade of the new century that Wise acquired most of his choicest books. These, together with his exceptionally extensive collection of nineteenth-century manuscripts, gave the Ashley Library its character and were to be the inducements that led to its acquisition by his country in 1937. Just as he had been fortunate in beginning to collect when first editions, in their original state, of such authors as Shelley, Keats, Wordsworth, and Byron, were to be got cheaply, so now again he was lucky in his opportunities—just when he had more money to command than in the earlier years.

For there now 'dribbled on to the market' (to use Stock Exchange terms much affected by Wise, as also by others in the Rare-Book Trade) a remarkable 'run' of Elizabethan quarto plays in the fine original condition that means so much to students of old literature. Wise was one of the men foremost to appreciate the bibliographical importance of copies as first issued. The precious printings from the Elizabethan presses that now came to light, fresh and eloquent witnesses to the English drama at its most virile epoch, were enough to excite the rivalry of long-pursed collectors. Rivalry there was, especially from such American millionaire bookmen as Robert Hoe (son of the famous inventor of the Rotary press), William A. White (a New York merchant), and later Henry E. Huntington (railway president and financier). The recurring fights over several years were not less keen because they were waged without fuss or publicity. But it behoved an Englishman to secure these treasures, or have them forever lost to his country. And Wise it was who, by his insistence and shrewd acceptance of expert advice, won the noiseless and unseen battle for books—outbidding his American rivals for the pick of the plays. In the balance-sheet of his career, it is this achievement that figures impressively on the credit side. His quiet collecting during this decade, often through agents, ultimately gave the nation possibly its last chance to secure in mint condition many of the important original editions in English poetry and drama from 1650.

As that esteemed authority, Seymour de Ricci, happily put it in a letter to me on the subject: 'The British Museum numerically 'is rich beyond praises. But there are hardly a dozen of their Eng-'lish first editions which can compare in condition with the Wise 'copies. Many valuable "firsts" in the Museum are in the sad 'condition of St Peter's statue in the Vatican, slowly destroyed 'by the kisses of admiring worshippers. To add the whole of 'the Wise Library to the British Museum would be to give the 'Keepers of that Institution exactly what they need the most: 'books they might save from the hands of Twentieth Century 'readers for the benefit of the year 2,000.'

Of this enthusiastic assessment of the entire Ashley Library, some qualification will be made. But it illustrates the arguments ultimately urged upon those responsible for buying the collection for the nation. A useful idea of his book-buying during this important period can be given by the following list of his acquisitions through one agency only, that of Messrs Quaritch (to whose bibliophile chief, F. S. Ferguson, I was indebted for it) between 1905 and 1908. The prices paid are very interesting as indicating the relatively small cost of his library compared with the sums at which we shall see it came to be valued, and the amount for which it was bought for the British Museum. Within a few years he was to see the values of such books rise far beyond even his calculations.

Wise's portrait-frontispiece of himself to the second volume of his 1905–8 *Ashley Library Catalogue* (Chapter 11)

III

In this list of Wise's acquisitions, all the books are first editions; but he had nearly all of them bound or rebound in whole morocco.

AUTHOR	TITLE	PRICE £. s.
Edmund Waller:	*Instructions to a Painter* (1666)	6.
Sir W. Davenport:	*Poem upon his Sacred Majestie's Most Happy Return* (1660)	6. 10.
George Wither:	*Vaticinium Causuale* (1655)	8. 8.
Ben Jonson:	*Ben: Jonson his Volpone* (1607)	60.
John Day:	*Humour out of Breath* (1608)	63.
Samuel Daniel:	*The First Fowre Bookes of the Civile Wars* (1595)	25.
Giles Fletcher:	*Christ's Victory over Death* (1640)	20.
Sir W. Alexander:	*Doomesday* (1614)	24. 10.
Drayton & others:	*Sir John Oldcastle* (1600)[1]	105.
William Cowper:	*Poems* (1782–5)	45.
Michael Drayton:	*Idea* (1593)	36.
George Chapman:	*The Conspiracie and Tragedie of Charles Duke of Byron* (1608)	20.
Ben Jonson:	*The Alchemist* (1612)	39.
John Still:	*Gammer gurton's Nedle* (1575)[2]	180.
Thomas Preston:	*A Lamentable Tragedie . . . of Cambises King of Percia* (n.d.)	169.
Thomas Nash:	*Have with you to Saffron-walden* (1596) ...	99.
„ „	*Nashes Lenten Stuffe* (1599)	111.
„ „	*A Countercuffe given to Martin Junior* (1589)[3]	18.
[George Peele]:	*The Battell of Alcazar* (1594)	60.
P. B. Shelley:	*Queen Mab* (1812)	53.
Alexander Pope:	*The Dunciad* (1728)	55.
Ben Jonson:	*The Fountaine of Selfe-Love* (1601)	60.
John Marston:	*The Malcontent* (1604)	70.
Sir W. Davenport:	[Various Plays in Three Vols] (1639–61)	50.
Shakespeare:	*Romeo & Juliet* (1637)[4]	30.

[1] Actually 1619. This is one of the Seven Spurious Plays attributed to Shakespeare, and reprinted in the Third Folio.
[2] Attributed to Wm. Stevenson by Pollard and Redgrave (1926).
[3] Attributed to Pasquill of England by Pollard and Redgrave.
[4] Not kept for the Ashley Library.

AUTHOR	TITLE	PRICE £.
George Peele:	*The Love of King David and Fair Beth-sabe* (1599)	151.
Philip Massinger & Thomas Dekker:	*The Virgin Martir* (1622)	30.
Edmund Waller:	*Pompey the Great* (1664)	12.
John Bale:	*Enterlude of Johan the Evangelyst* [?1560]	51.
John Cooke:	*Greenes Tu Quoque* (1614)	49.
Robert Greene:	*A Pleasant Conceyted Comedie of George à Greene* (1599)	109.
Anonymous:	*Everie Woman in her Humor* (1609)	103.
„	*An Enterlude of Welth and Helth* (1558)	105.

But, deeply satisfying though such buying must have been to Wise in the light of rare-book values after the 1914–18 World War, he did not always know what wonderful prizes were being thrust upon him by Fate. He was never really master of Elizabethan bibliography. While he explored the physical make-up of his own rarities perseveringly enough as a rule, his was never the wide and confident knowledge of the Elizabethan specialist; and his bibliographical works often suffered for lack of studious comparison with other copies of the same rarities.

For example: it is a matter of history that when the trio of Elizabethans, Chapman, Jonson, and Marston, so brilliantly collaborated in the comedy *Eastward hoe*, played by the children of Her Majesty's Revels at Blackfriars, there was an unexpected and alarming sequel. Offence was taken by the Court at a gibe against the Scotch; with the result that Chapman and Marston were thrown into prison. No doubt Marston was the offender. Ben Jonson, however, although he denied authorship, chivalrously joined his collaborators. Theirs was a pretty plight. They were in danger of having their ears and noses slit—which is unpleasanter than having your purse opened in the law courts to-day in the rare cases in which authors have the courage to be bold. But Jonson and Chapman set influential friends to work. The trio were released—the occasion being celebrated by Rare Ben feasting his partners in a proper Elizabethan merry-o. Perhaps they sang his song to Caelia that ends:

'Tis no sin, love's fruits to steal;
But the sweet thefts to reveal:
To be taken, to be seen,
These have crimes accounted been.

Anyhow, the gibe against the Scotch occurs in the scene where Seagull is telling vulgar fables about the wonders of Virginia and its fortunate inhabitants whose chamber-pots and dripping pans were of pure gold, and who gathered rubies and diamonds by the handful on the seashore. 'And then you shal liue freely 'there without Sergeants, or Courtiers, or Lawyers, or Intelli-'gencers,' says Seagull with a back-kick at the Court. Then followed the gibe:

Onely a few industrious Scots perhaps, who indeed are disperst ouer the face of the whole earth. But as for them, there are no greater friends to English-men and *England*, when they are out an't, in the world, then they are. And for my part, I would a hundred thousand of 'hem were there, for wee are all one Countreymen now, yee know; and wee shoulde finde ten times more comfort of them there, then wee doe heere.

This passage was deleted as soon as the play began printing in 1605. The only copy known to contain it is the very one that was acquired by Thomas James Wise; and to the Ashley Library Percy Simpson, the editor of Oxford University's magnificent *Jonson* edition, had to go in 1932 for a complete version of the play. But, although in his *Catalogue* Wise briefly dismisses his copy as the first issue of the first edition (presumably because of the title-leaf, about which he was mistaken), he was unaware of the treasure he possessed. With his fondness for ecstatically describing at length the reasons for the rarity of his acquisitions, it is inconceivable that he would not have brought out these facts had he known the interesting story about his unique possession.

The truth is that he was all at sea about *Eastward hoe*. He indulged in what is known as 'making-up' copies—i.e. completing defective copies of rare books by transference to them of the required parts from other defective copies of the same books. His *Eastward hoe* is an example of a made-up copy in which the third title-page issued has been put to the first issue of the text

—and the only known copy of such first issue at that. His mortification when these things were revealed to him after the publication of the *Ashley Library Catalogue* was great.

An Elizabethan student, thinking to be helpful, once gently broke the 'news' to him that one of his Massingers suffered from much the same defect. 'Yes, I know, confound it! I made it up myself,' was the candid avowal.

But Wise's library has many other good things proving that he sometimes bought more by luck than by judgment, and that he was more fortunate than he knew. How cheap, for instance, his *Volpone or the Foxe* at sixty pounds. Here again he was unaware that, of all the copies known of this famous first edition, only his own and the British Museum's specimen (that is inscribed by Jonson to Florio) contains the shy and pleasing verses signed N. F.—the tribute of Nathan Field, an actor who had been given his chance to appear in one or two of the great dramatist's plays. Apart from this, Wise's copy of *Volpone* is distinguished for other features.[5]

His copy of Thomas Preston's *Lamentable Tragedie mixed full of plesant mirth . . . of Cambises King of Percia* [n.d.] is worthy of note for a reason other than its scarcity. It came out of a quarto volume containing seventeen plays of the late sixteenth century that for thirty years was bricked up in the chimney corner of an Irish farmhouse. The lucky find, when split into seventeen lots and sold by auction in 1906, realized two thousand six hundred and two pounds—Wise paying one hundred and sixty-nine pounds for Mr Preston's mixture of tragedie and pleasant mirth.

Wise's buying of rare books continued until about 1930, but decreasingly as he completed his individual collections of authors' original editions. Some of his later acquisitions before the rare-book boom included Charles Lamb's *Blank Verse* (1798), forty-five pounds; George Chapman's *Bussy d'Ambois* (1607), twenty-two pounds, and his *Revenge of Bussy d'Ambois* (1613), twenty-eight pounds ten shillings; Robert Greene's *The Spanish Masquerado* (1588), forty-three pounds; Milton's *Comus*, four hundred and twenty-one pounds; and John Lyly's *The Woman in the Moone* (1597)—the last-named recaptured from America (Hoe collec-

[5] See Simpson's admirable commentaries in the Oxford *Ben Jonson*.

tion) at one thousand three hundred and twenty dollars. A number of his Elizabethans came from the famous Rowfant Library that was founded on the collecting of that earlier delinquent Halliwell-Phillipps; and others were from the library of Swinburne, who loved Elizabethan first editions for their texts, not for their texture. Wherefore lamented Wise, who cared for condition above all things.

IV

It was in 1903 that Wise had the first great shock of his career—a shock that must have been premonition of the impending Nemesis. In that year appeared the first volume of the standard edition of *The Works of John Ruskin* edited by Sir E. T. Cook and Alexander Wedderburn. It was a monumental work in thirty-nine volumes exhaustively edited. Wise knew its able editors. As a Ruskin specialist himself, he had naturally been consulted by them; and, as naturally, he would be anxious to see what they had to say about certain rare pamphlets that he, and he alone, had been able to bring to light in his *Ruskin Bibliography*—although they had not been known to his predecessor in that field, the pioneer Richard Herne Shepherd.

There was *Leoni: a Legend of Italy* (1868), a poem that eighteen-year-old Ruskin had written and got printed, by influence, in *Friendship's Offering* to recommend himself to Miss Adèle Clotilde Domecq, daughter of his father's partner in the wine merchants' business of Ruskin, Telford, and Domecq. It was a useful combination which enabled John Ruskin to be a Samaritan and patron of the arts. Of the Sherry Trinity, Telford provided the capital; Domecq, the wine; and Ruskin senior, the brains. Miss Adèle Clotilde Domecq was not one of the clotted-cream damsels who sighed and palpitated over the heart-throbs of *The Keepsake* or *Friendship's Offering*. She had laughed over Ruskin's offering in 'rippling ecstasies of derision, of which I bore the pain bravely 'for the sake of seeing her thoroughly amused'.[6] There was not much likelihood of the pained young wooer having honoured the derided poem by a separate printing. So also thought Cook

[6] See his *Præterita*.

and Wedderburn, who for various reasons doubted the authenticity of an alleged first-edition pamphlet, and its stilted preface in style so unlike Ruskin's. Moreover, the printers whose name had been stolen for the imprint still had their old ledgers, which contained no record of the production.

Next (Vol. 2, page one hundred and one), Cook and Wedderburn were obliged to 'call in question' *The Scythian Guest* (1849), a poem which had also appeared in *Friendship's Offering*. As Ruskin's editors they were unable, they said, to guarantee the genuineness of this pamphlet purporting to be the first edition. Wise probably shivered. But worse was to follow.

In Volume 12, issued the following year (1904), the editors dealt with another of these mysterious pamphlets, *The National Gallery* (1852). They showed by textual comparison that the producer of it had printed the material from *Arrows of the Chace* (1880), back-dating it 1852 in order to pass it off as a first edition. 'It thus follows that the reprint *"of extreme scarcity"* is what is 'known in the trade as a "fake".'

But it was in their eighteenth volume (pages thirteen to fifteen) that Cook and Wedderburn lashed out with the indignation of jealous editors. Of *The Queen's Garden* (1864), they said:

This pamphlet, which figures in dealers' language as "of the extremest scarcity", is—like the separate issues of *Leoni* and *The National Gallery* . . . a fake. It purports to have been "printed in aid of the St. Andrews School Fund"; in which case the issue would obviously not have been limited to a few copies. It bears the imprint of a firm which now at any rate is "not known" by the Post Office. The first copy of it to appear was elaborately described in the *Bookman* for February, 1893 [signed "W", is the later comment], with a reduced facsimile of the title page;[7] the facsimile was also given among the illustrations accompanying the bibliography, edited by T. J. Wise. Several copies of it subsequently appeared in the market, and changed hands at very high prices—copies in remarkably clean condition. . . . It is thus clear that the pamphlet is not what it purports to be, but is a clumsy "fake". The person who put it upon the market, not knowing that Ruskin had revised the lecture in 1871, had his "original edition of the utmost scarcity" set up from the later edition.

---

[7] The impudence and cleverness of this 'elaborate description', or puff, in friend Robertson Nicoll's *Bookman* is astonishing, but not untypical of Wise's publicizing of his wares.

These four pamphlets were not friendship's offerings from
Thomas James Wise. They were his productions done for commerce. In his publicizing of them he stressed the fact that one
had sold for forty-two pounds—a figure that must have been
considered very satisfactory for a thing whose cost price we can,
on his own evidence, put at about half-a-crown. All four pamphlets are now condemned as forgeries on evidence independent of
that of Ruskin's meticulous editors.[8] The important point, however, is that the unmasking of Wise's spurious nineteenth-century
pamphlets was really begun in the *Athenæum* in 1898 and, to a
greater and more pointed extent, by Cook and Wedderburn
from 1903 to 1912. But some thirty years had to elapse before
their damning verdicts were upheld by typographical tests, or
paper analyses, or both; and the forging was revealed to have
been extended to other authors' works. Did Cook and Wedderburn suspect Wise of being the fabricator or concerned in the
fabricating? And why did not their sarcastic rejection of these
four pamphlets immediately lead to the exposure of the whole
ramp, the evil but profitable traffic in which continued until
1934?

These are questions that will naturally be asked. By the way
Cook and Wedderburn linked Wise with *The Queen's Garden* and
quoted his publicizing statements as to its extreme scarcity, it
does look as if Ruskin's editors had some sort of suspicion of
Ruskin's bibliographer. But suspicion was one thing: tracing the
origin of the fakes or making any charge, direct or indirect,
against a man like Wise—a reputedly wealthy merchant and well-
known collector—was another. They were doing their duty to
Ruskin by branding the things. In the absence of more proofs
(that thirty years later were to be obtained by methods they
never dreamt of) they left the perpetrator to Time.

As to the second question: the apparent failure of the book-
collecting world to profit by the revelations of Cook and
Wedderburn is a more complicated subject. Carter and Pollard,
who indicated their indebtedness to Ruskin's editors,[9] point out
that the denunciations of the four pamphlets are 'scattered in

[8] *An Enquiry, op. cit.*
[9] A statement attributed to Graham Pollard by the *Daily Express* of 17 August 193 is:
'I hit on the clue that there was something wrong with Wise's famous catalogue of books
'when I was doing some work on Ruskin . . . . Carter and I began an investigation. . . .'

small-type notes' through Cook and Wedderburn's great work, and that collecting interest in Ruskin was beginning to diminish. Cook and Wedderburn's startling notes averaged some six hundred words for each of the pamphlets dealt with; in one case extending to a page-and-a-half. But in thirty-nine bulky volumes, however, the revelations were somewhat buried, and seem to have escaped general notice. Those who read and appreciated their importance kept their counsel, probably mystified and also impressed by the absence of tangible proof against the perpetrator. Nevertheless, for a considerable time Wise must have been on tenterhooks. But his luck held. The danger passed—though the sight of that edition of Ruskin's works on his shelves was like the writing on the wall to Belshazzar.

V

In 1905 and 1908 Wise produced the first of his two catalogues of the Ashley Library. It was an imposing affair in two large quarto volumes, with more margins than print, and including two hundred illustrations on vellum. The first volume had for its frontispiece the well-known 'true and livelie portraiture' of Sir Walter Raleigh; the second, a lesser-known but probably truer portrait of Thomas James Wise (reproduced here). The Catalogue describes some seven hundred items, compared with approximately seven thousand in the eleven-volume *Ashley Library Catalogue*, which he produced between 1922 and 1936. Considering the comparative smallness of the Library at the beginning of the century, and the fact that he was then embarking on a more ambitious plan of rare-book collecting, it is not easy to account for the sumptuous character of this earlier and obviously temporary catalogue. It may have been in the nature of a shop-window affair in connexion with his roles of rare-books dealer and collector. There may have been a secondary object: to give some of the forged pamphlets an appearance of authenticity by cataloguing them among the genuine things forming the nucleus of the Library. Such pamphlets as *Cleon* and *Gold Hair* (both works of Robert Browning in issues now condemned) were not only described as first editions, but were given prominence by having their title-pages reproduced from copies 'in the Library of Mr Buxton Forman'.

Similarly, publicizing in *Literary Anecdotes* his false Reading edition of Mrs Browning's *Sonnets*, Wise reproduced the title from 'a copy of the rare original in the Library of Clement K. Shorter'. These were things that Wise alone had brought to light, the purported 'discovery' of the Reading *Sonnets* being both highly important and romantic. Why not have reproduced the title-pages of his own copies? The explanation is obvious: the appearance of authenticity would be increased by showing them off in the libraries of other collectors. It was like slipping a naughty poem into a priest's pocket with the title plain to see, and exclaiming: 'Look! It is all right. Even the Church reads it.'

VI

About 1906, Wise's long and successful association with the firm of Hermann Rubeck led to an important development. He entered into partnership with Hermann's son, Otto P. Rubeck, in another essential-oil business, with works at Rotherhithe, and offices in Mark Lane. Of this business, trading under the name of W. A. Smith and Co., Wise was the chief of the two partners. It was a successful enterprise—especially in consequence of the World War, excess profits tax being paid. It contributed substantially to the resources of the collector-dealer.

Otto P. Rubeck, one of the very few people able to speak from close acquaintance with Wise in the early period of his career, was not very communicative in an interview I had with him. He thought there could be very little public interest in Wise's early life in the city. As to the activities which made Wise famous, Rubeck was disappointingly unenlightening. Emphasizing that his own private enthusiasm was for farming, particularly stock-breeding, he conveyed the impression that book-collecting and bibliography were things outside his knowledge. Nevertheless, he sold in 1890 to the British Museum four of the pamphlets which 44 years later were to be condemned as forgeries or suspects, appeared as a member of Wise's Society of Archivists and Autograph Collectors, and was in the schedule of

contributors to do a monograph on the autographs of Sir Walter
Scott (a subject for an expert). It is evident, therefore, that before
he passed to bulls he had an interest in books which subsequently
faded. However productive his bulls may have been, the sterility
of Rubeck's recollections did accentuate the remarkable way in
which Wise's early career seemed to be veiled.

VII

Late in 1907, a mean-looking four-page pamphlet measuring
six-and-a-half by four-and-a-quarter inches gave to the collecting
world '*A Song*. By Elizabeth Barrett Browning. Privately
Printed.' Here is the song, in which the poetess made amorous
play rather more in the style of *The Keepsake* than in that of the
better sonnets of her uneven poetry:

> *Is't loving to list to the night guitar,*
>   *And praise the serenading;*
> *Yet think of nought when the minstrel's far,*
>   *But of beauty and of braiding?*
> *Is't loving, to bask 'neath tender eyes—*
>   *'Neath other, on their removing,*
> *And join new vows to old perjuries?*
>   *Ah no! this is not loving!*
>
> *Unless you can think when the song is done,*
>   *No other's worth the pondering—*
> *Unless you can feel when the minstrel's gone,*
>   *Mine heart with him is wandering—*
> *Unless you can dream that his faith is fast,*
>   *Thro' months and years of roving—*
> *Unless you can die when the dream is past—*
>   *Ah no! this is not loving!*

This effort Mrs Browning considerably altered and expanded
into the poem 'A Woman's Shortcomings'. The tiny four-page
pamphlet of the original *Song* was issued without any statement
as to printer or publisher: it was still in copyright in 1907. Wise
describes his copy without indication of his having any connexion
with it. But he is able to say that it is in the original state as
issued, and (although there is no certificate) that it was limited to

twenty copies. He gave copies to Gosse, Wrenn, and the British Museum. Gosse, sending his thanks (3 August 1908) for the E. B. B. stanzas, says: 'I have determined . . . to begin buying 'books again, so as to fill up some of the gaps in my little collec-'tion. I know you have your special friends to think of, but if 'you would occasionally think of me, I should be grateful. I feel 'that I have been falling rather out of the game. But these things, 'nowadays, never seem to offer themselves.' Wise, in sending Wrenn his copy four days later, threw in this letter from Gosse as one would throw a scrap to a good dog, suggesting that the two might be bound together, as the letter would add a bit to the importance of the poem. Nothing wasted. Apparently he got hold of the original manuscript of the *Song* (in the letter to Wrenn he says he is binding it up with his own copy; but this MS. is missing from the Ashley Library), and could not resist the temptation to put it into print and make a first-edition trifle. But from the facts of the covert publishing and the existence of the copyright, it is presumably a piracy. It is not unfair to class this 'shortcoming' with printings by others that Wise loftily sneered at as 'miserable things'.

As for Gosse's request to be remembered, that came timely. For within a few months Wise was almost neck-deep in a treasure-trove such as booksellers dream of after jolly nights with the clique.[10] And then it was that Gosse was so useful.

---

[10] 'Clique' is the term for the inner fraternity of antiquarian booksellers in England.

CHAPTER 12

THE TWO SWINBURNES: SURPRISES IN THE POET'S STUDY

Up jumped, with his neck stretching out like a gander,
Master Swinburne, and squeal'd, glaring out through his hair,
'All Virtue is bosh! Hallelujah for Landor!
'I disbelieve wholly in everything!—there!'

With language so awful he dared then to treat 'em,—
Miss Ingelow fainted in Tennyson's arms,
Poor Arnold rush'd out, crying 'Sæcl inficetum!'
And great bards and small bards were full of alarms;
Till Tennyson, flaming and red as a gipsy,
Struck his fist on the table and uttered a shout:
'To the door with the boy! Call a cab! He is tipsy!'
And they carried the naughty young gentleman out.

Robert Buchanan: *The Session of the Poets* (1860)

I

ONE DAY IN 1872 a grave-looking middle-aged man with large drooping moustaches knocked at the door of a house in Dorset Street, Portman Square, London. He inquired in his low, almost reverential, voice if Mr Swinburne was in. The heavy-bosomed landlady was sure he was, from the racket going on above. She invited the caller—so unlike the others—to *walk up* to the first floor. He proceeded upstairs with dignified mien. But he soon halted at an amazing sight. There on the landing, dancing about stark naked, was a small youngish man of slight figure, from his head streaming an enormous shock of red hair——. This elfish rhapsody in a London lodging-house was the occasion of Theodore Watts-Dunton's first and fateful meeting with Algernon Charles Swinburne.[1]

[1] This is, I believe, the first printed account of the meeting. It derives from Watts-Dunton on his relation of it to his wife, and also to Sir Edmund Gosse who subsequently recalled it to him in a letter via Wise (29 April 1913) when objection was being made (instigated by the poet's sister Isabel and his cousin Mrs Disney Leith) to Gosse's description of Swinburne's physique (see page 170).

For some thirteen years Swinburne had led a Bohemian existence, chiefly in London. It had been a life of intense creative
effort as a poet, mingled with periods of the wildest excesses—
also of illnesses. His sister Isabel once to Wise thus summed up
the scandalous tales that for long were told of this stage of the
poet's career: 'I know what was said about him, and what a
'trouble he had been. He got among bad companions and was
'very reckless and foolish. But really he was not bad. Please do
'believe this. The worst was a man named Powell,[2] whose con-
'duct was most disgraceful.'

In this stage Swinburne's original and vitriolic personality, his
brilliant and amusing conversation, his gifts as a poet, had caused
him to be hailed and petted by men of reputation long before he
was discovered by the public. The little man with the mass of
flaming hair, green eyes, large head, and slight body and limbs
—the poet who could caper so funnily and write such deadly
invective—the frail elf who could outshriek Hitler, swear like
any Billingsgate porter, and pen exquisite verse to childhood,

A baby's feet, like sea-shells pink,

was described as a 'tropical bird', a 'crimson macaw among
owls': terms which have become permanent labels for that
eccentric and likeable character.

But his trouble was, he would but he could not emulate the
free robust lives of his heroes among the Elizabethan poets and
dramatists. He was more akin to his admired Villon, Baudelaire,
Rimbaud, and Mallarmé, and would be as Bohemian. He wanted
to drink and love with the zest with which he talked and hurled
off his poetry. He had the spirit; but, for one thing, he was
unable to cope with the spirits. There was his boon companion,
Sir Richard Burton, one of the few men who could fire the old
type of elephant gun from the shoulder; who could get up from
a long spell of translating the *Arabian Nights*, and drink a bottle
of brandy at a sitting: whereas Swinburne was under the table
after a few glasses.

He was, as he said, 'a bit of a bibliomaniac'; not much of one,
but enough to have responded to Wise's curiosity about his
Elizabethan quartos, and to have taken a temporary interest in

[2] i.e., George E. J. Powell (1842–82), a young Welsh squire and rake, for several years
Swinburne's crony with whom he visited France.

the collector. I used to frequent Robson's bookshop, now no more, where Swinburne was remembered as a regular customer when the establishment was in Cranbourn Street, Leicester Square. He always arrived in a cab for his usual afternoon with the proprietor. He would descend, uttering torrential maledictions on the fog or something, trip into the shop, and through to the private room at the back. There, rare books would be produced, together with—in view of the 'young gentleman's' known habits—bottles. The spirits flowed with the talk, which was glorious when it turned as usual to the Elizabethans. Nothing could restrain Swinburne on his pet theme—at least, not until the spirits and his legs began to disagree: also as usual. Then, making a faltering exit, he would be assisted by the bookseller and the staff into his waiting chariot; the while he cursed cab, cabby, cabhorse, and cabstand, in one magnificent flow that would have left Ben Jonson, Chapman, and 'foul-mouth'd' John Marston envious and speechless with laughter.

Probably Swinburne then went to his lodgings for one of those apologies for a meal of which Justin Huntly McCarthy had an unforgettable experience. 'Come to lunch,' the poet once said to him with more cordiality than calculation. On the appointed day McCarthy arrived, to find that lunch consisted of a tin of biscuits, a pot of jam, and a bottle of hock. The poet's landlady was wont to lament: 'Mister Swinburne, Sir! he haven't 'eat anything for days. A nice beefsteak 'ud do 'im a power o' 'good.'

This way of living could not go on: he had not the physique to keep pace with Burton and his sturdier cronies. The brilliant tropical bird was a jaded macaw—a bedraggled, dying creature —when in 1879—seven years after the undress introduction described above—with the consent of his mother Lady Jane Swinburne, he went to live with Theodore Watts (who later hyphenated the Dunton to his surname) to become the 'centre of his world' at The Pines, Putney. Watts, who in 1874 had given up his profession as a solicitor for the more congenial occupation of literary critic, mediated in the disruptive affair between the William Morris enterprise and its Pre-Raphaelite partners, and at various times acted with great tact in some delicate matters for Dante Gabriel Rossetti and Swinburne.

Under his care and influence the poet was weaned from brandy to two bottles of light beer daily (because ale had been Shakespeare's drink), and wheedled into a new life of serenity and health that lasted for thirty years in the peaceful haven at Putney. There, says Sir Edmund Gosse, he was 'The book-monk of a 'suburban Thebais. All the charming part of his character 'blossomed forth anew. . . . He became less amusing and stimu-'lating, although perhaps more lovable than he had been in his 'tumultuous youth.'[3] Of that tumultuous youth that gave us the noble lines of *Atalanta in Calydon* and the lyric passion of *Poems and Ballads*, Swinburne once wrote from The Pines to his mother (1885): 'What stuff people talk about youth being the happiest 'time of life! Thank God . . . I am very much more than twice 'as happy now as I was when half my present age just twenty-'four years ago.'

The loss of Swinburne from his circle of Bohemians, however, led to stories comparing him to a songster that had been captured and was pining silent and sad in its cage at The Pines. After the deaths of the poet and his 'devoted companion' (Gosse in the *Dictionary of National Biography*), these stories were resurrected and pointed with sneering criticism of Watts-Dunton—culminating in the scandal of George Moore's *Avowals*. As illustrative of the influences at work is this curious challenge to Wise by Gosse (6 October 1909): '. . . I only do hope that you will succeed, 'some day, in wiping the slime of T.W-D. off the pure marble of 'Swinburne's memory. You are surely going to prevent that he 'should go down to posterity as the Hero-Friend. . . .' But although Wise had his own prejudices against Watts-Dunton without needing the incitement of others, he shied at airing them in print. Nor did it suit his taste to clean any marble of memory, pure or otherwise.

These new sidelights on Swinburne and his satellites are by way of introduction to a full account of Wise's great haul at The Pines. This book has sufficient aims without trying to settle that other controversy.[4] But in due course, doubtless, there will

---

[3] *Life of Algernon Charles Swinburne* (1917).
[4] John Lawrence Lambe wrote a long letter to the *Morning Post* of 9 January 1920, headed 'Swinburne and Watts-Dunton. "A Campaign of Slander."' The differences between the references to Watts-Dunton in Gosse's *D.N.B.* article on Swinburne, his *Life* (*op. cit.*) of the poet, and in his private correspondence are striking.

be written the complete story of The Pines and the enigmatic
character of the unpicturesque Watts-Dunton, to whose helpful
friendships with Swinburne, Rossetti, and Tennyson, there are
plenty of tributes by the sharers of them.

II

Swinburne, who died at the age of seventy-two on 10 April
1909, left to his friend and housemate, Watts-Dunton (aged
seventy-seven), all his money and also his library, papers, and
copyrights. There at once followed a great clearing-up at The
Pines, of which business Wise in the second volume of his
Swinburne Bibliography gives but an inadequate account. 'Immedi-
'ately after the funeral Watts-Dunton invited me to join with
'him in the examination of the books and papers. . . .' The fact
is that it was an old-standing arrangement for him to have first
hand in the deal for the realization of the estate. On his two visits
to Swinburne he had formed a shrewd estimate of the contents
of the poet's library, and had staked first claim with Watts-
Dunton, to whom he made the usual gifts of his privately-printed
pamphlets, and generally made himself agreeable. The elderly
critic shared the common idea of Wise as being a wealthy merchant and keen collector.

That clearing-up in Swinburne's library was a revelation—
even, apparently, to Watts-Dunton after thirty years of life
with the poet under the same roof. It was a most exciting experience for Wise. He never forgot his astonishment, and delighted to
give descriptions of the business to his friends. The poet had been
a prolific worker, and from the time when he left Oxford—on
Jowett's advice, and without a degree—he had preserved the
bulk of his original scripts, so many of them on the favourite
blue foolscap. They included some things that most men would
not have dared to preserve. The library's lower bookshelves and
the corners were heaped with parcels containing letters, manuscripts, circulars, bills, and printers' proofs, bundled away from
time to time as Swinburne cleared his study table. Among the
manuscripts was much unpublished—and in some cases unpub-
lishable—poetry and prose from the poet's best period. The

'These new glimpses of SWINBURNE and his hopeful satellites are by way of introduction to a full account of Wise's great haul at The Pines' (Chapters 12 and 13).—The POET, with WATTS-DUNTON on guard

selecting and editing of these for publication meant a long-drawn-out task. Watts-Dunton was aged.

So in the room where the poet had spent the long and peaceful autumn of his life, still pouring out his lyrics and his learning, the old critic and the middle-aged bookseller and collector sat them down and did their deals. The latter's account—as usual when it comes to personal matters—is not very clear. But in the result, over a long period of visits, Wise got 'all I wanted':[5] the bulk of the papers, including everything unpublished, and some copyrights, for a sum of 'about three thousand pounds', which figure may safely be taken as the maximum. The treasure was removed in cabs to the Ashley Library at Heath Drive; but, for much of it, only temporarily. Those were exciting months over which the dealings were spread, with the private bookseller jubilant and uncontainable to Gosse about the 'glorious treasures' he was bringing away from Putney. The confidential friend thought the prices paid for them were generous; but he was assured that they were ridiculously low. 'Everything of Swin-'burne's, whether MS. or printed, is a "gilt-edged security".' With ready money and expert judgment, Wise—to use his own description—talked to Swinburne's elderly heir 'as a business man'. What that meant we shall soon see. Watts-Dunton was sometimes annoyed, as when he expostulated: 'You are very much too cock-sure.' The dealer merely laughed to himself, and passed on the joke to his confidant.

There was also Swinburne's collection of books that included Elizabethan quartos and other fine things. Wise had his pick of these at prices satisfactory to him; then, for the second helping, he introduced his client, John H. Wrenn, spending his annual holiday in England.

First of all Wrenn was shown over The Pines. To the Chicago business man it must have been impressive. Heavy with comfort and bestrewn with Victorianism, the walls and passages were crowded with Pre-Raphaelite art—that of Dante Gabriel Rossetti chiefly. The summer scene from Swinburne's study window, the garden away from the madding crowd of Putney Hill, was

---

[5] A London bookseller ******* ******* managed to get a foot in, and secured as many as one hundred and two MS. pieces—greatly to the surprise and chagrin of Wise; who, however, in the result was satisfied that he skimmed the cream for himself.

something to make the heart leap. The narrow lawn backed by trees formed a natural setting for a life-size statue—a replica, formerly in Rossetti's garden, of the Vatican Venus, standing so white against the brilliant verdure.

Wrenn now attuned, as awed as a girl at her confirmation, the three settled down to business in the study, unconscious of the mocking spirit of Swinburne, who sometimes never bothered to cash his publishers' cheques.[6] 'After some pleasant conversation,' records Wrenn in a solemn declaration, 'he 'allowed me to purchase . . . the poet's own copy of the original 'Quarto Edition, printed at Pisa in 1821, of Shelley's *Adonais*. . . . 'I also obtained from Mr Watts-Dunton the holograph manu-'script, fully signed, of Swinburne's Sonnet on Shelley, which 'has now been added to the Elegy. The whole forms one of the 'choicest and most attractive souvenirs imaginable of the two 'great Poets.'

It is the simple phrase 'he allowed me to purchase' that makes the American's record so revealing. After Wrenn had finished writing this statement on a blank flyleaf of the *Adonais*, Wise indited, signed, and dated, a corroborative note that he had been present on the above occasion, etc., etc. With two such testimonials to his veneration Wrenn replaced the immortal elegy in its fireproof and morocco-bound case, and returned to Chicago—a happy man.

Indeed, all three were happy, Wise most of all. Throughout his accounts of the three-thousand-pound deal for the bulk of the Swinburne manuscripts, etc., there was always an undertone of vaunting it as a matter of only literary importance to him. Of course many an author would be glad to know that his literary remains were to be so carefully preserved, even though he might pray for sterner discretion. But it is necessary to do justice also to Wise's commercial ability.

The three thousand pounds outlay to Watts-Dunton (if it was so much) was soon recovered. Within a short time Wise had resold some fifty of the manuscripts, mostly published, to Frank T. Sabin, a leading London bookseller, for three thousand two

[6] When Mrs Watts-Dunton was left a widow, she scrapped the remainder of Swinburne's books, and converted his study into her bedroom. Some of the visitors to The Pines were shocked and showed it. But, as she observed when displaying to me the charms of the boudoir: 'After all, Swinburne's gone. It is I who am living here.'

hundred and three pounds seven shillings. From William Heinemann, who paid Watts-Dunton five thousand pounds for the
Swinburne copyrights, Wise received nine hundred pounds in
respect of the publishing rights in the new manuscript material
he had acquired, in addition to other sums. The scripts and
association books he sold to Wrenn in the first four or five weeks
alone of the hectic turnover totalled seven hundred and thirty-
seven pounds nineteen shillings.[7] There were sales, through
another London bookseller opportunely visiting the U.S.A.
about that time, to American bookmen—two only of which
brought three hundred and forty-five pounds. Items disposed of
among his other private clients doubtless yielded similarly-
appreciable sums. Last, but not least, came the proceeds of printing the unpublished material in seventy-six of the privately-
printed Ashley Library editions, for single copies of which he
asked and got as much as ten pounds. The figure of seventy-six
does not include his Swinburne forgeries and suspects. And after
his Pines account had shown such handsome profits in cash
transactions, the 'residuary legatee of the so-called Pre-Raphaelite
School' (as Gosse flamboyantly described him) was left with
his own superb collection of original Swinburne manuscripts
and first editions into the bargain. It was a most profitable
clearing-up.

As an example of Wise's commercialism in dealing with
Swinburne's manuscripts, that of the poet's important *Essay on
Blake* (1868) was broken up, and leaves inserted in some twenty-
five Swinburne first editions (genuine and spurious) sold to
Wrenn 'to add a bit to their value'—as the dealer explained in
another similar instance. The fact that the Blake manuscript
showed considerable differences from the printed text did not
save it. Nor was even this piece of jobbery skilfully done. Four
pages of the Blake material were inserted in *A Midsummer
Holiday and Other Poems* (1884), whereas a MS. sonnet from this
book of Swinburne's verse was placed in his *Bride's Tragedy*
(1889). But this vandalism was not so tragic as his treatment of
the unpublished manuscripts of the Brontës.

[7] This figure, derived from Wrenn's own memorandum, does not include the one
hundred and eight pounds he paid for the *Adonais* and Swinburne's sonnet on Shelley
aforementioned—this purchase having been made direct from Watts-Dunton, the payment
apparently being through Wise.

III

Wise says 'fortune smiled upon my adventure' because
Edmund Gosse became interested in the haul of the poet's
literary remains, and offered editorial help. Fortune not only
smiled but had a hearty Olympian laugh over what was a sensation in its day.

In 1896 Wise had included a tentative bibliography of Algernon Charles Swinburne in his *Literary Anecdotes*, giving the titles
of four poems which 'A.C.S.' contributed to *Fraser's Magazine*
between 1849 and 1851. The bibliographer did nothing more
about the matter then. In 1912, however, something made him
search still further in the files of the magazine, there to find more
poems by A.C.S. The earliest had been done in 1849, when
Swinburne had just completed his eleventh year. Wise leapt to
his discovery and its possibilities for him. It was not quite a
record in precocity, he calculated. Chatterton had begun poet at
the age of ten years and six weeks; and Ruskin when ten years
and eleven months. But it was pretty close.

The discoverer exulted, 'hurried the good news' to Gosse,
and rushed transcripts to the printers—to make two of his
privately-printed 'first editions' entitled *Juvenilia*, by Algernon
Charles Swinburne; and *The Arab Chief A Ballad*, by Algernon
Charles Swinburne. 'These Swinburne juvenilia are imitative in
the extreme,' pontified Wise in his preface (borrowing Gosse's
terms without acknowledgments), 'and exhibit small promise of
'the wonders to come. But they are biographically interesting,
'and, after all, are immeasurably superior to the incoherent
'vapourings of Shelley's early muse.'

Gosse was also excited over Wise's discovery. 'I have little
'doubt of their being by our A.C.S., but it is very curious that
I can get no evidence of any kind,' he wrote to Wise (2 Aug.
1912) '. . . Half of them are quite new to me, and I am unable to
'guess what induces you to attribute them to Swinburne . . . I
'demand from you as full information as it is in your power to
'supply. . . .' But the little doubt was pooh-poohed away. Certainly the poems came in the nick of time. Gosse was just sending his memoir of the poet to the *Dictionary of National Biography*

and was able to include the discovery thus: 'He [Swinburne] was 'in fact, now writing verses, some of which his mother sent to '*Fraser's Magazine* . . . but of this "false start" he was afterwards 'not pleased to be reminded.'[8]

What a day was that when Wise through his private-printings, and Gosse through the *D.N.B.*, could display little Algernon as a poet-just-turned-eleven! And what a nuisance it was that he never wrote those poems!

No sooner were the Ashley booklets and the *D.N.B.* article off the press than Gosse realized that there had been a ghastly error—as did others, including Watts-Dunton, who was a very wideawake veteran. Then began a dithering exchange of daily letters between the biographer and the bibliographer; interspersed with charmingly polite missives from Watts-Dunton about that 'monstrous attribution'. It was found that the verses were included in a volume entitled *Metrical Miscellanies* by A.C.S. (1854), which sent Wise (on the suggestion of Watts-Dunton, who was having him on a string) scurrying to the British Museum Library's catalogue in search of an 'A. C. Stokes'. It was also found that one of the *Fraser's Magazine* poems by this mysterious A.C.S. had been dated from the Carlton Club (a fact Wise had either overlooked or failed to appreciate); which, as Gosse said, made the Swinburne attribution 'fall through', since 'little boys of eleven years of age do not 'date their effusions "from the Carlton Club"'.

It was all 'damnably' annoying. 'I am altogether in your 'hands,' wrote Gosse to Wise (29 March 1913). 'Your judgment 'is paramount. Only I should hate that anyone but ourselves 'should reveal the mistake. Fancy how it would look to wake 'up and read, "Messrs Wise and Gosse know so little of their 'business that . . . [etc.]." Keep the Old Man of Putney Hill 'quiet.'

Wise would have liked to keep the whole 'damned thing' quiet. Gosse, however, insisted on writing a formal letter to *The Times* (to which Wise declined to add his signature) to announce the new 'discovery' that the discovery was not really a discovery. But the Press and critics were not to be put off; the *D.N.B.* had been made the vehicle for false

---

[8] This was afterwards corrected in the reissue of the *D.N.B.*

history. Those were days when a literary problem or discovery
had not such formidable rivals of topical interest as, say, the
particular complexion favoured by some third-rate film actress.
The controversy over the injured 'A.C.S.' and the other mysterious 'A.C.S.' grew hot.

The now-defunct *Globe*, printed on pink paper, became almost
crimson in its efforts to solve the identity of the other 'A.C.S.',
whose verses had been fathered on Swinburne. After much
Sherlock-Holmesing, the *Globe* did it (8 April 1913); inspired,
I believe, by Watts-Dunton, who had solved the riddle a few days
earlier. The 'A.C.S.' who had actually written the *Juvenilia* and
The Arab Chief, and was the author of elusive *Metrical Miscellanies*, was triumphantly proved to be Sir Anthony Coning-
ham Sterling, K.C.B.—a minor poet, but a major soldier; he
had been Brigade-Major and Assistant Adjutant-General of
the Highland Division in the Crimea.[9]

The 'Old Man of Putney Hill' could not be kept quiet. At
first he had been led—of course, by Wise—into the error of
supposing that the wrongful attribution was originally due to
Richard Herne Shepherd in his pioneering *Bibliography of Swinburne*. But he went into the matter more closely, exploded the
charge against Shepherd, and blew up Thomas James Wise
instead, writing to him (10 April 1913): 'By the by, the familiar
adage, "Give a dog a bad name", etc., can certainly be applied
'to Shepherd . . . I have pretty well ascertained that the first
'ascription of the *Fraser* poems to Swinburne does not lie at
'the door of this man. I cannot trace it earlier than 1896, in the
'second volume of *Literary Anecdotes*.' Watts-Dunton's vindication of Shepherd and the taunt (undoubtedly directed at Wise)
are particularly interesting in view of what follows in my sketch
of Shepherd.

The curious feature of the whole affair, and the one most
relevant to this study, is that Thomas James Wise, the cause of
all the trouble, never himself emerged to take his major share of
responsibility. Gosse was hard-pressed by severe critics, including the poet's sister, Miss Isabel Swinburne, who was furious
with him, and James Douglas. What was Gosse's authority for

---

[9] These printings of the two poems, being made without the authority of the author,
are piracies.

the attribution and for the tale of the poet's cultured mother sending such rubbish to *Fraser's?* What did he mean by it? Gosse, made 'quite ill', was left to the lashing storm. As he said (and unfortunately believed), Wise was paramount. But bibliography is the handmaid of biography. The biographer was entitled to state his authority—as he briefly did in the letter to *The Times* announcing the 'discovery' that the discovery was not really a discovery. Except for this one reference, Wise escaped; thus proving once again his peculiar elusiveness in avoiding the consequences of his errors.

IV

All the same, it was very mortifying. When he came to correct the attribution in his later works, Wise made the peevish comment: 'It is difficult to understand why Swinburne, when the 'poems were brought directly under his notice in my *Bibliographi-* 'cal List* of 1897, and there distinctly cited as his, did not himself 'deny their authorship.' Perhaps not so difficult. If he ever saw Wise's *List*, he would have noticed that two of the poems fathered on him at the tender age of twelve, just when he was a queer little elf going to Eton, began:

> *Where shall I follow thee, wild floating Symphony?*

and

> *Oh! Sing no Song of a joyous mood.*

Another specimen of the minor A.C.S.'s muse:

> *Then don't despise the working man, he's strong and honest too,*
> *And he would rather governed be than seek to govern you;*
> *But lack of proper guidance at last may make him mad,*
> *And when the best don't govern him, he'll call upon the bad.*

Swinburne, even when settled down to the light beer and the heavy sobriety of the peaceful Pines, retained enough of the elfin spirit to enjoy such delicious jokes—and to leave them for posterity to enjoy.

CHAPTER 13

WATTS-DUNTON'S SURRENDER: MORE SECRETS OF 'THE PINES' VENUS

He's tough, ma'am, tough, is J. B. Tough, and de-vilish sly.
Charles Dickens: *Dombey and Son*
O, what a tangled web we weave
When first we practise to deceive.
Sir Walter Scott: *Marmion*

I

'YOU ARE A consummate diplomatist, and in your skilful hands 'everything in our tangled skein is coming straight,' Sir Edmund Gosse once wrote to Wise (6 June 1915) with reference to some trouble with Miss Isabel Swinburne concerning the critic's *Life* of the poet. How consummate, how astute even, Gosse amply experienced in his collaboration with Wise when the collector-dealer came to turn his rich haul of manuscripts from The Pines into hard cash. A lively correspondence ensued between the two men. It shows how Gosse revelled in editing Swinburne's unpublished work, writing prefaces, and detecting his collaborator's howlers; while Wise got on with the sorting of the treasure, the printing, and the dealings—about which the literary partner was not told what has been revealed here. Wise had his own tangled web from which to extricate himself.

There was a fearful instance in the early days of his negotiations for the Swinburne material. It is reported to Gosse in the following letter:

23, Downside Crescent,
Hampstead. N.W.
July 10. 1909.

My dear Gosse,

Many thanks for proof of 'Twilight'. I spent all last evening over the MS. of this, & it now reads quite differently. Will send you revise next week.

Bought some more MSS. from your "Reptile" friend[1] on Thursday,
& am going on Monday for more. He rather pressed me to take the
autographed "Tombeau" at 12/12/—. But I stuck to 'No', and told
him "all or none". It ended looking very much like "*all*".
Now for some fun. He had got a copy of my S[winburne]. Bibliography,[2] & pointed out to me

"Sonnets on Browning"

"Grace Darling"

&

"Bulgarie"

"These are *damned* things [said Watts-Dunton]: they are all 3 forgeries
& piracies. I shall write to the Athenæum & denounce them!"
I told him that to do so would do him much harm, as his note
would be replied to, & it would end by being shewn that he knew
nothing about S's books at all.
That I could produce S's *written permission* for the Br[own]ing
Soc^ty to print the Death Sonnets, and also a copy with presentation
inscription to Christina Rossetti, bought by me from Wm. R. after
Christina's death.
That I could also produce *S's letter to myself* giving me leave to print
"Grace Darling", & a second letter thanking me for copies of it.
"Oh, yes," he said, "I remember, they are all right."
As to "Bulgarie", I said, the MS. was sent for publication to the
P[all]. M[all]. G[azette]., but held back from publication. Possibly the
P.M.G. people may have struck off a few copies before returning the
MS. to S. *That* would not be either 'forgery' or 'piracy'!—"Yes, I do
remember something of the sort: I think I wont trouble about them"!

Ever yours

Thos. J. Wise

However much he might pretend this episode was funny, it
can hardly be doubted that it came as another horrid shock to
hear Watts-Dunton threatening to denounce these '*damned*'
pamphlets in the Press. It was another warning of the coming
Nemesis. But Wise soon recovered his aplomb. The way this

---

[1] i.e., Watts-Dunton. It is a sample of the abusive references to him in this correspondence.
[2] Wise's original and tentative *Swinburne Bibliography* (1897). Was he surprised to find
Watts-Dunton had it? This letter is reproduced literally from Wise's script. Italicized words
represent words underlined by him. My interpolations made for clarity appear within
square brackets.

unexpected indictment was met provides a remarkable and all-sufficing revelation of his 'consummate diplomacy'. Probably Gosse appreciated the 'fun', being deluded into believing that the critic who was so intolerable to him had been effectively quashed. But let us dissect the letter, examining the things with which Watts-Dunton was counter-threatened.

If, as alleged, Wise could show Swinburne's authority in writing for the Browning Society to print the *Sequence of Sonnets On the death of Robert Browning*, that document could only have referred to the quoting of the sonnets in the Society's annual *Papers* (see No. XII, 1890) among a collection of obituary notices and poetical tributes. It is doubtful whether he possessed even that authority, for he was not the editor of the *Papers* (his interest in the Society had waned by 1890); and the document was not among his Swinburne correspondence in 1937. Moreover, although two annual volumes of *Papers* were issued after Browning's death in 1889, they contain no reference to any such pamphlet having been produced for the Society or for anyone else. That it was *not* done for the Society Wise himself admitted ten years later in his 1919 *Swinburne Bibliography* (Vol. i, page four hundred and twenty-seven) when he said the pamphlet was seen through the press 'upon the poet's behalf' by Harry Buxton Forman. Therefore, if the thing was printed for the poet and not for the Society, the statement to Watts-Dunton about the letter of permission was misleading.

Wise backed up the threat about the letter by suggesting that he had the copy of the pamphlet presented by Swinburne to Christina Rossetti, which copy is described in his catalogues as 'highly treasurable'. It is indeed very interesting. But the nation, which bought it with the Ashley Library, will hardly treasure it so highly; because it is another fake—a kind of fake that in other circumstances he was known to denounce with his characteristic vehemence. In the first place, it is not an inscribed presentation copy, as implied by his note: 'Upon the recto of the first 'leaf is the following inscription', etc.

There is no inscription on any page of the pamphlet itself. What is there is a single sheet of Pines notepaper pasted on the first leaf; and the sheet bears this message in what appears to be Swinburne's handwriting:

The Pines
Putney Hill. S.W.
Oct. 3–90

Dear Miss Rossetti
    I send you a little poem of which the subject may perhaps interest
you, and am always
                            Very sincerely yours
                                A. C. Swinburne.

Now, if Swinburne wrote that note, it is almost a certainty that
it does not refer to the pamphlet in which it is inserted. He would
hardly refer to an important sequence of seven sonnets, written
on so memorable an occasion as the death of Robert Browning,
as 'a little poem'; and it is unlikely that he would make the
casual and not very complimentary suggestion that the subject
'may perhaps interest' the poetess. Moreover, if the pamphlet
really was privately printed for him, and if this letter dated
3 October 1890 really does refer to it, there was a long delay in
sending the gift. Robert Browning died on 12 December 1889:
the sonnets appeared in the *Fortnightly Review* issue for 1 January
1890, from which the pamphlet could be promptly printed.

    But what of Wise's later tale that Forman saw the *Sequence
of Sonnets* through the press for Swinburne? In view of this
definite attribution and also the statement that Herbert Gorfin
bought copies from Forman's widow, further light was sought.
What Forman's son Maurice had to say was not conclusive.
On the other hand, Gorfin managed to find the counterfoils of
a cheque-book that showed him to have paid on 17 February
1920 three pounds eleven shillings to Mrs Forman for two copies
of the pamphlet; and on 27 February 1920 eighteen pounds to
Wise for ten copies. The significant facts emerging are that:
(1) when Wise described the private printing in his 1896 'List
of Swinburne's Scarcer Works' (*Literary Anecdotes*) he said
nothing about Forman having seen it through the press for the
poet; (2) he met Watts-Dunton's denunciation of the pamphlet
by implying that the Browning Society printed it; (3) Forman
was dead when Wise came out in 1919 with the new tale that his
friend was the producer; and (4) when Forman's 'magnificent
copy' of this 'excessively rare' item was sold for forty-five
dollars in New York (1920) nothing was claimed in the cata-

logue description about its owner having produced it for Swinburne. But if the thing was regular, and it was done for and with
the consent of the poet, how strange that the British Museum
did not receive a copy from either the author or the producer.
Its copy, together with three other items, was the gift of G. A.
Phillips, of Ilford, Essex, on 9 May 1891.

Wise knew that what he put forward as an author's inscribed
presentation copy of *A Sequence of Sonnets* ill-supported his false
representation. When he came to boost it in his *Swinburne
Bibliography*, quoting the poet's purported inscription, he was
shrewd enough to see that the reference to 'a little poem' would
not pass muster. So he altered the tell-tale word—the all-impor-
tant word in a note of one sentence—and printed 'Dear Miss
Rossetti, I send you a little book . . .' etc. He says he bought this
copy now shown to be a fake from William Rossetti. Be that as
it may, whoever was its fabricator, Wise misled Watts-Dunton
about it; he gave two conflicting accounts of the pamphlet's
origin, one of which involved Forman but was not made until
that friend was dead; the fake presentation copy does not prove
that Swinburne knew of or consented to the private printing.
These facts together with the almost certain reproduction from
the *Fortnightly Review* strongly suggest that the thing is a piracy;
and the weight of the circumstantial evidence is heavily against
Wise.

It seems as if he was determined to catch at every thread, no
matter how weak, to link the production of the private-pamphlet
issue, the *Sequence of Sonnets*, with Swinburne. He records in the
Ashley Library Catalogue (VI, page one hundred and seventy-seven)
the possession of another copy, and says: 'Inserted at the com-
'mencement of the pamphlet is an A.L.S. of three pages from
'Browning's son to Watts-Dunton, conveying his thanks for the
'gift of a copy of the Sonnets.' But examination of the letter
shows that Browning's son neither conveyed thanks nor mentioned any 'copy' of the sonnets. All he did was to add to the
main and quite different subject of his letter this sentence: 'I
'have been deeply moved by Mr Swinburne's beautiful sonnets.'
As he was writing from a London address on 2 January 1890,
and as the sonnets had appeared in the *Fortnightly Review* of the
previous day's date, there can be little doubt that he was refer-

ring to the publication in that periodical. Had he been acknowledging the gift of a presentation copy of a private pamphlet
he would surely have been more explicit.

Next we come to the *Grace Darling* pamphlet. Reasons have
already been given in Chapter 10 for inferring that this is also
a piracy. But Wise held over Watts-Dunton the threat that he
could produce Swinburne's letter giving permission to print it.
In none of the poet's few letters to Wise, printed or unprinted,
in the Ashley and Wrenn Libraries, is there any such permission. Wise must have known that he could not produce the
boasted authority, because, for the purpose of printing, he
handled his brief correspondence from Swinburne in the same
year (1909) in which this revealing episode with Watts-Dunton
occurred.

As to the *Ballad of Bulgarie* pamphlet, Wise's plausible surmise
that possibly the *Pall Mall Gazette* people may have struck off
a few copies is proved by himself to be false because in his
Swinburne Bibliography (Vol. i, page four hundred and fifty) he
jocularly admits that he printed it without the poet's consent.
The absurd suggestions that the *Pall Mall Gazette* might have
printed the thing, and that that would not have been piracy,
should be noted.

In short, then, Watts-Dunton was right to describe all three
pamphlets as 'damned things'. They were not both 'forgeries
'and piracies', as he loosely said; they will henceforth be classed
as piracies. But the point as illustrating Wise's consummate
diplomacy is that in each case he warned off Watts-Dunton's
threatened denunciation in the Press by counter-threats based
on falsehoods and misrepresentations. It may be wondered why
the indignant housemate of Swinburne retracted his charges and
allowed himself to be coerced into silence. He was an old man of
seventy-seven, described at this time as physically feeble, though
mentally very active. But he was faced by a younger man—one
clever and formidable, who was, moreover, buying the bulk
of the inherited treasures. So, what with Thomas J. Wise's
counter-threats and his gold, the aged Watts-Dunton wilted
and surrendered.

In view of what has been said in Chapter 7 about Swinburne's
brief correspondence with Wise, and in view also of how he

held it over Watts-Dunton, it is interesting to see Gosse's
reaction to the collector's proposal to rush the letter into print
and to show them off in one of the earliest of his seventy-six
privately-printed Swinburne pamphlets. The letters were drawn
from the poet by the gifts of reprints and the suspect *Cleopatra*
pamphlet. Wise much desired a preface to them to be written
by Gosse. But the critic was not obliging to that extent. He
perhaps guessed what Wise would expect him to say. Anyway,
the request was emphatically refused in this reply (2 January
1910):

... Don't you think before working off these seven letters of Swinburne,
it would be worth while to look still more carefully for the six or seven
other letters which you have mislaid? You cannot have lost them, and
the collection would be so much more valuable if it contained fourteen than seven letters. There cannot be any cause for hurry, and I
would suggest that it would be far better to wait while you hunt your
papers thoroughly.

These letters, of course, are of great biographical and bibliographical
value; you have however used much (or nearly all) of this already in
your 'Bibliography'. . . . I do not see my way to writing any prefatory
words.

But Wise did not wait to hunt further for the missing letters,
probably for good reason. With the exception of a short note of
thanks (for a 'beautiful and curious' Shelley reprint) left unprinted, no more were found among his papers on their removal
to the British Museum; although he had years earlier sold to
Wrenn one of the so-treasured letters which was also a brief
acknowledgment for another Shelley reprint.

II

The accounts Wise gave to Gosse of his dealings at The Pines
after the deaths of Swinburne and Watts-Dunton make a rather
sordid tale, and the vituperative epithets he applied to 'W.-D.'
come ill from the writer who says of him in the preface to the
Swinburne Bibliography: Vol. I: 'I am glad to take this oppor-
'tunity of expressing the gratitude I feel to my dead friend for
'the kindliness and goodwill he at all times exhibited in his

'transactions with me,' etc. Watts-Dunton, old and feeble as he
was, had been anxious to get as much money as he could for the
literary property Swinburne left him. Because the inheritor tried
to get 'an extra pound or two' in some of the deals, Wise concluded that he was being 'squeezed'. He therefore determined,
he told Gosse, no longer to consider his old friend's interests,
but to make bargains as good as he could—notwithstanding his
admissions that he was having the best of matters already and
that the beneficiary was ignorant of values in certain cases. But
if events at The Pines had been exciting then, they were almost
violently thrilling when Watts-Dunton passed away on 6 June
1914.

Wise again busied himself there 'to get a look in on *our own*
a/c'. Generally his letters compare unfavourably with those of
Gosse; but the scenes of jealousy and hysteria at Putney
prompted him to descriptions from which Hogarthian pictures
may be conjured up. The Pines was likened to Hell, with the
three females who were there continually on the verge of coming to blows, labelling this and that as theirs, pulling 'Tom'
here and there to secure his championship.

'Your reports of the Watts-Dunton ménage are marvellous,'
once commented Gosse. 'Now people seem to be getting a little
'over the sort of terror which W.-D. managed to spread around
'him, I receive from strangers as well as friends dreadful stories
'of the way in which—of late years particularly—he bullied
'A.C.S., whose patience and modesty were heavenly. Still it is
'possible to write as that man Coulson Kernahan does some-
'where this month, as if W.-D. was a great gentleman, putting
'up with an eccentric pauper.' And again (28 June 1914): 'What
'you so very amusingly describe of affairs at The Pines is
'deplorable and monstrous. But continue to give me the
'wretched particulars.'

The young widow was eventually left in possession of the
home of Watts-Dunton. Wise continued visiting, but henceforward accompanied by Mrs Wise. 'Why did she always come
'here with him, or stick in the room if I went to their house?
'Tommy and I were old friends; and naturally I wanted to see
'him alone,' was Mrs Watts-Dunton's subsequent complaint to
me. I had no suggestion to make. But the housekeeper had,

when her mistress discussed the matter with her at the time.
The worthy Mrs Tibbitts's advice, according to the widow, had
been: 'Well, ma'am. Perhaps it would be better if you didn't
'put on that pretty short frock of yours, and wear those high-
'heeled shoes when they come next time.' These matters, however, are incidentals, if not unenlightening. The essential fact
for the collector-dealer was that the second clearing-up at The
Pines was disappointing as compared with the first. He could not
boast this time of journeying back to Hampstead with taxi-cab
loads of manuscripts and books. The old solicitor had left his
remaining treasures—his Pre-Raphaelite pictures, original correspondence, etc.—vested in trustees, to be sold in due course by
Sothebys. Perhaps he had learned his lesson: certainly he learned
something of the large profits made on the re-sale of some of his
Swinburne manuscripts—much to Wise's annoyance, as is
evidenced by his correspondence. On this occasion, therefore,
he only secured (through the widow) a few items, including a
much-desired and important Dante Gabriel Rossetti letter.
Afterwards, his visits became infrequent as his fame blazed forth,
and ultimately ceased.

    ✱✱✱✱✱✱✱ ✱✱✱✱✱✱✱✱—a friend of Wise who designed to write
a life of him[3]—was the subject of another typical note from
Gosse (6 July 1914) about the same time as the previous one:
'. . . The enclosed (which tear up) is from ✱✱✱✱✱✱✱ ✱✱✱✱✱✱
'✱✱✱, who used to be a devoted hanger-on of The Pines, but fell
'from his allegiance a little! His attitude to *me* has changed: he
'leaves the dead lion that he may pat the living dog. . . .'

    Drawing the veil over these dubious allegiances, it will be
instructive to consider the results of the scramble for Swinburne's property, especially as Wise was much concerned to let
it be known privately that his 'friend' Watts-Dunton had hardly
any financial resources of his own, and practically lived on the
poet.

    Swinburne's effects were sworn for probate at twenty-four

---

[3] It never materialized. Various circumstances suggest that the portrait of Wise would
have been executed in whitewash. The proposed artist asked Herbert Gorfin to send him
all the original documentary evidence existing of his transactions with Wise concerning
the fraudulent pamphlets, etc., coolly proposing that they need not be returned, as the
owner would no longer require them. In such a case Gorfin declined to part with his
documents.

'She will never tell any stories about the ménage in Cheyne Walk, or about the odd trio at The Pines, or about Tommy's visits. No! She will never tell, will this Venus.'—The scene from Swinburne's window, with the Vatican Venus which came from Rossetti's garden (Chapters 12 and 13)

thousand two hundred and eighty-two pounds ten shillings and eightpence, Watts-Dunton being the sole legatee. But Wise estimated that with the subsequent sale of the manuscripts and books, the estate realized about thirty-five thousand pounds— a likely enough figure.

Watts-Dunton's estate in turn was returned at twenty-two thousand nine hundred and thirty-four pounds six shillings and tenpence, which again in Wise's opinion was a considerable undervaluation.

Wise's profit from the re-sale of the Swinburne manuscripts, books, and copyrights, plus the proceeds of his publishing and the value of the treasures he kept for himself, was probably little short of ten thousand pounds. This is a reasonable estimate based on known transactions, only a few of which have been instanced.

III

It is in connexion with the private printing of the unpublished Swinburne manuscripts that the Gosse-Wise correspondence is such a revelation—not merely of the enterprise, but of the characters and relationships of the two friends. Sir Edmund Gosse was as intimately acquainted with the literary development of the poet as with the man himself. He was most eager to assist with the material unexpectedly brought to light. His warning to Wise (18 April 1913) is significant. 'Remember! that I know more 'about Swinburne than any other man living—more than his 'sister, more than Watts-Dunton, more than even you. I know 'much that will die with me. I have an almost religious wish to 'leave for posterity the materials for a genuine picture of him 'at his best.'

How much more Gosse knew of the poet's work and life than did Wise, the latter came to appreciate. He was frequently rescued from errors by his collaborator from 1909 onward, during the years in which the Swinburne pamphlets were privately printed by Wise from his acquired manuscripts. The results of his adventuring alone and unaided were the production of at least two pieces—including the *Blest* (1912) pamphlet —as first editions, only to be told that they had already been

published. Then there was the affair of Adah Menken, the actress
who shocked or delighted Victorians by a performance of
Mazeppa in semi-nudity, and who had literary tastes and aspirations. Swinburne's friendship with her afforded Thomas Wise
opportunity much to his taste for annotating his *Bibliography*
of the poet. He indulged himself even to the extent of giving her
five husbands, the first unnamed; although her latest biographer
(Bernard Falk, in 1934) limits the marriage list to four. But what
is one more or less among the 'lovable' Menken's many husbands and reputed lovers—as to which latter (Swinburne in
particular, possibly) Wise and others presumed too much. Gosse
in his *D.N.B.* article had said *inter alia* that the poet became
intimate with Adah—whatever that was meant to imply, for he
used the adjective indiscriminately—after she left her fourth and
last husband; and he flatly denied that Swinburne partly wrote
either her verses *Infelicia* or the poem *Dolorida* addressed to her.
His letter (12 June 1919) to Wise, who did not wholly accept
its criticisms, has several points of interest:

I hope you will consent to make the changes I have indicated on
these proofs. I think you ought to do me the justice to quote, or refer
to, what I said as long ago as 1912 on the subject of Menken (*Dict. of
Nat. Biogr. Supplement*, vol. iii, p. 461). I was attacked for it venom-
ously by the ladies, but it was true, and I cannot think why you should
be afraid to support me now.

I do not think that you have even looked at what I then wrote: or
you would not now make the mistake of supposing Menken's publication of *Infelicia* in 1868 to 'precede' her acquaintance with Swinburne
in 1867.

The whole episode ought to be treated, if at all, very delicately and
above everything accurately. I am minutely acquainted with the very
extraordinary incidents of it: I do not think that any one else now alive
is. There was not the most distant similarity between her relations with
Rossetti (who only saw her twice on business) and with Dumas (who
swore on oath that he did not know her and that the photograph was
an impudent fake) and those with Swinburne. Her relations with
Dickens I am sorry to see you mention: I wish you had not done so.

As you well know, Shorter's pamphlet[4] was almost entirely made up

---

[4] i.e., *Adah Isaacs Menken: A Fragment of Autobiography*, by Algernon Charles Swinburne,
1917. Privately printed by Shorter. Wise did not do Gosse the 'justice' to mention his
in many ways admirable biography of the poet in the *D.N.B.*

of material which I had entrusted to you and which Shorter impudently *stole* in your house.

The correspondence of the two men devoting their energies to Swinburne for such opposite purposes resembled a game of battledore and shuttlecock in its exchange of thanks and compliments—from the one side, for the prefaces, notes, and information which Gosse bestowed with enthusiastic generosity, interspersed with sundry rarities for the Ashley Library; from the other side, for pamphlet first editions (genuine and spurious), 'lovely' grapes, and an occasional manuscript. 'You really are 'a very terrible man,' Gosse wrote innocently (9 April 1901), acknowledging some gifts which included the pamphlets *Laus Veneris* and *Samuel Prout*, the former now classed as a suspected forgery, and the latter as a piracy. Again (19 August 1909): 'But I know your masterly way, and that it is useless to resist you.'

But for all the other's masterly way, it was Gosse who held the whip in their literary partnership; and he sometimes flicked it smartly about the 'obstinate beast'. An example is provided in an undated letter [? July 1919] about the manuscript, acquired by Wise, of Swinburne's uncompleted joke in French that George Meredith—to whom the author read it—described as 'the fun-'niest rampingest satire on French novelists dealing with English 'themes that you can imagine. One Chapter "*Ce qui peut se 'passer dans un Cab Safety*", where Lord Whitestick, Bishop of 'Londres, ravishes the heroine, is quite marvellous. But he '[Swinburne] is not subtle.' Wise wanted to print this effusion, and got one of his helpers to translate it for that purpose. The horrified Gosse protested:

What an extraordinary man you are! You will leave nothing untouched, and you not merely rub the dust off the butterfly's wings, but you scrub them to a skeleton. What is this that you suddenly start on me about a *translation* of Swinburne's pleasant jest? And why in the name of ******, do you apply to ***** ***** in the matter? If there is a question of this kind, am not I, as your colleague, worthy to be consulted? A man like ***** *****, a quite inferior person, should not be consulted on a delicate point of this kind. I cannot understand you having any dealings with him at all. Why do you do so?

"La Fille du Policeman" was a joke, a piece of playful extravagance.

Such a merry trifle cannot be "translated"! The whole fun of the thing was the bad French, the absurdity of the supposed Parisian view of English social life. What on earth has driven you to the amazing proposition of having it "translated"? You seem to me sometimes, in regard to Swinburne, to have immersed yourself so long in the merely bibliographical labour of dealing with his MSS., as to have lost all sense of humanity, of reality, in connection with him. You will leave nothing alone. It is incomprehensible to me that your sense of humour does not prevent you from crushing the very life out of the poor old poet by these pedantries.

It is high time that you put Swinburne altogether out of your view for a while, for you are losing all sense of proportion and all range of values in connection with him.

There were some values whose range Wise was never in danger of losing—whoever the authors concerned might be. In this case his project to make a pamphlet of *La Fille du Police-man* was abandoned in the face of Gosse's caustic criticism.

A startling revelation of Wise's ideas of annotation, in contradiction of his personal opinion, drew this objection from Gosse (6 April 1919):

... But why ... do you consider this anecdote "a myth"? I can conceive no possible reason for doing so. But as you do hold this, you ought not to say "is almost certainly true".

And a few days later (16 April 1919):

... What on earth do you mean by: "It is Leslia not Lesbia, Brandon'? You are surely not ignorant of the reason why Swinburne chose the name Lesbia?

Whether at their next meeting the critic enlightened Wise about Sappho and the Isle of Lesbos is not revealed. But the correction saved him from appalling error in one of the most notable of his bibliographical records; and a year later, in Vol. 2 of his *Swinburne Bibliography*, he was able to pull Shorter's leg for suppressing that passage about 'The small dark body's Lesbian loveliness.'

Gosse supplied prefaces for the writings of other authors besides Swinburne that Wise printed, in addition to numerous notes. What literary man will not recognize the peculiar attitude of mind and approach that drew this mild protest (30 November 1913)?:

My dear Wise, I was amused at your suggestion that it would only take me "ten minutes" to write this introduction!! It has taken me many days and numerous visits of reference to public libraries. There is no single work in any language where all the information I have brought together here is to be found. "Ten minutes", indeed!

This preface will be of use to whoever ultimately collects Borrow's *Kjæmpeviser* into one volume. If that is Clement Shorter, I daresay he will steal the greater part of it, and forget to acknowledge the source, —in the true Borrovian manner.

Again and again Gosse vehemently protested against Wise's habit of rushing pieces of poetry and prose to the printer to turn into privately-printed first editions, without saying anything about their origin, or where they had appeared serially, or giving them proper editorial treatment. For example, thanking Wise for the pamphlet *Pericles and Other Studies* (27 February 1914):

. . . This is a delightful addition to Swinburne literature. But I must gently,—yet earnestly,—reproach you for putting it out without any explanation whatever. . . . I myself, although I have made a considerable study of Swinburne, have no idea of the provenance of one of these articles. The value of the volume is, therefore, very much diminished. To myself, for instance, in writing Swinburne's life, it has hardly any value. You must be punished for bringing out a book in such an imperfect form, and the punishment is this: you must write out on a sheet of paper exactly where and when each of these papers appeared first, and send it to me that I may bind it into the "Pericles" volume, which will then become useful as well as curious.

The explanation of Wise's reticence was that this was one of the things he was privately printing without Watts-Dunton's authority; for on being enlightened about the hocus-pocus Gosse replied the next day: 'I shall, of course, keep "Pericles" 'most carefully under lock and key.'

IV

The fact is that Wise did not always know what treasures his great coup at The Pines brought him, or (more frequently) how to deal with them when he had got them—except, of course, commercially. A bundle of MS. poetry proved that he had been

'entertaining a bevy of angels unawares' when it was examined
by Gosse. No wonder that the critic was hailed as a wonderful
chap. Strictures on and punishments for Wise's failings notwithstanding, the correspondence became affectionate, expressing the
most tender solicitude for each other's health and well-being.
Wise would lament the plaguiness of his 'local trouble', as he
called it. Gosse, with more humour, would report: 'What is the
'matter with me is gravel in the kidneys. I must exercise patience.
'I shall meditate on the verses you have sent me, and sketch an
'introduction in my head. As the hymn says, "Out of my stony
'griefs Bethel I'll raise."' The collaboration between the two
friends seemed to be of the happiest and the most genuine
character.

And yet, the 'extraordinary man', who would leave nothing
untouched, must needs rub the bloom off his most valuable
friendship. Gosse lent his unpublished manuscript of Swinburne's
The Cannibal Catechism to Wise, who said he would get Clays to
produce for them ten copies—unseemly and unprintable as it
might be. But he printed at least double the number.

Of the proofs of another proposed private printing, Gosse
wrote (13 December 1909):

> I wish I could persuade you to destroy this utterly valueless frag-
> ment, which ceases before it begins, and is neither intelligible nor
> characteristic.
> I will have nothing to do with it, and I think [the] presence of it
> among the valuable and interesting posthumous pamphlets which you
> have brought out would be a calamity.

The fragment referred to was Swinburne's *A Criminal Case*.
In reply to this emphatic condemnation, Wise agreed that his
critic was right, and promised to have 'the types dispersed',
implying that he would give way to his friend and adviser's
urgent entreaty, and not produce the thing. Yes! the types
were dispersed—but only after Wise had printed off his usual
edition.

He occasionally sold to Gosse a rare book. Probably the
'duplicate' explanation came in here: Gosse would have been
shocked had he known that his friend and collaborator was a
secret book-dealer. Very friendly it was of him to spare his

duplicates from the wonderful Ashley Library. On one occasion Gosse wrote (25 July 1914):

... But a bookseller called Gorfin has offered me a collection of eleven early Landors, quite an interesting lot (he says you know them) for which he wants eighty-five ponnds. I have told him that I must wait a little before deciding. Do you think they are worth that, and that I ought to give it? I have got the money, but I am not in the habit of going busters. I shall be most grateful for a word of advice.

Wise agreed that he knew the Landors, and advised his dear friend to buy them. So the unsuspecting Gosse went 'busters'. But the books belonged to Wise all the time. It was as his agent for sale on commission that Gorfin offered them to Gosse.

V

The original arrangement with Watts-Dunton (who also inherited the Swinburne copyrights) was that Wise should, in addition to the purchase price for the manuscripts, pay fees for the right to produce them as his private pamphlets. He states in his *Bibliography* of the poet (Preface, Vol. 2) that the fee was thirty pounds each; but in the following letter, written at the time, he tells Gosse the figure was twenty pounds. But this plan (affecting only 'the first few' MSS., it is contended) was soon found 'inconvenient'—owing, he says, to the quantity of material that kept coming to light. Then 'for the bulk of 'the unpublished papers I paid prices which included the value 'of the copyrights'. Apart from the different statements as to the amount of the fee, the implication that separate copyright payments did not apply to the 'bulk' of the papers is hardly consistent with the report to Gosse about 'my flow of twenty-'pound cheques to Putney'. But the dealer's printed account of his commerce at The Pines is neither very clear nor convincing. What is beyond question, because below we have his own admissions, is that there was in some cases evasion of paying the agreed fees for the right to print pamphlets, which were consequently produced without Watts-Dunton's knowledge. One reason he gave to Gosse (13 November 1913) for this procedure was that the illicit printings included material which would lead Watts-Dunton (now eighty-one years old; his health fast breaking up) to express undesirable views! Wise had previously claimed (15 November 1909) that although Watts-Dunton could prevent publication he had no legal rights over private printing. Wise's attitude rather than accuracy about Copyright Law is shown in this extraordinary letter to Gosse:

23, Downside Crescent,
Hampstead. N.W.
27–10–09

My dear Gosse,

You ask why I pay W.-D. for printing these tracts. I do so because I feel morally bound to do so. He has no legal right or power to stop me printing them privately. As I bought "unpublished poems" without executing any legal instrument reserving to him the copyright, I have full legal right to PUBLISH them, & to register the copyright against him. He would have no claim upon me at law.

But I happen to conduct my actions upon the lines proscribed [sic] by my own ideas of right & wrong. I'm not going to be a cad because he has been a cad. When I bought those MS. [sic] it was under the distinct verbal understanding that I was not to publish one. Of course a "verbal understanding" could not be maintained in a court of law. But the old man accepted my word as being as good as my bond, & my word is sacred. I have never broken yet a promise I have once given.

I asked him "May I privately print [?]" He replied "not without my consent". Naturally I imagined that such 'consent' would be freely given. When I had made arrangements I asked for consent. He replied: "Pay: those proposed pamphlets will be very valuable: what do you 'offer to give me?" Hence my flow of twenty pound cheques to Putney.

The foregoing refers to the series of *Border Ballads* & the two *prose stories*. The Mazzini and the prose essays were sold to me without one word of comment or restriction. Thus with them my hands are free, & I'll see him ——— before I pay him a Cent for their a/c. But as a fact I don't propose that he shall see them at all.

Ever your
Sincere Friend
Thos. J. Wise

I will now put the *Mazzini Ode* to press, & send you proofs in due course. I mean to print a pamphlet or two of *Letters* also. No use to ask his consent for this, so shall do *without it*.

On Saturday I mean to talk as a *business man* in regard to the remaining MSS. and the Books. It's got to be "*All or none*"!

There is no doubt that Thomas James Wise did, as he says, conduct his actions by his own ideas of right and wrong. Here we have his own expression of those ideas. But he knew the Law, especially regarding copyright, better than this letter implies. He knew that he was privately printing the pamphlets for sale, although Gosse did not understand the trading aspect of the affair. It may be wondered why Wise went to all the trouble of this specious arguing. Was he exercising his 'consummate 'diplomacy' to hoodwink Gosse. Or was he doping his conscience? The things he produced without Watts-Dunton's knowledge or consent would be piracies. How many there were it is difficult, perhaps impossible, now to say. They were, according to him, a minority of the seventy-six privately-printed Swinburne pamphlets.[5] Gosse's faith in Wise's integrity was above suspicion. Nevertheless, he was obviously perplexed at times, as when he wrote (10 October 1909):

... As long as there is a mystery about these books, I should be sorry to cause you any possible inconvenience by distributing or even showing them. I keep my own copies locked up. . . .

VI

Apparently Wise made the same condition about keeping the things secret when he sent some of the private printings to the British Museum Library. Dr A. W. Pollard, then acting Keeper of Printed Books, in an undated letter written in 1909, assured him: 'Those Swinburne things seem awfully jolly. I have put 'them into an envelope labelled "Privately printed editions of 'poems, &c by Swinburne presented by T. J. Wise. Not to be 'catalogued until published in some other form," and they will

----

[5] In addition to these there were ten Swinburne pamphlets produced by Wise which are now condemned as forgeries or suspected forgeries. Their title and other details are given on pp. 341–5. Two—*Siena* and *Cleopatra*—have been dealt with in preceding chapters.

'be stamped and kept in a cupboard in the Keeper's room next 'to a set of Kelmscott Press books. . . .' But by the mischance that so often attends on dubieties, two of the items—*Liberty and Loyalty* and *M. Prudhomme*—did get catalogued. Wise, ever on the alert, saw them in the B.M. Catalogue, and drew attention to the disregard of his 'strict stipulation', as he described it to Gosse (9 November 1912). Dr Pollard apologized, adding that the entries had been removed.[6]

But what was a mystery to Sir Edmund Gosse is a mystery no longer. We have just seen Wise admitting that in certain cases he deliberately evaded paying Watts-Dunton the agreed fees for the right to produce booklets from the manuscripts acquired after Swinburne's death. Moreover, he did not wish his printings, although they were in limited editions, to become generally known for a while; because it was his plan to sell these MSS. as being unpublished—which he did in 1915 for the handsome price of nine hundred pounds to William Heinemann, whose firm so desired to have new material in their Collected Edition of the poet's work.

These were dark circumstances of which Dr Pollard could hardly be aware; and perhaps his confessed enjoyment of *M. Prudhomme* momentarily distracted his attention from the mystification about the printings. But there were other pamphlets coming into the British Museum Library which had been exciting the curiosity of the acting Keeper so blandly deferential to the generous and wealthy collector who might one day leave his superb Elizabethans to the Beloved of Bloomsbury. From 1888 to this time (1909–10) in the chronology of Wise, the British Museum had acquired twenty-five pamphlets now condemned as his book-forgeries, suspected forgeries, or piracies.[7] Of these, ten were works of Tennyson, of which one was bought by the Museum, and nine were given to it by Wise; one by George Eliot bought (as already shown) from Wise's fellow-employee

---

[6] Eight Swinburne pamphlets were thus sent by Wise in September 1909, and others on different dates, including *Liberty and Loyalty* and *M. Prudhomme*. They were made accessible in the B.M. Library in January 1920.

[7] This is one more than listed by Carter and Pollard, as I have included Tennyson's *The Antechamber* (1906) which is almost certainly a piracy. The pamphlet bears no source of origin, or *raison d'être*, or printer's imprint. It was donated to the British Museum in 1908 by Wise, and appears in a list supplied to me of printings by him which he gave to a near relative in 1909. (See Appendix II.)

Schlengemann; and five by Swinburne, of which one was bought from Otto Rubeck (another of Wise's colleagues), and four were given by Wise. Mark the names of the three authors I have selected from the writers of the twenty-five pamphlets. For about this very time Dr Pollard was contributing the article "Bibliography and Bibliology" to the eleventh edition of the *Encyclopædia Britannica* (Cambridge, 1910) into which he slipped this significant commentary:

. . . The type-facsimile forgeries are mostly of short pieces by Tennyson, George Eliot, and A. C. Swinburne, printed (or supposed to have been printed—for it is doubtful if some of these "forgeries" ever had any originals) for circulation among friends. These trifles should never be purchased without a written guarantee. . . .

'Type-facsimile forgeries of short pieces by Tennyson, George Eliot, and Swinburne, printed for private circulation'—half the total of the British Museum's copies of such things having come from Thomas J. Wise direct! Meditating in the Keeper's Holy of Holies, whose outer door is cunningly concealed from the meandering public by dummy book-backs, did Dr Pollard wonder. . . . ? G-g-great G-g-god and p-p-Panizzi! But if there was a doubt it could only have been momentary; though the time was to come when the worthy Keeper smiled shyly at the surprise of one researcher into Wise's mysteries on finding that suggestive note buried in the twenty-nine tomes of the *Encyclopædia Britannica*.

VII

During the writing of this and the previous chapter The Pines saw another clearing-up, consequent upon the death of Mrs Clara Watts-Dunton. Her mother, Mrs Reich, was an old friend of the bachelor Watts-Dunton. Clara, when a pretty, golden-haired girl of sixteen, was taken by her mother to visit the 'great critic'; to whom she went, some years later, as his secretary. Then in 1905, when she was about twenty-seven, she married the seventy-two-year-old Watts-Dunton of the solemn air, the soft tread, the kindly manners, and the walrus moustaches. Thus 'I—little more than a girl in years—became *chatelaine* at The

'Pines,' she said—although its keys were at first retained by the
official housekeeper. For four years the two old men and the
rival *chatelaines* lived their diverse lives regulated by The Hours,
a time-table sacred in the villa: then Swinburne departed. Five
more years of The Hours and Watts-Dunton also departed,
leaving the house of mysteries and eloquent treasures to be
reigned over by his young and attractive-looking widow.

Now, only the draped Venus survives—so stolid, so unlike
Rossetti's 'stunners', as he called his beautiful models. And she
cannot tell any stories about his ménage in Cheyne Walk, or
about the odd trio at The Pines, or about 'Tommy's' visits.
No longer is heard the little poet's high-pitched voice, floating
through the open window, inquiring 'Where are my bloody
boots?' or reciting, as he so often did with immense gusto, his
original version of old Bill Barley's refrain:[8]

Ahoy! Blast your eyes, here's old Bill Barley. Here's old Bill Barley,
blast your eyes. Here's old Bill Barley on the flat of his arse, by the
Lord. Lying on the flat of his arse, like a drifting old dead flounder,
here's your old Bill Barley, blast your eyes. Ahoy! B***** you!

So my account of The Pines ends with an echo of the days
when Swinburne 'with language so awful he dared then to treat
'em'.

[8] Swinburne was much given to reading aloud and quoting from his adored Dickens.
Old Bill Barley was one of his favourite characters. But he preferred his own to the version
that the author admittedly made more polite (*Great Expectations*, chapter xlvi). Mrs Watts-
Dunton frequently overheard the poet declaiming it.

CHAPTER 14

PAYING OFF OLD SCORES AND FINDING A SCAPEGOAT

Had I the gifts of wealth and luxury shared,
Not poor and mean, Walpole, thou hadst not dared
Thus to insult me. But I shall live and stand
By Rowley's side, when thou art dead and damned.

Thomas Chatterton

I

IN TELLING OF the sequels to The Pines coup, the year 1910 has been skipped. It marked the final stage in Thomas James Wise's residential progress from Holloway to Hampstead—the once favourite dwelling-place of London's merchants and authors. Wise bought a house in Heath Drive—No. 25—'a devilish difficult place to find on a foggy night,' E. V. Lucas described it truly enough; as also thought others who approached it the wrong way. Heath Drive is a quiet dignified road that, like Keats Grove on its south-eastern side, slopes to the top of the hill whence Joanna Baillie's Georgian house views with sleepy contempt the sprawling monstrosity of London. The casual stranger passing No. 25 Heath Drive, standing shy and respectable behind its stout, well-groomed hedge and square of sacred turf, would have been astonished to learn that people journeyed across the seas to visit it: that its first-floor back room housed one of the world's finest private libraries. What masks are the house fronts of mankind!

Here celebrity came to Thomas James Wise and his Ashley books and manuscripts—that family of his dreams, of his toils, and of his pleasures.

These were still laborious days for him. He plunged into his varied pursuits with the zest of a healthy man who has disciplined himself to waste nothing of energy or time, each day adding to his fortune, to his library, and to the fast-accumulating piles of booknotes and descriptions. We get a hint about him in

191

one of Gosse's notes (26 April 1913): 'Please read this letter 'carefully. You must forgive me for saying that I think, in your 'excessive haste about everything, you do not take the trouble 'to read my letters.' The admonition was a little exaggerated in its severity. Gosse's letters were not neglected. They brought too much valuable information to the groping and often perplexed commentator.

It was perhaps in one of these 'excessive hastes' that Wise failed to exercise his usual far-sighted judgment as a buyer, and refused a bundle of Robert Louis Stevenson manuscripts offered to him for the comparatively trifling sum of one hundred and twenty-five pounds—only to see R.L.S. a few years later become a rabidly-collected author, and these same MSS. to realize thousands of pounds. Such tales of lost opportunities can be told by all collectors and dealers.

II

The year 1912[1] inaugurated an important phase in the career of Thomas James Wise; for it was now that he began to occupy himself almost exclusively with enterprises that were to bring him fame beyond his pleasantest dreams, although they were followed by shocks unequalled in his worst nightmares. For the present, he was in comfortable circumstances financially; thanks largely to the success of his book-dealing and publishing, and also to his own City business of W. A. Smith & Co. In the previous year he had confided to Gosse that he was going to withdraw from commerce, and devote himself to his cataloguing. 'I shall be glad when you can throw off the burden of business 'and live entirely with the muses,' replied the critic, who on 12 August 1912 was hailing the news 'that you had freed your- 'self from the chain of business. You are so wise to do this 'betimes.'

His enterprises now were the production of the bibliographies

---

[1] While distinguishing this as the year in which Wise began his ambitious series of bibliographies and catalogues, it will have been noted that he had already compiled bibliographies of Ruskin (with Smart 1893), Browning (1897), Swinburne (1897), and Tennyson (1908). Those of Browning and Swinburne, however, were preliminary studies —now to be greatly expanded.

and catalogues which form such an imposing monument to his industry and skill—to his astuteness and unscrupulousness. These works, with all their faults, are unmatchable as the performance of one man: there is nothing like them for range of interest in the whole of the vast literature on literature. 'See Wise' will be one of the commonest references made by researchers and students.

All his life he had been learning about rare books and their histories. Every volume bought, whether for himself or for one of his private clients, had taught him something. As a pathologist examines a human body on the mortuary table, so Wise would lay each book before him, probing, exploring, collating—until all the secrets of its mechanism, as created by the printer and author long ago, were revealed to him, and described in his scrawling script. Thus were his data accumulated.

Now that he had a library full of scarce editions in the finest state and manuscripts of great curiosity and literary value, there remained the last part of his life's work: to compile records that would accomplish the twofold object of making his collection more widely known, and of making available the information it yielded. That was to be his crowning achievement. His catalogues and bibliographies would be the coping-stones, stuccoed with romantic decorations, to the library he had built up with such patience and shrewdness.

Incidentally, they would afford him the opportunity to pay off old scores against men with whom he had worked, and to whom he was indebted for services and inspirations which he did not deem it convenient to honour, lest perhaps his own achievement should be diminished. And, remembering those forged pamphlets and piracies, he determined also to have a scapegoat at hand on whom to plant them if need should arise.

III

Wise once said in an interview:[2] 'I am a bibliographer by 'choice and intention. I simply drifted into book-collecting 'because books and manuscripts formed the tools necessary for 'my job—and so tools had to be acquired.'

[2] In *The Strand Magazine* for September 1930.

The second part of this statement is an example of his aptitude for giving a twist to facts according to circumstances. At other times he would declare that he was first a collector—as early as in his teens. This was the fact: his ideas about bibliography were then negligible. What happened was that he first began collecting and dealing in books. Then he developed the ambitious plan of forming a collection that should specialize more and more in first and early editions of English poetry and the poetic drama. But he was soon faced with a most perplexing and formidable difficulty—the lack of information; although in the cases of a few authors he had the original efforts of pioneer bibliographers (Forman's work on Shelley has been cited) to build upon.

Having decided upon the authors he would collect, how was he to know all the works they had written, their earliest appearances, and what were the physical make-up and contents of the books? An author might have written a score of known books; but he also might have written a dozen unknown works— juvenilia and anonymous pieces. How could he say he had a complete collection of this or that author's works if he lacked the fugitive writings?

It was then that Wise came to appreciate the need of authoritative and exhaustive bibliographies whose purpose it is to tell these things, and provide exact descriptions of rare books and pieces. With this understanding came also the realization that he would have to compile his own. Now to make a really serviceable bibliography the compiler must have before him not only all the author's first editions in their original variations and in the complete state, but also as much of his manuscript material as possible—since clues to fugitive pieces are often only discovered in letters and obscure references. Thus Wise found himself collecting books and manuscripts from which he gathered bibliographical data, and compiling bibliographies which helped his book-collecting and dealing. It was a bibliophilic merry-go-round, on which he was always going to the end to reach the beginning. It was a highly exciting game. To discover a work that an author has slipped surreptitiously into the world of letters has an inexpressible thrill.

What allurement would there be in the drudgery of literary

'Thus "I—little more than a girl in years—became
chatelaine at The Pines"'—(Chapters 12 and 13) Mrs
CLARA WATTS-DUNTON

research if authorship were without its freakish moods and hidden impulses?—if Shakespeare had not written the *Sonnets* to the still mysterious 'Mr W. H.'; if the marvellous boy Chatterton had not written the poems fathered on the imaginary 'Thomas Rowley'; if Shelley had not made into paper boats a proscribed and anonymous pamphlet to float on the hazardous sea to Ireland; if Sir Walter Scott had not baffled a delighted world as 'The Author of Waverley'; if . . . but the adventurous tale is unending.

'When I was a young man,' Wise said, 'bibliography was 'something new. Scholars spent their days in linguistic research '—tracing the history and origin of words. The Oxford English 'Dictionary of 1888 is an outcome of this activity. . . . The study 'of the texts of the Classics was what everybody went for: look 'at the enormous number of reprints that came out then. But 'the editors were compelled to ask themselves what text was the 'most reliable one to reprint. Who could tell them? The biblio-'grapher! Nowadays, the good editor has to be a good biblio-'grapher. And that—that is my answer to the man who cries '"First editions! What a lot of nonsense it all is!" Sweep away 'into the dust heap the early editions of our English classical 'writers, and in many cases you destroy the records of the inti-'mate history of their mental and spiritual development.'

That was a characteristically energetic defence of book-collecting in which is much truth. If bibliography was hardly new in Wise's day, it was certainly circumscribed—both in its information and in its use. And its development into the science it has now become, with such magnificent results—by scholars like A. W. Pollard, W. W. Greg, and J. Dover Wilson—dates from the 'eighties. In that development Wise played his part—a rather more popular part, perhaps, as appealing to the wider interest of book-collecting.

He had been fortunate. In the 'seventies and 'eighties his contemporaries—mostly older men—like Dr Furnivall, Dr Richard Garnett, Richard Herne Shepherd, Harry Buxton Forman, F. S. Ellis, Colonel Prideaux, Walter B. Slater, Stopford Brooke, R. A. Potts, Wm. Rossetti, H. B. Wheatley, John Morgan, Professor Dowden, and Thomas Hutchinson, were all concerned in the awakened interest in bibliography and its potentialities. Some of these made an informal committee to advance the subject, one of the chief objects being to arrive at a common system of recording bibliographical descriptions. Wise told me that the 'final' plan then drawn up was the one he had always adhered to in his own works.

These enthusiasts, with others, used to meet at the house in South Audley Street, London, of R. A. Potts—a connoisseur who paid all the costs of printing specimens, etc. It is not difficult to conjure the picture of Wise in this conclave of ardent bookmen gravely discussing whether line endings should be distinguished by vertical or sloping strokes, whether advertisement pages should be counted as part of a book, and such minutiæ of the subject. Wise, the junior member, was all ears and eyes —tremendously keen, but modest and deferential in the presence of his elders and betters, some of whom were famous men of letters. He bided his time.

The day of his dominance was to come.

There are some people who are successful only in turning knowledge into more knowledge; there are others who have the knack of turning it into hard cash. Wise, collecting books and compiling his bibliographical data on wide and original lines, determined that the knowledge he set himself to gain should enhance the value of the rarities he acquired to get that knowledge—with a substantial side credit on account of his private book deals. The data had assisted him in his collecting and dealing; now, set out in imposing volumes, that data would make impressive advertisements of his library and publications.[3]

These pursuits, subtly interdependent, thus served a double purpose.

IV

One of the first scores he was to settle, after he began in 1912 to devote himself to his compilations, was with Dr Furnivall, from whom he received his first directions in bibliography— the very man who had also favoured him by the introduction to Browning. Wise, in his tentative work on the poet (1897), had

---

[3] An example occurs in Wise's preface to his *Borrow Bibliography*, in which he draws attention to the 'attractive series of Pamphlets' comprising his own privately-published issues which he traded (see page 105).

been obliged to catalogue Furnivall's earlier *Bibliography of Robert Browning* (1883); and he did so without comment. But now that his master had passed away (Dr Furnivall died in 1910), he vented his feelings in the added note:

Although the name of Dr Furnivall alone appeared upon the title-page as the compiler of the Bibliography, the spade-work was done almost entirely by me under his direction. It was my first lesson in bibliography. But it was always Dr Furnivall's habit to take full credit for any undertaking in which he was the smallest degree concerned. In the present instance Dr Furnivall's share of the labour mainly consisted in "compiling" and annotating the work done by Mr J. T. Nettleship and myself.

The custom whereby the pupil makes some return to his tutor by doing anonymous spadework has the sanction of antiquity. The system does not work out so unfairly in the long run. The master uses his pupil, who derives practical experience thereby; the pupil, in the fullness of time and with the privilege of age and reputation, uses his own students likewise. And so on—like Swift's fleas.

But examination of Dr Furnivall's original work of 1883 reveals that he was most punctilious, not merely in making acknowledgments of assistance, but in specifying the individual contributions of his helpers. In his forewords he thanks eleven of these helpers, including Richard Garnett, Austin Dobson, J. T. Nettleship (whose name appears as the author of one section), and especially 'Mr Richard Herne Shepherd, the well-known bibliographer'; the extent of whose honorary efforts is indicated by nearly forty notes. Wise's name is not mentioned; nor is there a single note initialled as contributed by him—though he may have been included among the 'and other friends' thanked.[4] It does not look as if he played any substantial or constructive part in this pioneering bibliography of Browning.

V

Another score to be settled was with one Fred Hutt, the youngest of three brothers—all booksellers.

[4] Furnivall was never ill-disposed to Wise, however cautious. See the episodes related in Chapters 3 and 10.

One day in 1888 he had called at Fred Hutt's shop, which was situated in Clement's Inn Passage. The bookseller knew where there was a copy of that excessively scarce book, the original edition of *Pauline* (1833), Browning's first work, a copy of which Wise had failed to get from its author, as related. Would Wise give fifteen pounds for it? 'Yes! gladly,' replied that excited customer, who departed rejoicing. When Wise went the next afternoon for the book, Hutt was very sorry, but the owner had held out for twenty pounds which he (Hutt) had paid, knowing how much Wise wanted the item. He trusted there would be no objection to a charge of ten per cent for his trouble. 'Certainly not,' said Wise, who was just going to write a cheque when, he says, 'it evidently dawned upon Hutt that he had let me off too lightly. He applied another squeeze,' mentioning ten shillings paid in cab fares to secure the prize, and hoping that there would be no objection to refunding this. 'Of course I will,' replied Wise; who adds that he 'gaily' handed over his cheque for twenty-two pounds ten shillings. Very gaily, we may be sure; for the astute collector-dealer was confident enough of the future rise in value of his prize.

But he alleges that a week or two later he learned from another bookseller that Hutt only paid two pounds ten shillings for the rarity and that it was in his possession all the time the business was under discussion. 'I was perfectly satisfied with the price I 'had paid,' comments Wise, 'but was naturally annoyed at having 'been the victim of lies and trickery. I made it my business to call 'upon Hutt and tell him what I had heard. Instead of flushing 'with shame and embarrassment, his face assumed a radiant 'look. . . . He was proud of his "smartness".'

There is something comic about the virtuous indignation of the last sentence. But there are other aspects of the matter. It is on the occasional deals in rarities that a bookseller like Hutt would expect to recoup himself for months of labour, continuous buying, and perhaps inadequate daily sales of small items. If it was the case that he originally asked fifteen pounds for the very rare *Pauline*, and then—finding Wise an eager client for it— jumped up the price to twenty-two pounds ten shillings (including cab-fare) by false assertions, his action is not to be defended. Nevertheless, we have only Wise's account of the episode.

He was, as he admits, perfectly satisfied until learning the hear-say story that the book had already been bought for two pounds ten shillings by Hutt (who in the meantime might have sent it elsewhere on approval, or even have sold it and had to repur-chase). Why should Wise concern himself with Hutt's profit and the report of a possibly rival and envious bookseller when he was so content with the final price of twenty-two pounds ten shillings that he 'gaily' paid it? Even assuming that all he says regarding the transaction is true, the point is that he could thus vent his spleen some forty years later on the dead bookseller knowing the colossal bargain he had obtained, and when criti-cism had better have been stilled. For only six years after the purchase, as he exultantly proclaims in telling the story, he saw three hundred and twenty-five pounds given for another copy of this same first-edition *Pauline*; whose market-price reached the fantastic figure of three thousand pounds in the very year that he published his reminiscence. In any case, the episode is unworthy of the space and importance given to it in the introduction of his *Browning Library* (1929).

Nor does the story of petty revenge end here. Three years later Wise found occasion for another kick at the bookseller. In his *Byron Bibliography* (1932) he says: 'Charles Hutt commenced 'business as an employee of Hodgson, of Chancery Lane. Unlike 'his brother Fred, he was a "straight" man in every way,' etc. And that was Fred Hutt's account settled.

VI

It was Richard Herne Shepherd (1842–95) who seems to have been selected by Wise to be the scapegoat at hand in case of emergency. Shepherd has a place in the *Dictionary of National Biography* as a bibliographer and man of letters. It was largely he who, in the 'seventies and 'eighties, turned the interest of biblio-graphy to modern authors; whereas formerly collectors and builders of libraries had confined themselves to the old and classical authors. With his *Bibliographies* of Ruskin (1897) Dickens (1880), Thackeray (1881 and 1887), Carlyle (1881), Swinburne (1883), and Tennyson (1886), he explored uncharted fields. Nor was it in bibliography only that Shepherd was a pioneer. By editing the then comparatively unknown Elizabethan dramatists Chapman, Dekker, and Heywood, he brought these authors to wider recognition. Strangely enough, all his bibliographies appeared without his name on their title-pages; and his valuable work for Elizabethan literature was similarly veiled. Whether this was due to his own modesty or to the grudging spirit of his publishers it is difficult now to decide. He was a publishers' hack and a handyman to antiquarian booksellers. Few publishers' hacks get their reward, either for merit or otherwise. But if he was imposed upon by many there were a few who bestowed kindness on the poor scholar. Delving into the past, I find a little bundle of his letters in neat faded script, concise and elegantly grateful for a patron's goodwill. They refer diffidently to his literary pursuits, and report with boyish enthusiasm (at the age of forty-three) encouraging progress with his 'lady-love', as to whom he is hopeful '*que demain l'heure du berger sonnera*'.

An eccentric character was Shepherd,[5] a tall, angular man, often shabbily dressed, with shoulders rounded from long nights of poring over books. He was remarkable for the possession of a most beautiful voice and gentle manners. One of his idiosyncrasies was his persistence in walking always in the middle of the streets—in defiance of the shouting and gesticulating jehus of London's cabs and other horse vehicles. His familiar figure, as he made his perilous perambulations from his home (at one time in Chelsea, and for years at the Bald-faced Stag in Kingston Vale, Putney[6]) to the British Museum, would be pointed out with the mixture of respect due to scholarship and that contempt for misfortune and eccentricity which characterized Victorian snobbery.

But snobbishness and meanness are not confined to any age. When Wise came to publish the correspondence of Swinburne in a series of little books, he entitled them respectively *Letters from Algernon Charles Swinburne* to Thomas J. Wise—to Edmund Gosse—to William Morris—to Sir Richard Burton, etc. But

[5] Little of a personal nature has been recorded of him. The picture here is derived from unpublished correspondence of his and also from details supplied by probably the only man now living who knew him well.

[6] Not the inn of that name in the Finchley Road, as stated elsewhere.

the poet's correspondence with Richard Herne Shepherd is merely *Letters on the Works of George Chapman, With an Introduction by Edmund Gosse.* However, Gosse did the gentlemanly thing, acknowledging the recipient of Swinburne's letters as a pioneer, and our indebtedness to 'this unfortunate man' for a 'most valuable contribution to literature'.

Shepherd's was a pathetic case of a kind only too common in literary history. Grandson of a clergyman, he was a man whose learning and devotion to literature were more profitable to others than to himself. Many another man has boomed himself into repute and affluence for achieving far less in literature than did Richard Herne Shepherd—the anonymous toiler. His career was one long desperate struggle, not made easier by resort to alcohol. He died in 1895, poverty-stricken, in an asylum.

When Wise, always loath to admit he owed anything to this ill-fated man of letters, came to compile his *Swinburne Bibliography*, he made the following carping reference to the dead pioneer:

Against the errors in Herne Shepherd's elementary Bibliography Swinburne himself afterwards warned me.[7] But I had already gleaned sufficient knowledge . . . to make me aware that the gleam of light thrown from the lamp of Shepherd was far too dim to enable me to espy the smaller trifles which . . . had been dropped by Swinburne, and were rapidly sinking beneath the accumulating dust. Of these— then unheeded, and unless promptly rescued, soon to be forgotten, waifs, but now highly valued treasures—Herne Shepherd knew nothing.

For very good reasons! Shepherd's *Bibliography* knew nothing of those forged or doubtfully authentic 'trifles'—Swinburne's *Dead Love*, the *Laus Veneris*, the *Cleopatra*, the *Siena*, and the *Dolores*. How could Shepherd, who died in 1895, guess what 'highly-valued treasures' they were to become, even had he got to know of them? As for their 'sinking beneath accumulating dust'—surely this was the wrong figure of speech. Wise meant 'salt' (not 'dust'), that useful commodity to which Maurice Buxton Forman referred in *The Times* Literary Supplement (12 July

---

[7] The poet seems to have developed a prejudice against Shepherd on account of his *Swinburne Bibliography*, compiled without any assistance from him. He was annoyed to find himself wrongly described therein as editor of *Undergraduate Papers*, and possibly also by the details given of Robert Buchanan's successful libel action arising out of the *Devil's Due* row. Swinburne's prejudice was made the most of by Wise.

1934), when he backed up Wise's story (in an interview to be quoted) of how Forman senior salted down 'remainders' of pamphlets.

It was Wise who knew all about those 'waifs'—whose values were to be artificially created by the authoritative descriptions in his Ashley Library Catalogues. He was their begetter.

VII

One of Shepherd's predilections was for hunting after Press contributions by authors, like Tennyson and the Brownings, in whom he was interested. This recording of juvenile and anonymous trifles hidden in magazine files is not without value. But Shepherd's obsession for printing some of his finds and perhaps making a few hard-earned and badly-needed shillings eventually secured for him the sobriquet of 'literary chiffonier', given by his biographer in the *D.N.B*—a description which, when applied in his lifetime by the outspoken *Athenæum* (together with more offensive epithets), was punished by a British judge and jury's awarding him one hundred and fifty pounds damages for libel against that paper.

It is a fact, however, that Shepherd did make a few unauthorized printings of this sort of trifles; to which proceeding some of the authors objected.[8] It was on these cases that Wise fastened greedily.

Outside of, as well as in, the Ashley Catalogues, their compiler built up a tale of rascality and untrustworthiness against Shepherd, suppressing all credit due to him as a pioneer.[9] The charges were supported by little or no evidence. An example is provided by the four-page Swinburne item entitled *Unpublished Verses*, of which Wise contemptuously says that, though 'constantly offered 'as a "First Edition,"' it is the 'merest rubbish' and an 'impu-

---

[8] The few things Richard Herne Shepherd printed were mostly out of copyright. The position was clearly stated by the judge in his summing-up in the case against the *Athenæum*, when he said 'The legal right of the plaintiff [Shepherd] to publish Mrs Browning's earlier 'poems was undeniable; but there were some rights which it was very bad taste to assert'. This case was decided in 1879; two years later Dr Furnivall was acknowledging Shepherd's generous and voluntary contributions to the first *Bibliography of Browning* (see above, page 197).

[9] See page 168 for Watts-Dunton's vindication of the 'dog given a bad name'.

dent piracy'. Shepherd is saddled with responsibility for the thing; and Wise asks:

Did Shepherd find some scraps of Swinburne's rough draft carrying the lines, and, ignorant of them, imagined them to be unpublished? I think not; but if so—how did he in 1888 know that they were written in 1866? My own opinion is that he traded upon the frequent ignorance of collectors concerning the contents of the books they buy, and carefully selected an extract from one of the Poems which should read pleasantly, and at the same time not readily be identified.

Why did Wise put foward the theory of *Unpublished Verses* originating from a rough draft, only to reject it? His alternative theory may be dismissed. The stolen poetry was not a 'carefully selected' extract: it consists of a jumble of lines in an order different from, and some of them in versions far inferior to, those in Swinburne's published poem *Hesperia*: they might well have been the rough draft of part of that poem. From Wise's suggestion it looks as if he knew more about the matter than he said. Of this there is a striking piece of circumstantial evidence. In the catalogue of books and MSS. sold at Sotheby's on 15 March 1911, was described a copy of *Unpublished Verses*, with the statement that the following notes appeared on a fly leaf:

These verses were originally intended for *Poems and Ballads*, Second Series [this was a slip], but the MS. sheet was mislaid. The MS. afterwards came into the possession of Mr Wise, who had fifty copies printed for presentation. Mr Wise tells a very different story to the above.

Where that important copy is now, who was the writer of those explicit notes, and what was his authority, it would be highly interesting to know. Since Wise asked questions incriminating Shepherd, here are three more: (1) What evidence had he that Shepherd printed the leaflet (several reasons can be advanced against that supposition)? (2) How comes it that he who described it as the 'merest rubbish' and an 'impudent piracy' was formerly trading in the fake? and (3) Is the truth of the matter this: that, eventually discovering that the jumbled lines had formed part of the composition of *Hesperia*, and were therefore liable to be recognized as neither unpublished nor a first edition, Wise denounced the fake, threw it on to Shepherd, and used it as another means to belittle and besmirch? There is no direct evidence to convict Wise in this particular case. But there is the circumstantial evidence of that copy catalogued by Sotheby's; and there is also the evidence that he sold copies of the piracy to his agent, Herbert Gorfin— once in a lot of fifteen.

Thus in his books and in conversation Wise lost no opportunity of making out Shepherd to be worse than he was—pursuing with relentless design a pioneer bibliographer to whom he was greatly indebted, but whose lamp, as he cynically complained, was 'too dim' to expose some of the fraudulent 'trifles' Wise himself had imposed upon the book world.

An even more remarkable case is that connected with Tennyson's poem *The Lover's Tale*, of which Herne Shepherd reprinted unauthorized editions in 1870 and 1875. The earlier was voluntarily withdrawn; and against the later an injunction was obtained by the poet. Shepherd was perfectly frank in his *Bibliography of Tennyson* about these printings of his, and gave the details of their suppression. But he defended himself strongly against the charge that he printed these things to cater for collectors of rare and curious books. 'What he was interested in was poems which 'were unobtainable among their authors' current volumes, and 'his whole series of reprints reflects this harmless passion for '"literary rag-picking".'[10] But about 1890 his 1870 edition of *The Lover's Tale* was copied with a predated title-page by the manufacturer of the nineteenth-century forged pamphlets; and Wise in his Catalogues was at great pains to plant this forgery of his also on Shepherd. It is a case of a forger cutting the throat of a not very wicked pirate.

When the bubble was pricked in 1934, Wise brought out the scapegoat ready at hand—as we shall see when that year is reached in this history. The scapegoat was also produced then by Maurice Buxton Forman, who theorized:

I wonder whether Herne Shepherd, and possibly others, knowing how keen he [the writer's father] was, manufactured small pamphlets with the sole object of planting them on him? It is not a nice thought, but it seems to me by no means impossible.

Buxton Forman was right: it was not a nice thought. All

[10] *The Enquiry* (*op. cit.*).

things considered, it was indeed a very ugly thought—to suggest the poor unfortunate scholar as the villain of the piece, or pieces. And if Richard Herne Shepherd did put out a few unauthorized printings, who was Wise to stone him?—Thomas James Wise, the plump and prosperous dealer, with his record as the producer of over fifty fraudulent and suspect printings, and his career of piratical publishing extending from the 'eighties to 1914.

CHAPTER 15

REVELATIONS GRAVE AND GAY

The truth seems to be that it is impossible to lay the ghost of a fact.
You can face it or shirk it—and I have come across a man or two who
could wink at their familiar shades.

Joseph Conrad: *Lord Jim*

I

IN ADDITION to the general cataloguing of his books and manuscripts, Wise was now compiling exhaustive bibliographies of
Coleridge (for the Bibliographical Society) and of George Borrow. His interest in the Romani lad was largely the result of
another Shorter-Wise haul of an author's manuscripts through
tracing the writer's descendants. In this instance the unpublished
MSS. were bought wholesale from the executor of Borrow's
stepdaughter, Mrs MacOubrey, and were now being sent hot
to press for publication by Wise in 1913 as first editions in forty-
four of his privately-printed pamphlets. His *Bibliography of
Borrow* (1914) followed close on their heels; and whether or not
so designed, it did in fact serve as a sale catalogue of the pamphlets. It helped him to get the profitable price of eighty pounds for
ten of the titles.

One of Wise's Borrow items has a threefold interest. It illustrates firstly, John Gibson Lockhart's little way with his contributors when editor of the *Quarterly Review*; secondly, Borrow's
sturdy independence; and thirdly, Wise's little way with his
possessions. Lockhart in 1845 sent a copy of Richard Ford's
Handbook for Travellers in Spain for Borrow to review. It was just
the thing for the happy man who while he had sold the Holy
Scriptures to the Spanish bought pleasant adventures at the
same time. Besides, Ford was his friend. To his dismay Lockhart
found that although Borrow had sent him a delightful paper, it
was really another 'capital chapter' of his *Bible in Spain*, with
'hardly a word of "review" and no extract giving the least

'notion of the peculiar merits and style of the *Handbook*'. This he confided to Ford wistfully. Editors, of course, are the accursed darlings of misfortune. The well-minded Lockhart braced his shoulders, and decided that 'I could easily (as is my constant 'custom) supply the humbler part myself, and so present at once 'a fair review of the work, and a lively specimen of our friend's 'vein of eloquence *in exordio*. But, behold! he will not allow 'any tampering.' Ford smiled. Borrow blasted Albemarle Street to Gibraltar, and wrote the following skit:

> *Would it not be more dignified*
> *To run up debts on every side*
> *And then to pay your debts refuse,*
> *Than write for rascally Reviews*
> *And lectures give to great and small*
> *In pot-house, theatre, and town hall*
> *Wearing your brains by night and day*
> *To win the means to pay your way?*
> *I vow by him who reigns in* ———
> *It would be more respectable!*

The manuscript of this skit and Borrow's 'review' as set up in type in 1845, but not published, were among Wise's acquisitions from Mrs MacOubrey. He says that this 1845 review, of which only 'two copies would appear to have been struck off', is the rarest of all Borrow's first editions. So! if it is a first edition, then he is wrong to describe (as he does in the *Ashley Library Catalogue*: Vol. I) his 1913 privately-printed publication of the review as the first edition: that publication, titled *A Supplementary Chapter to the Bible in Spain*, would be merely a reprint. The 1845 review, however, appears to be one of the proofs sent to Borrow by Lockhart after he had supplied his 'humbler part' by inserting some quotations from Ford's *Handbook*: in which case Wise's 1913 publication happens to be the first edition proper. There can only be one *editio princeps*. There cannot be a dead heat between something proofed in 1845 and the same thing printed in 1913. Wise could not have it both ways.

In this year of the Borrow publications Wise wrote to Gosse apparently putting forward someone as a successor to Alfred Austin in the vacant Laureateship. Gosse's reply (4 June 1913) is, as usual when he was irritated with 'Tom', first bland, then cuttingly abrupt:

. . . Asquith has sent for me to talk to him about the L'ship, to-day. I suspect he is a good deal pressed. The person you so kindly name is not a candidate, and could not be thought of. Nor is Y., so far as I know, in the "running" at all. . . .

That Wise's letter is missing is a pity; for it would be interesting to have verbatim his attempt at influencing a Prime Minister who could be relied upon at least not to repeat the crass idiocy of some past appointments to the office. Wise had once confessed to Gosse that he feared he was 'utterly unable to judge in 'the slightest the value of a poet's work'. His seeking to advance a candidate for the Laureateship is indicative of the now steadily increasing sense of his own importance and power. It is surmise, based on reasonable grounds, that his nominee was William Watson[1] who was subsequently given the rather cruel consolation prize of a knighthood.

II

But perhaps the most important event of the Wise chronology in the year immediately preceding the World War of 1914–18 was connected with Herbert Gorfin, whom we left in Chapter 9 helping the cashier at Hermann Rubeck's to dispatch books to his American and other customers. In the years that followed, the small office-boy advanced in station as well as in stature.

From 1898 young Gorfin was permitted to sell on commission books and pamphlets for his master. Gorfin found that certain pamphlets by the Brownings, Swinburne, Ruskin, and others, sold very well to collectors and dealers if only a copy or two were available at a time. They were somewhat vaguely referred to as 'remainders' of small editions, often printed, it was said, for their authors' use. He knew that a considerable stock of these easily-handled booklets was owned by Wise, who had once volunteered to him this explanation of how he came

---

[1] Watson had been among the lesser candidates passed over when Lord Salisbury made the political appointment of Austin as Laureate (1 Jan. 1896). Robert Bridges succeeded in the office 17 July 1913.

by the things: 'That they had been found in a publisher's ware-
'house in sheets when the premises were being cleared out previ-
'ous to demolition. That a workman, more astute than the
'generality of his kind, recognized them as being of some impor-
'tance and possibly of value, and got into communication with
'Wise through another party; and that he—Wise—bought the
'whole collection for a few pounds.' Incredible as it may sound,
this is the story Gorfin believed until the exposure.

The junior having decided to launch out for himself as a
bookseller (but with a shop, for the world to see): 'Look here,
'Herbert,' said Wise to him one day, 'as you know, I've been
'dealing in these pamphlets now for quite a long time, have made
'plenty out of them, and am getting a bit tired of them. What
'about taking the remainder over from me at a nominal price,
'and dealing with them in future on your own?' So the industrious apprentice, eager to become a rare-book seller, laid out his
savings and capital—over four hundred pounds—in a stock of
over seven hundred of Wise's nice 'clean' little pamphlets,
five hundred and seventy-seven of which were later to be proved
forgeries, suspects, or piracies. Considering that these constituted
Wise's remaining stock after years of profitable dealing, the final
figure indicates the large scale of the ramp.

Then came Gorfin's next great adventure. In 1912, backed by
a small stock of books (including those 'gilt-edged' securities,
the forged pamphlets he had been buying since 1909) and a large
stock of confidence, Herbert Gorfin opened a secondhand-
book shop in Charing Cross Road, London.

Confidence? Had he not a powerful friend and backer? There
followed two years of successful building-up of the Charing
Cross Road business, during which Mister Wise kept close
touch, visiting the young bookseller several times a week to sell
items and to arrange deals on commission. All was going fairly
for the young man, although there were times when his confidence was shaken.

He gave this example. Wise had an option on a rare first
edition which he suggested that Gorfin should offer to a West
End firm for one hundred and eighty pounds. Gorfin protested
that the price was not nearly enough for a book of which less
than half-a-dozen copies were known. He spent several strenu-

ous hours negotiating with the rival bookseller, who eventually
agreed to buy at four hundred and sixty pounds. The young man
joyously proceeded to find Wise, who became 'purple and speech-
'less with surprise and annoyance that he had made such an
'undervaluation'. He said he would consider the matter, and
finally decided not to sell. His agent, who presumed that the rare
book was afterwards sold to America direct, described this
episode with bitterness—not only because he had come to terms
with the other bookseller, but because he received no consideration in respect of his dealing. He had been promised a commission of ten per cent on the one hundred and eighty pounds and
twenty per cent on anything he could get above that figure.

Suddenly the barometer of friendship and fortune fell to zero.
In 1914 Gorfin's association with Wise became less cordial and
useful owing to the former's dissatisfaction over the Landor
deal with Gosse; Gorfin objecting that he was asked to sell
Wise's books without handling them.[2] Then came the World
War, which swamped the young bookseller's business, as it did
so many businesses.

Of their personal relations, Gorfin said that when they were
alone Wise was most charming in his attitude to him. His disposition was so friendly, indeed so affectionate, as to seem almost
paternal. With it all was a jocular intimacy that was born of
their long office familiarity at Hermann Rubeck's. 'But the
moment we ceased to be alone, when it came to showing and
'proving friendly relations before others, then Wise's attitude
'changed. His manner became cold and aloof. He was the client
'and master; I was the servant. Before long I realized that I was
'merely regarded as a tool'—which is exactly what the young
man was in the hands of his masterful patron, who bullied or
suavely cajoled according to the mood or the ticklish job in
hand.

Thus the experienced bookman of many parts and the young
bookseller of the dashed hopes went their ways—the former
heading for celebrity; the latter for the trenches. But destiny had
not done with their association.

[2] See pages 184 and 185.

'SIR EDMUND GOSSE'S friendship was one of the luckiest of the many boons that befell Wise. There were times when he was positively humble to the "literary gent" as he described the critic'—caught here by the camera as he fondles a kitten and talks with THOMAS HARDY in the garden of the master's home, Max Gate, Dorchester

III

On the 29th of July 1913, *The Times* achieved one of its historic coups by publishing under the heading 'Charlotte Brontë's Tragedy' a series of long-hidden love letters from the authoress to Professor Constantin Heger, the originals of which the professor's son had just lodged with the British Museum as a gift to the nation. So the secret was out at last. Something of it had been guessed for a long time. Mrs Gaskell, Charlotte's biographer, had left too much unexplained regarding Miss Brontë's two years as a teacher at the Brussels *pensionnat*, which ended with Madame Heger's estrangement and the suffering girl's departure. Now here was the story: revealed by the heroine, not by the novelist, in all the intensity of her passion and anguish—when she could find 'neither rest nor peace day and night' for the longing to hear from her professor; when, if she sleeps, '*Je fais des rêves tourmentants.*' The 'Reason' she also put into verse that is little known, and not yet included in her works:

> *Unloved I love, unwept I weep.*
> *Grief I restrain, hope I repress;*
> *Vain is the anguish fixed and deep,*
> *Vainer desires or means of bliss.*

> *Have I not fled that I may conquer?*
> *Crost the dark sea in firmest faith,*
> *That I at last might plant my anchor*
> *Where love cannot prevail to death?*[3]

This first publication of the love letters was the literary event of the decade. As they read them, men in their club chairs were stirred, women schoolteachers thrilled, and Brontë enthusiasts hurried to *Villette* and *The Professor* to fit the poignant letters into the blank spaces of those autobiographical works.

There were two person who, when they saw those generous columns in *The Times*, were particularly thrilled, but by far

---

[3] This, of course, did not appear among the newly revealed love letters. It comes from the Ashley Library MSS., and was privately printed by Wise in C. B.'s *Saul and Other Poems* (1913).

different emotions from those that touched the sensibilities alike of learned clubmen and repressed spinsters. Those two persons were Clement King Shorter and Thomas James Wise, who— as we have seen in Chapter 9—had made something like a 'corner' in Brontë manuscripts. *The Times* appended to Charlotte's letters (they were in French) English translations and notes by that authority M. H. Spielmann—prefacing the whole with the word 'Copyright'. Shorter was very angry, puffed down to Printing House Square, and raised loud protests. These were promptly silenced by the 'Thunderer', which next morning came out with this withering announcement:

Mr Shorter, while raising no objection to the acquisition of the letters by the British Museum or their publication by *The Times*, was a little disconcerted by the fact that the warning word 'Copyright' was added to our headline yesterday. Some while ago he purchased from Charlotte Brontë's literary executor [referring presumably to his deal with Bell Nicholls, see page 115] all legal rights in her unpublished correspondence, and he suggests that this would vest the copyright in the newly discovered letters in him. Whether this is legally correct in the case of letters now seventy years old, Mr Shorter must settle, if he cares to, with the British Museum authorities. So far as *The Times* is concerned, it was not intended to claim permanent copyright in the letters themselves, but only in the matter which accompanied them.

Whereupon King Shorter abdicated, retiring within himself; for which there was ample room. Wise, of course, did not go down to Printing House Square: he was not so concerned; and, as we have seen, he preferred to lie low when any bother was about. But a few months later he sent *The Times* transcripts, with Spielmann's translations and notes, to his printers, to make another of his privately-printed first editions, *The Love Letters of Charlotte Brontë to Constantin Heger* (1914). His prefatory note stated where the letters had appeared, brazenly added that Mr Spielmann's translations 'have also been reproduced in the following pages', and maintained that the copyright in the letters was the property of his friend Shorter, whose generosity, etc., etc. But it was not until 1938, twenty-four years later, that Spielmann learned to his surprise of the Wise publication and its wholly unauthorized use of his translations—'the cool bagging of my Brontë work,' he wrote to me. Nor could *The Times* then find a record of Wise making any communication regarding the use of the copyright translations.

It is unexpectedly late in Wise's career, now verging upon rectitude, to find him producing a piracy. Once again he could wink at his familiar shade.

IV

There came the World War of 1914–18. Its horrors did not tear into his family circle. Steadily he pursued his own aims. After the works on Coleridge and Borrow, he was able to publish in 1916 his *Bibliography of Wordsworth*; in 1917, that of *The Brontë Family*; and in 1918, that of *Elizabeth Barrett Browning*; in addition to a regular flow of his privately-printed first-edition pamphlets. Also during these years good bargains were made in books and manuscripts, for the luxury trade was badly hit; and so the Ashley Library increased its treasures. Amid these activities he was very active again in the City; for the War prospered his business in spite of the difficulties of the times. Even these were smoothed out by that valuable friend of whom he could secretly take advantage. The essential-oil dealer told his troubles about a shipment of cloves held up at Gibralter in a captured German bottom. Whereupon Gosse promised (5 October 1914):

If you did apply to the Admiralty Marshal, and if any difficulty arose, I will with the greatest pleasure put the facts personally before Mr Winston Churchill.

Whether Gosse interceded with Mr Churchill, then First Lord of the Admiralty and having his first historic tussle with the Germans, does not emerge. But he did use his influence in another quarter concerning a cargo of olives. So Wise's city affairs flourished as usual—as did his others.

As he worked in his comfortable library, sorting and cataloguing his treasures of thirty-five years of collecting, he might well pride himself on his skill and acquisitiveness. Closer study of the contents of his shelves surprised even him. The Ashley Library has two independent appeals: its magnificent first editions of early English poets and dramatists, and its wealth of manuscript material of the nineteenth century.

Wise had a partiality for what are termed 'human documents' telling of the scandals, the private confessions, the secrets, of authors. Now he had only to stretch out a hand and open his bookcases to expose the quivering souls, the comic figures, the ghastly skeletons, that always have made and always will make up the literary world. From these he covered the dry bones of his book descriptions with the living flesh of biography, giving life to his catalogues that will long outlast their purely bibliographical interest. What materials his eager hands had gathered! Documents in which men and women are stripped naked, souls searched and revealed—a welter of idylls and passions, jokes and despairs. I have handled many of these fragile letters and discoloured papers. And although some of them are now mockingly shrouded in the finest silk and morocco blazing with gold, it has seemed as if they were still wet with tears and kisses, or else shaking with the laughter or anger of their writers. Let us take a few specimens of their varied revelations. At—

SHELLEY'S noble generosity when expecting Keats in Italy: 'I 'intend to be the physician both of his body and soul. . . . I am aware 'indeed that I am nourishing a rival who will far surpass me; and this 'is an additional motive and will be an added pleasure.'

CHARLOTTE BRONTË, about her dead brother Branwell: 'All 'his vices were and are nothing now—we remember only his woes.'

KEATS'S suppressed poem entitled 'Sharing Eve's Apple', beginning:

> *O blush not so! O blush not so!*
> *Or I shall think you knowing;*
> *And if you smile the blushing while,*
> *Then maidenheads are going.*

MARY SHELLEY telling Mrs Leigh Hunt as one woman to another: 'If it were of any use I would say a word or two against your continu-'ing to wear stays. Such confinement cannot be either good for you 'or the child; and as to shape, I am sure they are very far from be-'coming.'

TRELAWNY philosophizing to Jane Clairmont: 'The "dream 'we call life" is a farce. . . . The only solace is that we are all in the 'donkey race.'

LORD BYRON relating for John Murray a scene between two of

his mistresses—Margarita Cogni and la Signora Segati: 'Margarita . . .
'replied in very explicit Venetian: "You are not his wife: I am not his
'"wife: you are his Donna, and I am his Donna: your husband is a
'"cuckold, and mine is another. For the rest, what right have you to
'"reproach me? If he prefers what is mine to what is yours, is it my
'"fault?"'4

JANE CLAIRMONT, the discarded mistress of Byron, in her diary:
'I have nothing left to do but fry in the sun for your amusement.'

MRS LEIGH HUNT as she saw Byron: 'Like a schoolboy who
'has been given a plain, instead of a currant, bun.'

THOMAS HARDY recalling the traffic perils in the London of
1867: 'It carried me back to the time of thirty years ago when I used to
'read your [Swinburne's] early works walking along the crowded
'London streets to my imminent risk of being knocked down.'

ROBERT LOUIS STEVENSON'S delightful letter in verse to his
friend Charles Baxter, beginning:

> *Blame me not that this epistle*
> *Is the first you have from me,*
> *Idleness has held me fettered;*
> *But at last the times are bettered,*
> *And once more I wet my whistle—*
> *Here in France beside the sea.*

CHARLES DICKENS back at slavery, after a jolly tramp and dinner
with Leigh Hunt: 'Oh, Hunt, I'm so lazy, and all along o' you. The
'sun is in my eyes, the hum of the fields in my ears—and a boy, redolent
'of the steam engine and sweltering in warm ink, is slumbering in the
'passage, waiting for "copy".'

GEORGE BORROW, who liked to air himself as a philologist:
'It must not be supposed that "Will" is the abbreviation of William;
'it is pure Danish, and signifies "wild".'

MARY RUSSELL MITFORD, to Dr W. C. Bennett about the
Brownings in Italy: '. . . They are kept in Florence by want of money,
'want so absolute that they cannot get to the Baths at Lucca. . . . A

4 Margarita Cogni was the young illiterate wife of a baker. The letter implies that her
rival 'la Signora Segati' was a woman of means. It does not bring out, nor does Wise's
annotation, that Marianna Segati was the twenty-one-year-old wife of Byron's landlord,
a draper. The long account is an example of the poet writing up to his reputation as a liber-
tine. It had already been published before Wise devoted four-and-a-half closely-printed
pages of his *Catalogue* to quoting it: thus illustrating both his manuscript-collecting and
his book-making.

'ship that was to have brought them money brought an account
'against them instead. This looks as if it were a bookseller. But surely
'he [i.e., Robert Browning] could earn money. Ah, dear friend, how
'right and wise it is in you to remain where you are, and what you
'are' [i.e., a bachelor].

GEORGE MEREDITH anticipating Swinburne's poems coming
out: 'I have heard "low mutterings" already from the Lion of British
'prudery.'

ROBERT BROWNING, reporting that Landor is established close
at hand (in Italy): 'I believe I am to have the poor dear old man
'permanently "added to my portion", as the Methodists phrase it.'

HARDY, again, on the riddle of Browning: 'The longer I live the
'more does Browning's character seem the leading puzzle of the Nine-
'teenth Century. How could smug Christian optimism worthy of a
'dissenting grocer find a place inside a man who was so vast a seer
'and feeler when on neutral ground?'

SWINBURNE, with a typical characterization: 'Swift I take to
have been Dante's bastard by a daughter of Rabelais.'

HENRY JAMES concerning Joseph Conrad: 'Born a Pole, and
'cast upon the waters, he has worked out an English style that is more
'than correct, that has quality and ingenuity. . . . Unhappily, to be
'very serious and subtle is not one of the paths to fortune.'

WILLIAM ROSSETTI, hugging himself upon the reflection that
he had got portraits of his sister and his 'dear loving old mother' into
the National Portrait Gallery: 'Christina had to be there one day, as
'a matter of course; but I greatly applaud myself on having thus wafted
'in my mother by a side-wind.'

Limerick writing was one of the milder amusements of Victorian authors and artists. Dante Gabriel Rossetti was always
doing it.[5] Here is one against him by his friend, John Payne—
him of the emasculated *Arabian Nights*:

[5] William Bell Scott once complained that the artist had sent him a limerick accusing
him of Atheism and immoderate use of whisky toddy (Rossetti reproving immoderation!),
adding that he couldn't prosecute him as the libel was not printed, but 'we shall have to
nab him some day'. Whereupon Gabriel retorted with this one, the MS. of which is not
in the Ashley Collection:

> *There's a scandalous bard called Rossetti,*
> *Who never his friends will let be,*
> *Till five hundred pounds*
> *And cost without bounds*
> *Shall quiet this rough-tongued Rossetti.*

There's a joker called Dante Rossetti,
Who thinks he paints better than Etty.
His ladies in paint
Look all ready to faint
But au fond *they're plain Molly and Betty.*

which was true enough, as Gabriel would agree; for did he not know his 'stunners' *à fond*?

The Ashley Library material is notable also for its light on the curious recreations of the Pre-Raphaelites. Wise says in his prefatory note to the privately-printed *Letters addressed to Algernon Charles Swinburne* (1919): 'All are interesting, but some of the 'expressions and allusions contained in three from Sir Edward 'Burne-Jones and D. G. Rossetti render the publication as a 'whole of these particular letters impossible. But the letters are 'by no means unimportant, and cannot be entirely disregarded. 'I therefore see no sufficient reason why they should not be 'preserved in the pages of a private pamphlet [for which Wise 'found a ready sale]. The only alternative is to destroy them.' The arguments contain the usual proportions of Wisedom and hypocrisy. He did not print the Swinburne effusions that prompted these letters. Nor did he destroy the equally scabrous replies they drew—all of which remain in the Ashley Collection at the British Museum. When, as is probable in the course of time, the Wise collection is split up, these things will go to their final resting-place on the shelves *Librorum Prohibitorum* in the Bloomsbury mausoleum.

There was an occasion when William Morris, on approaching the age of thirty, suddenly grew so very stout that he burst a pair of trousers. This was for years an unfailing cause of hilarity among the grown-up children of the Pre-Raphaelite Brotherhood. Burne-Jones and Rossetti drew realistic pictures of the 'Affair of the Bags' after Swinburne had exploited it in a squib 'which', says Wise after printing it as one of his publications, 'can never be included in any edition of his published verse'.

One of the Brotherhood (*circa* 1886), in a letter to 'My Dear 'but Infamous Pote', acknowledges the 'dreadful' gift of Swinburne's last letter, and his own fearful anxiety lest it should get out of his pocket and be seen. For 'its genius, my dear Sir, is

'such that I wouldn't destroy it for the world, and to keep it is
'destruction. It lies before me now with its respectable edge of
'black, and its wicked contents, like—if the simile may be
'accorded me—a sinful clergyman.' It appears further from the
letter that the enjoyment of the circle (including the 'Jewjube'
—i.e., Simeon Solomon) at Swinburne's effusion was so intense
that they spent the morning in illustrating it with drawings
'such as Tiberius would have given provinces for'. The classical
allusion explains why sending them through the post 'seemed
dangerous', and so 'we burnt them'. To show how much
Swinburne and Tiberius would have liked his illustrations, here
is the artist's description of one which escaped the flames:

> It was my own poor idea, not altogether valueless, I trust. A clergy-
> man of the established church is seen lying in an extatic dream in the
> foreground. Above him a lady is seen plunging from a trap door in the
> ceiling, ***** ** ****** ******* **** ***. How poorly does this
> describe one of my most successful designs. But you shall yet see it.

So much for the recreations of the Pre-Raphaelites. Nothing of
this stuff is fit to be published among the works of the respective
authors, says Wise unctuously. It could be privately circulated
for his gain, however; and the copies of his pamphlets are now
scattered far and wide, for anyone to reprint and disseminate also.

V

While Wise was busy during the War, there appears to have
been some disposition to be faithless to his old printers, Clay
and Sons. Between 1916 and 1918 nine of his publications were
produced by another firm. These may have been experiments
with a view to a change. However, he returned to Clays until
1922; when came the break with the good printers who had
innocently served him so long and so well in producing his
'private' pamphlets—both illegitimate and legitimate. On this
subject the comment to me of Cecil Clay is interesting. 'There was
'no official break with Clays as far as I know, and you see after
'1921 we had no printing works in London. The manager whom
'Wise always saw died in 1928 or thereabouts; but this should

'not have stood in Wise's way if he was prepared to go out of
'London. . . . Whatever the cause of Wise's change of printers
'you can rest assured it was not due to any suspicion on the part
'of the firm that its previous transactions with him were of an
'unsatisfactory nature.' (10 March 1938.)

But we have only arrived at 1918 in the chronology of Thomas
James Wise, for whom the post-war years were to hold such
remarkable developments.

CHAPTER 16

JOSEPH CONRAD: WISE TAKES
A *CHANCE*

The story [of the faked first edition of Chance] *once more proves what I have before asserted, that easy as it appears to be to fabricate reprints of rare books, it is in actual practice absolutely impossible to do so in such a manner that detection cannot follow the event. Even when the volume is of so recent a date that the necessary types and paper are both procurable, the human element fails, and, as in the present instance, a blunder is committed in spite of the exercise of the most meticulous care.*
Wise: *Bibliography of Joseph Conrad*

I

AFTER THE WORLD conflagration of 1914 to 1918 came the boom that follows war as vultures follow the dying beast to gorge on its still warm carcase. Europe passed from a nightmare of bloodshed to an orgy of gambling, dissoluteness, and extravagance. There were plenty of people who had amassed money. Now, when wealth was accumulated as never before in history, was the fever of spending and the delirium of making.

After the Napoleonic Wars the nation that came out most advantageously began coveting and buying the treasures, artistic and literary, of impoverished countries. Now history was repeated —with this difference: after Napoleon had run his short and fearful course, it was the British who could buy the Continent's illuminated manuscripts, Velasquez Venuses, and Elgin Marbles. Now it was America who could swoop down on Britain to gratify the desires of her culture for treasures in which she had a family interest. Vastly poorer in those treasures than was the Britain of a century earlier, she was much wealthier financially. So books, manuscripts, pictures, sculptures, even some of England's lovely old buildings, were captured by the irresistible dollar: many of them to be formed into magnificent collections, and finally swept with princely gestures by their millionaire-owners into the State's keeping for the benefit of the people.

It was wonderful history-making in those ten years that followed the World War; future American generations will be grateful to the collectors and libraries of 1918–28 for their enterprise. Although the ignorant lamented and protested against the transfer of cultural possessions from the old country to the new, it can be proved that Britain could well spare the greater part—even ninety-five per cent—of what America gained; for which, let it be emphasized again, she paid well. That the exchange was a fortunate one, those familiar with American scholarship are convinced by what has already been done with the English books, manuscripts, etc., acquired in the historic ten years.[1]

In the boom the rare-book field became affected with much of the gambling fever of the Stock Exchange. Collecting, for a time, ceased to be the exclusive pursuit of book-lovers and students, rich or poor. Into the arcadian field came bustling speculators ludicrously disguised as bookmen, who grasped the possibilities of the American demand and the popularized interest in old books and manuscripts due to the rising prices. They bought and bought with abysmal ignorance of what they were buying, in order to unload at the right time.

Many books that formerly were priced in shillings were now cheap at as many pounds. The first editions of immortal authors, that used to sell—and slowly enough—for a few pounds, now sold for hundreds. The exciting competition was increased, and values were forced up, by the elaboration of minute points of difference between copies of the same first edition due to accidents of printing, by the discovery of freak copies, and (more justifiably) by the appreciation of volumes bearing some association with their writers or their celebrated friends by reason of inscriptions, corrections, etc. As for original letters and manuscripts, fantastic prices were commonly reached—the amazing record being that of fifteen thousand four hundred pounds paid by A. S. W. Rosenbach for the script of *Alice in Wonderland*.

[1] American acquisitiveness in respect of English literary treasures continued to a decreasing extent after 1928, and of course it had been successfully active long before 1918; but there never was before, and probably never will be again, such a period as the ten years of the boom.

How that would have astonished the author—as it amazed his jolly nieces, my neighbours of boyhood days.

In the wider distribution of money that followed the 1914–18 World War, many of the old rich became the new poor. In some of the ancient homes of England a long reign of cloistered calm and careless affluence ended with the new economic conditions and the alarmingly increasing demands of taxation. Some of their little-known libraries, as matured as the wine in their cellars, were broken up and cast into the welter of the London sale-rooms. Others—more than generally known at the time—were ravished secretly: the old volumes, in their mellowed calf or original boards, packed into metal cases and rushed across the Atlantic. No one was wiser, except the dealer with his cigar and the straitened landowner left with a fat cheque and an uneasy mind. Ruffled and bewigged ancestors looked down fearfully from their frames, for the next visitors were to be the picture dealers.

Oh, yes! they sold well. The Americans loved anything which came from a turreted and famous mansion. Why not? Here were good things: to covet them was a grace, not an offence. The owners needed cash. By the time their mortgages and arrears of war income-tax had been paid through prosperous family lawyers, and allowance made for the death duties staring in the face of the living, there was not much left.[2] The libraries crossed the Atlantic; to be, on the other side, marvelled over and superbly indexed by experts whose care and efficiency would have left gasping the learned but easy-going librarians of the Stately Homes.

But it was not only the veteran first editions of mellowed libraries that went soaring in value. There were not enough of them to meet the hungry demand. So the first editions of contemporary authors were seized upon as the next best things—a few justly enough; more with little reason. It was in this traffic that the silly limit was reached. Some of these books had been published only a short time before in first printings known to have run to hundreds and thousands of copies. The supply at all

---

[2] The British war bill was the heaviest of all combatants—thirteen thousand five hundred and seventy-eight million pounds, against Germany's ten thousand three hundred and forty-one and America's eight thousand million.

times exceeded the demand, temporarily inflated though it was, and 'forced' by those who hoarded copies. Sums ranging from fifty to two hundred pounds were frequently paid for first editions of popular novelists and dramatists that before many years had passed were to be hardly sellable at prices about seventy-five per cent less.

With all the publicity these ephemeral wonders obtained, there were even some writers with aspirations to be best-sellers who thought that the collecting field was a short cut to their goal. More than one pushful author endeavoured to stimulate artificially the collecting demand for his very mediocre writings. It was a crazy time, the most cynical comment on which was that made by George Bernard Shaw, who advised Mrs Patrick Campbell to sell the personal letters he had written to her and make money while the going was good.

II

All this is very interesting history, the reader may say; but where does Thomas James Wise come in? The answer is that he had come in before the history-making began. With his shelves well filled with rare first editions and manuscripts, he could watch the soaring prices of the boom, knowing that the value of his library was being doubled, quadrupled, and more. Except for an item now and then to fill a gap, some desirable thing to adorn his collection (such as the first issue of *Paradise Lost*, which cost him six hundred pounds in 1924), he kept out of the mad competition and its fancy prices. Furthermore, he could sit back and see the labours of his earlier years bearing remarkable fruit. The concentration on books having special points of interest, on freak copies, on original issues in fine state, etc., was partly the result of his influence. His buying for himself tended to decrease after the war;[3] although his secret business as a bookseller continued.

Those who were selling and buying in the feverish rare-book

[3] When returning a questionnaire to *The Bookman's Journal* for its *Record of British and American Private Collectors* (1927) he specified his desiderata as 'Byron and Byroniana mostly just now'.

market eagerly consulted the bibliographies he was producing. In these, the points as to rarity were elaborated with all Wise's enthusiasm and that lavishness of evidence, drawn from MS. sources, which give his reference books much of the interest of biographies. His authority was increasingly cited; and he himself was frequently referred to personally by strangers—rarely in vain. Thus, whereas formerly Wise and his collection had been known to only a small circle of connoisseurs, now his name as a collector and bibliographer became familiar to many people in Britain, the Empire, the United States, and other countries. To this larger public he loomed out of an obscure past—affluent, successful, a genius at the collecting game, a wizard at bibliography.

He held aloof from the new craze for collecting almost every contemporary author who got into the newspapers. His shrewd judgment as a rare-book dealer warned him that many of these boosted first editions of second-rate novelists and poets had only a passing interest and value. Nevertheless, although he had chosen to specialize in the old poets and dramatists, the fame of outstanding men like Hardy, Conrad, and Kipling, and the amazing prices paid for copies of their rarities, caused him to tack to the fashionable wind—led to the opening of his library to a few selected rare first editions of modern novels. Here he was following the crowd. His literary perception and his scholarship have been much vaunted. But no instance can be found—not even that of Swinburne—in which Wise saw the promise of an author's early work and backed his judgment by collecting him when he was obscure and unheralded. *A Pair of Blue Eyes* did not lure him at first; the original *Almayer's Folly* was like any other man's; and certain lilting songs and amusing barrack-room tales (that came out in paper-covered booklets, soon to disappear) found no welcome in the Ashley Library—until they had become desirable things to be dearly bought.

III

In one of his compilations Wise makes reference to the merciless exploitation of Joseph Conrad after his death. I have a memorandum of Wise telling Edmund Gosse: 'I'm *sick* of the

'way these brutes are trading on Conrad—particularly the *******
'crowd, who are selling to the Yankees everything they got out
'of Joseph Conrad, or can scrape together,—books, letters, and
'aught else.' But he said nothing of what happened *before* the
author's death.

Wise was perhaps moved to collect Conrad by the example
of Richard Curle, who was a close friend of both parties. Curle
had himself been assiduously engaged in making a complete
collection of original Conrad editions, etc., the author generously assisting and inscribing many of the volumes. Immediately
the boom began, the values of Conrad first editions soared. Wise,
realizing the possibilities, determined to include him among his
collected authors, for reasons which may be gathered from what
he wrote in the introduction to his *Conrad Bibliography* (1920):
'No excuse is required for such a volume. Not only are the books
'of Joseph Conrad collected more and more at ever-increasing
'prices, but the bibliography of these books is itself some-
'what complicated and offers many pitfalls.' In this case,
however, he did not want mere first editions: he wished to
emulate the example of Curle and to have a collection of inscribed
copies—************************. This was arranged in a
way that was made worth while to Conrad, who also sold to
Wise all his manuscripts done from 1918 onward—at least nine
of which, in addition to a case of original letters from the author,
were disposed of privately by Wise.[4] The former merchant-
captain had had a lean time after he left the sea to become an
author. Now, with an increasingly expensive family, it was not
surprising that he should avail himself of some of the side profit
of the enthusiasm for his writings. But Conrad fondly believed
that the manuscripts he sold to Wise were remaining in the
Ashley Library.

The inscriptions written by the author for Wise in his Conrad
first editions were often of a bibliographical character. Actually
the old sea rover so brilliantly metamorphosed into the novelist
was about as qualified to make bibliographical statements as
was the essential-oil merchant to handle a windjammer in a

---

[4] One other, that of *Laughing Anne*, was retained in the Ashley Collection. I find Conrad
writing to 'Dear Mr Wise', sending the fifty-three-quarto-page MS., and also the corrected
typescript, of the play, and asking one hundred pounds for them, the letter being signed
'Yours faithfully'.

typhoon. Conrad's occasional irritation with the business can be surmised from the way in which some of the inscriptions were made: such as:

> Signed for T. J. Wise
> Joseph Conrad.

That bald statement hints a meaning best expressed in seaman's language. The mood varied in a few cases; and the author would perform his well-paid task with more 'friendly regards'. As an example of the inscriptions, take this one in Wise's copy of *The Inheritors*:

> This is a copy of the first American edition, which was before the English edition, the imprint of Heinemann being merely stamped for publication purposes.

So this is Joseph Conrad, the sensitive temperamental writer, who, ever after he left the sea, lived for his art, developing a secret self in which he lived to weave his pictures and fantasies. So this is Joseph Conrad solemnly writing his own bibliographical data. I try to imagine Conrad as I have seen him in his study, bending over his table, the powerful shoulders hunched, the hand with its long fingers and whipcord veins seizing his gargantuan fountain pen—for what? To compose bibliographical certificates to the rarity of copies of his own books! The mockery of it all. For the true picture is that of the calculating dealer suggesting careful inscriptions which in Joe's generous script would make the volumes so valuable. These passages from Conrad's unpublished letters give a direct view of the jobbery:

> (1 Aug 1920) 'Dear Mr Wise, . . . I keep the bound MS. (perfectly 'beautiful) till you come to claim it. I'll also write then the *note* accord-'ing to your wishes. . . .'
>
> (Undated) 'Dear Mr Wise, . . . Our friend *.*. was here yesterday, 'and I have signed your copy of S.L. [i.e., *The Shadow Line*] I hope in 'the way you wished it. . . .'
>
> (By his secretary: 17 December 1920): 'Mr Conrad asks me to say that he 'has written something in " *Victory*" which he hopes is what you wanted. 'He naturally could not write the same words quoted in the Biblio-'graphy, and wrote about the Play and Film instead. . . .'

Thanks to the continuance of his commercial good fortune, Wise never knew what these inscriptions he got Conrad to write

'It was *Chance* that raised Joseph Conrad into the rank of best-sellers; and it is *Chance* that provides a remarkable illustration of how chancey a bibliographer Wise could sometimes be' (Chapters 16 and 17)—The last photograph of the novelist taken June 1924 in his garden at Bishopsbourne

meant to him in cash. But he had a shrewd idea ************
****
****
****
****
******************* [5]
****
****
****
****
******

IV

The popularity of authors is not always due to readers' recognition of their best work. The overrated *John Inglesant* was made a best-seller by a photograph showing Gladstone holding a copy in his hands. It was *Chance* that raised Conrad into the rank of best-sellers; and it is *Chance* that provides a remarkable illustration of how chancy a bibliographer Wise could sometimes be.

The novel was first printed with a title-page dated 1913; but, publication being postponed until the following year, that title-page was removed and replaced by one dated 1914. A number of copies, however—some fifty, says Wise—got into circulation with the 1913 title; and these constitute the first issue of the first edition.

Then comes a mystery about which there have been many rumours and head-shakings. A forger got to work, printed off leaves reproducing the 1913 title-page, and inserted them in copies of *Chance* in place of the 1914 title. By chance, it was none other than Thomas James Wise who first revealed the hidden hand of the forger; and it was the forger's failure to reproduce exactly the genuine article that led Wise to write the weighty pronouncement which I have selected to head this chapter. It is possibly the sardonic echo of his regret, remembering his efforts with sundry nineteenth-century pamphlets.

Once informed of the foregoing facts, no one need be gulled. In copies of the genuine and valuable uncancelled 1913 issue of

[5] **.

P

Chance, the title-page bearing that date is part of the sheet on which that section of the book is printed. On the other hand, the forged 1913 title-page and also the publisher's substituted 1914 title-page are both inserted leaves pasted on to stubs in the joints, or back of the books. Wise made the matter crystal clear in his *Bibliography of Conrad* (1921) when he said:

> *The separately inserted title-pages with the note dated 1913 . . . are forgeries. Regarding this there can be no question, and copies of the book in which they occur are worthless from the point of view of the collector.*

Nothing could be more explicit, or typically dogmatic.

But by still stranger chance, it was Thomas James Wise who later, in his *Ashley Library Catalogue* (1926), described a most remarkable copy of *Chance* in his possession. It had the 'right' 1913 title-page, but *pasted in*; and this he accepted as a genuine first issue.

> A copy such as the present [he adds in the catalogue], the genuineness of which is supported by the author's signed certificate, is good enough. But in view of the doubt and uncertainty which must necessarily cling to any copy not certified in this manner, the only safe plan to follow is to accept no specimen of the book [he means as a genuine first issue] in which the title-page does not form an unsevered portion of the first half-sheet.

In brief, let Wise's copy be the unique exception to his own despotic rule: all because the obliging Conrad had been procured to write in the volume:

> The title-page of this book is a genuine copy of the original title dated 1913, at first removed, and subsequently restored to the volume.

If there is one thing certain in this uncertain affair, it is that this is not Joseph Conrad speaking and certifying, although the statement is in his script. The voice is that of another dictating to the novelist. Why this forcing of things to the extent of getting Conrad to write a certificate of genuineness for which he was hopelessly unqualified as compared with Wise? For that certificate to have any bibliographical value it needed to be signed by the expert, by Wise himself, who was able to expose the *Chance* forgeries. Did it never occur to the shrewd collector that the ruse was transparent: that as a guarantee, it was sheer humbugging? Or did his desire for inscribed rarities become such an obsession as to overwhelm his judgment and make him oblivious of the farce?

The final light exposing the hollowness of the business is this: that when the Ashley Library came to be moved to the British Museum, this strangely exceptional copy was missing. The inference is that, notwithstanding what he had set out in his Catalogue, Wise was taking no chance with his very extraordinary *Chance*.

Another first edition of a Conrad novel came under suspicion as having been the subject of a book faker's attentions. This was *A Set of Six*, a doubtful copy of which had been exposed through my Journal[6] as differing from Wise's volume. 'I do think that 'these frauds should be prevented—if it be possible to stop them,' he observed to me when expressing a wish to see the copy. This was duly borrowed from the obliging owner, J. C. Thomson; and 'a sort of inquest' was held on it by Wise, Clement Shorter, and G. E. Webster of Methuen's. It is not for the verdict that the case is mentioned here, but (in the light of subsequent events) for the sequel. Thomson, a typographical and paper expert of thirty-five years' experience, wrote to me: 'I neither agree nor 'disagree with Mr Wise's conclusions, but his reasons are 'ludicrously inadequate. It is but too apparent that he has no 'practical knowledge of printing and no technical knowledge of 'paper.'

Wise's connexion with Conrad did not end with the collecting of the highly-manufactured association items as described. There was the usual burst of privately-printed first editions. Clement Shorter was, for once, first in the field in 1918 with five booklets. These prompted a collector of the author's works—a man of limited means—to write to Conrad protesting against their publication in small privately-issued editions that he found difficult to procure. The kindly author took the stranger's protest to heart, and was sympathetic. He explained that he had allowed Shorter the privilege feeling that he owed him a good turn, frankly told about the forthcoming Wise printings, and indicated his intention to communicate the correspondent's 'special grievance' to them: adding—

---

[6] See *The Bookman's Journal*, Nos. 59 and 62 (1920) and 63 and 65 (1921).

'I also wish to say that I regret very much that you and other collec-
'tors should deem themselves treated unfairly. I acted in ignorance for
'which I can hardly be blamed as I am not a collector myself. That
'particular range of emotions is a closed book to me. I never collected
'anything in my life, not even postage stamps, as so many boys do.
'This is no doubt regrettable, but I am afraid I am an imperfect human
'being, mentally and morally, in other ways too. Pray forgive my
'imperfections.'

Wise came along with a rush in 1919, producing ten booklets over his imprint—none of which he sent to the British
Museum. Then, ten more of these privately-printed Conrad first-
edition pamphlets were produced (1919–20)—strangely enough,
although from the same printing press, over the imprint of Conrad this time. I sought an explanation from Richard Curle. His
reply, while missing the chief point of inquiry, supports some of
my contentions:

I presume that the reason why no copies were deposited at the British
Museum was that there was quite a run on the pamphlets and that a
number were given to Conrad. I was out of the country when the first
series was done, but I remember that Mr Wise paid Mr Conrad a
handsome fee for permission to do the second series. In fact the whole
relationship was friendly from beginning to end. I can only suppose that
no more pamphlets were printed partly because twenty seemed quite
enough, and partly because there was practically no more available
material.

The law's requirements apart, the fact that there was 'quite a
run' on the pamphlets seems a strange excuse for failing to send
copies to the British Museum, considering that these things were
usually purported to be done from idealistic motives of preservation. The printings were mostly of contributions written by
Conrad for periodicals. They omit to state where the pieces first
appeared—as one would expect a bibliographer to be most careful to state. Wise's production of these minor writings did not
meet with the sanction of his mentor any more than had the
printing of some of the Swinburne extravagances. Gosse was
silent for a long time regarding the Conradiana, but in due course
(22 January 1928):

'Of course I approve of your letter, and am indignant at the impu-
'dence of these pirates. But—I cannot resist very gently reminding you,

'that it was *yourself*, in your generous good-nature, that began it! If
'you had not, in order to put money into Conrad's pocket (which had
'a hole in it) started printing, as pamphlets, absolutely worthless frag-
'ments of his prose, all this would never have happened!! You are
'hoist on your own petard. But the greed of these new dirty scoundrels
'is limitless.'

Of this flick of the old whip it only remains to be said that financial benefit for the author was certainly not the motive that
prompted Wise's private publishing. The reference to Conrad's
pocket touches more pathetic matters than perhaps Gosse was
aware of. But there was no such hole in the pocket of Wise or
of his critic—for which indeed they had reason to be truly
thankful.

The 'handsome fee' which Curle says was paid by Wise to the
author for the right to print the second series of booklets was,
according to Conrad, two hundred pounds. As the ten editions
were certified to be limited to twenty-five copies each, the copyright charge per copy works out at sixteen shillings, to which has
to be added twelve and sixpence which Clays state was approximately the average price then of producing each—making a total
cost to the publisher of twenty-eight shillings and sixpence
per booklet. We have seen (Chapter 8, p. 105) Wise suggesting
to Gorfin prices averaging twenty-four pounds apiece for his
Swinburne private-printings, and himself obtaining eight pounds
each from another bookseller for the minor Borrow pamphlets.
On these figures it is not unreasonable to suppose that the 'handsome fee' paid to Joseph Conrad showed a handsome profit.

V

In 1920, Mrs Flora Virginia Livingston, of the Harry Elkins
Widener Memorial Library, Harvard University, wrote and
printed a thirty-two-page pamphlet entitled *Bibliographical Data
Relating to a Few of the Publications of Algernon Charles Swinburne*.
Mrs Livingston's notes were the 'outcome of a painstaking
examination' of Wise's *Bibliography of Swinburne*. As a result of
checking the bibliography by various Swinburne collections in
the United States, 'information has been gathered which was

'not known to Mr Wise'. In spite of her painstaking examination, however, the true character of certain Swinburne publications now condemned as forgeries or suspects was not revealed.

But the significance of the pamphlet is that it was respectfully but determinedly critical of one who was widely accepted as an infallible authority above suspicion. To Wise it may well have seemed the horrid writing on the wall again—not so clear and denunciatory as when Cook and Wedderburn's work was done; but still, a hint of the kind of investigation that might follow any day. In print he dismissed his critic with 'A thoughtless sugges- 'tion was made by Mrs Livingston in her hopelessly ill-informed 'and misleading pamphlet'.

Subsequently Mrs Livingston compiled an admirable *Bibliography of Rudyard Kipling* (1927), in which she boldly stated that two Kipling pamphlets, *White Horses* (1897) and *The White Man's Burden* (1899), now classed among Wise's productions, were piracies. It was more writing on the wall; and Wise's reaction is not surprising. In 1937, Mrs Livingston wrote to me:

I was unfortunately one of the first persons who criticized his work in print, and he never forgave me. I proved all my statements by the books themselves in our library, and he afterwards incorporated all of them in his own bibliography. . . . But he never forgave me, and considered me an 'ignorant, ill-informed person. . . .' My experience with him is very interesting, but what I could say, and think, would hardly be fit to appear in print. He was a great man, and a curious one —a *mystery*. But why get angry when errors are pointed out? We all make them, and most of us are only too glad to have them pointed out.

CHAPTER 17

PORTRAIT OF A DICTATOR

They dwell in the odour of camphor,
They stand in a Sheraton shrine,
They are 'warranted early editions'
These worshipful tomes of mine;—

In their creamiest 'Oxford vellum'
In their redolent 'crushed Levant'
With their delicate watered linings
They are jewels of price, I grant.
                    Austin Dobson: *My Books*

I

MENTION OF WISE once provoked Joseph Conrad to an unex-pected outburst on an occasion when I was visiting him at Bishopsbourne. At the time there was a proposal under discussion that I should include something of Conrad's in a little series of unpublished works. When we came to the subject in the course of conversation, the *Secret Agent* was mentioned. This led Conrad to suggest that I should use his unprinted play *Laughing Anne*. Suddenly there came to me the recollection that Wise possessed the original script of the piece. I was a young man with a considerable appreciation of the respective achievements of these two who were so much my senior. Lest anything should be done which might lead to misunderstanding, I recalled that Wise owned the original manuscript.

In an instant the calm of Conrad's study was broken as by a tropical storm. 'Wise! Wise!! What has it to do with Wise?' exclaimed Conrad with a passion that startled me. 'Wise! Wise!! 'he only owns the paper. The work is mine'—and Conrad's powerful shoulders went up: his face was tense with emotion. I began to say something tactful. It was no great matter anyhow. Moreover, I was a guest. But before I could say much, Conrad's

233

momentary irritation vanished; and, flinging himself on to the settee beside me, he put his arm round my shoulders: 'Of course you must have *Laughing Anne* now—poor dear Anne.'—He would let Thomas Wise know his intentions.—There would be no need to trouble him for the manuscript—another copy was available.—Then came the summons to lunch; and we joined a merry family group.

It seemed as if in this matter I was fated as Laughing Anne herself. No sooner was I back in London than the storm blew up from another quarter. Wise wrote (14 March 1923) furiously upbraiding me because, instead of consulting him, I had discussed the printing of Conrad's play with the author. He added that I had given him a lesson, and henceforward he would take care to keep unpublished things out of his catalogue. Being able to reply that I knew of the unpublished work long before his catalogue appeared, that the choice of *Laughing Anne* was Conrad's, and that it was no concern of mine what was omitted from the Ashley Catalogues, I could write with calm confidence. By return post came an apology and an assurance that *it was not on my account that he had resolved not to catalogue anything unprinted by either Rudyard Kipling or Robert Louis Stevenson.* It was a complete about-face. These uncatalogued manuscripts he presumably sold. Certainly they were not retained in Wise's collection.

So much for his attitude towards unprinted material; especially in the cases where he had acquired the paper on which it was written—which is a very different thing from possessing its copyright.

II

One certainly needed to have Laughing Anne's sense of humour when dealing with Wise. His talks and correspondence with me suggested the acrobatics of a thermometer plunged alternately into boiling and iced water. One day I might be a 'wonderful chap'. Another day: 'If you had only referred to my biblio-'graphy, you would have saved ***** making yourself and the 'magazine ridiculous.' Another day: 'You are doing a useful 'work. . . .' And another time: 'Why do you do this?' So the weathercock of praise and criticism revolved. The great thing in life was to keep your eyes glued on the score or so of works by Thomas J. Wise. Then you and everybody who wrote for you would be infallible. One of his habits when dealing with correspondence is illustrative of his character. In his impetuosity he would sometimes reply to correspondents by writing—in his slapdash script—terse and not always polite remarks in red ink on the margins of their letters. The addition of a line or so at the end, and his signature, completed the reply. The lurid result may be easily imagined. He liked to look on the ink when it was red. He often saw red.

But if his correspondence was stimulating, there were some who must have found his hasty letters a serious matter—judging by the stories he told me. If a book whose bibliographical points had been elucidated by Wise was contrarily described in a book-seller's list, the perpetrator was always likely to receive a sting-ing letter. And the merest suspicion of a 'wrong 'un' (i.e., a spurious manuscript or a faked book) raised the devil. At least two prominent members of the Antiquarian Book Trade were summoned to the Presence, and, concerned for their reputations, attended: to spend an embarrassing half-hour in the Ashley Library—that is, according to its owner.

Such episodes as these were described to me by Wise with a show of righteous indignation, mixed with quizzical enjoyment of the discomfiture caused. They left the impression that, had he been the Mikado or the Queen in *Wonderland*, instead of the dictator of bibliography and a London produce merchant, all the suspects, guilty or innocent, would have had their heads chopped off within twenty-four hours of the receipt of their catalogues.

But there was something in his exultant way of describing his inquisitions, usually with some inexplicable hiatuses, that made me resolve never wholly to believe, still less to repeat, the accounts. Nor was I the only visitor to the Ashley Library to make such a resolution. In print, the case was different. There, when it came to personalities, Wise either damned with safety or was caution personified. For he rather prided himself on his knowledge of the law on libel and copyright.

One of these stories concerned a London bookseller who was invited to the Ashley Library to produce some original Shelley

letters he allegedly had for sale, the genuineness of which Wise
suspected. The manuscripts were accordingly produced. 'I im-
'mediately saw that they were forgeries,' Wise told me. 'So I
'tore them up, handed the fragments back to *******, and said:
'"Now then! You are at liberty to sue me for destroying your
'"property."'[1]

This dramatic affair in the most sensational Lyceum traditions
could only have been improved by the inclusion of a 'curse you,
villain' and heavy snortings. I have made an exception to my
rule by repeating the story because Wise himself told it to so
many people that it has become a legend in the rare-book world
—a legend calculated to be highly creditable to the collector.
Side by side with it ought to be set these facts: that this bookseller, whose name has always been freely mentioned in the
telling of the story, was one of Wise's best customers for the
Ashley Library private printings; that he enjoyed Wise's hospitality; and that he was the recipient from the compiler of a copy
of the *Ashley Library Catalogue*. The regard was evidently mutual,
for he once, in a book, gave a testimonial to the destroyer of
other people's forgeries, describing him as 'that most dignified
'and honoured of book-collectors, Mr Thomas James Wise'.

It may be wondered what his relations were with booksellers
who meant so much to him, but whose secret rival he was. Outwardly he was suave and agreeable, but apt to be patronizing
and overbearing in some cases. That he had his antagonisms is
evident from complaints to Gosse, who on one occasion replied
(22 May 1913): '... I am truly glad that you have resisted ******.
'Why should he and ***** enjoy a little joust together, and you
'be made to pay for it? I hope it will teach them a lesson. . . .'
Wise was once involved in an episode which he related in a letter
now missing. Gosse's balm was not without its usual blister
(20 April 1920): '... The story you tell me about the Knock
'Out makes my blood boil. What an infamy! . . . I think, how-
'ever, that it will be said that you, as you knew the circumstances,
'should not have lent yourself to the imposture. I do not know
'why you gave fifty pounds for a pamphlet which is not rare and
'which is not intrinsically worth a twentieth part of that sum. . . .'

[1] It would be interesting to have the pretty legal point involved decided at one of those
Moots they hold in the Inns of Court.

III

As he was in his correspondence, so he appeared in personal intercourse. His talk was voluble, and often amazingly free in criticism of other people and things that roused his quick temper. At this time (from 1919 onwards) when he was widely regarded as a sort of bibliographical Sherlock Holmes or a Napoleon of book-collecting, I was seeing him with some regularity either at his house or in town—almost invariably to discuss some matter of bibliography. He was, both in manner and actuality, a dictator; and—like all dictators—during his little reign he wore the mantle of autocracy and omniscience with superb confidence, assisted (though not always) by diplomacy and also by a joviality that came of natural pleasure in his success. Neither in appearance nor in temperament was he the mellowed, dreamy, philosophizing bibliophile of fiction and occasional fact. No Sylvestre Bonnard was he. He looked, in truth, what he was: the astute business man, but a business man with an instinctive flair for books and collecting.

He was short and plump. His chubby face was pink and shaven. The shrewd eyes with their beady pupils could laugh humorously behind their spectacles, but they could also glitter mercilessly. The mouth and chin were of determined set. But it was the eyes that mirrored the man himself. An interviewer, Augustus Muir, said that Wise 'Looks at you as though reading a date on a title-page'. True, but a date can be read at a glance. Those eyes probed, fathomed, weighed up with the same intensity that revealed to him a book's bibliographical secrets from its make-up. Behind them was the opportunist experienced in pitting brain against brains.

His memory was prodigious. To date a book or event was as easy as striking a match. His brisk movements about his library, the way he would take a volume from here and there, reeling off a fund of anecdotes, were things that rarely failed to impress a visitor, and sometimes left him bewildered.

There was one theme on which his loquaciousness dried up: that was the subject of Thomas James Wise. In my anxiety to do justice to the subject of this biography and to test my personal judgment of the man by that of others, I sought the opinions of several who could justly describe themselves as close friends of the collector-dealer. All remarked on his reticence about himself —especially about his early days—and their inability to draw him out on any matter relating to himself on which he did not choose to be expansive.

One of the friends and admirers of Wise in his later years was de Vincheles Payen-Payne, who supplied valuable information for the *Swinburne Bibliography* and voluntarily gave much experienced help with the proof-reading of the *Ashley Library Catalogue*. His recollections were:

> The revelations about Wise came as a painful shock to me, and the whole thing is such a mystery that I do not dwell on it. I visited him frequently—usually on Sundays. I always found him most charming. He was very entertaining and full of talk. But somehow, when you had left him, and came to think over the talk, you realized that he hadn't told you nearly as much as you thought he had; that the things you expected and wanted to hear, especially about himself, never followed. He was *un faux bonhomme*.[2]

IV

My first impression of the Ashley Library was one of surprise. It was at Heath Drive, Hampstead, that it was seen as the fulfilment of a long-worked-for idea: there that visitors from many lands saw it in its fame. It seemed to me incredible that his thousands of treasures were contained in that one comfortable room some thirty-five by twenty feet—that the closely packed bookshelves in the ornately glazed cases embraced all the brilliant eloquence of the verse and prose, all the burning passion of those human documents, which were described in the owner's catalogues.

Truly here was 'infinite riches in a little room'. But the Ashley books are rarely of the bulky kind. The poetry and drama of his collecting often made their shy appearances in the world thin and poorly clad. Garbed anew in rich Levant moroccos of

---

[2] 'One who affects to be a good easy man: a hypocritical old fellow'—Clifton and Grimaux's *Dictionary* (1923).

many colours, with gold decoration and lettering, they became outwardly as well as inwardly 'slim gilt souls' of literature. And packed in scores to the yard of shelf room, they presented an unnatural air of newness and serried splendour—a marshalled and imposing array, but lacking the warm and careless intimacy, the literary atmosphere, of other private libraries I have known.

Binding and rebinding became something of an obsession with Wise. Far too few items were kept in their original condition; for the exceptions the best slip cases or book boxes were made. His bookbinders' bills in themselves represented a small fortune. Few collectors achieve success without making blunders that later are smiled at and blushed for. Wise tells this story against himself. In his early days he bound Shelley and Byron first editions in red and blue moroccos respectively; and, as he said —'mighty proud I was of them.[3] But not many years had passed 'before I appreciated my folly; and the lesson once learned, I 'lost no time in discarding the lot'—which appeared to him years afterwards, on the shelves of booksellers and collectors, like ghosts to remind him of his error. Morocco is excellent in its place and in due proportion. But his passion for it never moderated. The lesson of the socialistic red Shelleys and the aristocratic blue Byrons was never wholly learned; for Elizabethan plays issued without covers and merely stabbed, were later bound for him instead of being preserved in slip cases in their original and interesting condition.

A. E. Calkin, of Rivières, who did most of the Ashley binding, recalls that Wise never kept receipts for the large and frequent payments he made always immediately on receiving his accounts; but that he relied mainly on his remarkable memory. Of this he once gave effective proof. At the bindery one day after the object of his call had been achieved, he asked if his account was ready. As it happened, it was just then waiting to be posted. It included among numerous items the charge for a binding at which Wise instantly demurred, saying that it had been paid on such and such a date. Inquiry at once showed that the charge had been included by accident, and that the client's

---

[3] He said in his *Bibliography of Byron* that they were bound by Fullford. But if the order was given to that printer the work was perhaps farmed out. See footnote page 31.

recollection was correct. In view of the mass of diverse detail he had to keep in mind: Hermann Rubeck's business, his own City company, his private bookselling, and the tremendous ramifications of his bibliographical pursuits: the little incident is illuminating.

The Wrenn collection, so largely formed by Wise, also gave scope for his binding and rebinding obsession. The considerable work involved was nearly all done by Wise's binders, and paid for by him. The settlement with friend and client Wrenn was a private matter.

V

During the years covered by this and the previous chapter—namely, 1918 to 1921 inclusive—the production of the privately-printed Ashley Library pamphlets practically came to an end. In 1918 there were nine; in 1919 thirty; in 1920 fifteen; and in 1921 two. In addition, with Gosse he edited Swinburne's *Contemporaries of Shakespeare* (1919) and *Selections from Shakespeare* (1919), and in 1920 he completed his edition of the five-volume Wrenn Library Catalogue. Also in this period were published his *Bibliography of Landor* (1919), the *Swinburne* (1919–20), the *Conrad* (1920–1), and the *Keats* (1921), which works put him on a still higher pinnacle of authority. Materials for the last-named works had been accumulating for years.

Like most of his own works, these four met nothing but praise in the limited specialist Press in which they were reviewed. It is a characteristic of bibliographies that their merits are readily perceivable, whereas it takes time and usage to reveal their defects. Wise's compilations are, and will probably always be found, extraordinarily interesting and useful. If they have already proved to be often fallible bibliographically, they are invaluable for their commentaries historical and biographical on the books and authors in which he specialized. It is significant that he was regarded by most of his colleagues on the Council of the Bibliographical Society rather as a collector than a bibliographer, and as something of an amateur. But he was a collector with a marvellous alertness for the biographical relation and the bibliographical revelation. And the fact that he was firstly the collector and dealer and secondly the bibliographer accounts for both the merits and the defects of his works.

I once asked him of which of his compilations he was proudest. He shied at the question, and countered by asking which of them appealed most to me. At that time his *Bibliography of Byron* had not appeared, and I plumped for the *Swinburne* because of its added biographical interest. The choice seemed to please him. The *Byron* (1932–3) is a rival for the same reason; although both works contain errors that a more judicious and less dogmatic bibliographer would have avoided.

After 1921 less than half-a-dozen of the privately-printed pamphlets were issued. For this there were several reasons. For one, his easily-handleable material was giving out. Then his financial position was flourishing, thanks to the war. With his growing reputation in the rare-book and literary worlds foreshadowing honours and still dizzier heights of attainment, he doubtless felt that his smaller trading ought to be dropped—as the manufacture of the nineteenth-century forgeries had been stopped at an earlier stage in his career.

There was one other reason. He was about to begin the production of his magnum opus, to crown a life's successful effort achieved by sheer industry, not a little genius, and ruthless determination.

CHAPTER 18

HIS *MAGNUM OPUS*, SUPER-FIRSTS, AND HIGH HONOURS

For, whosoever hath, to him shall be given, and he shall have more abundance: but whosoever hath not, from him shall be taken away even that which he hath.

Matthew xiii. 12

I

WISE's MAGNUM OPUS was, of course, his *Ashley Library Catalogue* in eleven bulky quarto volumes, the first two of which came off the press in 1922, and the remainder at fairly regular intervals between then and 1936. It was meant to be an imposing affair that would enhance the value of his collection. It received a most flattering welcome. He afterwards said that he had no idea the *Catalogue* would meet with such success. As it was to cost five hundred pounds to produce the edition of each part, most of which he expected having to pay, he originally intended to confine the work to five volumes. Finding that all the copies for sale were promptly subscribed, he allowed himself to 'spread a bit'; so that in the end the eleven volumes only 'landed me', he added, 'in a loss of one hundred pounds each'. Even if that was the balance-sheet result, it was a profitable investment.

It is Wise's own testimony that every word of the *Catalogue*, as well as of his other formidable bibliographical works, was written by him. The wonder is that they were not more inaccurately done.[1]

He secured such well-known bookmen as Augustine Birrell, Edmund Gosse, John Drinkwater, E. V. Lucas, R. W. Chapman, A. W. Pollard, and D. Nichol Smith, to write introductions. Gosse's advice and help in the picking of the team were, of

---

[1] But he had a number of assistants who mostly gave their services gratis. The names of three who helped him with his proof-reading are known to me.

course, in request. But when he learned that Clement Shorter was in the list of those Wise proposed to approach he was furious and declared he would not write an introduction. One of his letters on the delicate subject has several points of interest, though the hint that Wise must not offer to pay for the 'great' compliments was disregarded in at least one case; in which the worthy bookman tactfully preferred that 'what you suggest' should be commuted for a book, adding: 'A cheque will be all gone in no time to meet the bills for the children's boots.' But to Gosse's advice:

 . . . Now, as to the preface to the new volume of your catalogue, I feel very much puzzled what to say. It is a great compliment for any one to be asked to write an introduction to one of your volumes, and would be a still greater compliment if you had not made (in your too-easy good-nature) such a mistake with the first introduction of all. I think you might ask ****** to do it, but I feel very strongly that the invitation must come direct from you, not through me. You are, of course, quite at liberty to tell him that you write at my suggestion. But, I assure you, there must be no suggestion of payment. The whole point of these little introductions is that they are voluntary.

 I will tell you what the difficulty is about ******. He is sure to be pleased to be asked, and equally sure to say 'Yes'. But he says 'Yes' to everything, he cannot say 'No'. The result is that he involves himself in endless engagements; and often delays, and often alas! scamps what he promises to do. You must weigh in your mind these pros and cons. . . .

Wise, thus guided by his faithful 'overlord in all that pertains 'to literature or criticism', found that the bookmen generously responded to his invitations, inspired no doubt by the wealth of treasures being revealed in the *Catalogue*. With the exception of a few good-humoured reservations, these learned ushers presented handsome tributes. In fact, the eleven volumes provide one of the prettiest assortments of such bouquets ever brought together. When poor Drinkwater's turn came, as early as Volume IV, he was handicapped because the 'thunder of praise' had already been stolen by his predecessors. Everyone was pleased—most of all Thomas James Wise.

But it takes time to digest a feast such as he had put before his kings.

II

Wise's bibliographies of a few authors had given a good idea of the quality of his collection. Now that all his treasures were described under authors' names arranged alphabetically, a highly-coloured picture of the Ashley Library was presented. Very few great collectors—and Wise was one of the greatest—have been their own cataloguers. He did not make a very successful job of it. Apart from his judgments on major problems, his efforts to cope with Elizabethan typography reveal his limitations; some of the title-pages set out in the text, when compared with their reproduction in accompanying facsimile plates, show errors of transcription; the indexing is most faulty and inadequate. The collection deserved to have been catalogued by an expert, but in that case we should have missed many naïve revelations of the owner's character.

In accord with the Bible's unidealistic principle quoted at the head of this chapter, Wise was the recipient of many gifts of rarities and of presentation copies from authors. In some cases the donors were named in his catalogue; in others Wise is silent. Whatever the reason for acknowledging some gifts and not others, the discrimination is further witness to the way he conducted his actions, as he said, by his own ideas of right and wrong.

'A book which has been admitted, in equal terms, to this 'Valhalla,' wrote Dr R. W. Chapman when ushering in Vol. VII of the *Ashley Catalogue*, 'takes on something of the divinity of 'its surroundings. . . . It is in a fair way to being a collectors' 'book.' Perhaps it was in this large hope that certain authors were so lavish in sending him presentation copies of their writings. Even George Bernard Shaw, Wise's 'playboy' acquaintance of former Shelley Society days, joined in adding 'more abundance'. He wrote in a gift copy of *Saint Joan* (referring to a recent Academic honour bestowed on Wise): 'Worcester 'ought to make ME an honorary fellow for supplying you with 'so many crude attempts at my masterpieces.' But if every author who presented his 'crude attempts' had been so honoured, Worcester College would have had a surfeit of Hon. Fellows.

T. J. Wise

Pages (reduced) of two other letters from Wise to the author. In the one, the Faker—not the Forger—is the theme; in the other, wise shows his humour

Another G. B. S. 'masterpiece' was inscribed 'Hot from the press'; and another 'To T. J. Wise—absolutely the first copy' —conjuring up a picture of the impatient author waiting at the printer's for the first turn of the press, then hurrying with the ink-wet sheets to the folders and stitchers, to ensure that the Ashley Library got the *absolutely first* copies of the editions printed.[2] Nothing less than this could have assured the strict accuracy of Shaw's laughing claim.

Here it must be recorded that the highly-gratified and lauded collector-dealer was himself generous in presenting his own bibliographies and catalogues to those who had been, or might be, useful. If not all the recipients could be expected to use them as he hoped they would be used, he liked to have their recognition in full measure. One well-known author whom he named to me **** ******* 'did not seem to care, so I ceased sending him my books'. For ever after, the bibliographer spoke of that author in the most disparaging way.

Wise was not very tolerant—least of all outside his enthusiasms. For instance, he did not care for Anthony Trollope, and, unlike other collectors, refused to find a place in his library for a single book or manuscript of that author. His typical comment to me was that 'all the fuss about him is simply due to one man' —a singularly ungenerous reference to Michael Sadleir, Trollope's biographer and bibliographer, and also a shocking exhibition of ignorance.

III

A feature of Thomas James Wise's library was his method of rounding off a collection of an author's first editions by gathering all important books directly relating to them. These he called '-ana'. An example is that of the Shelley section, in which his Shelleyana, excluding documents, number approximately one hundred and fifty items. If there is anything in Dr Chapman's pleasant theory that the mere inclusion of a book in the Ashley Library made it partake of something of the greatness of Wise's illustrious editions, then the presentation copies of contem-

---

[2] They were mostly the author's private editions, as he himself has described (see page 35).

porary authors and the items constituting the considerable
'-ana' were indeed richly endowed.

These '-ana' became the fellows of Wise's superb Elizabethan
first editions, of his Popes, Drydens, Priors, and other authors
already mentioned here. They shared the glory of the only perfect copy of the second earliest English comedy, *Gammer gurton's
Nedle* (1575), of the best copy extant of Milton's *Comus* (1637);
of one of the two known copies of Dekker's *A Rod for Run-
awayes* (1625); of the only known copy of Pope's indecent
parody, *A Roman Catholick Version of the First Psalm. For the
Use of a Young Lady* (1716); of one of the two known copies of
Congreve's *An Impossible Thing* (1720)—the authorship of which
he claimed as his discovery; and of the only known copy of
Edward FitzGerald's first and suppressed book, *Casimir Dela-
vigne*.

But it is invidious to single out a few titles, or even authors.
An idea of what are the riches made known by the *Ashley Catalogue* can be conveyed more quickly by the following figures. Of
eighty-eight first editions described, thirty-seven are claimed by
Wise to be the only known copies; of eighteen, he claimed that
only one other copy of each was known; of ten, that only two
other copies of each were known; and of twenty-three, that less
than half-a-dozen copies of each were known. More important
still, of these rarities, fifty-eight were said to be not in the British
Museum Library. As to manuscripts, he had amassed over three
hundred; while the autograph letters in the Library, many of
the highest interest, ran into thousands.

Considering the importance of some of the Ashley books, and
also the doubts about others, it is regrettable that Wise did not
make a general practice of giving the provenance of his rarities.
And had he emulated the example of Narcissus Luttrell, the
seventeenth-century collector, in stating the prices he paid for
his books, what an astonishing difference would be revealed
between the cost of the collection and the estimated valuations
subsequently put on it. But to have given provenances and
prices would have been awkward in some cases, and especially
undesirable in the event of having to change his secret plan for
the ultimate destination of the library.

Some comparisons of the prices and ultimate values of individual items have already been given here. Walter T. Spencer, the bookseller, has recorded that the earliest book he remembered selling to Wise was a perfect copy of Keats's *Poems* (1817) for ten pounds—a work for another copy of which, years later, three hundred and eighty pounds was paid by the bookseller, who added: 'Mr Wise once chaffed me about his "bargain" 'over tea when I visited him and Mrs Wise at his charm- 'ing house in Hampstead. . . . To me he has always been a true friend.'

It has been shown, in the case of *Eastward hoe*, how Wise erred through not comparing his rarities with others. His reputation as a bibliographer, and therefore the authority of his catalogues and bibliographies, suffers because of his judgments and his prejudices in favour of his own copies. Of the two issues of Thomas Middle- ton's *A Trick to catch the Old-one* (1608) Wise claims his example to be the first issue of the first edition; and he alleges that the copies in the British Museum, the Bodleian, etc., are of the second issue. But Dr A. W. Pollard, one of the ablest Keepers of Printed Books the British Museum has had, objected (in the Introduc- tion to Vol. IX) to this classification, considering it probable that the two variant issues were produced simultaneously. This was not the only instance in which Wise's weakness for theorizing on behalf of his own specimens was shown up by Dr Pollard. It takes a clever trick to catch the old-ones.

Wise could be amazingly inconsistent—the greatest sin in a bibliographer. There was the question of proof sheets. In 1907, when Robert Louis Stevenson's works were being edited, it was left to Edmund Gosse to decide whether or not a drama, *The Hanging Judge* (which had been set up in type), should be included. The decision was against it. 'A few copies of the proofs, printed 'upon one side of the paper only, were preserved,' says Wise, adding: 'In recent years these proofs of 1907 have come into 'the market and have realized prices far above their worth.' These proofs were thus frowned upon because Wise himself produced a private pamphlet of *The Hanging Judge* (1914), describing it as the first edition.

But see how he veers round when he comes to collate a four- page item—Swinburne's *Russia: An Ode* (1890). 'Three or four 'proof copies only were struck off,' he says in his note, 'and of

'these but a single example is at present known to have sur-
'vived.' It is clear from Wise's further annotation that these were
only proofs, yet in this case his 'unique' copy is labelled a first
edition.

The *Ashley Catalogue* contains this: 'To suggest that the correc-
'tion of every trifling error made whilst a book is at press constitutes a fresh "issue" is childish: such emendations furnish
'"minor varieties" of a volume: they do not result in fresh issues.'
Yet it was precisely by such 'childish' arguments that he represented some of his copies as being rare first issues of first editions.

There are lapses in his notes, although Edmund Gosse
repeatedly saved him from committing howlers. Of Dante
Gabriel Rossetti and Swinburne meeting at Oxford in 1857 he
says: 'Their intercourse soon developed into a more than
'fraternal comradeship.' Elsewhere he speaks of something
written on each side of the 'page' when he meant 'leaf'. In his
Bibliography of Borrow, Wise describes two rare pamphlets—
Targum and *The Talisman*—printed by the novelist in St Peters-
burg; and says that in each case the reverse of the title-page
bears a Russian quotation. The fact is that these 'quotations' are
nothing more than the usual 'Imprimaturs' of the censor
demanded by Russian law. His ignorance of Russian is excusable.
But if they were quotations, as he hastily assumed, it would have
been interesting to discover what ones Borrow had used—as a
careful bibliographer would have done by reference to someone
knowing the Russian language.

His transcriptions of documents he possessed are generally
marked by inaccuracies. An example is that of the Dickens
letter to Leigh Hunt of 12 May 1840, in which he has

painter	for printer
eyes	„ ears
pocket	„ palm
okam engine	„ steam engine

IV

But the vagaries of his bibliographical and editorial methods
would require volumes in which to explore them. I have only

given some illustrative examples. With the publication of the *Ashley Catalogue* from 1922 onwards, Thomas James Wise became a celebrity in the book world. Soon followed the academic and other recognitions that were so dear to him. Before recording these, however, one other and little-known activity in his career deserves mention as showing his diversity of interests. In 1922 the firm of Edwin Healey & Co., postage stamp merchants in the City, became Healey and Wise, Ltd. The 'Wise' in the firm represented both Thomas James, who acquired a substantial share, and his younger brother, retired from the ranks of the Army. The dealer in and collector of rare books was no stranger in the trade catering for that other hobby —collecting stamps. Gorfin, after setting up as a bookseller, did a little side business in foreign stamps for the firm in which Wise and his brother were interested. He recalled many visits to the General Post Office to fetch parcels of stamps from Harry Buxton Forman for his former master.

In 1922 Wise became the president of the Bibliographical Society, holding that office for two years.

The year 1924 saw the bestowal on him of an Honorary Fellowship of Worcester College, Oxford.

In 1925 appeared his first and (as shown) inaccurate entry in *Who's Who*.

The year 1926 brought the crowning distinction when he was made an Honorary Master of Arts of Oxford University.

In 1927 he was elected a member of the Roxburghe Club (founded 1813), the most exclusive institution of book-collectors in the world.

After the death of Edmund Gosse, Wise did much towards making the sale of his library (1928–9) a success. He showed his commercial acumen in advising the insertion of autograph letters received by Gosse in relevant copies of their authors' books. The collection brought twenty-six thousand six hundred and fifteen pounds at Sotheby's.

In 1929 Wise made over to the Bibliographical Society his copyright in the Ashley catalogues and others of his bibliographical works. His membership of the Society dated from 1907; he was nominated to the Council in 1908, becoming vice-president in 1919.

In 1930 appeared the long *Strand* interview with the founder of the Ashley Library that has been quoted. The only point remaining to be noted is the statement: 'He clearly remembers 'his meeting with George Eliot.' Considering how fond Wise was of telling in print and conversation of his associations with Browning and Swinburne (whom he pestered for their recognitions of some of his forged pamphlets), it is remarkable that there is no other mention of this meeting with the authoress. It could only have taken place when Wise was twenty years of age, or earlier, and before he had got into the Browning and Shelley collecting circles. The claim is about as substantial as others he concocted. Here is another of the authors that was the subject of his specialization. The George Eliot *Brother and Sister* pamphlet, dated 1869, is now condemned as one of Wise's forgeries, having been manufactured about 1888. As late as 1910 he could sell a surplus stock of twenty-three copies to Gorfin, and a further copy in 1912. The George Eliot item *Agatha* (1869) is classed as one of Wise's suspected forgeries. He sold a copy to Wrenn as a first edition, and passed that description in the Wrenn Catalogue (1920); but he called it the second edition in his own. This is another pamphlet which he alleged was seen through the press by Buxton Forman on behalf of the writer— a claim not made, however, until Forman was dead. In this case also is the coincidence of Wise being able to sell a batch of nineteen copies to Gorfin in 1912. Compare these sales figures with the details he gave in a letter to Gosse, who was deluded into buying the *Brother and Sister*, and who preserved the letter in his copy as a certificate of value. It said that twenty-five copies only were produced of each of the things. No wonder scores of bookmen like Gosse were duped.[3]

From 1924 to 1931, Wise also issued a series of ten large catalogues descriptive of his individual collections of the books, manuscripts, and '-ana' of Shelley, Swinburne, Wordsworth and Coleridge (together), Byron, Conrad, Landor, the Brontës, the Brownings, Dryden, and Pope. In these there was the wealth of

[3] Another example of the publicizing through friends: 'She actually printed privately 'for her friends two little garlands, *Agatha* (1868) and *Brother and Sister* (1869), which are 'the only "rare issues" of hers sought after by collectors, for she was not given to biblio-'graphical curiosity.'—Edmund Gosse in his essay on George Eliot in the first number of the *London Mercury* (1919), and later included in *Aspects and Impressions* (1922).

commentary and description that characterizes his bibliographies and the library's eleven-volume catalogue. Indeed most of the material was the same, having been 'lifted' from the earlier works. The duplication has the effect of making his considerable contribution to the literature on books appear at first glance double what it was. Again he was fortunate in securing bookmen like Roger Ingpen, C. H. Wilkinson, & H. F. B. Brett-Smith, to write the introductions not supplied by himself. Particularly interesting is that of Mr Brett-Smith's to *A Pope Library* (1931), supplying this reminiscence: 'He [Wise] has been known to 'describe the library of a famous collector of the last century, in 'the words of Charles Lamb, as a "ragged regiment".' It is not necessarily the prettiest regiment that provides the best soldiers. There was no room in the crack Ashley Regiment for the old warrior such as Lamb described, which reads the better because we know 'the topography of its blots and dog's ears and can 'trace the dirt in it to having read it at Tea with buttered 'muffins, or over a Pipe, which I think is the maximum'. Wise's conversational disparagement referred to that worthy scholar in eighteenth-century literature, G. A. Aitken. The story becomes more pointed with the explanation that both the Ashley and the Wrenn Libraries owed much to Aitken.

CHAPTER 19

BYRON ROMANTICS

As for the ladies, I have nought to say,
A wanderer from the British world of fashion,
Where I, like other 'dogs, have had my day',
Like other men, too, may have had my passion—
But that, like other things, has pass'd away,
And all her fools whom I could *lay the lash on:*
Foes, friends, men, women, now are nought to me
But dreams of what has been, no more to be.

Don Juan: 2, CLXVI

I

WISE'S PARTIALITY for what are called 'human documents' has been shown. He glowed with the passions of his heroes; his books flourished on their frailties. Of all his 'divine sinners', none fascinated him more than Lord Byron, whose scandals (as he hinted when in the depth of them) would be the more devoured the more they were damned. And it was while Wise was immersed in the bibliography of Byron that he chanced on what he insisted was an unknown love affair of the poet's, complete with baby.

Byron and his Julias and his Haidees are beyond the barb of scandal. They are deep in the slumber that wakes to no fresh gust of surging passion. But a new draught of the old intoxicating wine could add flavour to the *Byron Bibliography* and the *Ashley Library Catalogue*. It was sampled by Wise for his first volume of the *Catalogue* in 1922. That taste muddled him then—as we shall see. It was not until 1931, however, that the wine went to his head.

It had come from the well-stocked bins of Harry Buxton Forman's library. One evening, years back, while browsing among Forman's books, Wise found a red-clothed volume entitled *The Unpublished Letters of Lord Byron*: edited by H. S. Schultess-

Young, issued by Richard Bentley & Son, Publishers in Ordinary to Her Majesty, 1872. Unpublished letters of Byron? Issued by Bentley? Never heard of? It was a bolt from the blue to him who prided himself that he knew Byron's bibliography from the poet's first essay, the *Fugitive Pieces* of 1806, to the last of the many piracies of his *Don Juan*.

Now Forman, keen book-hunter that he was, knew this to be a volume of rarity and potentiality.[1] So Wise realized. For him how potential! They had one of their usual deals. Forman, who had bought it at the gift price of four guineas from Bertram Dobell (what days those were!), took a nice margin of profit; and still Wise bought cheaply. Thus the book found itself transferred to the Ashley Library. Its heady wine had to mature a little longer before the great libation.

II

It is necessary here to tell a tale within a tale—a romance of publishing. About 1872 a bright young fellow of twenty, by name Schultess-Young, went to Richard Bentley, and arranged with him to produce the *Unpublished Letters of Lord Byron*. These copies of letters derived from two aunts of the young man— Miss Julia Puddicombe, of Bovey Tracey, near Torquay, and a Mrs Clark, 'of Scroop House' [place not stated]. Of these ladies it would be most desirable to have further knowledge. Remarkably enough, the enthusiastic editor was able to inscribe his volume, by permission, to Mrs Thérèse Black, 'the Maid of Athens'—his 'sincere and obliged friend'. What a link! She, the fourteen-year-old beauty, of whom Byron had written:

> *Maid of Athens, ere we part,*
> *Give, oh give me back my heart!*
> *Or, since that has left my breast,*
> *Keep it now, and take the rest!*
> *Hear my vow before I go,*
> *Ζωή μου, σᾶς ἀγαπῶ.*

[1] The British Museum Library was lacking a copy until 1937, when it acquired the Ashley Library.

A notable book truly. No doubt Richard Bentley, Publisher in Ordinary to Her Majesty, felt a secret pride in producing such a valuable contribution to Byron literature, and scoring against his friendly rival, John Murray the Fourth, grandson of the poet's famous publisher. But while the printing-press was turning out the momentous book, Bentley struck a horrid snag. He discovered that some of the letters had already been printed, the Murray copyright in them having expired, and that others—new ones—had been obtained from one of the aunts without permission to use them. Moreover, nineteen others were spurious—the work of the notorious forger De Gibler, who about 1848 declared himself to be an illegitimate son of the poet.

As a man of honour, jealous for his high reputation, Bentley immediately stopped publication. Eventually, of the edition of seven hundred and fifty copies (of which half had already been bound), seven hundred and forty were destroyed; and into pulp went the youthful tribute of Schultess-Young to the now fading beauties of 'the Maid of Athens'. Thus, of his ill-begotten book, which is nevertheless a work of great interest, only ten copies were preserved of the entire edition; and of these, one came by way of Harry Buxton Forman to ensnare Thomas James Wise, the ardent bibliographer of Byron.

III

Wise, describing the book for the first volume of his *Catalogue*[2] (1922), quoted from Schultess-Young two passages from a series of seventeen letters to 'dearest L——' that the editor had copied from the documents of one of the aunts.

This was practically the first revelation of the 'dearest L——' love affair in the life of Byron.[3] But there were features about both it and the Schultess-Young book that perplexed Wise, and called for inquiry. He must go into this new scandal more thoroughly when he came to compile the *Bibliography of Byron* he had so long projected, and which was to conclude his biblio-

---

[2] Repeating the details in *A Byron Library* (1928).
[3] Though Bertram Dobell had contributed a short note about the Schultess-Young book to *Notes & Queries*, 14 November 1891.

graphies. It should be a two-volume work: the last word on the subject. But the 'last word' in bibliography is never final.

It was in 1931 that Wise again began to study the alleged letters of Byron to 'dearest L——'. In the whole seventeen, which date from 2 August 1811 to 1 August 1817, there is only one passage which can with certainty be said to mention a child as the result of their 'imprudence'.

This passage is given by Wise with two other quotations all run together as if the three were from one letter. I here give the three extracts, more fully and correctly, under their respective dates:

St James's St: Oct 30. 1811

Dearest L——,

I do not understand your letter or your quotations but only know that I *love* you, and you know I shall never marry you, for which you have reason to be thankful. I wonder whom I shall espouse, for I must take up the conjugal *cross* some day, and perpetuate the name of Byron better than by my rhymes. I sent you a copy of the *Childe* which you have never acknowledged. . . .

St James's St [no date]

. . . When I leave England I will not forget the things you ask for, and regret that you cannot accompany me, which is impossible, not for the sake of my character, but yours. . . .

Feb. 29, 1813

Dear L——,

What do you mean by *ungrateful?* I am not, who ever of your acquaintance may be, but am damned and dunned to death by Christians and creditors, though God knows, I am bad and poor enough; but I did not expect you to be implacable. The child ***** is dead, and I do not regret it, though a bastard Byron is better than no Byron. You are about the only woman who has caused me a remorseful moment; and when I say I am sorry for our mutual imprudence (to say nothing else), I do not express the compunction I feel. . . .[4]

These were the kind of 'human documents' that highly stimulated Wise. But he must investigate. Now, the first place to which the researcher naturally turns in such a case is the House of Murray, 50 Albemarle Street, where are fascinating relics just

---

[4] The asterisks in this extract are from Schultess-Young, and apparently indicate excisions.

as Byron left them, and also archives of inestimable literary value.
The courtesy of the successive Murrays to the researcher is
famous. Their House has become almost as much a national
institution as the British Museum.

Sir John Murray, the fifth John, responded promptly to Wise's
appeal, and was able to refer to the late Richard Bentley, son of
the publisher who had so drastically suppressed the *Unpublished
Letters*. There ensued among the three parties a correspondence
that has something of the flavour of the Delicate Investigation
into the conduct of Queen Caroline. In the course of two-and-a-
half months this Wise-Murray-Bentley correspondence totalled
between two and three hundred pages. It is lively witness alike
to the kindness and substantial help accorded to the bibliographer
and to his own persistence.

Sir John Murray took the view that the letters to 'dearest
'L——' were suspect. Wise argued (sometimes at the rate of
two letters a day) that they were so Byronic, had so much realism
in them, that such a young man as Schultess-Young could not
have invented them. Briefly, he was prepared to accept them
as based upon genuine letters, but crudely castrated—manip-
ulated so as to prevent identification of the aunt from whom
they were obtained.[5] There is a hint of Wise's psychology in
classing the young editor with the poor banished insects in
Shelley's *Sensitive Plant*:

> . . . .*whose intent,*
> *Although they did ill, was innocent*

and for his part, were he the Schultess-Young of eighty (Wise
assured Sir John Murray) he would not be ashamed of having
been the Schultess-Young of twenty. He would merely regard
himself as having been very foolish.

Sir John Murray, steeped in the traditions of a family so linked
with English bards and Scotch reviewers, and gallantly true to
his forebears' loyalty to Byron, did not like Wise's quotation of
isolated passages from the letters. 'Why emphasize Byron's
worst qualities?' he asked. He persisted in his belief that the
letters to 'L——' were suspect, and read like the forgeries of

---

[5] This was pure theorizing. The aunt, as also her documents, was then, and remains, a
mystery.

'The Shelleyites found themselves in debt. . . . There ensued a most unphilosophical row' (Chapter 5)

'Wise hit on what he insisted was a new love-affair of Byron's, complete with baby' (Chapter 19)

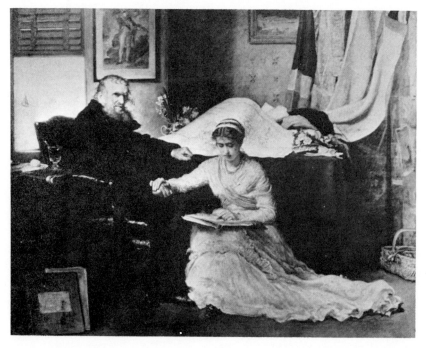

'That hardy adventurer Trelawny was still "walking the earth without greatcoat, stockings, or underclothing, this Christmas"' (Chapter 2).— Here he is in Millais's *North-West Passage* (Tate Gallery), posing at the age of over 80 as the old sea-captain

De Gibler. And he made a shrewd hit with the point that not one of the originals had come to light. That is a significant circumstance, considering how well the poet's correspondence has been preserved.

Yet Wise argued on—insistent but tactful. As to the 'bastard' 'Byron better than no Byron' phrase, he pointed out that 'bastard' was a favourite word with the poet; who often spoke of his daughter Allegra as 'my little bastard', or 'the little bastard'. So the controversy went on behind the scenes; and the proofs of the troublesome pages passed backwards and forwards, corrected and recorrected, revised and re-revised; until the day came when the three correspondents were more or less agreed—in differing. Wise wrote a joking postscript, conjecturing what a pleasant time the printer's clerk would have marking up his bill for 'corrections'!

And the oddest thing of all was Bentley's comment at the end of this Delicate Investigation: 'Curious that Wise, Forman,[6] 'and Schultess-Young, should—the three—happen to be living 'very near each other.'

IV

So Wise had his way. A few months later, in 1933, the second volume of his *Bibliography of Byron* came out—complete with the isolated quotations from the letters to 'L——':[7] the poet 'damned', as he was wont to say, with a new scandal, and fathered on another bastard.

But are the letters to 'L——' genuine? Here are some examples of discrepancies that, weighed together, are sufficient to condemn the letters. Those that show date discrepancies are instances of how easily a forger might err through over-confidence in his knowledge:

(1) In the alleged letter to 'L——', dated 30 October 1811, he speaks of having sent a copy of the *Childe* which had never

6 Maurice Buxton Forman, son of Harry Buxton Forman. He had lately retired from the Postal Service in South Africa; and did some research for Wise into the mystery of Schultess-Young's aunts. Schultess-Young died on 2 May 1933, aged eighty-three.

7 After having assured Sir John Murray that he would not dream of printing an opinion in disaccordance with his on the subject.

been acknowledged. Perhaps for good reason. *Childe Harold* was not published until 29 February 1812. Even by 17 November 1811, only a portion of the first Canto of the poem had been printed.

(2) There are unlikely references to Byron's leaving England. One is in the second extract from an undated letter, which Schultess-Young placed between correspondence dated 18 January 1812, and 2 February 1813. An earlier letter (30 November 1811) says: 'As I should be sorry not to see you again, I 'will give you a flying visit before I again leave England.' But Byron had only returned from his Grand Tour in July 1811. And he could not have been anticipating the flight of 1816, because he was not then married.

(3) Augusta Leigh was very much in Byron's mind at the time of the separation from his wife. He was her constant correspondent, and keeping a journal for her.

(4) The first of the alleged letters to 'L——', addressed from Venice, is dated 10 November 1816. But Byron did not arrive in Venice until the night of 11 November 1816.[8]

(5) On his arrival in Venice, disturbing news of Lady Byron's intention to take their daughter out of England awaited him; and his first urgent care was to instruct his solicitor to stop the move.

(6) Almost immediately on his arriving in Venice he was love-making with the libidinous Marianna Segati.

(7) While we know Byron could write cynically enough about his love-affairs to his friends (often as a pose), there is a want of gallantry in these letters that would hardly be expected—if they were really written to 'about the only woman who has caused 'me a remorseful moment'.

(8) In the letter of 2 January 1817, Byron is made to say 'you will not accept money from *me*. That cursed pride of yours 'will ruin you one day.' Yet the next epistle says her 'letters are 'full of complaints about your station, your poverty, and myself'. There is inconsistency here.

(9) In none of the letters or journals of Byron is there reference to a mistress named 'L——', notwithstanding his habit of discussing and recording his love-affairs.

---

[8] See Hobhouse's *Recollections of a Long Life*.

(10) Wise's only argument to support the authenticity of the letters to 'L——' is their Byronic language and cynicism. But the forger De Gibler had sufficient ability to imitate the poet's manner of writing, and plenty of material to derive from.

Bearing these things in mind, and remembering Sir John Murray's further argument that not a single one of the originals has come to light, Wise's judgment in so confidently accepting them as genuine lays him open to criticism. And, considering that he had consulted Sir John Murray and received so often his opinion that the letters were suspect, it is surprising that there is no disclosure of the dissentient view, which ought to have been recorded, however much it might have been disavowed.

His enthusiams for 'dearest L——' and her baby had this sequel. In 1930 a firm of New York publishers produced in elaborate style a book entitled *Seventeen Letters of George Noel Gordon Lord Byron to an Unknown Lady 1811–17*. They were the letters to 'dearest L——'. And Wise, in his eleventh and last volume of the *Ashley Library Catalogue* (1936), sniffily called it 'this sensational book'—this from the man who had been responsible for its being seized upon as sensational.

V

In the latter part of Wise's career his reputation for unmasking the evil-doings of forgers and fakers became something of an obsession with him. This is not to be wondered at considering the admiration excited by his successes as a bibliographical detective. In 1931, for example, he was the means of exposing a forged Charlotte Brontë manuscript (which would have involved her integrity if it had been genuine), and also a faked Shelley association first edition of *Queen Mab* (with signature and important annotations purporting to be by the poet, but really the work of De Gibler).[9] Both of these items would have sold for very high prices in the salerooms had it not been for his intervention. It must be emphasized that his keen perception combined with wide knowledge were often most effective in spotting fraudulent 'rarities'. But these activities were not

[9] For my accounts of both see the American *Bookman* for May and July 1931.

always successful or wholly admirable. There was a remarkable instance in this same year that throws much light on his methods and motives.

A firm of London booksellers sent him on approval a copy of *The Giaour* (1813), on paper water-marked 1805, that did not bear the name of the author Lord Byron, and that they described as 'undoubtedly the earliest issue of the first edition, 'hitherto unrecorded'. As such it was of the highest importance to Wise—not only as a rarity for his library, but also as affording him the opportunity of announcing its discovery in his forth-coming two-volume *Bibliography of Byron*. But was it that, he asked himself?

He had to accept as genuine the sheets carrying the letterpress. But he came to the conclusion that it was 'hardly possible' for this to be an example of an earlier edition than the accepted first edition bearing the poet's name, advanced various arguments why Byron and his publisher John Murray would not have issued this particular poem anonymously, and decided that the copy before him was that of an unauthorized edition

produced for his own benefit by the printer, T. Davison, whose conscience must have been as elastic as were the consciences of Caw-thorne, Ridge, and Sherwin, each of whom is known to have followed the same dishonest practice.

Thus judged Wise. Abbreviating a long and involved story, all these conclusions were found, by reference to Sir John Murray's Albemarle Street archives, to be wrong. The copy proved to be the earliest printing of the poem, to the title-page of which the author's name was subsequently added: the claim of the booksellers was substantiated. Thus the despised infidel is now promoted to the place of honour—first in the bibliography of the poem.

But before this result ensued, Wise noticed that the copy was bound in wrappers which he alleged were of modern brown paper; and he also said that the end-papers were not the original ones: 'What immediately excited my suspicion . . . was the fact 'that the book was obviously in Faked Wrappers.' Here was a stick with which to whack the booksellers, as was now his habit whenever chance offered: he laid it on heavily. The firm's chief replied with frankness and serenity that the copy, when they acquired it, was bound in new half-calf covers which they replaced by 'the wrappers you now find on it. These came from 'a later edition of the poem and are contemporary.' Reasons were then given justifying the firm's claim for the priority of the book —reasoning much more impressive than Wise's had been against it.

Wise was not readily turned from his views either on the book's relation to the accepted first edition or on the question of the wrappers. He wrote a long account of the matter that he intended should be sent to the Press as another exposure, and should also add excitement and glory to his Bibliography of Byron. This account constituted a damaging attack on the book-sellers, and contained some glaring misrepresentations of facts. But it was more damaging to Thomas James Wise, for he con-tradicted himself—as when he began by asserting that the book had been offered to him 'as uncut in the original wrappers', and later on tried to cover himself against this wilful misstatement by admitting that the booksellers 'did not say in so many words 'that the wrappers were "original"'. He also convicted himself of insincerity when he said: 'That Messrs —— acted in good 'faith cannot be questioned. The honoured name under the 'shelter of which the firm conducts its business precludes any 'suspicion of dishonest intent'—marginating this sneer with the subsequent comment: '****** will not see the bulge in my cheek 'where the tongue curls.' Nevertheless, he had some qualms about his publicity design, and determined to get the advice of others before proceeding with the alleged exposure.

So this document was at once circulated among at least four friends, three of them eminent in literature and bibliography. The first to reply was ******** ******, who hailed him 'God 'be with thee, little David', and compared the trade to 'a very 'Goliath and a Hydra to boot'; shied at pronouncing on the issue (either because of his official position, or for some other ungiven reason); and sought an invitation for himself and his wife to spend another of those 'jolly evenings'[10] with the

[10] He was not the only one to pass such evenings in the Ashley Library and listen to Wise's rattling talk. Following a like occasion, another well-known man wrote to Dear Tom: '. . . I hope I did not tire you last night? I enjoyed myself immensely, and came 'home laden with treasure. I find I have not got . . .' naming some of Wise's printings. Had he rubbed the gilt off these gingerbreads, he would have been aghast to find among his mementoes of the jolly evening were some fraudulent nineteenth-century pamphlets manufactured by the genial host.

collector-dealer. It certainly was a further case where 'little David' needed to be saved from himself and possibly also from getting into a public mess. This letter was hardly what he wanted, pleasantly biblical and adulatory as it might be to him. But the other three experts, in the kindliness of friendship, were more helpful. While agreeing with Wise about the wrappers—i.e., on the facts he stated; for they did not see them—these correspondents gently advised him against seeking publicity for his indictment; showed the weaknesses of his case, especially the 'good faith' admission; and pointed out the risk of an action-at-law against him by the booksellers.

In the face of such unanimity of disinterested counsel, Wise abandoned his plans—both as regards publicity for the affair and also the use of this damaging document in his Byron *Bibliography*. He had cause to rejoice that he had been restrained, for in the meantime the Murray archives had proved that the book, originally belittled by him, was what the booksellers had claimed for it. The issue about the wrappers remained an open one: they no longer existed to clear it up. It is curious—considering Wise circulated a number of influential bookmen to the detriment of the firm, and left behind such a dossier[11]—that instead of preserving the book as acquired he destroyed the wrappers, the part cause of the trouble, and had it rebound in the inevitable levant morocco.

The final light on this affair is that Wise made use of it to beat the booksellers (wholly vindicated in their claim for the item's priority) down to half the price they originally asked (i.e., from one hundred pounds to fifty pounds) for a rarity which in the end he described as 'believed to be unique', and which provided him with one of the most interesting of the Byron discoveries credited to him and revealed in his *Bibliography* of the poet.

VI

One other tale to close this chapter of Byron romantics. In the *Bibliography of Byron* (Vol. I) is described a copy of the second

[11] This dossier of thirty-five documents, including Wise's suppressed indictment in MS., the correspondence indicated, and even his paid and cancelled cheque for the rarity, are among the papers of the author.

authorized edition of his *English Bards and Scotch Reviewers*. Wise says it was a gift to him from Sir Sydney Cockerell, the former curator of the Fitzwilliam Museum, Cambridge. This copy of *English Bards* contains the following inscription:

> Byron—Athens—at Theodora Macri's—January 1810. Sun shining Grecianly—Lemon trees in front of the house full of fruit—damn the book! Give me Nature and two eyes opposite.

Now, Theodora Macri was the Vice-Consul's widow, with whom the poet lodged when a young man of twenty-two in old Athens. The 'eyes opposite' would be those of her daughter— the same 'Maid of Athens' to whom reference has already been made as Mrs Thérèse Black, the dedicatee of Schultess-Young's birth-strangled *Unpublished Letters*. An inscription like that, when in Byron's writing, and linking it with those tender love-filled days of 1810, made it the kind of ensouled treasure for which collectors grow sentimental and pay fat cheques.

But the sad truth must be told. The inscription is a forgery of De Gibler again. The rascal!

Yet when Wise was first shown this 'desirable' association item by Sir Sydney Cockerell, he was enchanted with it. Both the script and the matter of the inscription deceived him; and he promptly offered one hundred pounds to call the darling his. Sir Sydney Cockerell, however, being doubtful about its genuineness, declined the offer. Later, on further investigation, his doubts were confirmed. And in the end he presented Wise with the thing as a clever example of the forger's art.

But, just as Homer nowhere admits that he ever nodded, so we may look in vain for any admission by Wise in his catalogue notes that he was so deceived as to offer one hundred pounds for this Byron fake. Seven days out of any week he would have scouted the possibility of his being misled by a Byron forgery of De Gibler's. Was he not equally misled by the Byronic colour and style of the letters to 'dearest L——'?

CHAPTER 20

THE PRETTY TANGLE OF MRS BROWNING'S LOVE SONNETS UNTANGLED

This Brat, to him that got it, I return;
Or, to the Parish, where the same was born;
Lest half the misbegotten in the Town,
To finde a father, at my doore be throwne,
   Writ by the Knave of Spades, or by his Clerk,
   And publisht by the Devil in the Dark.
                    Major Wither's Disclaimer (1647)

I

THAT WISE should be deceived by one of De Gibler's Byron frauds is strange, for his acquaintance with that clever rogue's art was considerable. The builder of the Ashley Library had come to be regarded as the final court of appeal in matters connected with book-collecting. He was generally looked up to as a great judge—one without the least commercial bias—a ruthless enemy of all forgers and fakers. Of his ferocious intolerance of any book or manuscript suspected of coming from their hands I had more experience than ever from 1931 to 1933, when he passed on to me information about such things. His repeated encouragements to me to 'block the path of the forger' and his zeal to assist were most impressive.

But what of his own secret forgeries? Had those offences become metamorphosed and innocent in the crowded hour of success and adulation? Or was his fierce righteousness a self-goading to drown the whisper of conscience? Or was it a gesture, a superb piece of acting, to bolster his reputation against the day of judgment? Forgotten they could hardly be—those rare little pamphlets by the Brownings, Kipling, Ruskin, R. L. Stevenson, Swinburne, Tennyson, and the rest.

The day of judgment? He had seen the writing on the wall after the *Athenæum* exposures in 1898, and again but more forbodingly when Cook and Wedderburn did their duty by Ruskin. More recently there had been Watts-Dunton's threat of denunciation, and Mrs Livingston's probing and querying. Luckily for him, one had been frightened; the other had not gone deep enough. But there again had been the disposition to question— to question him, Thomas James Wise, the leading collector and bibliographer of his day! Who else might be probing, investigating? How long before some determined researcher came across those damning pages in the thirty-nine volumes of Ruskin's Collected Works?

Such questions as these he perhaps often asked himself. Whatever fears he may have had, they were soon confirmed. The sword over him was now hanging by a thread.

II

On the 12th of October 1933, he received a visit from 'a 'young man named Pollard, who fired at me a string of questions 'about some pamphlets', and a day or two later sent a typed questionnaire. This was the gist of the matter as related to me by Wise shortly afterwards. The brief account was not complimentary to the visitor, and was vague—circumstances I put down to the extreme irritability which Wise appeared to be suffering. As he was then recovering from an illness, the subject was not pursued. His agitation was unmistakable.

Well it might be. It was his first *direct* intimation (as I subsequently learned) that his spurious nineteenth-century pamphlets were being subjected to investigation.

He had not seen Herbert Gorfin for some years. Their association had steadily waned, as Wise's fame grew and after the duplicity over those Landors in 1914. By 1923 it had entirely ceased. Now, after the disturbing interview with Graham Pollard, he had a pressing desire to renew the old friendship. He acted promptly. Gorfin must be found at once. Urgent letters (one in duplicate to different addresses) were sent to Lewisham, but failed to bring immediate response. In desperation to get hold of the partner of past deals, Mrs Wise even journeyed by hired motor-car to Lewisham, only to find he had left that place.

However, the quarry was soon run to earth: the inviting letters and telegrams reached him on the 16th and 18th of October. There was an urgent matter to discuss. It affected Gorfin a great deal, and himself slightly, urged Wise. He was anxious for his former assistant to come to tea. But the sudden hospitality availed little: the cups neither cheered Wise nor inebriated Gorfin, who knew what was coming after tea better than did his former Lord-and-Master-of-the-Outer-Office at old Hermann Rubeck's. It was too late now even for the consummate diplomatist.

Later in the autumn of 1933, he—accompanied by his wife, who remained in the waiting-room—called on Cecil Clay at the firm's London office. The interview between the managing director of the printing firm and its old client took place in the board room. They were alone. Wise soon came to the subject of the investigations into the pamphlets. Clay knew all about them now. The revelations had naturally come as a great surprise to him. His firm had facilitated the typographical researches of Carter and Pollard, but most unfortunately had not been able to give them just the information that would have revealed the forger's identity.[1]

Clay, describing the interview, gave me the following verbatim report of what was said. It is highly important. I quote his exact words, a copy of which he subsequently confirmed as accurate:

> Wise referred to 'those monstrous fellows' and asked: 'Can't you 'say you had nothing to do with these things',—meaning the pamphlets.
> I replied: 'How can I when you know we printed them for you. 'Aren't you rather giving yourself away?'

After this plain indication of the attitude of Clays, the interview quickly came to an end, and Wise returned to his library, to read and re-read what he had said in his books about these damned pamphlets which now threatened to blast his success. In particular, he turned to the long and romantic stories he had gathered round one of them—Mrs Browning's *Sonnets* (Reading:

[1] '. . . They [Messrs Clay & Sons] admitted readily enough the facts . . . proved that 'they had printed the pamphlets. But they were unable to give us any conclusive clue to 'the identity of their client, because they had preserved no ledgers earlier than 1911— 'nor is there any reason to suppose that anyone in their employ was privy to the fraud.' *An Enquiry, op. cit.* See also footnote 10, page 91 here.

1847)—because either he had been informed or had guessed that this one would occupy the key position in the impending attack.

III

Of the group of mysterious pamphlets which Wise had so desperately urged his printers to disavow, the purported Reading: 1847 edition of her love-inspired *Sonnets* had always been the most highly prized—alike for its rarity and for the famous story behind it. This story has long been known as 'a very pretty episode of literary history', the description of it by the teller himself, Edmund Gosse. In the light of other treatment of it and information, a truer description would be 'a very pretty tangle of literary history'. It is of interest to straighten out the tangle. Because here we have the most glaring example of Wise's opportunism—the masterpiece of his career of bamboozlement.

The sonnets were written by Elizabeth Barrett while she lay on her invalid's couch during the clandestine courtship which ended in the elopement with and wedding to Robert Browning in 1846. These events have become familiarized (and often over-sentimentalized in the case of Robert) as the romance of *The Barretts of Wimpole Street*—a romance more one-sided, it might be argued, than is popularly believed. Tender and varied are the manifestations of woman in her love-passion: awe-inspiring in their most exquisite raptures. But she is more concerned that the Adored behold understandingly than that he be awed. It is she who will enfold the passion in a cocoon of reverence if the lover but feed the flame. How well Elizabeth divined the wonder of it all as she put her secret thoughts into the sonnets:

> Say over again and yet once over again
> That thou dost love me. Though the word repeated
> Should seem "a cuckoo song," as thou dost treat it,
> Remember never to the hill or plain,
> Valley and wood, without her cuckoo-strain,
> Comes the fresh Spring in all her green completed.

But the time came when she wanted Robert to know how she had expressed in verse those dear feelings. Perhaps she felt the

eternal feminine need of assurance that he still beheld understandingly. It is the one reiteration of which woman never tires:
the litany of love.

There are several accounts of how Elizabeth's sonnets came to
the eyes of her Beloved. The best known is that by Gosse, made
public first in 1894, and printed again in 1896 in his *Critical
Kit-Kats*. He averred that it came with the authority and at the
desire of Browning, the circumstances having been related by
the poet to a friend (i.e., himself: a mystification which has con-
founded not a few) for future use. Gosse began his episode by
recalling that the love-sonnets 'were first given to the public'
in the 1850 edition of Elizabeth's *Poems in two volumes* where
they were styled *Sonnets from the Portuguese*—a disguising title
which it was mistakenly thought would divert attention from
their personal character. Here is the main part of the Gosse
account, omitting for the moment its unfortunate conclusion:

'. . . During the months of their brief courtship, closing, as all the
'world knows, in the clandestine flight and romantic wedding of
'September 12th, 1846, neither poet showed any verses to the other.
'Mr Browning, in particular, had not the smallest notion that the
'circumstances of their betrothal had led Miss Barrett into any artistic
'expression of feeling. As little did he suspect it during their honey-
'moon in Paris, or during their first crowded weeks in Italy. They
'settled, at length, in Pisa; and being quitted by Mrs Jamieson and
'her niece, in a very calm and happy mood the young couple took up
'each his or her separate literary work.

'Their custom was, Mr Browning said, to write alone, and not to
'show each other what they had written. This was a rule which he
'sometimes broke through, but she never. He had the habit of working
'in a downstairs room, where their meals were spread, while Mrs
'Browning studied in a room on the floor above. One day, early in
'1847, their breakfast being over, Mrs Browning went upstairs, while
'her husband stood at the window watching the street till the table
'should be cleared. He was presently aware of someone behind him,
'though the servant was gone. It was Mrs Browning, who held him
'by the shoulder to prevent his turning to look at her, and at the same
'time pushed a packet of papers into the pocket of his coat. She told
'him to read that, and to tear it up if he did not like it; and then she
'fled again to her room.

'Mr Browning seated himself at the table, and unfolded the parcel.

'It contained the series of sonnets which have now become so illus-
'trious. As he read, his emotion and delight may be conceived. Before
'he had finished it was impossible for him to restrain himself, and,
'regardless of his promise, he rushed upstairs, and stormed that
'guarded citadel. He was early conscious that these were treasures not
'to be kept from the world; "I dared not reserve to myself," he said,
'"the finest sonnets written in any language since Shakespeare's."
'But Mrs Browning was very loth indeed to consent to the publication
'of what had been the very notes and chronicle of her betrothal. . . .'

Another account[2] is by Dr F. J. Furnivall:

'Mrs Browning's *Sonnets* to her husband. She wrote these in London.
'One day she timidly hinted to Browning that she'd tried to express her
'feelings about him. He answered that he didn't think people should
'wear their hearts on their sleeves for daws to peck at, or something of
'the kind. This shut her up. When abroad she was one day late in put-
'ting on her bonnet to walk with him. He cald to her. Spying about,
'he saw a tiny roll of paper on her looking-glass or table, pounst on
'it, and said, "What's this?" unrolling it the while. "Only something
'"I wrote about you, & you frightened me from showing it to you,"
'said she.* And in her next edition the *Sonnets from the Portuguese* were
'printed.
    '* He told me this himself.'

These two accounts are as far apart in their divergence and
implications as the tropics from the North Pole. Whether Gosse
re-told in an artificial story what Browning related to him, or
whether the poet gave him the more romantic version he generally favoured, may never be known. It is comprehensible that
Browning would be explicit with the older friend who was so
useful to him, who founded the Society of adorers, and who compiled the first bibliography of his works. Furnivall tended to be
grimly realistic whether in literary history or in biography—
as witness his refusal to have Browning's footman ancestor kept
secret. Anyhow, his terse recital suggests that there was indeed
a time when Robert did not behold understandingly: when the
sensitive and ardent Elizabeth was rebuffed. The Beloved himself confessed as much several times: once to Leigh Hunt to
whom he wrote from Bagni di Lucca (6 October 1857): '. . . They
'[the Sonnets] were shown to me at this very place eight years

2 Corrections, etc. (for Sharp's *Life of Browning*, 1890).

'ago, in consequence of some word of mine, just as they had
'been suppressed thro' some mistaken word. . . .' Then again,
to Julia Wedgwood, wealthy spinster confidant, in 1864: 'Yes,
'that was a strange, heavy crown, that wreath of Sonnets, put
'on me one morning unawares, three years after it had been
'twined—all this delay, because I happened early to say some-
'thing against putting one's loves into verse: then again, I said
'something else on the other side, one evening at Lucca,—and
'next morning she said hesitatingly "Do you know I once wrote
'"some poems about *you*?"—and then—"There they are, if you
'"care to see them. . . ."' Browning's confession was made again
in 1881 in a letter to Dr Peter Bayne:[3] '. . . The "sonnets" were
'only known to exist, and seen for the first time by the person
'to whom they were addressed [i.e., to himself] two or three years
'after the writer's marriage. The reticency came from some mis-
'understood remark which seemed to doubt the depth and sin-
'cerity of such feelings so exhibited in verse. Fortunately some
'other long subsequent conversation did more justice to an
'exceptional case: and the next morning the writer said "Do
'"you know I once wrote some verses to you?" This was at
'Bagni di Lucca, after the birth of her child, a few months
'before. . . .'
Now these passages from Browning's letters also prove that
he first saw Elizabeth's love-poems in 1849 at Bagni di Lucca
when they were in manuscript. But what of Gosse's story
'coming with the authority of Browning', that the famous
incident of the young wife's shy gift occurred at Pisa in 1847?
How did he come to err on such an important point? This part
of the mystery may be untangled thus:
Gosse, frequently careless as to facts, was mistaken as to the
place—possibly owing to previous reference to Elizabeth's disclosure of her poems being made at Pisa; and put the date 1847
because the poets left there in April of that year.[4] For there was
extant a letter of Elizabeth's to Robert dated 22 July 1846, a

[3] See *The Times* Literary Supplement (15 November 1934).
[4] Gosse's version—especially when compared with the whole of Browning's to Miss
Wedgwood—reads as if written up on rather slight data, and that he originally believed
it occurred at Pisa. But even if he once had the facts right and subsequently altered them
to fit Wise's new information, this does not implicate him in the production of the Reading
pamphlet.

few months before the marriage, that promised him 'you shall
'see some day at Pisa what I will not show you now'[5]—a hint
at the revelation of her love-poems that actually was made later
when they moved to Bagni di Lucca. The Pisa error was first
printed by William Sharp in his *Life of Browning* (1890): he said
'It was here in Pisa, as I have been told on indubitable authority,
'that Browning first saw in manuscript those *Sonnets*. . .'[6]

These references were most probably known to Wise. It so
happened that in 1893 Gosse issued a catalogue of his library
which describes the 1850 edition of Mrs Browning's *Poems* as the
first in which the sonnets appeared; so it is a fair inference
that when the catalogue was compiled he knew nothing of the
'1847' pamphlet of them. But the forgery was certainly in print
before June 1893 (as is indicated by his letter presently to be
quoted); and Wise was only waiting the suitable moment
for the 'discovery' of it—to be followed by the customary
elaborate propaganda. As Gosse in the following year—viz.
1894—was to surprise the world with Browning's relation (in
the preface to Dent's issue of the *Sonnets*) of the 'pretty episode',
it was natural he should give his friend advance information
of what was coming, even if he had not confided the episode
previously. This was Wise's chance: it was just the opportunity
he wanted. So he told the critic that the Brownings, through the
instrumentality of Miss Mitford, had had the sonnets privately
printed in 1847, and that he had discovered a few copies. This
must have been a staggerer to Gosse. It meant that the 1850
publication was not the first edition of them, as everyone
believed, and as he himself had said in his Catalogue, and in-
ferred at the beginning of his account. Then, like the conjuror
who puts the Knave of Spades firmly in the pack and promptly
produces it from the back of his collar, Wise brought out a
copy of the precious pamphlet. There it was: 'Reading: 1847.'

---

[5] This was printed by Professor Dowden (in his *Robert Browning*: 1905), who was in
communication with Wise. It is very possible that Gosse knew of this letter; and, because
of it, either originally believed the 'pretty episode' occurred at Pisa, or was the more
willing to accept Wise's yarn.

[6] Prof. W. O. Raymond in a monograph 'The Forgeries of Thomas J. Wise and their
'Aftermath' (*The Journal of English and Germanic Philology*, Vol. xliv, No. 3) suggests
that this authority was Gosse. But the authority for the error might have been someone
else—e.g. Dowden (see footnote 5) or even Furnivall. Either case makes Gosse's 'Pisa'
statement innocent.

That was the clincher. He was adept at bringing out his clinchers:
we have seen how he hoaxed Swinburne and Browning with them
years before. What could the unsuspecting Gosse do in the face
of the pamphlet? What he did was to make of his amazing friend's
amazing new 'facts' what is clearly an addendum to the 'pretty
episode', as follows:

'At length she [Mrs Browning] was persuaded to permit her friend
'Miss Mary Russell Mitford, to whom they had originally been sent in
'manuscript, to pass them through the press, although she absolutely
'declined to accede to Miss Mitford's suggestion that they should
'appear in one of the fashionable annuals of the day. Accordingly, a
'small volume was printed, entitled Sonnets /by E.B.B. /Reading /Not
'for Publication /1847. /an octavo of 47 pages. . . .'

Thus was the spurious 'Reading: 1847' pamphlet produced
by Wise passed off as the rare first edition of the famous Sonnets.[7]
Thus was the 'very pretty episode of literary history' completed
by the bunkum about Miss Mitford's responsibility for the printing. It is clear, from Browning's letters quoted above, that the
details about the pamphlet's origin tacked on by Gosse were not
derived from the poet. From whom else could they have
emanated but from Wise—and in the way here reconstructed?
It was the Wise technique all over: first plant your yarn; next
produce the unknown pamphlet as clinching it; and then triumphantly record it in bibliographies and catalogues in order to
establish the all-desirable priority of the fraud.

For my reconstruction of the way in which this bogus Mitford
yarn came to be appended to 'literary history', there is substantia-
tion in a letter from Gosse to Wise dated 21 June 1893. This is
the earliest letter from the critic to the book-forger that I have
come across. The formal styles of address and ending indicate
that the acquaintanceship had not reached the stage of collaboration and warm friendship when 'Dear Mr Wise' became 'My

---

[7] But in manufacturing the forgery Wise made a major textual error which has gone
unnoticed. For the tenth line of sonnet No. XX—
                'Never to feel thee thrill the day or night'
his edition has the reading—
                'Never to feel the thrill the day or night'
If, as he alleged, Miss Mitford saw the proofs of her dear friend's Sonnets through the press,
it is fairly certain that she would have spotted so gross and stupid a mistranscription or
printer's error. So would Gosse have done, had he been involved in the production as
Miss Ratchford deluded herself he was.

'How strange the psychology of the man who, while writing thus of his affection for . . . the poet, yet knew that he had fabricated five spurious editions of the Brownings.' (Chapters 3 and 20).—Their portraits by Field Talfourd in Rome, 1859

Wise's bookplate, and a photograph of him taken by Herbert Gorfin, *c.* 1901

ship that was to have brought them money, brought an account against them instead. This looks as if it were a bookseller. But surely he [i.e., Robert Browning] could earn money. Ah, dear friend, how right and wise it is in you to remain where you are, and what you are [i.e., a bachelor].

GEORGE MEREDITH anticipating Swinburne's poems coming out, I have heard "low mutterings" already from the Lion of Skaal, in reply.

ROBERT BROWNING, observing that Landor is established at

dear Wise'—and even 'My dear Tom', if the fellow had not been too exasperating to the highly sensitive 'literary gent'; who eventually signed himself 'Yours affectionately, E.G.' The relevant portion of the letter is as follows:

29 Delamere Terrace,
Westbourne Square, W.

Dear Mr Wise, 21.6.93.
I perfectly understand and while chronicling the existence of the Mitford volume, I will do nothing to emphasize the value of it. Nor do I think I need borrow it from Forman. Like you, I hate borrowing valuable books. . . .

Yours very faithfully,
Edmund Gosse. [8]

It is reasonably certain, in view of the letter's date and purport, that the references concern what Wise had told Gosse about Miss Mitford having had the *Sonnets* printed in 'a small volume' at Reading. To analyse the letter: the cryptic assurance '*I perfectly understand*' has to be read conjointly with the final clause of the sentence, and connotes that Wise had been indulging in some characteristic mystification—which might be expected in the case of an upstart 'first edition' that so surprisingly contradicted the account 'authorized' by Browning. '*While chronicling the existence of the Mitford volume*' obviously relates to what it was proposed Gosse should append to the Preface he would then have on hand for Dent's edition, published the next year, of the *Sonnets* which he described as the 'very notes and chronicle' of Elizabeth's betrothal. '*I will do nothing to emphasize the value of it*': Wise could be confident enough of the rarity and consequently the pecuniary value of any such 'first' printing of the famous poems. To ignore the commercial side of it would be to leave Gosse's 'history' less open to suspicion of boosting the pamphlet, and more in keeping

[8] Gosse's letter, apart from demonstrating that he was so tricked into foisting the yarn into literary history, has another important bearing. It shows that in 1893 he did not possess a copy of this forgery: otherwise there would have been no question of need to borrow Forman's. This makes even more ludicrous Miss Ratchford's charge that Gosse was a co-partner in the 'Wise-Forman-Gosse forgery factory'. For is it likely—all other improbabilities apart—that an ardent book-collector like Gosse would not have had a copy of the factory's most valuable and 'desirable' production—its key piece—had he been a co-partner?

with a relation by the poet. The manufacturer was astute enough
to foresee the literary importance which would be given to his
new friend's chronicling. Finally, '*Nor do I think I need borrow it
from Forman*': Wise had evidently suggested that if Gosse
wanted a copy of Miss Mitford's purported 'Reading: 1847'
volume he could borrow Forman's. This was playing what was
to become the familiar trick of putting it across his friends by
parading their unquestioning acceptance of his fraudulent printings. We have seen (Chapter 11) how he reproduced the title-
pages of his forgeries, including this very one, in the libraries of
Buxton Forman and Clement Shorter. And Gosse, whose
qualities as an essayist and portrait painter in words were too
often unaccompanied by accurate scholarship, was content to
rely upon his glib informant's report: already he was, as he later
confessed himself to be, 'altogether in your hands. Your judgment is paramount.' So, apparently without troubling himself
even to examine this suddenly-revealed and pretentious pamphlet
which upset the bibliography of the *Sonnets*, the Mitford yarn
was swallowed holus-bolus and appended to his 'episode'.

How clever of Wise to get his 'discovery' woven into such
a romantic story, and by such an authority as Edmund Gosse!

IV

Clever, yes! But now he had to be cleverer. Here was another
tangled web to get himself out of—the most intricate and
horridest of his career. He must concern himself with the exceedingly interesting account he had given in his *Browning Library*
(1929) of how he came into possession of his two copies of this
'Reading: 1847' edition. About 1885, he had written, he became
acquainted with 'Dr' W. C. Bennett, an elderly bachelor and
author of some books of verse, who had been a great friend of
Miss Mitford. Bennett, an accountant, confided that he possessed
copies of the privately-printed *Sonnets* received from Miss Mitford when she lived at Three-Mile Cross, near Reading. Wise
was invited to Bennett's home at Camberwell to see the treasures:
1886 is the date of the visit stated in two other versions. The
remainder of the account must be given in Wise's own words:

I remember that the meal awaiting us was 'high tea', and that it consisted of hot buttered toast and sausages. After his landlady had cleared the table, letters and books were brought out, among them the much-longed-for *Sonnets*. One of the copies was in an old and broken half-calf binding, with the edges fortunately left untrimmed. But it had inserted the manuscript of the additional sonnet, *Future and Past*, which had been sent by Mrs Browning to Miss Mitford to complete the series of forty-four. I bought the tiny booklet for twenty-five pounds, and carried it home rejoicing. I also purchased one of the unbound copies . . . Shortly afterwards Dr Bennett sold the remaining copies. They were bought by Harry Buxton Forman, Robert Alfred Potts, Sir Edmund Gosse, the Rev. Stopford A. Brooke, John Morgan of Aberdeen, Mr Walter Brindley Slater,[9] and other friends to whom I hurried the good news. Dr Bennett received ten pounds for each. . . . Some years afterwards Sir Edmund Gosse sold his copy for fifty pounds. It went, I believe, to Charles B. Foote, of New York.

Gosse was dead when Wise came out with this expanded tale of how the copies were brought to light. But he told Gosse in 1913, recalling Bennett's friendship with Miss Mitford, that he purchased a number of things from the 'doctor' which had passed to him from the authoress, adding 'my copy of the Reading "Sonnets" was one of them'. The latter 'reminiscence' may have been made for the purpose either of reminding Gosse of, or preparing him for, the Bennett story which Wise was going to put forward *in print*. This he did, first and tentatively, in his *Bibliography of Elizabeth Barrett Browning* ultimately published in 1918 after being long on the stocks. But this preliminary version of the tale did not name the alleged buyers of Bennett's remaining copies. The above (1913) reference to his Reading *Sonnets*, which looks so casually made, is more significant than may at first sight appear. It provides further indirect evidence that Edmund Gosse never possessed a copy of the forgery;[10] and that Wise's statement about him selling his copy to a New York collector

<hr/>

9 In the dispersal of Slater's books at Hodgson's on 22 and 23 February 1945 appeared the largest (and almost complete) group of Wise's forgeries and suspected forgeries that has so far been sold together at auction. The fifty-seven items put up as a collection realized two hundred and thirty-five pounds. Copies of the two forgeries the Reading *Sonnets* and Tennyson's *Morte D'Arthur* were sold separately at forty-three pounds and nine pounds respectively. The Slater library made a total of £5,368.

10 Further evidence, that is, to Gosse's letter of 21 June 1893 above quoted (see also footnote 8).

for fifty pounds is untrue. For had Gosse been a purchaser when the 'good news' was 'hurried' to him, Thomas would almost certainly not have referred in 1913 only to his copy as bought from Bennett but to 'our copies'. It is the case, however, that some of the other collectors named did become possessors of the 'much-longed-for' *Sonnets* with the 1847 date.

But to return to Wise's highly detailed account of the 'high tea'. If his name is substituted for Bennett's in the second part we shall be nearer the truth. For the fact is that this further 'pretty episode', describing how he discovered and secured the rare 'Reading: 1847' *Sonnets*, is false. And in view of the threatened exposure of the pamphlet he knew that he must shift his tale. For in the autumn of 1932 there had been published *Letters of Robert Browning Collected by Thomas James Wise*, the originals of which had been included among the five hundred and seventy-one letters sold by Sothebys in 1913 for the sum of six thousand five hundred and fifty pounds. A keen-eyed reviewer in *The Times Literary Supplement* (28 September 1933) had quoted from the correspondence collected by Wise the very letter to Leigh Hunt containing the passage (given above) which proved that Browning first learned in 1849 of the existence of his wife's love sonnets to him—i.e., two years after their purported printing in 1847 at Reading. So thus, ironically enough, the recent publication of the letters Wise had collected forced his own hand.

But there was some delay. Early in November of 1933 he had a fall—injuring his head, according to a letter to me from Mrs Wise, who explained that he had been trying to do too much while recovering from an accident of eighteen months before. In due course, however, he made sufficient recovery to tackle the greatest problem he had ever encountered. Much was going on behind the scenes. For example, in this November 1933 Wise, through his agents, bought back the remaining stocks of pamphlets—including forgeries and piracies—that he had sold to Gorfin. The price paid for the recovery of the incriminating things was four hundred pounds—exactly the sum which, as already related, the former clerk had some twenty years earlier laid out on his master's nice 'clean' little pamphlets. An assurance was also given by the manufacturer of them that they would be destroyed. We may be sure they were, to no very sweet music either. Gorfin, in relating to me this unexpected transaction, could not remember the number of copies taken back. But he estimated their value to him, on the then market prices as two thousand pounds.[11]

V

In the spring of 1934 Thomas James Wise determined to meet the coming attack upon his spurious pamphlets before it was launched. To this end a long letter appeared over his name in *The Times* Literary Supplement that appeared on 24 May 1934. It was a piece of wriggling characterized by stupidity and audacity. Those intimates of his who were anxious for his reputation did not hesitate to express their disappointment with it. But it is important as being, with the exception of an interview and also another letter on a single phase of the subject, Wise's only public statement on the charges brought against his frauds.

The letter begins:

MRS BROWNING'S "SONNETS, 1847"

Sir,—The suggestion has been pressed upon me that this book, with an imprint "Reading [Not for Publication]" is an impostor, not printed until many years after 1847.

With cool strategy, he proceeded to anticipate the lines of attack that would shortly be made; though without naming the two investigators. There is an admission that no reference to the 1847 book appeared during Browning's lifetime. He recalled *The Times* reviewer's discovery of the letter which showed that 1849 was the date of the poet's first acquaintance with the *Sonnets*; and this 'constitutes a real difficulty in the acceptance of 'the 1847 book'. There followed an ingenious attempt to explain away how Gosse (in his story of the poems that was derived from Browning) came to include the yarn about the printing of the 1847 edition at Reading through Miss Mitford—a yarn, as has been shown, that was undoubtedly invented and supplied by Wise. After a couple of red-herring hints as to other unexplored

11 Herbert Edwin Gorfin died at Staplehurst, Kent, on 22 December 1942, aged sixty-five.

places that might reveal something to save his face, and some far-fetched supposition—all this wriggling led to the admission: 'I may be driven to the conclusion that the 1847 book is not 'authentic.'

But there was still the printing of the spurious 'Reading: 1847' edition to be accounted for. He asked:

With whom could this have originated? One name must be cleared out of the way at once; a name which would never have been brought into the matter but for a mistake of my own. In the introduction to 'A Browning Library' 1929, writing forty-three years after the event, I told the story of a visit to W. C. Bennett in 1886, and said that I acquired my two copies of the 1847 book from him; and earlier than this, in the first volume of my Ashley Catalogue, 1922, I said that my copies came to me from W. C. Bennett. What I actually brought away with me was his own sonnets, "My Sonnets", privately printed at Greenwich in 1843. The confusion of two such books may seem incredible, even after thirty-six years. It is to be explained by the subjects of our conversation. . . . My two copies came to me not from W. C. Bennett but from Harry Buxton Forman. From whom did he obtain them? Neither I nor his son Mr Maurice Buxton Forman can tell with any certainty, but how he may have obtained them I hope his son will be able to ascertain from an examination of his father's correspondence.

With this version Wise threw any reputation for veracity to the winds. Comparison of this account with his original one here given on page two hundred and seventy-seven shows to what degree of mendacity he would go. The rest of his letter matters little. There were unsuccessful efforts to combat the technical arguments about paper and type, which he knew were to be advanced to prove that the 'Reading: 1847' *Sonnets* could only have been printed more than thirty years after the date on its title-page. He concluded: '. . . I will leave further exposition . . . 'to those who have a more microscopic eye than I can boast of.'

But few would, or could, in any other circumstance have boasted a keener eye than Thomas James Wise.

VI

In *The Times* Literary Supplement for the following week (31 May 1934) appeared two letters on the subject. One was from Maurice Buxton Forman endeavouring to substantiate Wise's explanation that his copies of the spurious Reading edition came from Buxton Forman senior. This was an effort to help a friend in difficulties; but it did no good to Wise or to anyone else. The other letter was from Graham Pollard rebutting Wise's attempt to disprove the technical evidence against the genuineness of the 1847 edition of the *Sonnets*, and announcing that the book describing the tests, etc., which had been applied to that edition and other important poetical rarities would be published within the next few weeks.

The stage was now set for the drama.

CHAPTER 21

THE EXPOSURE AND SOME SURPRISING SEQUELS

The honest men in the Trade usually manage to damp the rogue's powder.
Wise (in *The Strand* interview, 1930)

I

THE RESULT of the investigation into Wise's spurious pamphlets was published on the 2nd of July 1934.[1] The authors, John Carter and Graham Pollard, were two professional booksellers. It must be rare, if not unique, in the annals of controversy for critics to be able to quote their opponents' reply in their original charge. At the end of the volume appeared a 'Stop press' section quoting from Wise's extraordinary letter, in which we have just seen him anticipating the attack.

The kind of forgery that the authors set out to expose was new. As shown in the foregoing chapters, the forger was much too ingenious merely to imitate rarities and to pass them off as genuine. He conceived the idea of printing conveniently small pieces by collected authors, and dating them earlier than any known first editions of them (often as issues privately printed for the authors, with a false imprint, or no imprint at all)—thus giving them a priority which is the essential of the rare. In this way were created new books that mostly could not be compared with any originals, and therefore required tests other than the usual ones to prove that they were not printed at the dates stated, but years later. Both the crime and the methods of detecting it were novel. The *Enquiry* which revealed them was a sensation of the day.

As Wise had foreseen, the pamphlet of Mrs Browning's *Sonnets* with the 'Reading: 1847' imprint, the foremost of the forgeries (one had sold for some two hundred and fifty pounds at auction), was the focus of attack. The investigators subjected this

---

[1] i.e., in *An Enquiry, op. cit.*

and more than fifty other suspected pamphlets to analyses, chemical (for paper) and typographical. They also applied where possible a third positive test, the familiar use of textual comparison, in addition to certain negative tests. The result was that twenty-nine of the pamphlets were condemned outright as forgeries, twenty as suspect of forgery, and five as piratical. Some of the printings were condemned because their paper was of a kind not in use at the dates on which they were purported to have been printed; some because they were printed from type used only by Clay and Sons (Wise's printers) and designed subsequent to the dates of the purported printings; and five on textual grounds. Some were condemned on account of both paper and type; and others on all three positive grounds. (The complete list of the *corpus delicti* including new information and additions made by other investigators will be found in Appendix II.) Various other peculiarities of these pamphlets were revealed. For example, while they purported to have been printed from 1842 onwards, none had appeared in book-auction sales before 1888. With one doubtful exception, not a single specimen alleged to have been printed for the author's private distribution bore a presentation inscription or had any other personal association with the author. Neither the British Museum Library nor any other national collection had received any of the pamphlets before 1888. Most of the printings either had been 'discovered' by Wise, or owed their reputation as collectors' items to his published works. And finally, extensive marketing of the spurious things was traced to Wise, who eventually sold stocks of some of them to his agent, Herbert Gorfin.

The investigators' conclusions were built up on detail, most of it highly technical. The work was a testimony to the patience and skill of its compilers. It vindicated Wise's office colleague, Herbert Gorfin. The investigators said that at first they imagined it possible that the forger was Gorfin: but he was only ten years old when the earliest independent evidence of their existence is found; and all of them had been produced by the time he was twenty-one. 'A few minutes' conversation was sufficient to con-'vince us not only that Mr Gorfin was not the forger, but that 'he had not the slightest idea that he was selling forgeries.' Tribute is paid to the high value of his assistance.

As for the master: in spite of the book's inferences, the Enquirers, for obvious reasons, nowhere charged Wise with the responsibility for the forgeries. They could not bring them definitely home to him. Their aim was to show the fraudulent nature of the pamphlets, and to emphasize his extraordinary commercial interest in them, and his patronage of them as rarities. The nearest they came to sharps was: 'We find it diffi-'cult to believe that Mr Wise cannot now guess the identity of 'the forger; but, as long as it remains a guess, he has followed a 'very proper course in making no suggestion.'[2]

II

The sensational character of the revelations, for all their bibliographical technicalities, made big-headline news for the more popular dailies, and evoked long and careful reviews from the staider journals. An interviewer posted down to Hastings, where Wise was recuperating. He is reported to have said (*Daily Herald*, 30 June 1934):

A large proportion of the books condemned are genuine. Those that are wrong were apparently printed in the middle and late 'eighties of last century.

At that time I was a young man in the twenties, hunting for books and seeking for knowledge about them.

These things were accepted as genuine at that time by such men as Buxton Forman, Sir Edmund Gosse, William Rossetti, Dr Garnett of the British Museum, The Rev. Stopford Brooke, and others.

If these men of age and experience accepted them as genuine, why should I, their junior, suppose them to be spurious?

He went on to say that Harry Buxton Forman had a habit of buying and 'salting down' small remainders of pamphlets, etc.,

---

[2] Their chief difficulty was the actual connecting of Wise with the printing of the spurious pamphlets, for Clays 'were unable to give us any conclusive clue to the identity of 'their client'. But even guesswork was unnecessary after 1939 when *Forging Ahead* (see also note page 91) quoted the independent testimony of the diarist Mr Y.Z. as to Wise in January 1888 'still proceeding on his wild career', and established that this statement referred at least to the forgery of Swinburne's *Siena* and to the suspect *Cleopatra* (pages 77–83 here). Also, more damning, when *Forging Ahead* quoted Cecil Clay's verbatim report of Wise 'giving himself away', and of the printers' chief frankly reminding him that they printed the pamphlets for him (page 268 here).

of authors he believed in, and disposed of these largely by exchange—a considerable number thus coming to him (Wise) in return for manuscripts, others being taken in payment of Forman's Shelley Society subscriptions. These pamphlets, Wise averred, were disposed of through Gorfin, who apparently wanted more:

> Forman said he could have them all, and I passed them over. I was only the vehicle. I was the messenger lad who took the goods for delivery. They were planted on Forman, and not on me.

After commenting that for the last two years he had heard 'subterranean rumours and remarks', he recalled the visit to him of Pollard, who said they had found some wrong things.

> I replied that I was very interested, and said I would be pleased to assist them in any way I could. He instantly said 'No, we don't want 'any help, but we would like to know when and from whom you 'purchased your own copies of certain pamphlets?'—a list of which he produced.
>
> I replied that to tell him offhand where and when I purchased the pamphlets, which cost a few shillings each between thirty and fifty years ago, was an impossibility because the copies I had in my library were frequently not the copies I received from Buxton Forman.
>
> The next day Mr Pollard sent me a typed list of about thirty or more pamphlets, and asked that I should fill in the source from which my copies came. This I should have done had I not heard, just at that moment, rumours of what was going on.

Next he offered his opinion that 'the things that are really 'wrong were produced by Richard Herne Shepherd'—forgetting that the two Kipling pamphlets were produced two and four years after Shepherd's death, and several of the others in 1895, when the unfortunate man died in an asylum. Wise wound up this public and self-contradictory statement with the irrelevant outburst:

> All my life I have been preaching against bad copies of books and teaching people to leave bad copies alone. That has done small booksellers a lot of harm and so they curse and hate me.

In private Wise at first continued the same line of peeved indignation and injured innocence. In a statement to me made on the 6th of July he referred to 'the disgraceful book which is now 'being talked about'. It was clever, and certain of its contents were of great value, he opined. But it was written in the worst of bad taste; and many of its references to him were absolutely untrue. Finally, 'I never held stock of any one of these pamphlets in my life'. He was not willing to enter on further discussion of the affair or to support his complaints by citing examples.

On the 12th of July, he wrote again to *The Times* Literary Supplement, saying that he had glanced hastily through the pages of the *Enquiry*, and 'I lose no time in writing to explain my 'position with regard to the pamphlets of which the authenticity 'is challenged'. But practically all he did was to deny, as he had denied to me, that he ever 'held stock' of any one of the condemned or questioned pamphlets, and to give an embroidered version of what he had said in the interview as to Harry Buxton Forman's remainders, and how they passed via himself (Wise) to Gorfin. Within his letter he quoted a longer letter to him from Maurice Buxton Forman which was an elaboration of his previous letter of 31 May 1934, and which named some of the people from whom Forman senior acquired remainders for 'salting down'. Maurice Forman echoed Wise's stupid and vindictive hint that Shepherd might be the culprit,[3] and wound up by fearing that he had been rather long-winded, but 'I type as I think, 'and my typing is not very expert!'

III

All this bluffing was typical of Wise in his everyday dealings —as revealed in various private papers made available to me, and also remarkably instanced here in relation to Watts-Dunton. But it was the last feeble bid. He could see in the glare of public print how hollow his explanations were: how poorly they impressed some of those whose concern it was—for the sake of their association with him—that he should make at least an arguable, if not a vindicating, defence. And when the bluffer's bid failed he retired into stubborn silence. But there were heard some strong voices in *The Times* Literary Supplement. To begin

[3] See page 204.

with, Herbert Gorfin gave the lie direct to the only 'position' Wise had taken up in defence of himself. He wrote (19 July 1934):

Sir,—Mr Wise states, in a letter in your issue of July 12, that he got his copies of those pamphlets which are shown in Messrs Carter and Pollard's book to be forged, from H. Buxton Forman. Among other material, I was selling these regularly on commission for Mr Wise from 1898 onwards, and I purchased from him what I understood to be the entire remainder in 1909–1911. In all our many transactions this connexion of the pamphlets with H. Buxton Forman was never mentioned, even by implication; and the suggestion that he was the source from which they came was only made to me, by Mr Wise himself, on October 14, 1933—two days after Mr Pollard had visited him and explained that they were forgeries. Mr Wise had previously given me a totally different account of their origin.[4]

The clinching evidence on page two hundred and seventy-eight of the repurchase by Wise of the remaining stocks of pamphlets for £400 was not brought out by Gorfin in the above letter —either because he was pledged to secrecy at the time of the transaction, or because he originally designed (before the inception of this biography) to print a narrative of his connexion with Wise; or possibly for both reasons. But the letter is of some importance for Gorfin's testimony that in all his 'many transactions' with Wise no mention or implication of Forman being connected with the spurious pamphlets was ever made. We have seen that Gorfin was at one time in the habit of going to Forman on behalf of Wise's stamp business.

Another correspondent, in the same issue of the Supplement, pointed out *inter alia* that neither Wise nor Maurice Buxton Forman stated explicitly whether the fifty-four pamphlets examined in the *Enquiry* were among the 'swaps' which Forman senior was said to have made with Wise.

But it was the letter from the Viscount Esher in the issue of 23 August 1934 that voiced the opinions of many thoughtful readers:

Sir,—Book collectors throughout the world are still waiting to hear from Mr Wise an explanation of the forgeries exposed by Mr Carter and Mr Pollard in their 'Enquiry into the Nature of Certain Nineteenth-

---

[4] Wise's 'totally different account' as he gave it to Gorfin appears on page 209.

Century Pamphlets'. Those of us who have bought the forged pamphlets for large sums of money cannot consent to leave the matter where
it is.

Mr Wise has said in an interview that 'a large proportion of the
'books are genuine'. It is only fair that Mr Wise should tell us collectors which are the genuine ones, and why. He must have evidence to
refute the careful examination made by Mr Carter and Mr Pollard.
That evidence should be produced. It is clear from the book that
Mr Wise played a great part in the distribution of the forged pamphlets,
and therefore must be more anxious than any of us to pursue the
enquiry. He presented twenty-three of them to the British Museum,
and fifteen to the Cambridge University Library. . . .

[The letter proceeds to state facts now familiar to readers of
this book, and continues:]

So far, therefore, the only explanation made by Mr Wise is to throw
back the provenance of the pamphlets on to Mr Buxton Forman. Does
he suggest that Mr Buxton Forman was the forger? Or, if they were
'planted' on Mr Buxton Forman, whom does he suggest they were
planted by? Mr Buxton Forman was a distinguished man of letters,
and his relatives will no doubt be able to tell us whether he was likely
to have forged the pamphlets or whether he was likely to have accepted
as genuine from somebody else (without mentioning his name or
credentials) over a long period of years a mass of unknown and valuable
pamphlets. Some evidence of these prolonged transactions must exist
and should be produced.

Nothing could be more explicit than that. It is perhaps not
strange, in view of what has been brought out here, that Wise
never broke his silence. But that Maurice Buxton Forman did
not respond to the invitation of Lord Esher's letter is more surprising. An explanation of why no immediate reply was forthcoming from Wise was supplied in the following issue of the
Literary Supplement by his wife, who wrote briefly explaining
that he was unfit to carry on any public correspondence, and that
his doctor had strictly forbidden him to do so.

There followed in the Literary Supplement[5] a most valuable
series of letters, some of which were as unexpected as they were
timely. Carter and Pollard in their *Enquiry* had erred very unhappily in dismissing as 'wholly fictitious' Edmund Gosse's

[5] Of *The Times*—8, 15, and 22 November 1934.

story of the idyllic episode (i.e., of Mrs Browning's surprise gift
to her husband of the love sonnets) just because he had been
unwise enough to add on to it Wise's invention about the
'Reading: 1847' edition and how Miss Mitford was said to have
had it printed. The letters amply substantiated that the first part
of Gosse's account of the episode derived from Browning himself; and John Carter made the proper *amende*. He could do so
without affecting the exposure of the unidyllic nature of the
'Reading' *Sonnets* pamphlet. That remained damned, but not
done for.

Later the same year Thomas J. Wise was asked on behalf of
the Roxburghe Club for an explanation of the matters brought
out in the *Enquiry*. In a statement to Lord Aldenham, then
President of the club, he excused himself from meeting its
members at his lordship's house on the 12th of December owing
to indisposition. He denied explicitly that he ever once had
aught to do with the production of the fraudulent pamphlets,
and argued that if they had been planted by one person, or had
made their appearance inside a brief period, those circumstances would have assuredly roused distrust. Instead—he explained—they were quietly slipped into commercial circulation
one by one over a number of years.[6] The statement was evasive,
yet gave away more than was intended. That it was not, as
hoped, deemed sufficing to the club was promptly demonstrated by two members suggesting that he should resign his
membership. This he did (10 December 1934) on the ground
of 'ill-health'.

IV

If the popular Press could find big headline-news in the exposure of Wise's nineteenth-century pamphlets by such novel
methods as paper and typographical detection (the latter through
a broken-backed f, a 'button-hook' j, and a tilting question
mark), the sensation caused in the book-world can be well
imagined. It came as a particularly painful shock to distinguished

---

[6] This is precisely the *modus operandi* I have explained and evidenced in Chapter 6,
which appears herein as it was written for the 1939 edition of this work. The statement
to Lord Aldenham was made known to me in 1946.

friends and acquaintances of Wise, to those who had lauded his impressive performances as a collector and bibliographer, and to his wealthy clients.

Some criticized the publication of the exposure during his lifetime—illogically ignoring the arguments that frauds ought to be exposed, and that at least the *Enquiry* gave Wise the opportunity to vindicate himself if he could. Among his other friends there was a disposition to suspend judgment, to wait for the oracle to speak. It was unthinkable that the wealthy collector, the builder of the finest private library of its kind, the stern chastiser of fakers, could have been responsible for the pamphlets.

In the meantime one leading firm of rare-book experts, who had had considerable dealings of an unimpeachable character with Wise, conducted a private and independent investigation 'just in case . . .' They went to the expense of having some of the pamphlets analytically tested for the paper content. But the verdict was just as damning.

And I cannot forget the charming naïveté of a leading and esteemed official of the British Museum Library, who rounded a discussion about Wise and the scandal, and the future of the Ashley Library, by observing to me: 'You know him well. 'Can't you get him to make a confession of exactly what he has 'done? It would get the dreadful business off his chest, and leave 'him in peace.'

It was easier to imagine a zoo spectator entering the cage of a bear racked with toothache, and trying to extract the molar with a motor-spanner.

V

Nevertheless there actually was some sort of attempt at the desperate remedy. It was made, however, by one who could claim the privileges of greater age and close friendship. Gabriel Wells, the bookseller of New York and London, discussing the affair with me in 1936, recalled that his friendship with Wise had lasted for twenty-five years:

One day [he said] I went to Heath Drive with the idea of making an end of the unsatisfactory position. Tom was very excited. He was willing to do anything. And I even drew up a statement, a confession, for him to sign, of his part in the business, and of his willingness to make recompense for any direct loss sustained through him. But the final decision was not to touch it—that it was best left alone.

Myself: But was Wise willing to sign this document?

Gabriel Wells: Oh, yes!

Myself: You are certain he understood it was a confession?

Gabriel Wells: Certain! But it was thought best to leave it alone; and there I left it.

Subsequently I sent Gabriel Wells a copy of the above note of our conversation, asking if he had any objection to my using it. At an interview which he requested, to discuss the proposal, he said that the only objection he had was to the use of the word 'confession', and that all else was accurate. He averred that there had been no confession, and that I must have misunderstood him. But my note was written within an hour of the conversation. While I print it as an accurate record of what was said, it is only fair to give equal prominence to his subsequent objection to the one word. It should also be recorded here that Gabriel Wells within a few months of the disclosure produced a pamphlet in defence of Wise. In this he maintained that the term forgery did not strictly apply in this case 'as no counterfeit was committed, only an act of piracy aggravated with the impropriety of imprint'. To this remarkable argument he added: 'I admit that 'this savors of quibbling.' The defence came in time for Wise to notice in the last volume of his great catalogue, and to refer to it as 'an able comment'.

There were, of course, other friends whose faith in Wise remained unshaken; and it is only fair again to give an example of their reasoning. One of these was a well-known North of England man whose library contained not a few purchases and gifts from Wise. Mr W. *********, who preferred that his name should be withheld for the present, supplied me with a series of notes from which I quote:

Mr Thomas J. Wise I knew quite well. I always called upon him when in London, and spent many happy hours in his company . . . [Referring to the attacked pamphlets:] Some of these he admitted to me were false; some he contended were genuine. But what hurt him was the implied accusation that he was responsible for the fakes. As he said, the book would have served a useful purpose had its chief motive not been an attack upon him. As it was he determined to investigate the whole problem, which would have involved an enormous amount of labour and research, going back some thirty years. His doctor at once told his wife that in his state of health such an attempt would kill him. His friends begged him to postpone it until his health improved, and after a few interviews in which he vainly called upon his memory for all the necessary details he had to give in, hoping to regain sufficient strength to tackle the work later. By that time his letters to me were in his wife's handwriting; he had a nurse who also acted as secretary; and on the two or three occasions I was allowed to see him the time was limited to a quarter of an hour. It was really a tragedy, for his failure to refute the charges has left in the minds of those who did not know him well, or at all, the impression that they were justified. And it must be said that there were some who exulted in knocking him off his pedestal. To those who really knew him the charges are unbelievable. . . . He was proved to be fallible—like every other bibliographer. But that he would live his laborious life knowing that some of the items in his Collection were frauds—and *his* frauds— is unthinkable. . . .

This, then, is the testimony of a personal friend of Wise— of one who, down to 1938, believed in his innocence.

VI

It is an unpleasant task to have to write of Wise's illnesses from the viewpoint of whether they prevented him from doing what was naturally expected of him. But in a biography whose only concern is with factual truth and faithful portraiture the implications of the letter just quoted ought not to be passed over. It is the case that he unfortunately was temporarily incapacitated for two or three periods after the spring of 1932.

I saw Wise on two of these occasions when he was confined to bed, but able to converse freely, dictate letters, and read. Once he was suffering from some epidermal trouble about which he told me; and, with bibliographer-like zeal for demonstration, he proceeded to show the locale of the trouble with as much unreserve as if I had been his doctor.

In spite of his illnesses, however, it is also the case that from

1933 (when he knew of the investigations being made) to 1936 there were periods when he was able to devote himself very effectively to tasks he had on hand. This aspect of Wise's last years was the subject of a note by 'Bibliographer' in *The Times* for 19 May 1937. In the previous day's issue there had appeared a letter signed 'A Personal Friend' (the pseudonym, as he informed me himself, of one to whom over many years the Ashley Library meant a great volume of work), protesting that Wise was a very sick man 'unable to enter into any controversy, 'in which condition he remained until he died'. In reply, 'Bibliographer' wrote:

With all due respect to 'A Personal Friend', there was no need for Mr Wise to 'enter into any controversy' about the forged pamphlets. He was well enough at the time to write a long (though largely irrelevant) letter to *The Times Literary Supplement* (12 July 1934) on the subject, and subsequently to see through the press the eleventh volume of the Ashley Catalogue. It did (and still does) seem to many people that he might have made the very brief statement of the facts which was all that was required.

As has been shown in the foregoing pages, Wise actually wrote twice to *The Times* Literary Supplement about the forgeries. And on my last visit to him in 1936 he was up and about his library—obviously not the lively man he had been, but able to discuss bibliographical matters with his old keenness.[7] On that occasion when his wife and his close friend ****** ****** were also present, he made no direct reference to the *Enquiry*, though the casual showing of a book containing a Tennyson inscription now caused him to forget the temporary ban on the subject; and he exclaimed bitterly: 'They will be saying next that that is wrong.' Mrs Wise uttered a gentle warning . . . and for the next few seconds in the Ashley Library there was an embarrassing stillness.

So that when Wise retired in obstinate silence behind the anxious and able care of his wife he was not, despite the two or three periods of disability, so handicapped that he could not deal with the challenge of the *Enquiry* if he would. The protest of 'Bibliographer' in *The Times* was justified. Although in his three

---

[7] His script in 1936, as evidenced by his inscription on Vol. xi of his Catalogue presented to the British Museum, is at least as good as it was ten or twenty years earlier.

public statements Wise affected to ignore that the *Enquiry* was
an unformulated attack on him, it is now clear that he was fully
conscious of its reflections on his honour. He could not help
being otherwise. In spite of the care of the authors to avoid
risks, the book was damaging to Wise's character and reputation: its inferences were clear. And it is difficult to believe
that it did not provide the opportunity for a successful action at
law (for which he had the means, too often an essential for re-
dress) if he was innocent or if the inferences were unfair or based
on serious errors of fact.

VII

The British Museum's copy of Wise's catalogue, *A Browning
Library*, has become particularly interesting by reason of certain
anonymous manuscript corrections made in defiance of one of
that institution's most stringent rules. These corrections are
concerned with the fraudulent 'Reading: 1847' edition of Mrs
Browning's *Sonnets*, and are designed by minimum alterations
to make the text agree in parts with facts that Wise subsequently
had to admit (see Chapter 20). On page eighty-three of *A Browning Library* is the following passage as originally printed by Wise:

This copy of Mrs Browning's *Sonnets* [i.e. Wise's own copy] was
formerly in the possession of Dr W. C. Bennett. It was given to him
by Mary Russell Mitford, to whom had been entrusted by the
authoress the task of seeing the book through the press. By Dr Bennett
it was sold to me.

By insertion in script of the word 'not' the last sentence has
been made to read: 'By Dr Bennett it was NOT sold to me.'

Page eighty-four bears this printed passage in continuation of
the description of Wise's own copy of the forged *Sonnets*:

Inserted also is the Manuscript of *Future and Past*, now No. 43 of
the *Sonnets from the Portuguese*. . . . The MS. had been forwarded by
Mrs Browning to her friend at the time of its composition, in order
that it might be added to the original forty-three and so complete the
series. Miss Mitford inserted it in her copy of the booklet, where it still
remained when I purchased the volume from Dr Bennett in 1886.

———— Sonnets. / By / E. B. B. / Reading : / [Not for Publication.] / 1847.

Collation : Foolscap octavo, pp. 47; consisting of Half-title (with blank reverse) pp. 1—2; Title-page, as above (with blank reverse) pp. 3—4; and Text of the forty-three *Sonnets* pp. 5—47. The reverse of p. 47 is blank. There is no printer's imprint. The head-line is *Sonnets* throughout, upon both sides of the page. The signatures are A to C (3 sheets, each 8 leaves).

The *First Edition.* Bound in dark brown levant morocco by Riviere, with panelled sides and gilt top, the remaining edges entirely untrimmed. The leaves measure 7 × 4¼ inches.

This copy of Mrs. Browning's *Sonnets* was formerly in the possession of Dr. W. C. Bennett. It was given to him by Mary Russell Mitford, to whom had been entrusted by the authoress the task of seeing the book through the press. By Dr. Bennett it was sold to me.
⎰ *NOT*
Inserted at the commencement is an interesting A. L. S. of 4 pp. 8vo, addressed by Miss Mitford to Dr. Bennett, containing much chatty news about the Brownings :—

〰〰〰〰〰〰〰〰〰〰〰〰〰〰〰〰〰〰〰〰〰〰〰〰〰〰〰〰

Inserted also is the Manuscript of *Future and Past,* now No. 43 of the *Sonnets from the Portuguese.* This sonnet was not included in the original series of forty-three printed in the volume of 1847, but was added in the edition of 1856. The MS. had been forwarded by Mrs Browning to her friend at the time of its composition, in order that it might be added to the original forty-three and so complete the series. Miss Mitford inserted it in her copy of the booklet, where it still remained when I purchased the volume from Dr Bennett in 1886.

A set of MSS. of the *Sonnets from the Portuguese,* consisting of the original

The manuscript corrections, on different pages, made by Wise in the British Museum's copy of his book A Browning Library *after the exposure of his spurious '1847' edition of Mrs Browning's famous* Sonnets (Chapter 21).

Here by the crossing-out of Miss Mitford's name in the last sentence, and the substitution in script of 'I', the sentence is made to read: 'I inserted it in her copy of the booklet, where it 'still remained when I purchased the volume from Dr Bennett in '1886.' The anonymous corrector forgot to repeat in the last part of this sentence the correction previously made on page eighty-three.

On pages eighty-four and eighty-five is this passage:

A third set of MSS., comprising the whole forty-four sonnets complete, was given by the poet's son, R. W. B. Browning, to Mrs George Smith, and is now in the possession of her daughter, Miss Ethel Murray Smith. When making this gift Pen Browning stated that the MSS. had been handed by his mother to her husband in 1849. But the statement was inaccurate.

The last sentence has been altered in script by crossing out 'in' in the final word, making it read: 'But the statement was accurate.'

These corrections, though completely reversing the meaning of the original text, are slight, it is true. But from their manner and matter, I have no hesitation in attributing them to Wise, with whose script and way of correcting proofs I am familiar. To have altered the text more completely would have involved extensive script corrections, thus providing more identification of the anonymous breaker of the British Museum's rule. There is no doubt, however, that at some period subsequent to the exposure of the forgeries, Thomas James Wise went to the British Museum Library, secured its copy of his own book, and there made the amendments repudiating the fiction with which he bolstered up the account of his 'discovery' of the spurious 'Reading' Sonnets. This eleventh-hour gesture, made in the silence of the British Museum Library, is not the least curious part of the story.

CHAPTER 22

WHY THE FORGERIES WERE DONE

When bright the brimming goblet gleamed,
And lightly laughed the eager wine;
The glow of Pleasure softly streamed,
And in its sparkles seemed to shine;
But when the cup was passed and drained,
And lay unheeded on the board,
With dark Remorse my heart was stained,
As was the vase with Liber's hoard.

Thomas J. Wise: *Verses*

I

THOMAS JAMES WISE died at his home in Heath Drive, Hampstead, on the 13th of May 1937 and was cremated at Golder's Green Crematorium on the 15th. His age was seventy-seven years and seven months.

For the most part the obituary notices of him were inadequate and contained errors of fact about his family and early career. An exceptional contribution—headed 'the British Museum and 'the Ashley Library'—was that by Arundell Esdaile to the *Library Association Record* for November 1937; which, though it contained little biographical material, said:

. . . Probably no one will ever know who the original forger was, nor does it now matter. . . .

The suggestion that it does not matter who imposed upon the book-world an extensive series of frauds which had the effect of falsifying the bibliographies of several leading authors may be of small concern to the general public; but it ought to matter a great deal to anybody writing about books and Thomas James Wise. But even more surprising were these further views vouchsafed to the perhaps not so credulous librarians:

. . . Wise stated that he and Buxton Forman were buying up just

298

such remainders in quantity, and marketing them for the benefit of the Shelley Society. . . . The statement is anyhow inherently probable and may be regarded as sufficient. . . .

Wise's statement, whomsoever it sufficed for and however probable it seemed to the person determined to believe it, was a deliberate lie. His Shelley Society private-printing ramp (the real cause of the society's virtual bankruptcy), and the way its debts were paid off, have been revealed earlier in this work from first-hand documentary evidence. The Esdaile notice concludes with a sort of invocation to its readers to—

. . . rejoice that the irreplaceable national record he spent his life in gathering has now, by his family's generosity, become a national possession. . . .

The circumstances of the 'generosity' by which the nation is said to have become possessor of the Ashley Library are fully brought out in the pages following.

True to its tradition, *The Times* (14 May 1937) gave a short memoir that was a careful and informed summary of his achievement as the builder of the Ashley Library. After an appreciation of Wise's skill as a collector, the notice said that in 1934 his credit as a bibliographer was gravely damaged when a large number of rare and valued pamphlets, whose reputation depended almost exclusively on his elaborate descriptions, histories, or discoveries of them, were proved beyond dispute to be spurious and manufactured many years after their purported dates. *The Times* continued:

Many people in the book-world were not satisfied that this was just a case of Jove having nodded. Wise was shown to have been intimately involved with the sale and distribution of the pamphlets to collectors and to libraries in Great Britain and America. In response to a general demand for an explanation of the source of the forgeries and of his repeated attestations of their genuineness, Wise first attempted to throw responsibility on to men no longer alive who had been his friends and co-collectors, and then, challenged to produce evidence for his statements, withdrew into obstinate silence.

This reference to the exposure of the pamphlets and its immediate consequences was resented by some of Wise's friends, although beyond the pseudonymous plea of 'A Personal 'Friend' (see page two hundred and ninety-three) their protests lacked the courage of public expression. The obituary columns of *The Times* are among the most valuable contributions to journalism. The reference to the nineteenth-century forged pamphlets was as essential in any true record of Wise as the mention of his honours. But the disposition to shirk the truth is symptomatic of the age.

II

After Wise's death there was naturally much inquiry regarding the future of the superb collection of books and manuscripts in his Ashley Library: the curiosity of the Press was but a reflection of the wide speculation in the book-world. Before 1921 a few of those closely in touch with him had gathered the impression that he intended to leave his Library to the nation. In that year his friend, Coulson Kernahan, submitted an article to me in which occurred the passage: 'Mr Wise's collection will one day 'go, I understand, to the nation.' I thought it fair to show a statement of that kind intended for publication to Wise, who expressed his wish that such an announcement should not be made public because in the then financial situation it was difficult to estimate what the circumstances would be when he 'cleared off the scene'. But what his wishes were, and would continue to be, nothing could change, he assured me. After a subsequent conversation, I believed—as did others—that the Ashley Library was destined to be given to either the British Museum or one of the two Universities—Oxford or Cambridge.

Wise, who had no children (but was survived by his wife and his brother), left a fortune of one hundred and thirty-eight thousand pounds gross. In his last will made in 1926 he lets it be known that by his previous will he had left to the British Museum some rare and valuable books that its library either did not contain or only possessed in poor copies. But he regretted that, owing to the extent that high rates of the death duty and income tax would lower the net amount of his estate, he did not feel warranted in fulfilling his original design, His directions, therefore, were that his Library was to be sold; but he expressly forbade its removal to and auctioning in America. But a codical of 6 January 1933, by which date Wise knew of the investigations being made into his spurious pamphlets,[1] further directed that his Library was first to be offered for sale to the British Museum at a price to be determined by his wife.

In due course negotiations were opened with the Trustees of the Museum. The sum to be paid was not readily arrived at. It was eventually announced that the Trustees had undertaken to buy the Library from the executors at a price which was not made public, but which the official announcement said 'is very 'much less than its estimated value'. The secrecy about the price was due to the condition made by the family. The Museum authorities would have preferred to state the figure. Wise's widow, who had throughout the negotiations been anxious for the Library to be acquired by the nation even at some sacrifice of her particular interest, gave to the Museum the handsome set of bookcases in which the Ashley books and manuscripts were contained.

The purchase price agreed is believed to have been about sixty thousand pounds, to be paid over a number of years.

The decision received considerable notice in the Press, which for the most part recognized the importance and desirability of the acquisition. There were some exceptions, however. For example, the *Daily Express* announced in a large streamer head-line: 'BRITISH MUSEUM TO GIVE BOOK FAKER MEMORIAL.' Those who had expected the Library to be given to the nation were naturally much surprised at the news.

But whether purchase or gift, scholars and experts welcomed the national acquisition of the Ashley books and manuscripts. It has already been explained in these pages that many of the Museum's rare Elizabethan first editions, copies of which Wise possessed in superb condition, were very much the worse for wear—hence the desire of the authorities to secure the Ashley Library's specimens, and also its items that the national institution lacked. Moreover, there was the collector's wealth of MSS. —the part of the acquisition that received much less notice, though it may well prove the more fruitful. A *Times* leader echoed the approval of responsible opinion with a nicety when it said:

[1] See page 285.

Wise's shortcomings in connexion with that unfortunate business [the series of forgeries], whether they were of omission or commission, are no doubt of considerable psychological interest, but it does not affect in the slightest the value and importance of the great library which he amassed with unrivalled acumen and taste.

Of the approximately seven thousand books and manuscripts a considerable number would be needless duplicates of copies already in the British Museum—especially those of the '-ana' Wise collected and the copies presented. The B.M. Library with its millions of volumes does not require mere duplicates, of which it has many. This was a factor that weighed in the negotiations, and eventually enabled the Trustees to assure the tax-paying public that they had paid less than the estimated value of the collection. Had they run the risk of letting it be dispersed at auction, it is doubtful whether the particular books they needed, and all the manuscripts and letters that it was at least equally desirable for them to have, could have been secured against open competition without payment of unduly high prices. On the other hand, the vendor's natural preference for the Library's finding a home in the British Museum, on acceptable terms, can well be understood. That had been the wish of its founder, who doubtless calculated the course of events, and who had friends able to direct them.

In all the circumstances, therefore, it was better that the authorities should take over the whole collection, so that the wealth of material in print and script should be available to the future generations of biographers, researchers, and students, who will be glad of it. The value of the Ashley Library had been conjectured at various figures from one hundred thousand to as much as two hundred and fifty thousand pounds—the higher figures based on the inflated prices of the boom. What it would have realized at auction in normal times is now purely a matter of guess. It is also a matter of speculation what its original cost was to Wise. It is most probable that even at the Museum's figure the sale price showed a large profit on his outlay. Such a result is not surprising in the case of a man whose genius for collecting was superimposed on great commercial ability and foresight, and who had made not a small part of his fortune out of dealing in books and manuscripts.

III

In the case of a library of any considerable size, it is a frequent experience that when it comes to be checked or moved, discrepancies between its contents on the shelves and as detailed in its catalogues are found. Items get lent out and not returned—though this is less likely to happen in the case of rare and valuable books. When the Ashley collection came to be checked for the purpose of negotiating its sale to the British Museum, it was discovered that over two hundred books and manuscripts described in its eleven-volume Catalogue were missing. Some of these were of minor interest; but there were forty-seven of the first importance whose absence—especially in one case—could not be otherwise than disappointing and surprising to the British Museum officials responsible for the checking, removal, and safe custody of the collection which is now housed at the Bloomsbury institution.

The missing items included the original letter from the Prime Minister (Mr Asquith) offering Swinburne a Civil List Pension of two hundred and fifty pounds a year. 'As an old Balliol man, 'it would be a peculiar privilege to me to secure this slight 'acknowledgment of the genius of the greatest of our Balliol 'Poets'—an offer which was promptly declined by Swinburne. Among other manuscripts lacking were nine by Joseph Conrad, four by Swinburne (including that of the *Laus Veneris*—indexed but not described), and two by Thomas Hardy. Of missing printed books were ten seventeenth-century first editions, including two by John Dryden, two by Thomas Shadwell, Thomas D'Urfey's *The Progress of Honesty* (1681), and gallant Congreve's *The Mourning Bride* (1697), in which the famous line, 'Music has Charms 'to soothe a savage Breast', first appeared. Of his own more or less legitimate productions he had not retained copies of no less than twenty-three of the forty-four privately-printed Borrow pamphlets.

Naturally, when the Library came to be checked by the British Museum officials, there was much interest regarding the fate of Wise's condemned or suspected nineteenth-century pamphlets. It was found that fourteen of them (four by Ruskin, one by

Swinburne, seven by Tennyson, and two by Thackeray) were also missing. The officials were told by Maurice Buxton Forman, who as a friend of the Wise family assisted in the final business, that three of the Tennysons were 'definitely destroyed' by Wise, and others in the list 'may also have been destroyed'.

But there was missing one book at whose loss the public, no less than the British Museum, might well feel the profoundest regret. Its removal from the collection was tantamount to the abstracting of one of the central and most lustrous gems in a king's crown. This was the manuscript of John Keats's sonnet, 'A Dream after reading Dante's Episode of Paolo and Francesca' [1819], written on a flyleaf of a copy of Cary's *Dante* (1814). This volume was made still more precious by bearing poor Keats's inscription to his sweetheart, Fanny Brawne, and his monogram drawn by himself; and also by containing a transcription by Fanny of the last sonnet written by the dying poet. No wonder Wise said of this: 'A more fascinating "association book" it would be difficult to imagine.' He was wont to display it to his friends with intense pride. And now it will not be seen in the Ashley Library—as acquired by the nation after the discovery that so many rarities were missing, although not with the knowledge that the collection contained important books shown here to be fakes. This Keats treasure was sold by Wise to the wealthy American collector A. E. Newton; at the dispersal of whose library in 1941 in New York it realized seven thousand dollars.

That so many of Thomas Wise's important first editions and highly desirable manuscripts were thus disposed of is evidence not merely of the extent of his business as a rare-book dealer, but of the fact that (in these cases, at all events) his commercial transactions were of more account to him than the leaving of the Library as described in the *Ashley Catalogue*—which is therefore not now a true record of the collection acquired by the British Museum.

IV

The fact that the range of forgeries perpetrated in the 'eighties and 'nineties remained so long unexposed (with the exception of the two in the *Athenæum* in 1889, and the four Ruskins by Cook and Wedderburn) is remarkable. The revealing entry of the Diary of Mr Y. Z. has shown that Wise's 'wild career' was known before 1888 to one man, and probably to a few others. But the full extent of that career could not then be realized because it had not run its course; also, it could not have been guessed what high prices some of the 'wrong things' would reach as the result largely of his subsequent clever publicizing. Moreover, as has been shown in Chapter 6, although some of the things indicated were in fact spurious, they were apparently regarded as piratings. A piracy does not sound nearly so dreadful as a forgery. Also, was he not a prosperous collector? His 'wild career' was perhaps dismissed as an unwise escapade, of which the less said the better. The Diary was a reliable confidant.

But it is now evident that in the course of time the authenticity of some of these rare nineteenth-century pamphlets that kept coming into the market in such remarkably fresh condition and so lacking in inscriptions or provenance became questioned among the more careful and observant bookmen (we have seen Dr Pollard's warning in the *Encyclopædia Britannica*). An expert well qualified by long experience told me that some of the better-informed booksellers have always been shy of handling certain of these items because they had suspicions of them. Wise, as a dealer, had an alert ear for the whispers of the rare-book trade. He himself demonstrated his intimate knowledge of it. So we have this extraordinary position: that all the time his fame as a collector, as a bibliographer, and even as a scholar, was increasing, and while he was honoured for his achievements, *he knew there were those who knew* that some of the rare pamphlets he had 'discovered', and whose reputation he had established so interestingly in his catalogues, were wrong. What is more, *he knew there were those who knew* that he had had a connexion with these pamphlets that was at least suspicious.

Suspicion is one thing, however: proof is another.

Wise proceeded on his way superbly confident. With a cynical appreciation of snobbery, he realized how useful a shield was the reputation for possessing wealth. He was always believed to be very rich. In his younger days as a commercial clerk he was a reputedly 'well-to-do young merchant'—on a salary of under six pounds a week and at times admittedly hard pressed to meet his book bills. At the London offices of his printers he was known as 'the millionaire who brought those funny little things 'enclosed in beautiful leather cases to be printed'. There was no anxiety to correct these useful impressions except when circumstances demanded otherwise: as when **** ******, well-known man of letters, hard-pressed and badgered, unsuccessfully sought his financial aid for a literary venture—a worthy enough cause, as Wise regretfully agreed, pushing across the whisky decanter to the disappointed petitioner. The imposing catalogues, the discriminating gifts of them, the scornful denunciations of poor copies, suspect books, and fakes—all these were like defensive weapons. He became a formidable object to attack—if he could be attacked; for, really, there was so little evidence about the origins of these pamphlets of which certain rare-book dealers were so shy and some non-commercial experts so roundly condemnatory.

On the other hand, there were some booksellers, and even collectors, who at times felt that Wise carried too far his dictatorial assumption of infallibility, his domineering insistence that his own books or arguments, and not theirs, were the right ones. Thus his bibliographical theories (not all of them disinterested) were sometimes seriously disadvantageous to others. But the antiquarian book trade is one that seems to bring to its close fraternity a prescience and patient philosophy—if not always from the insides of books. The attitude of the critics of Wise was that 'We shall see all in good time'.

And in good time, inspired by the clues left by the literary editors, Cook and Wedderburn, it was two of the younger generation of booksellers who so brilliantly instanced the truth of Wise's saying which heads the previous chapter. His was a haunting secret that he carried for nearly fifty years, never knowing when might be exploded the mine whose train he knew was laid in the *Collected Works* of John Ruskin. The more amazing, therefore, were his aplomb and diplomacy which produced that *faux bonhomme* of Payen-Payne's description. An example is this statement he made to me as an afterthought to his account[2] of the committee of bookmen who planned a

2 See page 196.

system of recording bibliographical details: 'In my long series
'of Catalogues and Bibliographies I have adhered strictly to the
'decisions then arrived at; but the forgery and faking practised
'during the last few decades have necessitated some small
'divergence from the original plan.'[3]

V

Why did Wise perpetrate his forgeries and fakings? This is a
question on which there has been much speculation. Various
face-saving theories have been tentatively advanced, though
without any support for them by either evidence or argument.
The weakness of these often hastily-projected theories may be
exemplified by the observations of George Bernard Shaw
appended to the useful notes he sent me regarding his contacts
with Wise:

I shall read your book with interest to see what you make of the
Great Exposure. Were the alleged forgeries really jokes of his which
the dealers took seriously? Or facsimiles manufactured as such like
the Shelley Society ones? The printers must have believed this. No
other defence seems possible; but T.J. never made any defence. The
collector complex usually ends in forgery, as in Collier's case.

The fraudulent pamphlets were not facsimilies, whatever the
printers may have believed. And the collector complex does not
end in forgery any more usually than the author complex ends
in lunacy.

These Shavian pearls of wisdom aside, the joke explanation is
the weakest of the theories. Wise throughout his career was far
too purposeful a man to waste his energies in acquiring the
necessary technique, and in the labour of publicizing the frauds,
for the mere pleasure of caprice. The records of controversy, of
surreptitious printings and veiled authorships, include many
examples of pieces put out as jokes for the delectation, or discomfiture, or mystification of others. But the makers of the jokes
have invariably let some intimate friends into the secret, or left
some contemporary evidence of them as such, even if the things

---

[3] He added: 'For example, watermarks and class of paper (laid or wove) might be
'stated with advantage; and . . . a facsimile of every title-page is highly desirable. . . .'

were not openly acknowledged when the interest had fizzled out. Besides, if Wise produced the forgeries and piracies as jokes surely when he was put in the dock of public opinion he would have said so, knowing that the honest explanation is corroborated sooner or later. Was Shaw's idea of fun serious? Did he really think the humour lay in Wise's efforts to trap authors like Browning and Swinburne into admissions that his fraudulent productions of their work were legitimate, and in his hard lying about the high prices he had paid for them? No! It is dear George Bernard's defence that is funny. He had to have his little jokes.

Another and more favourite theory is the vague one that it was an aberration—that Wise manufactured the spurious pamphlets and piracies for the satisfaction of 'putting them over' experts. But this explanation is almost an insult to his keen intelligence and shrewd instinct. The same reasoning that cancels the 'joke' excuse applies here.

Other explanations are that he manufactured the things to use as levers for ingratiating himself with their authors, and that he desired the triumphs of 'discovering' the rarities. He did use some of them for the first purpose; and he probably also gloried in secret over his triumphs. But these were the results or sequels of the enterprises rather than the original purposes of them. Not all the falsifications were usable for these ends. Moreover, if those were the reasons that prompted him, he could have lessened his offence by refusing to make money out of them.

The latter consideration brings us to the argument most frequently heard from Wise's apologists—namely, that the profit he made out of the forgeries was so small that he would have not risked for it his fame as a collector and his reputation as a bibliographer. This is putting the cart before the horse. The forgeries were begun when he was twenty-six or twenty-seven years of age and only learning his bibliography from Furnivall, Herne Shepherd, and Harry Buxton Forman—when he had not compiled a single bibliographical work, and when he was only known as one of the numerous enthusiastic book-collectors of the Browning and Shelley circles. The theory involves the premise that the young cashier, when he began the forging and pirating, envisaged the high and unique position he was to attain in his mature years. This is a very improbable assumption; because, purposeful and persevering as he was, his subsequent celebrity and success were not unfortuitous.

And were the profits so small on things that Mr Y. Z.'s records show him producing at a cost of about half-a-crown apiece? When Wise said that Dr Bennett sold the 'discovered' Reading *Sonnets* at ten pounds apiece, it is not unreasonable to conjecture that this figure represents his prices to Forman and some of the others to whom he 'hurried the good news'. When his clever publicizing resulted in this forgery realizing as high a price as two hundred and fifty pounds, and Ruskin's *Scythian Guest* sold for forty-two pounds, it cannot be supposed that he, with his keen commercial mind, did not benefit still more by the high prices he worked up.[4] True, for reasons that have been shown (see Chapter 6), he at first sold the things cheaply enough to get them into circulation. But he had reserve stocks on which to draw when their market prices rose; for, as late as 1910—after he had satisfied his own private clientele and also sold some on commission through Gorfin—we find him disposing of as many as forty-one copies of one spurious pamphlet alone to his agent. The numbers printed must in some cases have been out of all proportion to their purported 'rarity'. Recalling that the Wrenn librarian has estimated the cost to John H. Wrenn of the forgeries and piracies at over one thousand pounds, that Wise had other wealthy clients on his private list, that after years of skimming the cream he sold off remaining stocks of the 'wrong' things to Gorfin from 1909 to 1912 for some two hundred and eighty-nine pounds,[5] it is obvious that the profits must have been very appreciable—running into thousands of pounds, apart from the kudos he gained for the 'discoveries'. The full total will probably never be known. But in years to come, when the locale of more copies is known, it will be possible for industrious researchers to form a better idea of the extent and financial results of the

[4] Graham Pollard is quoted in the *Daily Express* of 17 August 1937, as saying: 'We do 'know that he [Wise] would put a forgery in a sale, get two booksellers, unknown to each 'other, to bid for it. It would be sold to him for, say, fifty pounds. He would have to pay 'the fees to auctioneer and bookseller. But then, with a price fixed for a pamphlet, 'he would produce other copies to collectors—fakes too—and sell them.'

[5] This was the sum of an incomplete list of purchases. There were other sales of pamphlets to Gorfin. The stock which Gorfin bought for four hundred pounds, as described earlier, to set up as a bookseller in 1912 included legitimate printings by Wise.

forging and pirating by Wise of over fifty nineteenth-century pamphlets.

He was, as we have seen, originally prompted to it by his experiments in facsimile reprintings. But, although he prided himself on his success in making these indistinguishable from the rare originals, he saw the dangers of detection. It was then that he conceived the highly ingenious plan of manufacturing small pieces and antedating them as first editions which could not be compared with any originals. They soon began to make profits, and at a time when the young cashier wanted all the money he could get.

It is my carefully-considered judgment that the basic motive of the long system of frauds was gain; to which later, possibly, was added desire for the kudos of 'discovering' the exciting rarities —kudos dear to the vanity of the ambitious collector-dealer. The psychological interest in the case, however, is not why he fell, but how he rose to fame after the fall.

Consider the superb audacity with which we have seen this Jekyll of the book-collecting world and Hyde of the printing press carrying himself during the many years he held the secret that, partly known as he knew it was, must one day be revealed. Consider the clever way in which he ingratiated himself with men who could serve his purposes, how usually he steered clear of controversy, how he bluffed antagonists and bamboozled patrons and helpers, and how his explanations involving friends and acquaintances in his misdeeds were not put forward until they were dead or dying. Consider how, living through this anxious and tortuous scheme of things, he magnificently realized the triple accomplishment of making his fortune, building a fine library, and rearing his rather flashy reputation. And considering these things, we see behind the varied achievements an uncanny genius.

Not the least strange of many features of the story are the coincidences of some of the references made by ushers of the Ashley Catalogues in their Introductions. Arundell Esdaile, who contributed the concluding one (dated from the 'British 'Museum, October, 1935') to the eleventh volume of the *magnum opus*, described himself as 'the last man in of Mr Wise's eleven', opining that he enjoyed 'some of the normal pleasant 'irresponsibility of a man in that (once too familiar) position'. One of his swipes was:

> ... Bibliography is the new tool which the last two generations have forged for the better understanding of books. It is not a small credit that Mr Wise has played some part in forging the tool and exemplifying in one of the richest fields what use it can be put to. ...

Then there is the quotation made in 1930 by C. H. Wilkinson, Dean and Librarian of Worcester College, Oxford, in his introduction to *A Dryden Library*. Wise was then at the very height of his glory. Did he wince, feel a chilly premonition, when he found his kindly introducer quoting, as a sort of text, this from *The Rambler*, No. 4?:

> There have been Men indeed splendidly wicked, whose Endowments throw a Brightness on their Crimes ... because they never could be wholly divested of their Excellencies; but such have been in all Ages the great Corrupters of the World.

Whether, remembering the unscrupulousness that Wise's career reveals, and the way he used and abused valuable friends, his 'wickedness' is regarded as 'splendid', depends upon the individual regard for honesty and truth and the sacredness of friendship. But that there were many 'Excellencies' in his achievement as a collector, that his 'Endowments' had their own 'Brightness', cannot be denied to Thomas James Wise, who staked for himself a threefold claim in the annals of fame as

THE BUILDER OF THE ASHLEY LIBRARY,

THE MOST PROLIFIC OF BRITISH BIBLIOGRAPHERS,

AND THE FORGER OF THE NINETEENTH-CENTURY PAMPHLETS.

POSTSCRIPTUM

The author regrets that the further Wise 'dossier' (which provided case 3 in his letter, headed 'Executors and their Duty', to *The Times* Literary Supplement of 24 June 1944) regarding a Robert Louis Stevenson document cannot be included in this edition. It will be the main subject of a future publication at the appropriate time.

APPENDICES

1. Notes by GEORGE BERNARD SHAW, with the AUTHOR'S replies.

2. The Bibliography of the BIBLIOGRAPHER, listing his bibliographies, catalogues, private-printings, forgeries, piracies, etc.

3. NECROLOGY.

¶ *These notes by George Bernard Shaw were written in a copy of the issue of this biography published in America in* 1939 *under the title of* Forging Ahead, *and before its revision and expansion for the present United Kingdom edition. They were inscribed on end-papers, fly-sheets, margins, and other blank spaces. The page references in square brackets, since inserted, at the beginnings of the notes apply to this edition.*

¶ *When this Bernardized copy of my book was shown to me in* 1940 *by the*
****
****
****
****
****
****
****
****
****
****

The Author

APPENDIX I

With Bernard Shaw's compliments
Keep this, or better still, sell it; but if you give it to a charity
I will never speak to you again.[1]
Thanks for the loan of it.[2]
Ayot St Lawrence, Welwyn, Herts.
16/7/40.

On Thursday July the 4th 1940, at Clifford's Inn, I borrowed this
book from Alan Keen.

I was interested because I made the acquaintance of T. J. Wise in
the eighteen eighties at the Shelley Society.

I was a leading feature at all Furnivall's societies—the New Shakespeare (or Old Spelling) Society,[3] the Browning and the Shelley—
because as I was an inveterate public speaker, and could always be
depended on to enliven a discussion, Furnivall enlisted me without
consulting me, and never troubled me for a subscription. I hope I
had the decency to pay my way, as Furnivall always provided tea and
cake as well as discussion. I had never read a line of Browning's when
I was conscripted in this fashion; but I was full of Shakespeare and
Shelley.

The oddity of these bodies was that Furnivall's crowd was a Browning crowd to whom Browning was a religious leader; and Furnivall
openly scorned Jesus because, as he put it, "the fellow let himself be
spat upon without at least giving the spitter a black eye". I and the
late E. C. K. Gonner, still in our mischievous youth, used to egg him

---

[1] According to the *Evening Standard* of 28 February 1945 the inscribed copy of this
biography had been sold to another bookseller for over two hundred pounds.
[2] This note is written between the two lines here italicized that are printed on a loose
card.
[3] It was spelt 'New Shakspere Society'.

on to horrify the pious old ladies whose subscriptions kept the Societies going.

They followed him into the Shelley Society in all innocence; and when I, at the first meeting in the lecture theatre of University College, announced that as a good Shelleyan I was a Socialist, an Atheist, and a vegetarian, two of them resigned on the spot.

The Shelley Society was Furnivall's last invention in that line; and it brought Wise into the business for the first time.[4] He never spoke at the meetings; though his strong sense of humour and the remarkable promptitude of speech and decision which made him so successful in business would have made a speaker of him if his interests had been in the least polemical. They were wholly bibliographic. He soon had the Browning and the Shelley [Societies] producing the facsimilies of Pauline and Alastor which started him on his career as a practical joker and the hero of this book. I believe I have both of them somewhere.

After those early days I met him only once; but we kept up our acquaintance by correspondence, as he was keen on collecting the rehearsal copies of my plays as first editions, and could have them from me for nothing.

I have made a few marginal notes further on.

G. BERNARD SHAW.

[Page 29.] Wise was not "a stocky lad".[5] He had a slightly bullet head, and in his later years became portly; but at this time he was slim, well-proportioned, well-dressed, and passed as a university graduate.

[Page 30 . . . 'James Dykes Campbell'.] He was a very likeable gentleman. I must have had some correspondence with him; for he complained that he could not decipher my handwriting without a magnifying glass, and was surprised—when he did use one—to find that my letters were so carefully formed that I must have a conscience. This was for him an unexpected discovery.

[Written on the blank reverse of leaf bearing Furnivall's portrait.] Furnivall began as a Tennyson enthusiast, but developed into a Browningite, in spite of his extreme irreverence. He was a good sort;

---

4 This is hardly in accordance with the facts brought out here. The Browning Society was started some five years before the Shelley Society (see pages 40 and 61).

5 Shaw did not know Wise as a lad in his 'teens. Wise was twenty-seven years of age when they became acquainted. That he 'passed as a university graduate' is interesting in view of what I have recorded. However, the adjective got omitted in revision.

but his quarrels were outrageous. His abusive postcards addressed to Mr Pigsbrook (Swinburne) were typical of his transports of rage when he was contradicted.

When a faithful secretary of his died he not only broke up his Societies by insisting on their sharing in his demonstrations of grief, but actually separated from his wife because she objected. Yet this scandal could not make his friends dislike him. He could not behave himself in a controversy, always making such a fool of himself that it was impossible to feel angry with him.

As a friend he was irreproachable and entirely classless.

[Page 75.] It was not a "stage production". It was a recital of *Hellas* by Austin Podmore (a stupendous feat of memory) in St James's Hall with a full orchestra performing incidental music. Furnivall knew nothing about music, and engaged the orchestra recklessly at a

Top half of page 144 (reduced) of the copy annotated by George Bernard Shaw of the American edition of Thomas J. Wise in the Original Cloth, reproducing Shaw's script. The printed text appears in this book on pages 160–1.

cost which broke the Shelley Society. Wise was guiltless in this folly.[6]

[Page 84, 'the whiskered Victorian beaux' and 'the billowing 'petticoats'.] Rubbish! Desange's pictures of the Crimean war were the last of the whiskers; and the crinolines vanished early in the sixties. I well remember the shock I got when I first saw a lady without one. I was a small child then. As to the choruses, they wore tights and pinched their waists: a hideous combination. They did not know what a petticoat was.[7]

[Page 161, 'the peaceful haven of The Pines'.] Henry Salt and I once took a walk with Theodore round Putney Heath, and lunched at The Pines afterwards. Theodore treated Swinburne exactly like a tutor encouraging and patronizing a small boy. Also a little like the proprietor of a pet animal coaxing it to exhibit its tricks. Swinburne accepted these attitudes without protest, but would not perform before me; and I had to talk all their heads off to prevent the luncheon being a dismal failure. Swinburne was then an old gentleman with the body of a boy, carrying a disproportionately large filbert shaped head. His eyes were like shirt buttons. I got nothing out of him; but Salt had some words alone with him and found him voluble enough. Apparently I terrified him—"banged him into dumbness" as Shakespear puts it.

[Written on the blank reverse of leaf bearing portraits of Swinburne and Watts-Dunton.] Theodore's moustache is not black enough. He dyed it so immoderately that when he went to the theatre the dye "crept" and blackened everybody in the stalls.

---

[6] 'Stage' was a slip of the pen that has been amended. Whether or not Wise was 'guiltless in this folly' is an open question. Shaw's contention—adopting the excuse behind which Wise sheltered—that the recital broke the Society is incorrect: the indisputable evidence brought out by this book was before him. It was Wise's uncontrolled printing of facsimiles and off-prints that made the Shelley Society bankrupt and gave him the training for the production of the forgeries. Incidentally, the *D.N.B.* says Furnivall studied music in his younger days.

[7] Stuff! Soldiers of the 'fifties were *bearded*. Side-whiskers (or 'Piccadilly Weepers') belonged to the 'sixties, and hung on until late in the 'nineties. I did not mention crinolines: so that point is irrelevant. But they did not vanish 'early in the 'sixties', being worn well into the 'seventies. True the choruses were often in tights, but not always. Certainly in the late 'eighties the petticoats of the dancers billowed—very charmingly too, judging by contemporary pictures. In the 'nineties a great feature of the music-halls was skirt-dancing. But Bernard Shaw, thirty-two years my senior, was probably blasé about legs and petticoats when my interest in them began to be excited.

I met him first at William Morris's Hammersmith house. J. L. Joynes was with me. He was smoking at the fireside of Morris's study when we came in. Morris was not there; so we went into the dining room to find him. Joynes said: "Who is the chap in the study?" Morris looked puzzled; and Joynes added explanatorily "Like a little infantry major."—"Do you mean Theodore WATTS?" said Morris, utterly astonished by this view of him.

Watts (I never picked up the Dunton) believed that his sonnets were the final perfection of poetry and his gipsy novels immortal; but he was a friendly man and a serviceable friend. His advice was no use to me, as it was given when I was a journalist-critic; but it was good advice and meant as such.

There was a ridiculous side to Theodore; but he was a real good man.[8]

[Page 307. 'The weakest [of the theories] is that he did them as a 'joke'.] Not at all. His sense of humour had a good deal to do with his choice of this particular form of practical joke, which did not promise to be as lucrative as it proved. He forged nothing: all his literary material was quite genuine. He did not forge first editions: he invented imaginary ones. His fictions hurt nobody, and gave keen pleasure to collectors. Why should we be angry with him for making people harmlessly happy? Foolish people no doubt, preferring first editions full of mistakes to final corrected editions. But quite harmless, like T.J. himself.[9]

[Written on the blank reverse of end flyleaf.] P.S. When Wise's library became famous, and its destination was understood to be the British Museum, I promised him my collection of Ellen Terry's letters to me on condition that he acquired my letters to her, which had been sold to an American collector. Wise offered £200 for them, and would

---

8 Shaw's tribute to Watts-Dunton further rebuts the campaign of slander referred to on page 161.
9 That Wise's forgeries did not promise to be as lucrative as they proved—which is surmise and doubtful—means nothing. He may or may not have anticipated that his clever publicizing of the spurious pamphlets (see Chapters 6 & 9) would raise their values to the extent that single copies, which cost him about half-a-crown to produce, realized sums varying from five to two hundred and fifty pounds. What is proved here is (a) that he was immediately concerned to make them profitable to him; and (b) that, in fact, they became highly lucrative to him. Whether, had they lived, his friends and trusting clients would have been happy to know he had sold them fraudulent things, and whether he was 'quite harmless' in falsifying the bibliographies of so many famous nineteenth-century authors, are questions the reader may now judge for himself.

not go beyond that price (less than a third of what the American had paid for them) knowing that it would be a top price for them later on. The American died; and the letters passed to his son. Then Wise died; and I have heard nothing of my letters since.[10]

Meanwhile the Graham-Pollard[11] detection exploded; and Wise, instead of owning up to a series of practical jokes as such, first attempted a mystification, and then, when Lord Esher cornered him, threw in the towel by declaring, through Mrs Wise, that his doctors forbad further controversy. It then became known that his library was not bequeathed to the Museum; and it was no longer certain that the Museum would accept it in any case.

Thereupon I presented the Terry letters to the Museum, where they now repose.

[Written on the back endpaper.] P.P.S. Apart from the interest of his subject matter, I wish the author, if he issues an English edition, would consider my note on page 278 [i.e., the note above given on his 'joke' theory]. Wise humbugged his customers, who richly deserved it; but far from hurting them he added greatly to their pet pleasure.

Even the exposure was first class fun.

Then why write about him as if he was Jack Sheppard or Wainwright the poisoner ?[12]

G. B. S.

16/7/1940.

[*Revised for press*, 21 *June* 1945.]

---

[10] The offer was made to Wise by Shaw in 1933—a significant date (see Chapter 22, page 301). The American collector was Elbridge Adams.

[11] Should be 'Carter-Pollard'.

[12] The suggestion that these Notes by Bernard Shaw should be included here was first made to me on 27 Feb. 1945 by Dr F. E. Loewenstein writing from 'Shaw's Corner, Ayot St. Lawrence, Welwyn, Herts', with the intimation that G.B.S.'s permission would be forthcoming. As my publisher and a few friends also urged the suggestion, I saw no reason why the Shavian fancies should not take the stage alongside the shattering facts. The Notes are printed as originally written except for Shaw's revisions in proof, which consisted of a few minor textual alterations, a brief addition about Swinburne, and an unexpected deletion in the above P.P.S. of seven words after 'subject matter'.

I assume that the temper of his Notes was due more to the disappointment of our dear Methuselah that the book he had wished to read did not give a more flattering portrait, than to his reaction on finding his jolly beard twice pulled. However that may be, I did —as he desired—reconsider his remarkable 'joke' theory: with the result that it has been dealt with a little more fully in this edition (see pages 307–309).

But I have not written about Wise as if he were Jack Sheppard, though certainly Professor Dowden is here quoted as calling him a highwayman long before the forgeries were exposed. Nor have I written about him as if he were Wainewright. It has never been suggested that Wise poisoned his relatives and other people. His apologist ought not to put out these suggestive ideas lest he be taken seriously. In the research necessary to supply this biography of our greatest literary forger, I have expended sufficient time and labour without trying to make him an entirely different kind of 'hero'.

Apart from the interest of his reminiscences I find Bernard Shaw's theories about Thomas J. Wise rather monologically illogical. But 'first-class fun', of course.

W. P.

APPENDIX II

THE BIBLIOGRAPHY OF THE BIBLIOGRAPHER

A Record of his Compilations, Privately-Printed Publications,
Edited Works, Forgeries, Piracies, Etc.

I

BIBLIOGRAPHIES BY THOMAS JAMES WISE OF

John Ruskin (in collaboration with James P. Smart). 1893. Two
vols. Crn. 4to. Pp. (vol. I) 358 and (II) 276. Illustrations extra.
Copies 250.
Robert Browning. 1897. F'cap 4to. Pp. 252. Illus. ext. Copies 50.
Algernon Charles Swinburne (List of the Scarcer Works). 1897. F'cap 4to.
Pp. 118. Illus. ext. Copies 50.
Alfred, Lord Tennyson. 1908. Two vols. F'cap 4to. Pp. (I) 382 and (II)
220. Illus. on vellum ext. Copies 100 plus 5 on handmade paper.
Samuel Taylor Coleridge. Printed for the Bibliographical Society. 1913.
F'cap 4to. Pp. 328. Copies 500.
Coleridgeiana. Being a Supplement [to the Coleridge Bibliography]. 1919.
F'cap 4to. Pp. 40. Copies 500.
George Henry Borrow. 1914. F'cap 4to. Pp. 342. With Errata slip.
Copies 100.
William Wordsworth. 1916. F'cap 4to. Pp. 288. Copies 100.
The Brontë Family. 1917. F'cap 4to. Pp. 276. Copies 100.
Elizabeth Barrett Browning. 1918. F'cap 4to. Pp. 268. Copies 100.
Walter Savage Landor (in collaboration with Stephen Wheeler). Printed
for the Bibliographical Society. 1919. F'cap 4to. Pp. 448. With twelve
facs. extra.
Algernon Charles Swinburne. 1919–20. Two vols. F'cap 4to. Pp. (I) 528
and (II) 428. Copies 125.
Joseph Conrad. 1920. F'cap 4to. Pp. 128. Copies 150.
Joseph Conrad. Second edition revised and enlarged. 1921. F'cap 4to.
Pp. 144. Copies 170.

John Keats. [Included in the *John Keats Memorial Volume* issued by the] Keats House Committee, Hampstead 1921. 4to. (Pp. 209–15.)
George Gordon Noel, Baron Byron. 1932–3. Two vols. Crn. 4to. Pp. (I) 170 and (II) 166. Illus. ext.

II

CATALOGUES BY THOMAS JAMES WISE OF

The Ashley Library. A List of Books Printed for Private Circulation. . . . 1895. Crn. 8vo. Pp. 18. N.B.: There is said to have been an earlier issue, dated 1893, which I have not seen. The catalogue was reissued in 1897.
The Ashley Library. 1905–8. Two vols. Demy 4to. Pp. (Vol. I) 286, with 122 facs. on vellum ext.; and (II) 182, with 74 facs. on vellum ext. No certificate of issue or printer's imprint.
The Ashley Library. 1922–36. Eleven vols. Crn 4to. Dunedin Press. Vol. I (1922) intro. by Richard Curle. Pp. 286; Vol. II (1922) intro. by Augustine Birrell. Pp. 230; Vol. III (1923) intro. by Edmund Gosse. Pp. 226; Vol. IV (1923) intro. by John Drinkwater. Pp. 232; Vol. V (1924) intro. by E. V. Lucas. Pp. 226; Vol. VI (1925) intro. by A. E. Newton. Pp. 234; Vol. VII (1925) intro. by R. W. Chapman. Pp. 238; Vol. VIII (1926) intro. by David Nichol Smith. Pp. 224; Vol. IX (1927) intro. by Alfred W. Pollard. Pp. 350; Vol. X (1930) intro. by J. C. Squire. Pp. 238; Vol. XI (1936) intro. by Arundell Esdaile. Pp. 228. Illus. ext. in each vol. Copies 200 on antique plus 50 on handmade paper.
A Shelley Library. Intro. by Roger Ingpen. 1924. Crn. 4to Pp. 184. Illus. ext. Copies 160 plus 20.
A Swinburne Library. Intro. by T. J. Wise. 1925. Crn. 4to. Pp. 314. Illus. ext. Copies 160 plus 30.
Two Lake Poets. William Wordsworth and Samuel Taylor Coleridge. Intro. by T. J. Wise. 1927. Crn. 4to. Pp. 160. Illus. ext. Copies 160 plus 30.
A Byron Library. Intro. by Ethel Colburn Mayne. 1928. Crn. 4to. Pp. 174. Illus. ext. Copies 160 plus 30.
A Conrad Library. Intro. by Richard Curle. 1928. Crn. 4to. Pp. 88. Illus. ext. Copies 160 plus 25.
A Landor Library. Intro. by T. J. Wise. 1928. Crn. 4to. Pp. 128. Illus. ext. Copies 160 plus 25.

A Brontë Library. Intro. by C. W. Hatfield. 1929. Crn. 4to. Pp. 108.
Illus. ext. Copies 160 plus 30.
A Browning Library. Intro. by T. J. Wise. 1929. Crn. 4to. Pp. 160.
Illus. ext. Copies 160 plus 30.
A Dryden Library. Intro. by C. H. Wilkinson. 1930. Crn. 4to. Pp. 116.
Illus. ext. Copies 160.
A Pope Library. Intro. by H. F. B. Brett-Smith. 1931. Crn. 4to. Pp. 140.
Illus. ext. Copies 160.

NOTE: Wise's *Bibliographies* and *Library* catalogues concerned with
the same author are not identical. Although the principal contents are
much the same, each gives material not contained in the corresponding
volume.

III

PRIVATELY-PRINTED BOOKS, PAMPHLETS, ETC. ISSUED BY THOMAS JAMES WISE

An asterisk at the beginning of a title denotes that the publication
does not bear either Wise's imprint, or the Ashley Library book sign
at the end of the volume, or any other acknowledgment of its having
been issued by him.

Where the description 'Ist edn.' is appended, this is taken from Wise;
although in a few cases the claim is here challenged. Where there is no
such description, the printing is not recorded by Wise as a first, but
nevertheless generally is—unless otherwise classified: e.g., as a reprint.

Nearly all the publications bear statements that they were printed
for private circulation or distribution. Except in the cases where other
printers' imprints are indicated, the printers were Richard Clay &
Sons, whose imprint is often omitted. Where their imprint or that of
another printer, appears on a publication, the name of the firm is
given shortly. In the absence of a name, therefore, the printers may be
understood to be Clays—except in the few cases specified in the
footnotes.

With the exception of those specially noted, the publications bear
unsigned statements saying that the issues were limited to thirty copies
each. In some cases—like four of the collections of letters from Shelley
—three, four, or five copies were printed upon vellum in addition.
Where the number of copies issued is stated, the figures are those of
Wise. But see Chapter 8, Section V.

The letters S.S.P. at the end of items indicate that these pamphlets were printed from the Shelley Society Papers; and from the same type reimposed, plus the addition of preliminaries. It appears to have been Wise's practice to make these off-prints, giving some, if not all, of the authors of the Papers half-a-dozen copies. In some cases he sent a copy to the British Museum Library; but in others the required copyright copy was not supplied. In at least one case the author of a Paper did not consider it worth issuing separately in this form, and declined to accede to the request of Wise, who nevertheless produced it. In two or three other instances there is reason for doubting whether the authors' permissions were obtained (e.g., see the correspondence with him from Dr Garnett, John Todhunter, H. Buxton Forman, etc., in the British Museum Department of Manuscripts). All these off-prints appear in Wise's 1895 *List of Books Printed for Private Circulation* (see Chapter 10).[1]

The pagination figures indicate the numbers of leaves printed on, but do not include paper covers or boards which usually reproduce the title-page on the recto of the front cover.

MATTHEW ARNOLD:

Alaric at Rome. A Prize Poem. MDCCCXL. Type-facsimile reprint. Edited and with Preface by Wise. 1893. Clays. 8vo. Pp. 24. Limited 'to a few copies'—which Wise stated in his 1895 *List* numbered 35.

Letters from Matthew Arnold to John Churton Collins. 1910. Crn. 8vo. Pp. 12. Copies 20. 1st edn.

[*N.B.*: See also Section IV, additions to Forgeries, Piracies, etc.]

EDWARD AND E. MARX AVELING:

Shelley's Socialism. 1888. Demy 8vo. Pp. 30. Copies 28. S.S.P.

MATHILDE BLIND:

Shelley's View of Nature Contrasted with Darwin's. 1886. Clays. Demy 8vo. Pp. 22. Copies 28. S.S.P.

GEORGE BORROW:

A Supplementary Chapter to the Bible in Spain. 1913. 4to. Pp. 48. 1st edn.

Letters to his Wife Mary Borrow. 1913. Crn. 8vo. Pp. 40. 1st edn.

Marsk Stig. A Ballad. 1913. Crn. 8vo. Pp. 40. 1st edn.

---

[1] Sydney E. Preston, a member of the Shelley Society, told me that the private-printing (1886) giving extracts from notices of the first performance of *The Cenci* was produced for him by Clays. It is therefore not included here.

The Serpent Knight & Other Ballads. 1913. 4to. Pp. 36. 1st edn.
The King's Wake & Other Ballads. 1913. 4to. Pp. 24. 1st edn.
The Dalby Bear & Other Ballads. 1913. 4to. Pp. 20. 1st edn.
The Mermaid's Prophecy & Other Songs, etc. 1913. 4to. Pp. 32.
1st edn.
Hafbur & Signe. A Ballad. 1913. 4to. Pp. 24. 1st edn.
The Story of Yvashka with the Bear's Ear. 1913. 4to. Pp. 24. 1st edn.
The Verner Raven . . . & Other Ballads. 1913. 4to. Pp. 28. 1st edn.
The Return of the Dead & Other Ballads. 1913. 4to. Pp. 24. 1st edn.
Axel Thordson & Fair Valborg. A Ballad. 1913. 4to. Pp. 46.
1st edn.
King Hacon's Death, etc. 1913. 8vo. Pp. 16. 1st edn.
Marsk Stig's Daughters & Other Songs, etc. 1913. 8vo. Pp. 24.
1st edn.
The Tale of Brynild, etc. 1913. 4to. Pp. 36. 1st edn.
Proud Signild & Other Ballads. 1913. 4to. Pp. 28. 1st edn.
Ulf Van Yern & Other Ballads. 1913. 4to. Pp. 28. 1st edn.
Ellen of Villenskov, etc. 1913. 4to. Pp. 24. 1st edn.
The Songs of Ranild. 1913. 4to. Pp. 28. 1st edn.
Niels Ebbesen, etc. 1913, 4to. Pp. 32. 1st edn.
Child Maidevold, etc. 1913. 4to. Pp. 28. 1st edn.
Ermeline. A Ballad. 1913. 4to. Pp. 24. 1st edn.
The Giant of Bern, etc. 1913. 8vo. Pp. 16. 1st edn.
Little Engel, etc. 1913. 4to. Pp. 28. 1st edn.
Alf the Freebooter, etc. 1913. 4to. Pp. 28. 1st edn.
King Diderik, etc. 1913. 4to. Pp. 28. 1st edn.
The Nightingale, etc. 1913. 4to. Pp. 28. 1st edn.
Grimmer and Kamper, etc. 1913. 4to. Pp. 28. 1st edn.
The Fountain of Maribo, etc. 1913. 4to. Pp. 28. 1st edn.
Queen Berngerd, etc. 1913. 4to. Pp. 32. 1st edn.
Finnish Arts, etc. 1913. 4to. Pp. 28. 1st edn.
Brown William, etc. 1913. 4to. Pp. 32. 1st edn.
The Song of Dierdra, etc. 1913. 4to. Pp. 28. 1st edn.
Signelil, etc. 1913. 4to. Pp. 28. 1st edn.
Young Swaigder, etc. 1913. 4to. Pp. 28. 1st edn.
Emelian the Fool, etc. 1913. 8vo. Pp. 40. 1st edn.
The Story of Tim, etc. 1913. 8vo. Pp. 32. 1st edn.
Mollie Charane, etc. 1913. 4to. Pp. 28. 1st edn.
Grimhild's Vengeance, etc. Intro. by Edmund Gosse. 1913. 4to.
Pp. 40. 1st edn.
Letters to his mother Ann Borrow, etc. 1913. 8vo. Pp. 40. 1st edn.
The Brother Avenged, etc. 1913. 4to. Pp. 32. 1st edn.

BORROW Cont.

The Gold Horns, etc. Edited by Edmund Gosse. 1913. 4to. Pp. 28. 1st edn.

Tord of Hafsborough, etc. 1914. 4to. Pp. 32. 1st edn.

The Expedition to Birting's Land, etc. 1914. 4to. Pp. 28. 1st edn.

ANNE BRONTË:

Self-Communion. A Poem. Edited by Thomas J. Wise. 1900. Clays. 8vo. Pp. 52. Two leaves of facs. ext. 1st edn.

Dreams and Other Poems. 1917. F'cap 4to. Pp. 24. 1st edn.

CHARLOTTE BRONTË:

The Adventures of Ernest Alembert. A Fairy Tale. . . . Edited by Thomas J. Wise. 1896. 8vo. Pp. 40. Two leaves of facs. ext. 1st edn.[2]

Richard Cœur de Lion & Blondel A Poem. 1912. Crn. 8vo. Pp. 20. 1st edn.

Saul and Other Poems. 1913. Crn. 8vo. Pp. 20. 1st edn.

Letters Recounting the Deaths of Emily Anne and Branwell Brontë . . . 1913. Crn. 8vo. Pp. 24. 1st edn.

The Red Cross Knight & Other Poems. 1917. F'cap 4to. Pp. 20. 1st edn.

The Swiss Emigrant's Return & Other Poems. 1917. F'cap 4to. Pp. 20. 1st edn.

Darius Codomannus A Poem. 1920. Clays. Crn. 8vo. Pp. 16. 1st edn.

[N.B.: See also Section IV, additions to Forgeries, Piracies, etc.]

THE BRONTËS:

The Orphans & Other Poems. By Charlotte, Emily, and Branwell Brontë. F'cap 4to. Pp. 20. 1917. 1st edn.

REV. STOPFORD A. BROOKE:

*Inaugural Address to the Shelley Society. 1886. Clays. 8vo. Pp. 26. Copies 28. S.S.P.

ELIZABETH BARRETT BROWNING:

*The Battle of Marathon A Poem Written in Early Youth. . . . Reprinted in Type-facsimile with an Introduction by H. Buxton Forman. 1891. Demy 8vo. Pp. 104. Copies 54.

---

[2] An off-print from the type used for the printing of the tale in *Literary Anecdotes of the Nineteenth Century* (1895–6).

The Religious Opinions of Elizabeth Barrett Browning. 1896. 8vo. Pp. 30. 1st edn.

The Enchantress & Other Poems. 1913. Crn. 8vo. Pp. 30. 1st edn.

Epistle to a Canary 1837. Edited by Edmund Gosse, C.B. 1913. Crn. 8vo. Pp. 20. 1st edn.

Lelia A Tale. Pref. note by 'T.J.W.' 1913. Crn. 8vo. Pp. 36. 1st edn.

Letters to Robert Browning and Other Correspondents. Edited by Thomas J. Wise. 1916. Crn. 8vo. Pp. 56. 1st edn.

Edgar Allen Poe, A Criticism, etc. 1919. Clays. Crn. 8vo. Pp. 16. 1st edn.

Alfred Tennyson With a Defence of "The Dead Pan". 1919. Clays. Crn. 8vo. Pp. 20. 1st edn.

A Note on William Wordsworth, etc. 1919. Clays. Crn. 8vo. Pp. 20. 1st edn.

Charles Dickens & Other 'Spirits of the Age', etc. 1919. Clays. 8vo. Pp. 20. 1st edn.

[*N.B.*: See also Section IV, additions to Forgeries, Piracies, etc.]

ROBERT BROWNING:

Letters from Robert Browning to Various Correspondents. Edited by Thomas J. Wise. 1895–6. Two vols. Crn. 8vo. Pp. (I) 112 and (II) 112. Limited to 'a few copies for Private Circulation'. 1st edn.

Letters from Robert Browning to Various Correspondents. Edited by Thomas J. Wise. Second Series. 1907–8. Two vols. Crn. 8vo. Pp. (I) 108 and (II) 94. 1st edn.

Letters from Robert Browning to T. J. Wise and Other Correspondents. 1912. 8vo. Pp. 44. 1st edn.

The Death of Elizabeth Barrett Browning. 1916. Clays. Crn. 8vo. Pp. 24. 1st edn.

The Last Hours of Elizabeth Barrett Browning. 1919. Clays. 8vo. Pp. 14. 1st edn.

Critical Comments on Algernon Charles Swinburne & D. G. Rossetti, etc. 1919. Clays. 8vo. Pp. 16. 1st edn.

Letters from Le Croisic. Intro. by Edmund Gosse. 1919. Crn. 8vo. Pp. 20. 1st edn.

Edward FitzGerald and Elizabeth Barrett Browning. Intro. by T. J. Wise. 1919. Crn. 8vo. Pp. 16. 1st edn.

Some Records of Walter Savage Landor. 1919. Clays. Crn. 8vo. Pp. 16. 1st edn.

BROWNING Cont.

Reflections on the Franco-Prussian War, etc. 1919. Clays. 8vo. Pp. 16. 1st edn.

An Opinion on the Writings of Alfred, Lord Tennyson, etc. 1920. Clays. 8vo. Pp. 20. 1st edn.

Letters to his Son Robert Wiedemann Barrett Browning, etc. 1920. Clays. 4to. Pp. 16. 1st edn.

An Account of the Illness and Death of his Father, etc. 1921. Clays. 8vo. Pp. 16. 1st edn.

SAMUEL TAYLOR COLERIDGE:

Letters Hitherto Uncollected. . . . Edited with a Prefatory Note by Colonel W. F. Prideaux. . . . 1913. 8vo. Pp. 68. 1st edn.

Two Addresses on Sir Robert Peel's Bill, etc. Intro. by Edmund Gosse. 1913. 8vo. Pp. 40. 1st edn.[3]

Marriage. 1919. 8vo. Pp. 24. 1st edn.

JOSEPH CONRAD:

The Shock of War Through Germany to Cracow. 1919. 8vo. Pp. 20. Copies 25. 1st edn.

To Poland in War-time. . . . 1919. 8vo. Pp. 20. Copies 25. 1st edn.

The North Sea on the Eve of War. 1919. 8vo. Pp. 20. Copies 25. 1st edn.

My Return to Cracow. 1919. 8vo. Pp. 24. Copies 25. 1st edn.

Tradition. 1919. 8vo. Pp. 20. Copies 25. 1st edn.

Some Reflections Seamanlike and Otherwise on the Loss of the Titanic. 1919. 8vo. Pp. 36. Copies 25. 1st edn.

Some Aspects of the Admirable Inquiry into the Loss of the Titanic. 1919. 8vo. Pp. 44. Copies 25. 1st edn.

Autocracy and War. 1919. 8vo. Pp. 66. Copies 25. 1st edn.

Guy de Maupassant. 1919. 8vo. Pp. 20. Copies 25. 1st edn.

Henry James. An Appreciation. 1919. 8vo. Pp. 20. Copies 25. 1st edn.

*Anatole France. 1919. Clays. F'cap 4to. Pp. 20. Copies 25. 1st edn.

*Tales of the Sea. 1919. Clays. F'cap 4to. Pp. 12. Copies 25. 1st edn.

*The Lesson of the Collision [etc.]. 1919. Clays. F'cap 4to. Pp. 16. Copies 25. 1st edn.

*An Observer in Malay. 1920. Clays. F'cap 4to. Pp. 12. Copies 25. 1st edn.

---

[3] Not a first edition although catalogued as such by Wise. It is a combined reprint in different format of the folio brochures of the *Addresses* that Coleridge separately printed in 1818.

Books. 1920. Clays. F'cap 4to. Pp. 16. Copies 25. 1st edn.

Alphonse Daudet. 1920. Clays. F'cap 4to. Pp. 12. Copies 25. 1st edn.

Prince Roman. 1920. Clays. F'cap 4to. Pp. 44. Copies 25. 1st edn.

The Warrior's Soul, 1920. Clays. F'cap 4to. Pp. 40. Copies 25. 1st edn.

Confidence. 1920. Clays. F'cap 4to. Pp. 16. Copies 25. 1st edn.

Anatole France. ("*L'Ile des Pingouins*.") 1920. Clays. F'cap 4to. Pp. 12. Copies 25. 1st edn.[4]

CHARLES DICKENS:

Letters to Mark Lemon. [Preface by T. J. Wise.] 1917. Dy. 8vo. Pp. 16. 1st edn.

An Account of the First Performance of Lytton's Comedy "Not so Bad as We Seem", etc. 1919. Clays. 8vo. Pp. 16. 1st edn.

Notes and Comments on Certain Writings . . . by Richard Henry Horne, etc. 1920. Clays. 8vo. Pp. 16. 1st edn.

ARTHUR DILLON:

Shelley's Philosophy of Love. 1888. Clays. Dy. 8vo. Pp. 20. Copies 28. S.S.P.

EDWARD FITZGERALD:

The Rubaiyat of Omar Khayyam. A type-facsimile reprint of the rare first edition. 1887.

H. BUXTON FORMAN:

The Vicissitudes of Shelley's Queen Mab. A Chapter in the History of Reform. 1887. Clays. Dy. 8vo. Pp. 24. Copies 28. S.S.P.

The Hermit of Marlow A Chapter in the History of Reform. 1887. Clays. Dy. 8vo. Pp. 30. Copies 28. S.S.P.

Shelley "Peterloo" and "The Mask of Anarchy". 1887. Clays. Dy. 8vo. Pp. 32. Copies 28. S.S.P.

Rosalind and Helen. 1888. Clays. Dy. 8vo. Pp. 28. Copies 28. S.S.P.

Elizabeth Barrett Browning and Her Scarcer Books. A Bio-Bibliographical Note. 1896. 8vo. Pp. 32.[5]

---

[4] The last ten of the twenty Conrad privately-printed pamphlets bear the imprint of the author. But they were all printed for and issued by Wise—as explained on page 230.

[5] An off-print from the type used for the printing in *Literary Anecdotes of the Nineteenth Century* (1895–6).

RICHARD GARNETT:

Shelley and Lord Beaconsfield. 1887. Clays. Dy. 8vo. Pp. 24. Copies 28. S.S.P.

GEORGE GISSING:

Letters to Edward Clodd. . . . 1914. 8vo. Pp. 60. 1st edn.
Autobiographical Notes. . . . In Three letters to Edward Clodd. The Dunedin Press. 1930. Dy. 8vo. Pp. 16. 1st edn.[6]

THOMAS HARDY:

A Defence of Jude the Obscure. In Three Letters to Sir Edmund Gosse, C.B. The Dunedin Press. 1928. Dy. 8vo. Pp. 16. 1st edn.
Notes on "The Dynasts". In Four Letters to Edward Clodd. The Dunedin Press. 1929. Dy. 8vo. Pp. 16. Copies 20. 1st edn.

JOHN KEATS:

Ode to a Nightingale. Edited with an Intro. by Thomas J. Wise. Fullford, Printer. 1884. F'cap 8vo. Pp. 26. Copies 29. Reprint.

WALTER SAVAGE LANDOR:

An Address to the Fellows of Trinity College Oxford, etc. 1917. Crn. 4to. Pp. 20. 1st edn.[7]
To Elizabeth Barrett Browning and Other Verses. 1917. Crn. 8vo. Pp. 24. 1st edn.[7]
A Modern Greek Idyll. 1917. Crn. 4to. Pp. 16. 1st edn.[7]
Garibaldi and the President of the Sicilian State. 1917. Crn. 4to. Pp. 16. 1st edn.[7]

ANDREW LANG:

Lines on the Inaugural Meeting of the Shelley Society. 1886. Clays. 8vo. Pp. 26. Copies 25.
The Tercentenary of Izaak Walton. 1893. Clays. Crn. 4to. Pp. 16. Copies [? 30]. 1st edn.

JOSEPH BICKERSTETH MAYOR:

A Classification of Shelley's Metres. 1888. Clays. Dy. 8vo. Pp. 48. Copies 28. S.S.P.

[6] Not a first edition although so catalogued by Wise (see pp. 105, 106).
[7] Although these pamphlets bear no printer's imprint the typography resembles that in items produced by Eyre & Spottiswoode.

GEORGE MEREDITH:
Letters from George Meredith to Edward Clodd & Clement K. Shorter. 1913. Crn. 8vo. Pp. 40. 1st edn.

WILLIAM MORRIS:
Letters on Socialism. 1894. Crn. 8vo. Pp. 40. Copies 34. 1st edn.

W. KINETON PARKES:
*Shelley's Faith. Its Development and Relativity. 1888. Clays. Dy. 8vo. Pp. 24. Copies 28. S.S.P.

DANTE GABRIEL ROSSETTI:
John Keats Criticism and Comment. 1919. Clays. Crn. 8vo. Pp. 24. 1st edn.
Letters from Dante Gabriel Rossetti to Algernon Charles Swinburne, etc. 1921. Clays. Dy. 8vo. Pp. 16. 1st edn.

WILLIAM M. ROSSETTI:
Shelley's Prometheus Unbound. 1886. Clays. Dy. 8vo. Pp. 32. Copies 28. 1st edn. S.S.P.
Shelley's Prometheus Unbound Considered as a Poem. 1887. [Pt. I only.] Clays. Dy. 8vo. Pp. 50. Copies 28. 1st edn. S.S.P.

JOHN RUSKIN:
*Gold. A Dialogue Connected with the subject of "Munera Pulveris". Edited by H. Buxton Forman. 1891. 1st edn. Clays. Crn. 8vo. Pp. 28. Indefinite certificate [Wise states elsewhere 40 copies].
*Stray Letters from Professor Ruskin to a London Bibliopole. [i.e., F. S. Ellis]. 1892. Crn. 8vo. Pp. 104. Indefinite certificate. [Wise states 40 copies.] 1st edn.
*Letters upon Subjects of General Interest from John Ruskin to Various Correspondents. 1892. Crn. 8vo. Pp. 114. Indefinite certificate. [Wise states 40 copies.] 1st edn.
*Letters from John Ruskin to William Ward. Edited by Thomas J. Wise. . . . 1893. Two vols. Crn. 8vo. Pp. (I) 120 and (II) 110. Front ext. Indefinite certificate. 1st edn.
Letters on Art and Literature. . . . Edited by Thomas J. Wise. 1894. Crn. 8vo. Pp. 112. Indefinite certificate. 1st edn.
[Note: The Ashley Library book sign first appeared in the Ruskin series of Wise's publications and in this volume.]

RUSKIN Cont.

Letters from John Ruskin to Ernest Chesneau. Edited by Thomas J. Wise. . . . 1894. Crn. 8vo. Pp. 74. Front. ext. Indefinite certificate. 1st edn.

Letters from John Ruskin to Rev J. P. Faunthorpe, M.A. Edited by Thomas J. Wise. . . . 1895–6. Two vols. Crn. 8vo. Pp. (I) 116 and (II) 112. Indefinite certificate. 1st edn.

Letters from John Ruskin to Rev F. A. Malleson, M.A. . . . Edited by Thomas J. Wise. . . . 1896. Crn. 8vo. Pp. 116. Indefinite certificate. 1st edn.

*John Ruskin & Frederick Denison Maurice on "Notes on the Construction of Sheepfolds". Edited by Thomas J. Wise, 1896. Crn. 8vo. Pp. 56. 1st edn.[8]

Letters from John Ruskin to Frederick J. Furnivall, M.A. . . . *and Other Correspondents.* Edited by Thomas J. Wise. 1897. Crn. 8vo. Pp. 118. Front and another leaf facsimile ext. Certificate of 30 copies issued. 1st edn.

[N.B.: See Section IV, additions to Forgeries, Piracies, etc.]

H. S. SALT:

*A Study of Shelley's "Julian and Maddalo". 1888. Clays. Dy. 8vo. Pp. 34. Copies 28. S.S.P.
*An Examination of Hogg's "Life of Shelley". 1889. Clays. Dy. 8vo. Pp. 24. Copies 28. S.S.P.

PERCY BYSSHE SHELLEY:

*Prologue to Hellas. With an intro. note by Richard Garnett. Edited by Thomas J. Wise. 1886. Clays. Crn. 8vo. Pp. 30. Portrait front. ext. Copies 20. 1st edn.

Letters from Percy Bysshe Shelley to J. H. Leigh Hunt. Edited by Thomas J. Wise. . . . 1894. Two vols. 8vo. Pp. (I) 86 and (II) 80. 1st edn.

Letters from Percy Bysshe Shelley to Thomas Jefferson Hogg. Vol. 1. 1897. Crn. 8vo. Pp. 110. 1st edn. [Note: No further volumes issued.]

[N.B.: See Section IV, additions to Forgeries, Piracies, etc.]

---

[8] Reimposed, after corrections, from the type of *Literary Anecdotes.*

ROBERT LOUIS STEVENSON:
Familiar Epistle in Verse and Prose. 1896. Dy. 8vo. Pp. 20. Facs.
front. ext. Indefinite certificate [Ashley Lib. Cat. says 27 copies].
1st edn.

R. L. & FANNY VAN DE GRIFT STEVENSON:
The Hanging Judge A Drama, etc. With an Intro. by Edmund
Gosse, C.B. 1914. Crn. 8vo. Pp. 104. 1st edn.

HENRY SWEET:
*Shelley's Nature Poetry. 1888. Clays. Dy. 8vo. Pp. 56. Copies 28.
S.S.P.

ALGERNON CHARLES SWINBURNE:
The Saviour of Society. Intro. by Edmund Gosse. 1909. Crn. 8vo.
Pp. 36. Copies 20. 1st edn.
Of Liberty and Loyalty. Intro. by Edmund Gosse. 1909. Crn. 8vo.
Pp. 24. Copies 20. 1st edn.
In the Twilight. A Poem. 1909. F'cap 8vo. Pp. 16. Copies 10.
1st edn.
Letters from Algernon Charles Swinburne to T. J. Wise. 1909. Crn.
8vo. Pp. 32. Copies 20. 1st edn.
*To W.T.W.D. Written upon a flyleaf of a copy of *Sympathy,* etc.
[1909]. Post 8vo. Pp. 4. Copies 20. 1st edn.
M. Prudhomme At the International Exhibition. Intro. by Edmund
Gosse. 1909. Crn. 8vo. Pp. 28. Copies 20. 1st edn.
Letters on the Works of George Chapman. Prefatory note by Edmund
Gosse. 1909. Crn. 8vo. Pp. 44. Copies 20. 1st edn.
* Lord Soulis A Ballad by a Borderer. 1909. Crn. 8vo. Pp. 22.
Copies 7. 1st edn.
*The Marriage of Monna Lisa. 1909. Crn. 8vo. Pp. 16. Copies 7.
1st edn.
*The Portrait. [Pref. signed by Watts-Dunton, but written by
Gosse.] 1909. Crn. 8vo. Pp. 20. Copies 20. 1st edn.
*The Chronicle of Queen Fredegond. Pref. unsigned, but by Edmund
Gosse. 1909. Crn. 8vo. Pp. 74. Copies 20. 1st edn.
*Burd Margaret A Ballad by a Borderer. 1909. Crn. 8vo. Pp. 16.
Copies 20. 1st edn.
*Lord Scales A Ballad of a Borderer. 1909. Crn. 8vo. Pp. 16.
Copies 20. 1st edn.
*The Worm of Spindlestonheugh A Ballad by a Borderer. Pref. by
Edmund Gosse. 1909. Crn. 8vo. Pp. 24. Copies 20. 1st edn.

SWINBURNE Cont.

Border Ballads. 1909. Crn. 8vo. Pp. 24. Copies 20. 1st edn.

Ode to Mazzini. 1909. F'cap 4to. Pref. by Edmund Gosse. Pp. 24. Copies 20. 1st edn.[9]

Letters from Algernon Charles Swinburne to Edmund Gosse. 1910. Series I. Crn. 8vo. Pp. 40. Copies 20. 1st edn.

Letters from Algernon Charles Swinburne to Edmund Gosse. 1911. Series II. Crn. 8vo. Pp. 52. Copies 20. 1st edn.

Letters from Algernon Charles Swinburne to Edmund Gosse. 1911. Series III. Crn. 8vo. Pp. 44. Copies 20. 1st edn.

Letters from Algernon Charles Swinburne to Edmund Gosse. 1911. Series IV. Crn. 8vo. Pp. 40. Copies 20. 1st edn.

Letters from Algernon Charles Swinburne to Edmund Gosse. 1911. Series V. Crn. 8vo. Pp. 40. Copies 20. 1st edn.

A Record of Friendship. 1910. Crn. 8vo. Pp. 12. Copies 20. 1st edn.

Letters from Algernon Charles Swinburne to John Churton Collins. . . . Intro. by Edmund Gosse. 1910. Crn. 8vo. Pp. 44. Copies 20. 1st edn.

Letters on William Morris, etc. 1910. Crn. 8vo. Pp. 32. Copies 20. 1st edn.

The Ballade of Truthful Charles & Other Poems. 1910. Crn. 8vo. Pp. 32. Copies 20. 1st edn.

Letters on the Elizabethan Dramatists. Pref. by Edmund Gosse. 1910. Crn. 8vo. Pp. 48. Copies 20. 1st edn.

Letters from Algernon Charles Swinburne to A. H. Bullen. 1910. Crn. 8vo. Pp. 36. Copies 20. 1st edn.

Letters to Thomas Purnell & Other Correspondents. 1910. Crn. 8vo. Pp. 32. Copies 20. 1st edn.

A Criminal Case. 1910. Crn. 8vo. Pp. 16. Copies 20. 1st edn.

Letters Chiefly concerning Edgar Allan Poe from Algernon Charles Swinburne to John Ingram. 1910. Crn. 8vo. Pp. 36. Copies 20. 1st edn.

The Ballade of Villon and Fat Madge. Pref. by Edmund Gosse. 1910. F'cap 4to. Pp. 22. Copies 20. 1st edn.

Letters from Algernon Charles Swinburne to Edmund Clarence Stedman. 1912. Crn. 8vo. Pp. 64. Copies 20. 1st edn.

Blest and the Centenary of Shelley, Etc. 1912. Crn. 8vo. Pp. 8. Copies 20. 1st edn.

Letters from Algernon Charles Swinburne to Sir Richard F. Burton & Other Correspondents. 1912. Crn. 8vo. Pp. 30. Copies 20. 1st edn.

[9] The nine privately-printed pamphlets from *Lord Soulis* to *Ode to Mazzini* inclusive bear the imprint of Watts-Dunton. But they were printed for and issued by Wise as recorded in his *Bibliography.*

Letters from Algernon Charles Swinburne to Sir Henry Taylor &
Other Correspondents. 1912. Crn. 8vo. Pp. 40. Copies 20. 1st edn.
Letters from Algernon Charles Swinburne to Frederick Locker Lampson
& Other Correspondents. 1912. Crn. 8vo. Pp. 48. Copies 20. 1st edn.
Letters to the Press. Intro. by Edmund Gosse. 1912. Crn. 8vo.
Pp. 132. Copies 32. 1st edn.
The Cannibal Catechism. Pref. note unsigned, but by Wise. 1913.
Crn. 8vo. Pp. 14. Copies 20. 1st edn.
Les Fleurs du Mal & Other Studies. Intro. by Gosse. 1913. Crn. 8vo.
Pp. 114. Copies 32. 1st edn.
Letters to Sir Edward Lytton-Bulwer & Other Correspondents. 1913.
Crn. 8vo. Pp. 56. Copies 20. 1st edn.
Letters from Algernon Charles Swinburne to Stéphane Mallarmé.
Intro. by Edmund Gosse. 1913. Crn. 8vo. Pp. 40. Copies 30.
1st edn.
Æolus. 1914. Crn. 8vo. Pp. 16. Copies 20. 1st edn.
A Study of "Les Miserables". Intro. by Gosse, 1914. Crn. 8vo.
Pp. 60. Copies 30. 1st edn.
Pericles, & Other Studies. 1914. Crn. 8vo. Pp. 84. Copies 30.
1st edn.
Letters from Algernon Charles Swinburne to John Morley. Intro. by
Edmund Gosse. 1914. Crn. 8vo. Pp. 52. Copies 20. 1st edn.
Thomas Nabbes. A Critical Monograph. 1914. Crn. 8 vo. Pp. 16.
Copies 20. 1st edn.
Christopher Marlowe, etc. 1914 Crn. 8vo. Pp. 24. Copies 20.
1st edn.
Letters from Algernon Charles Swinburne to Edward Dowden, etc.
1914. Crn. 8vo. Pp. 44. Copies 20. 1st edn.
Letters from Algernon Charles Swinburne to Richard Monckton Milnes,
etc. 1915. Crn. 8vo. Pp. 80. Copies 20. 1st edn.
Lady Maisie's Bairn, etc. 1915. Crn. 8vo. Pp. 44. Copies 20.
1st edn.
Félicien Cossu. A Burlesque. Intro. by Gosse. Crn. 8vo. Pp. 32.
Copies 20. 1st edn.
Théophile. Intro. by Gosse. 1915. Crn. 8vo. Pp. 36. Copies 20.
1st edn.
Ernest Clouët. Intro. by Gosse. 1916. Crn. 8vo. Pp. 24. Copies 20.
1st edn.
A Vision of Bags. Intro. by Gosse. 1916. Crn. 8vo. Pp. 16. Copies
20. 1st edn.
The Death of Sir John Franklin. Pref. by Edmund Gosse. 1916.
Crn. 8vo. Pp. 24. Copies 20. 1st edn.

The Triumph of Gloriana. Intro. by Gosse. 1916. Crn. 8vo. Pp. 16. Copies 20. 1st edn.

Early Letters from Algernon Charles Swinburne to John Nichol. 1917. Crn. 8vo. Pp. 40. Copies 30 [but stated to have been suppressed to 10].

Rondeaux Parisiens. 1917. F'cap 4to. Pp. 30. Copies 35. 1st edn.

Weariswa' A Ballad. Intro. by Edmund Gosse. 1917. Crn. 8vo. Pp. 20. 1st edn.

The Italian Mother and Other Poems. 1918. Crn. 8vo. Pp. 24. 1st edn.

The Ride from Milan and Other Poems. Pref. by Edmund Gosse. Eyre & Spottiswoode. 1918. Crn. 4to. Pp. 20. 1st edn.

The Two Knights and Other Poems. 1918. Crn. 8vo. Pp. 16. 1st edn.

A Lay of Lilies and Other Poems. 1918. F'cap 4to. Pp. 24. 1st edn.

A Letter to Ralph Waldo Emerson. Pref. by Edmund Gosse. 1918. Eyre & Spottiswoode. Crn. 4to. Pp. 12. 1st edn.

Queen Yseult A Poem. Intro. by Edmund Gosse. 1918. F'cap 4to. Pp. 84. 1st edn.

Lancelot, The Death of Rudel, And Other Poems. Pref. note by Edmund Gosse. 1918. F'cap 4to. Pp. 32. 1st edn.

Undergraduate Sonnets. Pref. note by Edmund Gosse. 1918. Eyre & Spottiswoode. Crn. 4to. Pp. 16. 1st edn.

The Character and Opinions of Dr Johnson. 1918. Eyre & Spottiswoode. Crn. 4to. Pp. 12. 1st edn.

The Queen's Tragedy. 1919. F'cap 4to. Pp. 20. 1st edn.

Letters from Algernon Charles Swinburne to Richard Henry Horne. 1920. Clays. 4to. Pp. 20. 1st edn. [Note: Carries the printer's imprint of Clay & Sons for the first time in this Swinburne series of publications.]

Autobiographical Notes, etc. 1920. Clays. 4to. Pp. 28. 1st edn.

[*N.B.* See also Section IV, additions to Forgeries, Piracies, etc.]

JOHN TODHUNTER:

Notes on Shelley's Unfinished Poem "The Triumph of Life". 1887. Clays. Dy. 8vo. Pp. 28. Copies 28. S.S.P.

Shelley and the Marriage Question. 1889. Clays. Dy. 8vo. Pp. 20. Copies 28. S.S.P.

EDWARD JOHN TRELAWNY:

The Relations of Percy Bysshe Shelley with his two Wives. 1920. Clays. 8vo. Pp. 16.

The Relations of Lord Byron and Augusta Leigh. 1920. Clays, 4to. Pp. 16. 1st edn.

WILLIAM WATSON:
Lachrymae Musarum. 1892. Dy. 8vo. Pp. 18. Copies 100. 1st edn.
Shelley's Centenary. 1892. Dy. 8vo. Pp. 18. Copies 29.

THOMAS J. WISE:
Verses. 1883. Fullford, Printer. 8vo. Pp. 36. Copies 41.

WILLIAM WORDSWORTH:
The Law of Copyright. 1916. Crn. 4to. Pp. 12. 1st edn.[10]

VARIOUS AUTHORS:
A Romance of Literature. By Algernon Charles Swinburne and
Dante Gabriel Rossetti. Preface by Wise. 1919. Dy. 8vo. Pp. 16.
1st edn.
Letters addressed to Algernon Charles Swinburne. By John Ruskin,
William Morris, Sir Philip Burne-Jones, and Dante Gabriel
Rossetti. 1919. Clays. Dy. 8vo. Pp. 16. 1st edn.

IV

THE FORGED, SUSPECT, AND PIRATICAL
NINETEENTH-CENTURY PAMPHLETS

ISSUED BY WISE

The list below is compiled from Carter and Pollard's *Enquiry*,
which gives details of sales by Wise of all the pamphlets except Tennyson's *Morte D'Arthur* and Wordsworth's *To the Queen*. The statements
in heavy type following some of the titles are the censorship comments
since appended to the descriptions of the respective pamphlets by the
British Museum Cataloguer. Of the remaining pamphlets without such
statements, the British Museum Library either did not possess copies at
the time this book was written, or had not then recorded censorship. All
are catalogued by Wise as first editions, except George Eliot's *Agatha*.
The concluding words against each item indicate briefly the verdicts
of Carter and Pollard respecting the pamphlet. 'Condemned' means
that the item is classed as a proved forgery; 'piratical', that the item
is a piracy at least; and the other terms indicate that the respective
items are suspected forgeries.

10 Bears no printer's imprint. It appears to have been produced by a firm other than
Clays.

MATTHEW ARNOLD:

Saint Brandan. 1867. Crn. 8vo. Pp. 12. **The imprint is probably fictitious [1890?].**—'Highly suspicious.'
Geist's Grave. 1881. Sq. F'cap 8vo. Pp. 12. [1890?].—Highly suspicious.

ELIZABETH BARRETT BROWNING:

Sonnets. 1847. F'cap 8vo. Pp. 48.—Condemned.
The Runaway Slave. 1849. Dy. 8vo. Pp. 28. [In Verse]. The imprint is fictitious [1888?].—Condemned.

ROBERT BROWNING:

Cleon. 1855. F'cap 8vo. Pp. 24. **The imprint is fictitious [1890?].**—Condemned.
The Statue and the Bust. 1855. F'cap 8vo. Pp. 30. **The imprint is fictitious [1890?].**—Condemned.
Gold Hair. 1864. F'cap 8vo. Pp. 16. **The imprint is probably fictitious.**—Suspicious.

CHARLES DICKENS:

To Be Read at Dusk. 1852. 8vo. Pp. 20.—Condemned.

GEORGE ELIOT:

Brother and Sister. 1869. Crn. 8vo. Pp. 16. [1888?].—Condemned.
Agatha. 1869. (Second Edition.) Crn. 8vo. Pp. 16. **The imprint is probably fictitious [1895?].**—Highly suspicious.

RUDYARD KIPLING:

White Horses. 1897. Crn. 8vo. Pp. 12. **An unauthorized edition.**—Piratical.
White Man's Burden. 1899. Crn. 8vo. Pp. 12. **An unauthorized edition.**—Piratical. [Its status has since been changed by Carter and Pollard to that of a forgery of the genuine first edition.]

WILLIAM MORRIS:

Sir Galahad. 1858. F'cap 8vo. Pp. 18. **The imprint is fictitious [1890?].**—Condemned.

DANTE GABRIEL ROSSETTI:

Sister Helen. 1857. Crn. 8vo. Pp. 20. **The imprint is fictitious [1890?].**—Condemned.
Verses. 1881. Crn. 8vo. Pp. 16. **The imprint is probably fictitious [1894?].**—Suspicious, anyhow a piracy.

JOHN RUSKIN:

The Scythian Guest. 1849. Sm. 4to. Pp. 16. The imprint is fictitious [1890?].—Condemned.

The National Gallery. 1852. Dy. 8vo. Pp. 16.—Condemned.

Catalogue of the Turner Sketches. 1857. [1890?]. Pp. 20.—Condemned.

The Queen's Garden. 1864. Dy. 8vo. Pp. 20.—Condemned.

Leoni. 1868, Crn. 8vo. Pp. 16.—Condemned.

The Future of England. 1869. Ry. 8vo. Pp. 16. This is really another issue of an edition bearing the fictitious imprint Woolwich 1870. [London 1890?].—Condemned.

Samuel Prout. 1870. Crn. 8vo. Pp. 16.—Piratical.

The Nature & Authority of Miracle. 1873. Crn. 8vo. Pp. 16. The preface signed J.B.H. The imprint is probably fictitious [1890?].—Suspicious.

ROBERT LOUIS STEVENSON:

On the Thermal Influence of Forests. 1873. Dy. 8vo. Pp.16. [1895?] The imprint is ficticious.—Condemned.

The Story of a Lie. 1892. Crn. 8vo. Pp. 80.—Extremely suspicious.

Some College Memories. 1866. F'cap 8vo. Pp. 20.—Piratical.

ALGERNON CHARLES SWINBURNE:

Dead Love. 1864. Crn. 8vo. Pp. 16. Imperfect, wanting the wrapper. The imprint is fictitious [1890?].—Condemned.

Laus Veneris. 1866. Dy. 8vo. Pp. 28. The imprint is probably fictitious [1890?].—Suspicious.

Cleopatra. 1866. Sq. F'cap 8vo. Pp. 20. The imprint is probably fictitious [1890?].—Suspicious.[11]

An Appeal to England against the Execution of the Condemned Fenians. 1867. Fol. Pp. 2. The imprint is probably fictitious [1890?].—Very doubtful.

Dolores. 1867. F'cap 8vo. Pp. 24. The imprint is fictitious [1895?]. —Condemned.

Siena, 1868. Crn. 8vo. Pp. 16. The imprint is fictitious [1890?].— Condemned.[12]

---

[11] The British Museum cataloguer is a little out in suggesting this date for the probable perpetration of the suspect. It was done not later than 1887. See Chapter 6.
[12] Footnote 11 also applies to this item.

ALFRED TENNYSON:

Morte D'Arthur, etc. 1842. F'cap 8vo. Pp. 72.—Condemned.

The Sailor Boy. 1861. F'cap 8vo. Pp. 8. **The imprint is fictitious [1895?].**—Condemned.

Ode for the Opening of the International Exhibition. 1862. F'cap. 8vo. Pp. 8. **The imprint is fictitious [1890?].**—Condemned.[13]

Lucretius. 1868. Sm. sq. 8vo. Pp. 28. **The imprint is ficticious [1890?].**—Condemned.

The Lover's Tale. 1870. F'cap 8vo. Pp. 56. **The imprint is fictitious [1890?].**—Condemned.

The Last Tournament. 1871. F'cap 8vo. Pp. 56. **The imprint is fictitious [1895?].**—Condemned.

A Welcome to Alexandrovna. 1874. F'cap 8vo. Pp. 8. **The imprint is probably fictitious [1895?].**—Suspicious.

The Falcon. 1879. Crn. 8vo. Pp. 36.—Suspicious.

The Cup. 1881. Crn. 8vo. Pp. 48.—Suspicious.

The Promise of May. 1882. Crn. 8vo. Pp. 76.—Suspicious.

Carmen Seculare. 1887. Lge. Crn. 8vo. Pp. 16. **The imprint is probably fictitious [1895?].**—Very suspicious.

Child Songs. 1880. F'cap 8vo. Pp. 8.—Condemned.

WILLIAM MAKEPEACE THACKERAY:

An Interesting Event. 1849. F'cap 8vo. Pp. 16.—Condemned.

A Leaf out of a Sketch Book. 1861. F'cap 8vo. Pp. 24. **The imprint is fictitious [1895?].**—Condemned.

WILLIAM WORDSWORTH:

To The Queen. 1846. F'cap 8vo. Pp. 8.—Condemned.

EDMUND YATES:

Mr Thackeray, Mr Yates, and the Garrick Club, 1859. Dy 8vo. Pp. 16.—Condemned.

ALSO SUSPECT

WILLIAM MORRIS:

The Two Sides of the River. 1876. [1894?]. Crn. 8vo. Pp. 22. **The imprint is probably fictitious.**

ROBERT LOUIS STEVENSON:

Thomas Stevenson. 1887. 12mo. Pp. 22.

War in Samoa. 1893. Dy. 8vo. Pp. 28.—'Probably a Piracy.'

[13] In the British Museum's Music Catalogue with the press-mark H. 208.

ALFRED TENNYSON:
Ode on the Opening of the Colonial and Indian Exhibition. 1886. Dy.
4to. Pp. 8.
The Death of the Duke of Clarence and Avondale. 1892. Dy. 8vo.
Pp. 4.
England and America. 1872. F'cap 8vo. Pp. 6.

ADDITIONS TO THE *CORPUS DELICTI*

Since the publication of the *Enquiry* additions have been made by
other investigators to its list, as set out above, of Wise's printings
condemned or classed as highly suspect. Two have been added by
Roland Baughman of the Huntington Library, California, viz.—

MATTHEW ARNOLD:
Alaric at Rome. MDCCCXL. Dy. 8vo. Pp. 12. Printed separately
from the type of Wise's 1893 facsimile of the genuine 1840 *editio
princeps*, for which see Section III.—A forgery.

ALFRED TENNYSON:
Becket, A Tragedy. 1879. Crn. 8vo. Pp. 124. Imprint apparently
fictitious.—Suspect of forgery. [Note: Wise informed Sir Edmund
Gosse (14 June 1914) that he had bought from Mrs Watts-
Dunton for £20 Tennyson's *Becket* given by the author to her
husband.]
_____

Miss Fannie Ratchford of the Wrenn Library has established that
he issued:
ALFRED TENNYSON:
Idylls of the Hearth, 1864, **with a spurious title-page,** being the
ordinary first edition of *Enoch Arden* with substituted title.
_____

The following is a list of piracies, or printings suspect of piracy,
attributed to Wise and identified as such—mostly for the first time—
in this book. The titles here are not included in the foregoing record
of his privately-printed pamphlets, some of which—apart from the
admitted Swinburnes—were probably also issued without authority.—

SIR JAMES BARRIE:
Scotland's Lament. 1894. Dy. 8vo. Pp. 8. Copies 12. 1st edn.

CHARLOTTE BRONTË:
The Love Letters of Charlotte Brontë to Constantin Heger [translations and notes by M. H. Spielmann]. Pref. note by T. J. Wise. 1914. Crn. 8vo. Pp. 44. 1st edn.

ELIZABETH BARRETT BROWNING:
A Song. 1907. Post 8vo. Pp. 4. Copies 20. 1st edn.

JOHN RUSKIN:
Two Letters concerning "Notes on the Construction of Sheepfolds. . . ." 1890. Clays. Crn. 8vo. Pp. 32. 1st edn.

HARRIET SHELLEY:
Harriet Shelley's Letters to Catherine Nugent. . . . 1889. Crn. 8vo. Pp. 74. 1st edn.

PERCY BYSSHE SHELLEY:
Poems and Sonnets. Edited by Charles Alfred Seymour [i.e., T. J. Wise]. Philadelphia: 1887. Crn. 4to. Pp. 76. Copies 35. 1st edn.
Letters from Percy Bysshe Shelley to Jane Clairmont. 1889. Crn. 8vo. Pp. 112. 1st edn.
Letters from Percy Bysshe Shelley to Elizabeth Hitchener. 1890. Two vols. Crn. 8vo. Pp. (I) 174 and (II) 178. 1st edn.
Letters from Percy Bysshe Shelley to William Godwin. 1891. Two vols. Crn. 8vo. Pp. (I) 120 and (II) 118. 1st edn.

[A. C. STIRLING: but attributed to Algernon Charles Swinburne on title-page]
Juvenilia. 1912. Crn. 4to. Pp. 40. Copies 20.
The Arab Chief. A Ballad. 1912. Crn. 8vo. Pp. 18. Copies 20.

ALGERNON CHARLES SWINBURNE:
A Sequence of Sonnets on the death of Robert Browning. 1890. Sm. 4to. Pp. 14. 1st edn.
The Ballad of Bulgarie. Pref. note unsigned, but by Gosse. 1893. Post 8vo. Pp. 16. Copies 25.
Grace Darling. 1893. Clays. 4to. Pp. 22. Copies 40. 1st edn.
Robert Burns. A Poem. 1896. Dy. 8vo. Pp. 12. 1st edn.
Unpublished Verses [n.d.] Crn. 8vo. Pp. 4.

Also an incalculable number of Swinburne pieces printed, on Wise's own admission, without authority. (See pages 186 and 187), among those recorded under the private-printings.

ALFRED TENNYSON:

The Antechamber. Printed for Private Circulation. 1906. Globe 8vo. Pp. 24.

This item bears no printer's imprint or identification with Wise, who described it in his Tennyson *Bibliography* as the first edition. It was printed by Clays, and appears in a list supplied to me of productions by Wise which he gave to a relative in 1909. The B.M.'s copy was donated by Wise in 1908.

Also, Carter and Pollard have stated (*The Times* Lit. Supp., 1 June 1946) that further investigations have satisfied them that the following four pamphlets are 'members of the group' of Wise's forgeries.—

ALGERNON CHARLES SWINBURNE:

A Word for the Navy A Poem. 1887. Post 8vo Pp. 16.

The Question MDCCCLXXXVII. A Poem. 1887. Post 8vo. Pp. 16.

Gathered Songs. 1887. F'cap 4to. Pp. 36.

The Jubilee MDCCCLXXXVII. 1887. Sq. post 8vo. Pp. 24.

All four pamphlets have imprints purporting that they were published by 'Charles Ottley, Landon, & Co, London', and were printed by 'T. Rignall, Printer, Whitefriars'. These imprints are almost certainly as fictitious as others used by Wise. There is no such printer in the London directories of the period. *A Word for the Navy* is one more thing foisted on Richard Herne Shepherd by Wise in a long and unconvincing story told in his Swinburne Bibliography (Vol. I, p. 365 *et seq.*), which however is silent as to how the Swinburne material for the other three pamphlets came into the hands of the alleged publishers and printer. The British Museum Library's copies of the first three pamphlets were given to it by Wise on 11 December 1909, the year of his coup at 'The Pines' (see Chapters 12 and 13); and the fourth pamphlet reached the B.M. on 9 May 1891 through the 'G. A. Phillips' who at the same time sent Wise's piracy of Swinburne's *Sequence of Sonnets* (see p. 174).

V

WORKS EDITED, OR CONTRIBUTED TO, BY WISE

Robert Browning's *Pauline*. A page-for-page reprint by Clay and Sons, 1886, of the original edition of 1833. Edited, with a Prefatory Note by Wise. (See Chapter 3, Section III.)

A Reference Catalogue of British and Foreign Autographs and Manuscripts. 1893. Wise contributed Parts I and II and also edited the work; which was published by the Society of Archivists and Autograph Collectors. [See Chapter 10.]

Edmund Spenser's *Faerie Queene*. George Allen: 1894. Edited.

John Ruskin's *The Harbours of England*. George Allen: 1895. Edited.

Literary Anecdotes of the Nineteenth Century. By W. Robertson Nicoll and Thomas J. Wise. 1895–6. Two vols. Wise contributed new and important bibliographical material; including bibliographies of Swinburne and Robert Browning that were the bases of his later and fuller ones of those authors.

Robert Browning's *Bells and Pomegranates*. Ward, Lock: 1896. Preface and notes by Wise.

Algernon Charles Swinburne's *Border Ballads*. The Bibliophile Society of Boston: Massachusetts. 1912. Edited.

Swinburne's *Posthumous Poems*. Heinemann: 1917. Edited, in collaboration with Edmund Gosse.

Swinburne's *Letters*. Heinemann: 1918. Two vols. Edited, with Gosse.

Swinburne's *Contemporaries of Shakespeare*. Heinemann: 1919. Edited, with Gosse.

Selections from Swinburne. Heinemann: 1919. Edited, with Gosse.

Harold B. Wrenn's *Catalogue of the Library of the late John Henry Wrenn*, 1920. Five vols. Edited.

The Complete Works of Swinburne. Heinemann: 1925. Edited, with Gosse.

The Shakespeare Head Brontë. 1931–8. Edited, with John Alexander Symington. [But see footnote 2, page 116.]

N.B. in addition to the foregoing, Wise superintended the publication of the Shelley Society's type-facsimile; and also a few of the Browning Society's reprints.

APPENDIX III

NECROLOGY

A list of some of the principal persons with whom or whose works Thomas J. Wise was concerned. The dates of these contemporaries, as most of them were, are significant in the chronology of his career and in regard also to the references to some of them in his writings published after their death. As will be seen, all but four predeceased him.

	DIED
William Wordsworth	1850
Elizabeth Barrett Browning	1861
W. M. Thackeray	1863
Charles Dickens	1870
George Eliot	1880
Edward John Trelawny	1881
Dante Gabriel Rossetti	1882
Matthew Arnold	1888
Robert Browning	1889
Alfred Tennyson	1892
R. L. Stevenson	1894
Edmund Yates	1894
Dr W. C. Bennett	1895
Richard Herne Shepherd	1895
William Morris	1896
John Ruskin	1900
Algernon Charles Swinburne	1909
Dr F. J. Furnivall	1910

	DIED
John Henry Wrenn	1911
Judge Klein	1911
Professor Edward Dowden	1913
Theodore Watts-Dunton	1914
Harry Buxton Forman	1842–1917
Wm. Michael Rossetti	1919
Sir Wm. Robertson Nicoll	1923
Wm. Harris Arnold	1923
Joseph Conrad	1924
Clement King Shorter	1926
Sir Edmund Gosse	1928
J. R. Maylett (London manager of Clays)	1929
THOMAS JAMES WISE	1859–1937
Herbert Gorfin	1878–1941
Coulson Kernahan	1943
Walter B. Slater	(?) 1943
De V. Payen-Payne	1945

INDEX

This Index does not cover Appendices II and III

349

CONRAD, JOSEPH—*contd.*

Wise's private printings of, not sent to the British Museum, 230
cost and yield of the private printings, 231
and the author: a tropical 'storm' over Wise, 233–4
the sequel, 234
MSS. missing, 303
mentioned, 108, 252
Conrad, Joseph, Bibliography of, Wise's, 220, 225, 228, 240
Conrad, Joseph, executors of, 10
Constable, T. & A., 141–2
Cook, Sir E. T., Editor of Ruskin (q.v.), 151–4, 232, 267, 305
Cook and Wedderburn. See, Cook, Sir E. T.; Wedderburn, A.; and *Ruskin, John, Works of*
Cooke, John, 148
Cooper's Well, and Miss Cooper, 96
Copyright Act flouted, 103
'Cottonian' bindings, Mrs Southey's, 51–2
Countercuffe given to Martin Junior, A, T. Nash's, or Pasquill's, 147
Cowper, Wm., *Poems* by, 147
Crane, Walter, 131
Crimean War pictures, 318
Criminal Case, A, Swinburne's, 184
Crinolines, 318
Critical Kit-Kats, Sir E. Gosse's, 270
Curle, Richard, 10, 51, 225, 230, 231

D

Daily Express, protest against purchase of Ashley collection, 301; mentioned, 153 n., 309 n.
Daily Herald interview on the exposure, 284
Dale, Francis Richard, of City of London School, 27
Daniel, Book of, 144
Daniel, Samuel, 147
Danielson, Henry, 10
Dante, 216; Cary's *Dante,* 304
Darling, Grace. See *Grace Darling*
Davenport, Sir W., various plays in three volumes, etc., also *Poem upon his . . . Majestie's . . . Return,* 147
David and . . . Bethsabe, The Love of King G. Peele's, 148
Davison T., printer, 262
Day, John, 147
Dead Love, Swinburne's, 201
De Bruni, 41
Defence of Guenevere, Wm. Morris's, 143

DE GIBLER, Byron impostor and forger:
his wife or mistress, 23
and *Unpublished Letters,* 256, 258–61
bogus inscription, 265
mentioned, 17, 266
Dekker, Thomas, edited by R. H. Shepherd, 200; mentioned, 148, 248
Delicate Investigation, 258
"De Luna, Countess" (myth), 23
Dent, J. M., & Sons, 10, 273
De Quincey, Thomas, 52
Desange's pictures, 318
Des Graz, C. G., 10
Devil's Due, Swinburne's, row about, 201 n.
Devonshire Road (afterwards Axminster Road), Holloway, No. 127, 27, 33
Diarist's record, a. See Y.Z.
DICKENS, CHARLES:
and Thomas Powell, 45
and Adah Menken, 180
letter to Leigh Hunt, 215, 250
mentioned, 101, 133, 134
Dickensian allusions, 34, 39, 170, 190
Dickensian, The, 45 n.
Dickens, Bibliography of, R. H. Shepherd's, 199
DICTIONARY OF NATIONAL BIOGRAPHY:
misled by Wise as to F. J. Furnivall, 112
was Furnivall musical?, 318 n.
Swinburne, Gosse's *Life* of: mistake in 1st edn. (later corrected), 166–7
as to Adah Menken, 180
as to R. H. Shepherd, 199–202
Divorce of Wise's first wife, 139
Dobell, Bertram, 38, 255, 256 n.; behind his shop, 39
Dobson, Alban, 10
Dobson, Austin, 197; *My Books,* 233
Dodgson, C. L. (Lewis Carroll), his *Alice,* MS. of, 221
Dolorida, poem addressed to A. I. Menken, 180
Dombey and Son, Dickens's, 170
Domecq, Adèle Clotilde, and Ruskin, 151
Domestic scene, 135
Don Juan, Byron's, 254–5
Doomesday, Sir W. Alexander's, 147
Dorchester, Shelley find at, 67
Doubts of certain pamphlets, First, 141–3
Douglas, James, 168
DOWDEN, EDWARD, PROF.
his *Life of Shelley,* etc., 63, 69, 71, 74, 195
calls Wise a pirate, 70
British Museum Catalogue misled by Wise to libel, 71
Drayton, Michael, and others, 147